The Revolutionary War in the South

The Revolutionary War in the South:
Power, Conflict, and Leadership

Essays in honor of John Richard Alden, edited by
W. Robert Higgins

Duke University Press *Durham, North Carolina* 1979

To John Richard Alden

Contents

Part III. The Framework of Military Conflict in the South

Preface

John Alden is both the impetus and the reason for this book. With the exception of Bill Abbot, all of the other contributors were directed and encouraged through a doctoral program in Early American History by John Richard Alden. Alden then metaphorically adopted Abbot when his dissertation director died. Not only did all of these people work under the supervision of John Alden, but they also studied at and received the Ph.D. from Duke University. Although he taught at many different schools during his career, all of his doctoral students who completed their work studied with him in North Carolina.

In 1974 on a backcountry road in Tennessee, Jack Greene and I began to talk about the approaching conclusion of John Alden's teaching career. We mutually agreed that although John had produced great amounts of research and publication, he had limited his students to fewer than twenty. Why should not all of these people join in a single volume the ideas they had begun to study with John Alden? A collection of essays about the American Revolution in the South by a coherent body of investigators would be unique. Correspondence with the remainder of the former Alden doctoral students elicited strong support for the concept among a majority of them. Interest in participating in a volume which recognized John Alden's importance to the field of early America was voiced by a number of his friends. However appealing the essays by some of these scholars might have been, I decided that a limit had to be set and a coherent criterion was to include only those by individuals who had studied directly under John Alden. The one exception was Bill Abbot's offer to place John Alden's corpus within the historiography of the American Revolution.

After discovering that there was great interest in the project, with the help of Jack Greene and Don Higginbotham a firm and self-supportive skeleton for the proposed volume was diagramed. This formation has been rigorously followed from that time. As I depended upon them to help with the organization of the essay topics, I have depended heavily upon Don and Jack since that time. Both men have thoroughly read each submission and provided me with historical and literary critiques. Without their support this collection would never have reached publication as a single unit.

Ashbel Brice, director of the Duke Press, indicated his support of the project back in its infancy. His assistance has been continuous and in those times when a dozen strong-willed individuals' interests seemed to tear the life from the collection, he provided the necessary encouragement to send out yet another round of letters. Anne Poole was the editor who standardized our various idiosyncrasies. Margaret R. Moffett, my typist for several years, was responsible for the accurate typescript. My wife Eva B. Poythress, a former doctoral student of Don Higginbotham's and our unofficial secretary, shared the interest of all of us in the volume.

As stated above, however, despite the contributions of all of us, no word about the Revolution by any of us would have appeared without John Alden. It was he who, during a number of years, took a diverse collection of young men and instilled in them his high sense of historical accuracy, his lucid literary style, and his great humanity. Because he educated all of the contributors, it is only fitting that this volume be dedicated to John Richard Alden.

W. Robert Higgins

John Alden the Historian

The editors of this volume of essays written by John Alden's students wished to include a word about Alden's own writings. Since the appearance in 1944 of his study of John Stuart and the southern colonial frontier, Mr. Alden has written and published nine books, and he has edited and in part written two more. He has also published a number of articles and many book reviews. When invited to comment briefly and informally on this body of works, I wondered how it was to be done without raising a friend's hackles and offending his modesty by turns. The immediate recollection that John Alden is the most sensible and generous of men removed any uneasiness on that score. There remained, however, the far more troubling question of how to come up with something useful and more or less true.

Clearly the first thing to be done was to read, or reread, what John Alden has written. Not since I was a sophomore in college and worked my way through the novels of Sinclair Lewis, from *Our Mr. Wrenn* to *Bethel Merriday*, have I read sequentially and consecutively the works of a particular author. It is an interesting experience, and it can be an instructive one. Certainly anyone reading Mr. Alden's works in this way will learn much about the South in the eighteenth century and about the American Revolution. He will also learn something about John Alden the historian.

Once the books were read, it seemed only sensible to take a look at what historians have had to say about them. This proved to be a less useful exercise than one would expect. With certain notable exceptions—as in the case of James Ferguson's remarkable piece on Alden's *A History of the American Revolution* (1969) published in the *William and Mary Quarterly*—the reviews of Alden's books provided little in the way of insights or perspectives not readily accessible to anyone bothering to read the books themselves. This is in part simply a reflection of the general nature and function of book reviewing, but a case can be made that Alden's work has been peculiarly the victim of the blandly complimentary and faintly patronizing descriptive review.

As a matter of fact, what critics have said about Alden's writings reveals less about the man or his work than do Alden's own comments on the historical writings of others. The book reviews he has written over the years not only reveal things about Alden as critic and historian, they also tell us something about the nature of scholarly journals—or, to be more precise, about how book review editors of certain American historical quarterlies have functioned during the past three decades. Alden's first book was a study of John Stuart, the superintendent of Indian affairs in the South from 1763 to 1775. Its appearance immediately identified Alden as a specialist on Indian affairs, and for a time he was reviewing one book after another on Indians. Then came the publication in quick succession of *General Gage in America* (1948), *General Charles Lee* (1951), his edition of Christopher Ward's *The War of the Revolution* (1952), and a volume in the new American Nation Series entitled *The American Revolution, 1775–1783* (1954). Well before the appearance of the last of these volumes, he had become a prime reviewer of anything having to do with the military history of the Revolutionary War. He has now for more than a quarter of a century been reviewing books first on Indians and subsequently on battles, many—perhaps most— written by buffs and rank amateurs. If the quality and scope of his earlier biographies were not enough to tip off the editors, his more general works such as his volume on the Revolution in *A History of the South*, published in 1957, or his *Pioneer America* (1966) in *The History of Human Society* should have induced them more often to test his mettle as a critic with books of real substance. It has been their, and our, loss that they did not.

Yet it may be that both the man and scholar are better revealed in the way he has handled the very mixed bag of books on which he has been passing judgment since the late 1930s. Whatever the book he is reviewing, whether good, bad, or indifferent, trivial or important, Alden always gives in explicit language his judgment about how well or ill it is written and his opinion both of its validity and of its ultimate value. One soon learns what he expects of anyone who has set himself up as an historian and commits his words to the printed page. A proper historian must say what he has to say in clear and forceful language; what he does say must be accurate, sensible, and of some moment. A few of the books sent to him for review, ones as dissimilar as Arthur M. Schlesinger's *Prelude to Independence* (1958) and Alexander A. Lawrence's *Storm over Savannah* (1951), meet his test on every count. Of these, he is generous in his praise. Most of the rest do not measure up, and he always says so, regretfully and gently but firmly, and tells why.

The work of his students published in this volume and elsewhere makes clear that Professor Alden required of them what he has demanded of the writers whose books he has reviewed: that they investigate a significant aspect of eighteenth-century America not already adequately treated and report honestly and clearly on what they find. Certainly this is a standard he set for himself and fully met from the time he began to write history. One has only to sample a few pages of his studies of Stuart, Gage, or Lee to recognize this.

It is in his books that John Alden's views on history and the writing of history are best revealed. He has put the greater part of what he has had to say about the past between the covers of books rather than into articles, essays, or lectures. He is also one of the surprisingly few active historians of America whose books are numerous enough and of sufficient importance to form a real corpus of works worthy of consideration as such. Upon them his reputation as a historian will rest.

One should not conclude from the basic standards for the writing of history which Alden sets for his students, or for any other writer of history including John Alden, that he has himself ever been content only to be a good researcher and good reporter. He has always accepted fully the historian's responsibility to probe for meaning, to seek out hidden causes and identify unlikely effects. Still, his manner of studying the past remains at bottom simple and direct. There is nothing in any of his books to suggest that he ever aspired to cleverness, to novelty, or even to the sort of profundity that many historians are now wont to make a show of. In fact, the reader of his books and reviews is left with the impression that perhaps he does not see any of these things as altogether desirable attributes of serious historical writing.

Certainly in his own writings Mr. Alden has in mind something other than to confound, provoke, stimulate, or tickle our fancy. Like everyone else, he perceives that a number of interesting and important things happened in this country between 1763 and 1789. The Americans moved to the point of breaking with their mother country, they fought for and won their independence, and as a free people they went far toward transforming and reconstituting their institutions as they created a new nation state. In book after book, in those treating only a limited segment of all this, such as his study of Gage or of Lee, and in his more general works, Mr. Alden never shirks the straightforward but always difficult task of finding out and setting down what in fact happened. He wants to know how one thing led to another and how men shaped events. His first object always is to learn and to tell what people did and when they did it. The why's and the wherefore's may follow, indeed should follow, but only after he, and we, have got straight the who's, the what's, and the when's.

Mr. Alden is, of course, perfectly well aware that the force of all sorts of circumstances outside the control of the characters in his story limits their choices and circumscribes their activities. He just happens to be rather more interested in observing what they do with whatever freedom of action the fates—the economists and social scientists generally—leave to them. Social and economic change as described and analyzed by others tends to become in Alden's hands something to be taken for granted; it becomes the backdrop or context for the revolutionary generation's struggle for independence and political liberty. The forces shaping man's destiny need to be understood and taken into account, but the role humankind has played on the world's stage is, for Mr. Alden, the true stuff of history.

It is probably more than happenstance that much—but by no means all—of Alden's work has dealt either with the life of an individual or with military matters. Writers of conventional biography and of military history, like the old-fashioned novelist, focus upon decisions made, actions taken, and consequences suffered or enjoyed. It is people and not circumstances who decide, act, and suffer consequences—and usually in that order. For these writers to get things in their proper order is sometimes more difficult, often more important, and nearly always more rewarding than it is for most other sorts of historians. Confusing the sequence of events in a battle or a man's life may on occasion do no greater violence to the truth than mixing up the timing of things in, for instance, an analysis of some economic or political development or of a particular social process, but no other historian can achieve quite so much by simply putting events in order as the one who is writing a biography or the history of a military campaign. John Alden's powerful memory, his remarkable ability to get what happened straight in his mind and to keep it straight, his skill in writing narrative prose, and his view of the past as an arena in which people acted out their parts are all useful qualities for any historian, but they are particularly valuable for the biographer and military historian. Whether or not these personal qualities have determined the direction his writings have taken, they are all in evidence in his earliest works, and he has in fact spent his professional life writing the kind of history which seems best suited to his talents.

Alden's general approach to an historical problem is nowhere more evident than in his biography of Charles Lee. He chose to write an account of Lee's life because Lee's role in the Revolutionary War was important and because it has always been misunderstood. To establish the one and correct the other, he pieced together the story of Lee's military career in Europe and America. It is a good story, and Alden tells it well. He follows Lee from his days as a young redcoat in America during the French and Indian War, through his campaign in Poland where he played courtier to King Stanislaus, to his moment of glory as Washington's general, and ends with a full account of his court-martial, disgrace, and death.

Here and in most of Alden's other works, chronology—the story—is more than just a handy schema for the historian; it is the key to the puzzle and the primary vehicle for projecting the author's vision of the truth. Alden has always known that a person's actions are usually the historian's best clues to what sort of individual he was. As a biographer, Alden is thankful for the glimpses into Lee's character which Lee's own words and what others said about him provide, but he finds his Lee in the deeds of the man. Lee reveals himself through his dealings with Loudoun, Amherst, Abercromby, and Gage, with Clinton, Burgoyne, and the Howes, with Robert Morris, John Rutledge, Moultrie, William Henry Drayton, Rush, Reed, Richard Henry Lee, and especially with George Washington; through what transpired on that fateful day at Monmouth; and through the way he reacted to his rejection by Washington and the other American leaders after his court-martial. These are what Alden examines and reports on.

It should be noted, however, that as he tells the story of Lee's career, Alden is always in search of the mainspring of Lee's actions. He persistently probes for those traits of character and personality that lie beneath the surface of events. But he takes his evidence as he finds it, avoiding speculation about Lee's psyche or inner life. The tale itself he tells with care and precision but also with passion, for this is a book with a thesis. There are ancient wrongs to be righted and unacknowledged imbalances to be redressed. Charles Lee is to have his due even at the cost of questioning the great Washington's judgment, if not his rectitude, in the Monmouth incident. Whatever the book may lack in detachment and suavity of language so characteristic of Alden's other works, it makes up for in vitality. And like everything he wrote it starts at the beginning and goes to the end in a clear, accurate, and purposeful fashion. It is one of my favorites.

Three years before the Lee book came out Alden published a study of General Thomas Gage. In deciding to write a biography of Gage —or, rather, an account of Gage's life in America—Alden set for himself a problem quite different from anything he faced either in his earlier monograph on John Stuart, who as Indian superintendent was under Gage's command, or in his later work on General Lee, Gage's companion in arms in the French and Indian War. The book that resulted, however, exemplifies Alden's approach to the writing of history in much the same way that the Lee biography does.

Gage became commander in chief of British forces in North America in 1763 when the British government decided to keep an army stationed in the colonies in peacetime. He remained in command until his recall shortly after the battle of Bunker Hill in 1775. These were years in which the army in America was in the thick of things. British troops and their commander persistently sought to cope with the crucial and potentially explosive problem of the vastly expanded West. They provoked colonial resentment in their attempts to enforce the Quartering Act in New York and elsewhere. The army stood by while colonial mobs nullified the Stamp Act in the fall of 1765 and eventually forced its repeal by Parliament. In 1768 British troops occupied the city of Boston to strengthen the hand of the Massachusetts government after opposition to the Townshend Acts had reduced it to virtual helplessness. They perpetrated the Boston "massacre" of 1770, reoccupied Boston in 1774 to enforce the Port Bill, and in 1775 fired shots at Lexington and Concord and fought on Bunker Hill. A full account of what the commander in chief did to shape these tangled events should reveal a great deal about Thomas

Gage and about the role he and the British army played in America between 1763 and 1775.

Alden's account does inform us about both these things, but the book has as its main focus something else. The British government and the patriot leaders, not Gage, made the decisions and suffered the consequences in all of this. Gage is hardly ever more than an instrument of British policy or, alternatively, a victim of American resistance. Being the kind of historian he is, Alden finds himself telling the story that is there, the saga of Britain and her colonies moving step by step toward the breakup of the old empire and finally to open warfare. The book becomes not so much a biography of General Gage which happens to shed light on the coming of the Revolution as an account of the coming of the Revolution from which we learn how Gage rode before the great storm being raised by others.

Even though Alden kept Gage pretty much in the foreground throughout the book and made no attempt whatsoever to be comprehensive in his handling of the coming of the Revolution, when it appeared in 1948 the Gage volume offered as clear, concise, and perspicacious an account of the long road to Lexington and Concord as one could have found anywhere. It also presented new and valuable information on the role of the British army in the colonies after 1763. Since that time, scores of volumes, a number by Alden himself and by other leading American and British historians, have been written on one aspect or another of the dissolution of the old British empire before 1776. Alden's book on Gage has held up remarkably well through it all. It has never been made to look silly or even wrong in any important way. Nevertheless the spate of works published in the past twenty-five years on Anglo-American tensions in the 1760s and on the revolutionary movements in the colonies has rendered the Gage book a good deal less valuable than it once was.

As a matter of fact, Alden's less ambitious and less urbane volumes on Charles Lee and John Stuart are today more nearly indispensable for the student of eighteenth-century America than his book on Gage. It is fair to say, I think, that each of these is the definitive study of its subject. The Stuart monograph continues to be one of the most useful books we have on the Indians and frontier of the southern colonies in the crucial two decades before the Revolution. It is also one of the most readable. One can learn from it among other things what the tribes of southern Indians were, where in the old Southwest they lived, how they felt about and dealt with one another, and what were their relations with the French, the Spanish, and with the English colonists. In the opinion of one whose acquaintance with the historical literature on the American Indian is admittedly hardly more than a nodding one, Alden's volume on Stuart remains a very good place to start one's study of the southern Indians. Beyond that, and more important, it is a superb piece of work on the superintendent of Indian affairs and his office.

What Alden provides is a close look at an imperial administrator as he functioned over a long period of time. The full dimensions of the complex and shifting "Indian problem" with which Stuart had to come to grips from the 1750s until 1775 becomes clear. Many of the difficulties Stuart faced and the decisions he made had far-reaching military, political, and diplomatic implications. Furthermore, the policies Stuart formulated and pursued were shaped by a combination of pressures coming from the British government in London, from General Gage in New York or Boston, and from the governors and legislatures of the southern colonies. For nearly two decades Stuart mediated between the conflicting claims of his various superiors or clients and managed day by day the enforcement of the Indian policy thereby arrived at. This is the story Alden tells. No one else is likely to tell it again soon. A student of the time and place needs the book as much now as he did when it first appeared in 1944.

Something crops up in this first book of Alden's that is quite uncharacteristic of either the man or his work. While going about his business of laying bare the mysteries of Indian relations and imperial administration, he occasionally takes time out to deliver a lusty swipe at one of his elders whom he finds in grievous error about one thing or another. As chance or an alert editor would have it, one of the targets of Alden's strictures was sent the Stuart book for review in the *American Historical Review*. The distinguished reviewer, Clarence E. Carter, gave Alden a rap or two on his knuckles, but he recognized Alden's temerity for what it was, the exuberance of a historian with his first book and a new degree, and treated him for the most part as kindly as Alden has since treated many a less deserving young historian.

Mr. Alden's most important book, I believe, is his *The South in the Revolution, 1763–1789.* It was published in 1957 as Volume III in

A History of the South edited by E. Merton Coulter and the late Wendell H. Stephenson. Those who would dispute my characterization of it as his most important work may agree that nothing else Alden has written displays his talents to better advantage. The scope of the book allows him to demonstrate his ability to control enormous amounts of material and to work on a far broader canvas than in his biographical studies; at the same time, the subject matter demands a mastery of detail and a familiarity with a range of source materials not required for his other more general works, which include his synoptic history of the Revolution in the American Nation Series, his broadly interpretive *Pioneer America*, and the comprehensive treatment of the Revolution he published in 1969.

Leaving comparisons aside, there are claims one can make for *The South in the Revolution* and its author which no one would challenge. As the text shows, the man who wrote the book is master of a very large body of historical works devoted to the era of the American Revolution, and, like Merrill Jensen, another distinguished historian of the period, he has read for himself a great many of the documents upon which those works were based. Furthermore this volume in *A History of the South* leaves no room for doubt about Alden's ability to handle a subject as many-faceted and fundamentally important as the historical process through which the southern colonies and states passed between 1763 and 1789. It is a full and clear account of what historians knew about the period when Alden wrote the book, and it is also the statement of Alden's own view of the matter. It is his version of what happened and reflects his sense of what was important.

We see confirmed in *The South in the Revolution* as well as in his two other general studies of the Revolution Alden's view of man's role in history. The Revolution came because of decisions men made, because of things people in Britain and America did and did not do between 1763 and 1776. The actions and interactions of human beings were also what set the course and determined the outcome of the Revolution and then created the new federal union of 1789. It is perhaps sufficient to say of this that Alden's handling of the history of the American Revolution reflects his belief in the efficacy of human choice despite any limitations set upon it by conditions and circumstances. It would not be unreasonable, however, to raise the question whether the simple act of telling the story of a people's passage through an age of revolution may not be a way to avoid facets of the historical process, which cannot be confronted directly or described in concrete terms.

In responding to such a question perhaps one gets nearest the truth by conceding at the outset that Alden's work on the Revolution has not been primarily, or even secondarily, a quest for hidden meanings and unnoted connections. He has sought to learn what others have found out, to discover for himself certain things he feels are important to know, to understand, and to put it all together so that it makes sense and reflects the evidence. In his books on the Revolution he has shown himself the master of compression. I know of no more than three or four other American historians now writing who can in a few words reduce a very large and complicated matter to so clear and cogent a statement without falsification or oversimplification. This knack helps to explain, I suspect, why he is so very successful in writing military history. In this connection anyone interested in observing a craftsman at work should read his brief account of the battle of Yorktown in his 1954 book on the Revolution and then read the fuller account in his general history of the Revolution published in 1969. Each does exactly what is required and does it extremely well. The reader is left with the feeling that Alden's control of the material and his mastery of his craft are so complete that a ten-page, a fifty-page, and a two-hundred-page account of the campaign written by him would be equally clear, equally balanced, and equally true. His personal lens permits him to zoom in close and pull far back without ever blurring the focus or causing him to lose perspective. Nor is his gift for clarification and compression manifested only in his handling of military campaigns. His broad synthesis of the first 250 years of American history entitled *Pioneer America* is only the most striking proof of this. Incidentally, it was the one book of Alden's I knew nothing about. It is an elegant book, learned and wise. I hope it is being widely read.

In any evaluation of John Alden's work at this point in his career, there are I suppose a number of other questions that could and should be brought up and canvassed. Perhaps one ought to speculate a bit about Alden's place in the historiography of the Revolution and the eighteenth-century South. If one does this, a series of interrelated questions immediately comes to mind, such as how important and useful were his books at the time each appeared, how well have they stood the passage of time until now, and what are the chances of their being consulted, read, and appreciated a generation hence. Still another question along this line, or maybe it is only another way of asking the same ones, is whether John Alden has broken new ground, has made us see some important aspect of the past in a new way. And there are others.

My response to any and all questions such as these may not be entirely direct but it is emphatic. During his long career, Alden has explored unexplored territory, used much unused evidence, and told us things, important things, we did not know about eighteenth-century America and the South. He has added to the body of knowledge and expanded our understanding of the past. Furthermore, he has formulated a clear-eyed and comprehensive view of the American Revolution that is his own, hard won and secure. He has spelled it out with great skill and care in a whole row of books ranging from the strictly monographic to the grandly synthetic and broadly interpretive. From first to last, these books are sensible, serious, humane, intelligent, well written, and honest. Alden is a historian.

He is also a person of parts. Not long after I left graduate school and began teaching at the College of William and Mary, my mentor, Charles Sydnor, died. The history faculty at Duke University invited John Alden of the University of Nebraska to become a member of its department in Sydnor's place, which he did in 1955. Soon after his arrival in Durham he read my dissertation and sent me a letter. He wrote to tell me that he appreciated what a loss to me Sydnor's death had been and invited me to call on him for advice or help just as I would have called on Sydnor. This was an extraordinarily generous thing for Alden to have done. What's more, he meant what he said. For example, shortly before the Institute of Early American History and Culture published a little book of mine on eighteenth-century Georgia, Alden read the manuscript and made a list of factual errors three pages long. Some of the errors were real howlers that must have jumped out of the page at him but others related to the most obscure points. John Alden does indeed have a splendid memory and encyclopedic knowledge, but he did not make that list without hours of rooting around in the university library. There have been many other kindnesses since then.

During my years in and around the Institute at Williamsburg John Alden was on its Council much of the time. This was when I got to know him well, and we became friends. I have in recent months also come to know his work far better than before. It is therefore with some authority that I speak when I clear my throat and affirm that the affection, respect, and admiration that historians of early America accord the man and his work are fully merited.

W. W. Abbot

Part I. The Context of the Revolution in the South

Character, Persona, and Authority: A Study of Alternative Styles of Political Leadership in Revolutionary Virginia

Jack P. Greene   *The Johns Hopkins University*

i.

> *. . . this part [of the patriot], it is well known, is played in very different styles.*[1]

If the number and quality of leaders produced by a political culture are an important measure of its vitality, the political culture of revolutionary Virginia must be judged as one of the most vital in modern history. No other political society in revolutionary America or, indeed, at any later time in American history has produced so many gifted leaders. Patrick Henry and George Washington, George Mason and Thomas Jefferson, James Madison and John Marshall are only the most conspicuous of a whole galaxy of leaders contributed by Virginia to the revolutionary era. Various scholars have considered the intriguing question of why this particular political culture produced such a profusion of talent. They have, at least in a preliminary way, analyzed the social, institutional, and intellectual framework out of which it came.[2] To date, however, there has been

1. Alexander Grayden, *Memoirs of His Own Time* (Philadelphia, 1846), p. 288. The author is indebted to the members of The Seminar at The Johns Hopkins University and more particularly to Louis Galambos, Rhys Isaac, Jeffrey Mayer, Willie Lee Rose, Thad W. Tate, and Ronald Walters for their thoughtful criticisms.

2. See especially Charles S. Sydnor, *Gentlemen Freeholders: Political Practices in Washington's Virginia* (Chapel Hill, N.C., 1952); Daniel J. Boorstin, *The Americans: The Colonial Experience* (New York, 1958), 99–143; Robert E. and B. Katherine Brown, *Virginia 1705–1786: Aristocracy or Democracy?* (East Lansing, Mich., 1964); Keith B. Berwick, "Moderates in Crisis: The Trials of Leadership in Revolutionary Virginia" (Ph.D. dissertation, Univ. of Chicago, 1959); Jack P. Greene, *The Quest for Power: The Lower Houses of Assembly in the Southern Royal Colonies, 1689–1776* (Chapel Hill, N.C., 1963); Jack P. Greene, "Foundations of Political

no systematic examination of the character of political leadership, of how politicians acquired the cloak of prominence—and authority— and how they wore it. This essay seeks to illuminate these "inner compulsives of politics" in revolutionary Virginia through an examination of the relationship between styles of leadership and the foundations of individual authority as revealed by the careers of three men: Richard Henry Lee, Edmund Pendleton, and George Mason.[3]

These three men meet five important criteria for inclusion in this study. First, each belonged to the political generation that, born between 1721 and 1735, entered public life during the two decades prior to the Revolution and assumed a large role in the direction of public affairs during the 1760s. George Washington, Peyton Randolph, Robert Carter Nicholas, George Wythe, John Blair, Jr., Archibald Cary, Joseph Jones, and Benjamin Harrison V all fall within the same generation. This generation can be distinguished from an older one which included Speaker John Robinson, Richard Bland, Landon Carter, Charles Carter of Cleve, William and Thomas Nelson (the elder), and Benjamin Waller, all of whom died and/or retired during the 1760s and 1770s. It can be differentiated as well from a younger group, including Patrick Henry, Thomas Jefferson, James Madison, Thomas Nelson (the younger), Severn Eyre, Edmund Randolph, John Marshall, and John Monroe, all of whom entered politics after the revolutionary controversy had begun. Second, each of the three men had a career that spanned the entire era of the Revolution from 1760 to 1790, unlike Peyton Randolph or Nicholas, who were either more or equally prominent during the 1760s and early 1770s. Third, each achieved extraordinary success and widespread acclaim as a political leader. Fourth, unlike Wythe, each left behind a body of material large enough to permit consideration of the problem at hand, but, unlike Washington, not so large as to defy analysis in an essay of confined length. Finally, in both personality and role they were sufficiently different from one another to reveal divergent styles of leadership.

Power in the Virginia House of Burgesses, 1720–1776," *William and Mary Quarterly*, 3rd ser., XVI (1959), 485–506; and Jack P. Greene, *Landon Carter: An Inquiry into the Personal Values and Social Imperatives of the Eighteenth-Century Virginia Gentry* (Charlottesville, Va., 1967).

3. The quotation is from J. H. Grainger, *Character and Style in English Politics* (Cambridge, Eng., 1969), p. 11. This volume is one of the few systematic studies of styles of political leadership for any past society.

This essay employs four concepts—*role, persona, character*, and *style of leadership*—that have no very precise definitions or generally agreed-upon meanings. The definitions used here are set forth in the following propositions, which consist of an elaboration of the major assumptions on what the subsequent analysis is based:

1. Force of personality is not a sufficient condition for political leadership.

2. Each political system has standards of conduct by which leaders may be evaluated and traditional *roles* which incorporate those standards. The term "role" is here employed in its *vernacular* and not in its *technical* sociological sense.

3. These political roles—usually drawn from the past or from an admired contemporary model—exist independently of the actors who fill them and have readily identifiable functions within the political system. They in turn prescribe certain familiar postures or stances, here referred to as *persona*. These personae constitute the external representations—the faces—of the political roles they represent.

4. These personae have two important functions in the political process. First, quite as much as institutional structures, established procedures, or underlying ideologies, they help to give coherence to the "ragged world of politics." Because they have the sanction of tradition, they link the participants in the political process to the larger sweep of history and thereby provide an escape from the "mundane present."[4] They provide leaders with identity models through which they can explain to themselves and their audience who they are, what they stand for, and what their function is in the public realm. These personae also supply audiences with visible symbols of authority, symbols whose power rests upon their familiarity and acceptability and which provide an ideal standard against which the performance of individual leaders can be measured. Thus, to act coherently and to command authority each leader must assume and maintain an approved persona.

5. Second, these personae provide a link—that is, they help to mediate—between role, which exists outside the individual actor, and *character*, which may be defined for the purposes of this essay as that complex of salient mental and ethical traits that give distinctive configuration to each individual personality.

6. To achieve and maintain credibility—for his public behavior

4. Ibid., pp. 4, 33–34.

to carry conviction—among an audience to whom one has intimate and prolonged exposure (e.g., his peers in a legislative body or his constituents in a small electoral district), a leader must discover a persona that is—or can be made—congruent with his character.

7. The successful internalization of a persona may thus require a significant modification of character (e.g., the suppression of disapproved traits or the cultivation of approved ones) to achieve the necessary degree of congruity between character and the imperatives of the persona. Similarly, a leader with a powerful personality may significantly expand or change the shape and content of any given persona.

8. Exigency may also require the alteration of old or the creation of new persona, for to be viable a persona must have contemporary relevance as well as the sanction of—or at least congruence with—tradition. At the same time, exigency may also necessitate or stimulate character modification in individual leaders.

9. What is customarily referred to as *style* in a political leader may be defined as his distinctive "lustre" and his peculiar "form or mode of functioning" in the public realm: that is, his "characteristic way of performing duties," speaking, responding to problems, handling work assignments, and interacting with other participants in the political arena. Style is thus "a *form* of conduct created by an actor in communication with other actors." From the outside, it "is the observed quality and character of his performance"; from the inside, it is the leader's "bundle of strategies" for eliciting sympathetic resonances from other participants for the purpose of enhancing his self-esteem by adding to his public reputation and/or his record of political achievement.[5]

10. Because sympathetic resonances can be elicited most easily by a leader through the incorporation of an approved persona into his style, the style of leadership of an individual usually is thus a product of the interaction between his character and such a persona, an interaction that takes place within—and is invariably shaped by—a general context supplied by the exigencies of the time.

5. Ibid., p. 4; David Shapiro, *Neurotic Styles* (New York and London, 1965), p. 1; Hugh Dalziel Duncan, *Symbols and Social Theory* (New York, 1969), p. 33; James D. Barber, "Classifying and Predicting Presidential Styles: Two 'Weak' Presidents," *Journal of Social Issues*, XXIV (1968), 52–53; Alexander L. George, "Assessing Presidential Character," *World Politics*, XXVI (1974), 242–45.

ii.

*May the cause of liberty, be ever conducted with pru-
dence, but never benumbed by too frigid estimates of difficulty or danger.*[6]

Richard Henry Lee was born to public service. No member of his
political generation had a more distinguished or longer lineage.
Three generations of Lees, dating back to the 1640s, had played a
prominent role in the colony's affairs, while his mother's family (the
Ludwells) had exercised a powerful voice in Virginia politics since
the 1660s. Each of his five brothers had distinguished political careers. Of the two who were older, Philip Ludwell was a member of
the Virginia Council, while Thomas Ludwell, a lawyer, took a leading role in the revolutionary conventions and committees during
1775–76 and was a judge of the General Court under the new state
government. Of the three younger brothers, Francis Lightfoot represented Virginia in the Continental Congress, while William and
Arthur, after a decade of vigorous and conspicuous activity as opposition politicians in London, held important diplomatic posts on the
continent for the new United States government. Richard Henry
himself became a justice of the peace for Westmoreland County in
1757 when he was only twenty-five years old, and the following year
he was elected one of that county's two representatives to the House
of Burgesses, a post he held for the next eighteen years. Despite his
youth, he quickly—within a year—distinguished himself as one of
the most active and prominent members of the House. Selected as a
delegate to the First Continental Congress in 1774, he represented
Virginia in Congress from 1774 to 1779 and again from 1784 to
1788, serving as president of Congress in 1784, and, in between his
two stints in Congress, representing his county in the Virginia House
of Delegates. The capstone to this long political career was his appointment as one of the first two senators from Virginia in the new
Federal government in 1789, a post he held until his retirement in
1792.[7]

6. Richard Henry Lee in a speech in the Virginia Convention in 1775, as quoted
by Edmund Randolph, *History of Virginia*, ed. Arthur H. Shaffer (Charlottesville,
Va., 1970), p. 217.
7. See Burton J. Hendrick, *The Lees of Virginia* (Boston, 1935); Oliver Perry
Chitwood, *Richard Henry Lee: Statesman of the Revolution* (Morgantown, W. Va.,

His "antient and honorable family" was not, however, the only or even a very important ingredient in Richard Henry Lee's long-term prominence in Virginia politics. Among his own generation, there were many men of equally distinguished ancestry. Of them all, however, only Peyton Randolph and Robert Carter Nicholas carried a political weight that exceeded or matched that of Lee. Clearly, one has to look elsewhere for the primary sources of Lee's political authority. In his brief description of Lee in his *History of Virginia*, written two decades after Lee's death, Edmund Randolph, Lee's younger contemporary, offered some important suggestions. Lee, said Randolph,

had gained the palm of a species of oratory rare among a people backward in refinement. He had attuned his voice with so much care that one unmusical cadence could scarcely be pardoned by his ear. He was reported to have formed before a mirror his gesture, which was not unsuitable even to a court. His speech was diffusive, without the hackneyed formulas, and he charmed wheresoever he opened his lips. In political reading he was conversant, and on the popular topics dispersed through the debates of Parliament, his recollection was rapid and correct. Malice had hastily involved him in censure for a supposed inconsistency of conduct upon the Stamp Act; but the vigor and perseverance of his patriotism extorted from his enemies a confession that he deserved the general confidence which was afterwards conceded to him.[8]

As Randolph's description suggests, much of Lee's appeal as a political leader and an essential component of his style of leadership derived from his eloquence as a public speaker. He was widely admired for his "unique oratorical and histrionic talents" and was early "reckoned one of the first Speakers in the House of Burgesses." He had, said one contemporary, "all the advantages of voice . . . the fine polish of language . . . and all the advantages of gesture which the celebrated Demosthenes considered as the first, second, and third qualifications of an orator."[9] At the First Continental Congress John

1967); and Greene, "Foundations of Political Power in the Virginia House of Burgesses."

8. Richard Henry Lee to Silas Deane, Jan. 22, 1779, in *The Letters of Richard Henry Lee*, ed. James Curtis Ballagh (New York, 1912), II, 16; Randolph, *History of Virginia*, p. 184.

9. Grainger, *Character and Style*, p. 67; Harry Piper to Dixon and Littledale, May 29, 1773, Henry Piper Letter Book, 1767–76, Alderman Library, Univ. of Va. (Charlottesville); William Wirt, *The Life of Patrick Henry* (Philadelphia, 1836), p. 109.

Adams testified that "the Virginians" justly spoke "in Raptures" about the oratory of "Richard Henry Lee and Patrick Henry—one the Cicero and the other the Demosthenes of the age." Like the rhetoric of Demosthenes, that of Henry "did not smell of lamp-wicks . . . but of water-drinking and anxious thought." It was not informed by "the artifice of scholastic rhetoric": no "rules and forms and niceties of elocution" intervened to choke "his native fire" or blunt the natural power of his eloquence. By contrast, Lee's oratory was studied— "chaste—classical—beautiful"—so cultivated and harmonious as to make his hearers "sometimes fancy that" they were "listening to some being inspired with more than mortal powers of embellishment." When he spoke, it was "as if elegance had been personified."

Lee's effectiveness as a speaker was enhanced by his striking appearance—his "acquiline nose, and Roman profile" being "too remarkable not to have been noticed" at a great distance—and by the "gracefulness of his attitude (generally) leaning a little with his hat in his hand on the back of the front seat." As his younger contemporary St. George Tucker remarked, Lee's manner of speaking may have "approach'd more nearly to that of Cicero . . . than any other I ever heard," but Lee also seems to have had another, more contemporary model in William Pitt, Earl of Chatham. Like Chatham, Lee strove for theatrical effect. The Great Commoner stood before the House of Commons "with the eye that could 'cut a diamond', the black velvet, the bandages, the huge boot," while Lee, having "lost the use of one of his hands," kept it "constantly covered with a *black silk Bandage*, very neatly fitted to the palm of his hand, but leaving his thumb free."[10]

But it was not only Lee's self-conscious and dramatic presence as a speaker but also what he said and his day-to-day performance that commanded the attention and admiration of his fellow legislators. He was "a very clever Man," said one Virginia contemporary, "& an ornament to his Country"; "a masterly man," added John Adams, a "sensible and deep thinker," who, like both Cicero and Chatham, prevailed not simply "by reason of his eloquence" but by the power of his reason and his intellectual acuity: he seems both to have "rea-

10. *Diary and Autobiography of John Adams*, ed. L. H. Butterfield et al. (Cambridge, Mass., 1962), II, 113; *Plutarch's Lives*, trans. Bernadotte Perrin (London, 1919), VII, 211; Wirt, *Patrick Henry*, pp. 109, 125; St. George Tucker to William Wirt, Sept. 25, 1815, *William and Mary Quarterly*, 1st ser., XXII (1914), 256; Randolph, *History of Virginia*, p. 213; Grainger, *Character and Style*, p. 67.

soned well" and to have "had a quick sensibility and a fervid imagination." Like Cicero's, his rational powers were informed by extensive—according to the standards of the day—learning as well as a good memory. Educated at Wakefield Academy in Yorkshire, he was widely read in the classics, science, the Bible, the law, constitutional and political theory, parliamentary debates, and the polemics of contemporary politics.[11]

Sensible, learned, and affecting oratory was, however, only the most conspicuous of Lee's talents as a legislator: he also had a remarkable capacity for business. With enormous self-discipline, which he regarded as essential "for the depraved heart of man," he never shrank from hard work. Unlike Patrick Henry, who seems to have had an "insuperable aversion" to "the labours of the closet" and, according to Jefferson, "was the laziest man in reading I ever knew," Lee was an industrious and effective committeeman who at every stage of his political career wrestled with the most intricate problems and drafted large numbers of committee reports, state papers, and laws. During his long service in Congress, he was such a workhorse that "excessive writing and constant attention to business" left him "little time for the ordinary offices of life." To Henry, in October 1777, he complained of "the want of time to discharge with propriety an hundreth part of the business with which I am crowded. My eyes fail me fast, and I believe my understanding must soon follow this incessant toil." His contemporaries admired Lee's capacity for such hard work. "Fine parts," Henry wrote Lee the following December, "are seldom joined to industry, and very seldom accompany such a degree of strength and toughness" as Lee had exhibited in his devotion to the American cause.[12]

Henry's reference to Lee's "strength and toughness" calls attention to still another and even more important source of Lee's political authority. With Lee, as with Chatham, the "very vigour of his poli-

11. Harry Piper to Dixon and Littledale, May 29, 1773, Piper Letter Book; Page Smith, *John Adams* (Garden City, N.Y., 1962), I, 170; *Plutarch's Lives*, VII, 211, 215; R. H. Lee to [Thomas Shippen Lee], Apr. 7, 1787, in *Letters of Richard Henry Lee*, I, 418–19.

12. Lee to George Washington, Nov. 13, 1775, to Samuel Adams, Feb. 7, 1776, to Charles Lee, May 21, 1776, to Patrick Henry, Oct. 8, 1777, in *Letters of Richard Henry Lee*, I, 156, 167, 192, 325; *The Writings of Thomas Jefferson*, ed. Albert Ellery Bergh (Washington, D.C., 1903), I, 12; Hugh Blair Grigsby, *The Virginia Convention of 1776* (Richmond, 1855), pp. 132, 142.

cies" was the "*numen*," the presiding spirit, of his political personality. Within a year after his first entry into the House of Burgesses, he donned the mantle of the vigorous, independent "country" patriot who, ever suspicious of power, blew the whistle on corruption in the political establishment by demanding a strict examination of the treasury, the preserve of John Robinson, who, as speaker of the House and treasurer, was the most powerful politician in Virginia and so enormously popular as to be described as "the darling of the Country." By this act Lee quickly established his reputation as a man "hot, violent, and supercilious, in party; [and] very tenacious of his opinion."[13] Beginning in the mid-1760s, the contest with Britain provided Lee with a stage and a setting that could scarcely have been better contrived for the elaboration of a role that was so congenial to his personality. The Stamp Act, that wanton application of "the iron hand of power," so "warmed" his mind, he declared, as to produce "a fixt determination to exert every faculty I possessed both in public and private life, to prevent the success of a measure" that was "in the highest degree pernicious to my Country." For the next decade, he was the ever-vigilant patriot, the clarion who alerted his countrymen to the "unjust and destructive" measures of a "tyrannous administration" to impose its "slavish system" of "Colony Administration" upon the colonies.[14]

A vigorous advocate of firm and uncompromising resistance, Lee was an early and consistent proponent of a "union of counsel and action among" the "lovers of liberty in every province." "Whilst men in general, are thoughtless and indolent," he wrote John Dickinson in 1768, "spirit and wisdom are necessary to rouse and inform minds," and it was the special role of Lee and men like him to "rouse a spirit

13. Grainger, *Character and Style*, p. 68; Francis Fauquier to Board of Trade, May 12, 1761, CO5/1330, ff. 129–135 (Public Record Office, London); Jack P. Greene, "The Attempt to Separate the Offices of Speaker and Treasurer in Virginia, 1758–1766," *Virginia Magazine of History and Biography*, LXXI (1963), 11–18; David John Mays, *Edmund Pendleton, 1721–1803: A Biography* (Cambridge, Mass., 1952), I, 174–208; Joseph A. Ernst, *Money and Politics in America, 1755–1775: A Study of the Currency of 1764 and the Political Economy of Revolution* (Chapel Hill, N.C., 1973), 63, 74–75; An Enemy of Hypocrisy [James Mercer] to *Virginia Gazette* (Purdie & Dixon, Oct. 3, 1766).

14. Lee to ———, May 31, 1764, to Landon Carter, June 22, 1765, to *Virginia Gazette*, July 25, 1766, to [Edmund Jenings], May 31, 1769, to William Lee, July 7, 1770, and to Samuel Adams, Feb. 4, 1775, in *Letters of Richard Henry Lee*, I, 5–7, 17, 36, 46, 128.

that proving fatal to an abandoned Ministry may save the whole Empire from impending destruction."[15] "If the people will submit to abuse," he wrote Landon Carter in 1771, "let them do it with their eyes open; if they will pursue the wrong, after having been shown the right way, they will have only themselves to blame." The patriot at least would have the satisfaction of having done his duty: "Who fails in doing right," Lee later told John Adams, "fails nobly, because Virtue is its own and a very great reward." Indeed, the cause of virtue would be lost without "the strongest exertions," perseverance, and "vigor" on the part of patriots such as himself. He wanted to believe that virtue would ultimately "drive vice & folly off the ground," but his political experience taught him that "the cause of virtue, without proper means to support it, must often fail."[16] Hence, he had no use for the practitioners of "pedantic politics," for "time-serving Men," for the "Dealer in Expedients," or for "timid senseless politics." The stakes were too high for principle to be sacrificed to expediency: the colonies had to be as adamant in "the cause of Liberty, as so noble and exalted a principle demands." The "blessings of Liberty," he was persuaded, "flow not from timid and selfish policy."[17]

Vigor, for Lee, did not mean impetuosity. Although he introduced the motion for independence in Congress in June 1776, he was not an early advocate of a complete break with Britain, and throughout the years of war and Confederation he was vigorous in support of a moderate rather than a radical approach to most major political issues, including especially the movement to strengthen the federal government. "I remember when I once detested the moderate character [during the long political contest with Britain prior to Independence]," Lee wrote Samuel Adams in the fall of 1784, but at "this moment I think that moderation, wisdom, firmness, and attention, are the principles proper for our adoption: and highly becoming the

15. Lee to Landon Carter, June 22, 1765, to John Dickinson, July 25, 1768, to ————, Mar. 27, 1768, to Samuel Adams, Feb. 4, 1773, and to Arthur Lee, Feb. 24, 1775, in *Letters of Richard Henry Lee,* I, 8, 29, 26–27, 82, 131.

16. Lee to William Lee, July 7, 1770, to Landon Carter, Apr. 18, 1771, to William Lee, Sept. 20, 1774, to John Adams, Apr. 24, 1779, to Patrick Henry, Feb. 14, 1785, in *Letters of Richard Henry Lee,* I, 52, 56, 124; II, 47, 333.

17. Lee to Landon Carter, June 22, 1765, to John Dickinson, Nov. 26, 1768, to William Lee, July 7, 1770, to Landon Carter, Apr. 18, 1771, to William Lee, Sept. 20, 1774, to George Washington, Oct. 22, 1775, to Charles Lee, Apr. 22, 1776, to Samuel Purviance, May 1, 1776, and to Patrick Henry, Feb. 14, 1785, in *Letters of Richard Henry Lee,* I, 8, 30–31, 52, 56, 124, 183, 186; II, 333.

dignity of our successful situation." And Lee could be—and was—vigorous in support of unpopular measures. During the 1770s and 1780s, he strongly opposed large paper money issues and advocated a program of vigorous taxation, payment of British debts, and mild treatment of Tories—all positions that were unpopular with large segments of the Virginia political community and especially with the localist followers of Patrick Henry.[18] He endorsed John Adams's view "that person & property in America" should "be held sacred. I too love Liberty," he wrote his cousin in the year of his death, "but it is a regulated Liberty, so that ends & principles of society may not be disturbed by the fury of a Mob or by the art, cunning, and industry of wicked, vicious & avaricious Men." During the Stamp Act crisis, he played a conspicuous role in the "out-of-doors" opposition in Virginia's Northern Neck. He staged a public demonstration against the Stamp Act at Westmoreland Court House in September 1765 and the following winter organized the Westmoreland Association, a vigilante group dedicated to preventing the use of stamps, and personally led a massive march to Hobb's Hole in Essex County to force Archibald Ritchie, a Scottish merchant who had announced his intention of complying with the Stamp Act, to make a humiliating public recantation. Except for these early episodes in his career, however, Lee eschewed the part of the country patriot "who will be popular, right or wrong." Unlike John Wilkes or Patrick Henry, he seems to have lacked the inclination or the necessary breadth of appeal to secure a broad following among the public at large or to become a demagogue. His proper forum was the legislative chamber; his audience, his fellow legislators. Like Chatham and Charles James Fox, he was not the ideologue who would take his case to the country but a "parliamentary politician" who preferred to operate inside the legislative halls and within the small circles of the politically powerful. Even his newspaper essays were primarily directed toward his peers.[19]

Perhaps as much as anything Lee's insatiable desire for approval

18. Lee to Thomas Jefferson, Aug. 25, 1777, Aug. 10, 1778, to Patrick Henry, Nov. 15, 1778, to Samuel Adams, Nov. 18, 1784, Mar. 14, 1785, in *Letters of Richard Henry Lee*, I, 319, 431, 452–53; II, 294, 342–43; Grigsby, *Virginia Convention of 1776*, 142. The political divisions of the 1780s in Virginia are analyzed by Jackson Turner Main, *Political Parties before the Constitution* (Chapel Hill, N.C., 1973), 244–65.

19. Lee to ———, Oct. 10, 1785, and to Thomas Lee Shippen, Feb. 12, 1794, in *Letters of Richard Henry Lee*, II, 390, 576; Grainger, *Character and Style*, pp. 47, 68–77; Chitwood, *Richard Henry Lee*, pp. 36–42.

—his hunger for fame—among those he admired in the political arena underlay his powerful devotion to public life. It "has ever been my wish," he wrote Patrick Henry in 1777 while defending himself against attacks from his enemies in the Virginia legislature, "to deserve the esteem of virtuous men, and to stand well in their opinion." This yearning for esteem, wrote Landon Carter, made him "always open to flattery" and, in William Maclay's opinion, overly "ambitious and vainglorious." Indeed, his ambition for public fame was so great as to evoke distrust among his associates. He was a man, said James Mercer in 1766, "very happy in FACE, and good in expression" but "too great a slave to his ambition and desire" to be Speaker of the House. Moreover, that distrust seemed to be given some credence by his inconsistent behavior during the crisis over the Stamp Act. At the suggestion of a friend, Lee rashly, as he later explained, applied for the post of stamp collector before he had "reflected in the least on the nature and tendency of such an Act." He claimed to have recognized his error "a few days after" he had sent off his application and to have embarked upon his vigorous opposition to the measure "long before" his "application could possibly" have reached Britain. But the application and the prominent role he later took in opposition to the Stamp Act left him open to the charge that he did not discover the evil "consequences of the act until he was assured his application was not attended with success, so it is to be presumed his patriotick spirit was set on fire by envy and disappointment." Only after having failed in the closet, the charge went, did Lee feel compelled to seek his account with the people.[20]

To moderate men such as Edmund Pendleton, not only did a man thus compromised seem to be an "improper leader" of such an "incendiary stigma" as the march on Archibald Ritchie, "but the [excessive] number emploied" on that march—"about 600 men"—as well as the "Parade and noise on the Occasion" seemed to betray, on Lee's part, a willingness to sacrifice public order to personal ambition. No matter how intense his later patriotism, Lee's motives were thereafter always somewhat suspect. "As true a trout as ever swam, as staunch a hound as ever ran" was the Petersburg merchant

20. Lee to *Virginia Gazette*, July 25, 1766, to Patrick Henry, May 26, 1777, in *Letters of Richard Henry Lee*, I, 16–18, 298; Chitwood, *Richard Henry Lee*, 39, 225; *The Diary of Colonel Landon Carter of Sabine Hall, 1752–1778*, ed. Jack P. Greene (Charlottesville, Va., 1965), II, 1102–3; An Enemy to Hypocrisy [James Mercer] to *Virginia Gazette* (Purdie & Dixon, Oct. 3, 1766).

Roger Atkinson's estimation of Lee ten years later. But he added, as if he were not entirely sure of the accuracy of his evaluation, that he hoped it would be "possible [to] keep this gentleman firm & faithful in his country's cause & I *think* he will be so kept." The distrust arising out of Lee's ambition may have been deepened by a certain reserve. Though he appears to have interacted easily with other people, he seems to have kept all but a very few at some distance, and by his own testimony, he "endeavored not to take up friendships lightly." Though he always managed to vindicate himself and regain his authority, this distrust helped to lend plausibility to a number of vicious attacks on Lee during the late 1770s both in Congress and in Virginia.[21]

From the point of view of the public, however, Lee's ambition was entirely functional. No man seems to have striven harder to achieve some congruence between his public persona—as the vigorous, unselfish patriot—and his political behavior. For what he craved was not merely praise but praiseworthiness. He wanted not merely to be famous but to deserve fame, and this consuming "spur of fame," as the men of the Revolution phrased it, repeatedly seems to have driven Lee to sacrifice personal and family concerns to his political career. He began talking about retirement from elective office—which he "found . . . an hard service"—as early as 1770 after only twelve years as a legislator, and the wish to retire was a persistent theme in his correspondence for the remaining twenty-two years of his career. His complaints about overwork, the loss of "private enjoyments," and the adverse affects of his public obligations upon his "health . . . fortune, and . . . domestic happiness" were incessant. His long service in Congress took him away from home for as long as six to seven months at a stretch with the result that his plantation affairs were often in a "distracted state" and his family—he had nine children—suffered "immensely by my absence." He had only the utmost contempt for and resentment towards those "avaricious plunderers" among his colleagues in public life who used their position for personal enrich-

21.Edmund Pendleton to James Madison, Apr. 21, 1790, in *The Letters and Papers of Edmund Pendleton 1734–1803*, ed. David John Mays (Charlottesville, Va., 1967), II, 566; Atkinson to Samuel Pleasants, Oct. 1, 1774, in A. J. Morrison, ed., "Letters of Roger Atkinson, 1769–1776," *Virginia Magazine of History and Biography*, XV (1908), 356; Lee to William Whipple, July 1, 1783, to Samuel Adams, Apr. 7, 1785, in *Letters of Richard Henry Lee*, II, 246, 283. Italics added. See also *Diary and Autobiography of John Adams*, III, 367–68, for another, less credible analysis of the reasons for distrust of Lee.

ment, and his public service may actually have contributed to the diminution of a fortune that was never "very ample" for his large family. Indeed, he found himself forced to live with "the truest republican economy" when he was at Congress, at one point during the winter of 1777 being reduced to living upon the "scanty fare" of "wild pigeons" which were "sold for a few cents per Dozen."[22] As a consequence of the "distressing pressure" created by these and similar adversities, Lee "long panted for retirement." Whenever he came under attack from his political enemies in either Virginia or Congress, as he did in 1777, 1778, and 1779, this threat to retire became strident. "Where a man by being honest is sure to be oppressed— Where disgrace & ruin are to reward the most faithful services. When the discharge of duty raises up the angry and malignant passions of envy, malice, and all uncharitableness—It is best to retire until necessity has pointed out proper men and proper measures," declared Lee in 1779. As Cato in Joseph Addison's play had said in lines that struck deep resonances among eighteenth-century Virginians, "When vice prevails, and impious men bear sway, the post of honor is a private station."[23]

But Lee would never retire "absolutely" until his health forced him to do so. The true and virtuous patriot Lee aspired to be could not retire without violating both his public persona and his own self-image. For such men, duty demanded that comfort be sacrificed for great public ends. For one who had made the "generous, Roman resolution . . . at the hazard of life, fortune, and domestic happiness, to contribute, by every means to the perfect establishment of our Independence," it was impossible to "quit the service . . . untill . . . a proper peace upon proper principles" had been established, lest such an important work fall into the hands of "weak, ambitious, avaricious and wicked men." Having once put his "hand to the plough," he was

22. Lee to William Lee, July 9, 1770, to Landon Carter, Apr. 18, 1771, to Charles Lee, May 21, 1776, to Thomas Jefferson, Nov. 2, 1776, to Patrick Henry, Dec. 3, 1776, May 13, May 26, Oct. 8, 1777, to William Lee, Jan. 25, 1778, to Arthur Lee, May 27, 1778, to Patrick Henry, Nov. 15, 1778, to Arthur Lee, Feb. 11, 1779, to William Shippen, Jr., Apr. 18, 1779, to Thomas Jefferson, May 3, 1779, and to Samuel Adams, Apr. 6, 1783; Virginia Delegates to George Pyncheon and John Bradford, Oct. 16, 1777, in *Letters of Richard Henry Lee*, I, 52, 56, 192, 222, 228, 290, 302, 325, 332, 384–85, 410, 453; II, 30–31, 35, 44–45, 54–55, 381.

23. Lee to John Page, May 26, 1777; to Francis Lightfoot Lee, July 27, 1778, to William Shippen, Jr., Apr. 18, 1779, to F. L. Lee, Apr. 26, 1779, in *Letters of Richard Henry Lee*, I, 295–496, 29, II, 45, 49–51; Joseph Addison, *Cato*, Act IV, scene 4, ll. 140–51.

"bound to go through" no matter what the difficulties. In the cause of "public liberty," he was fond of remarking, "nothing is done whilst any thing remains to be done." Only after the "independence of America" had been fixed "on wise and permanent foundations," could Lee "with infinite pleasure . . . return to" his "farm and eat the bread of industry in freedom and ease."[24]

His sense of identity was, in fact, too deeply bound up with the public realm ever to permit him to be content in a private station. He might occasionally denounce politics as "the Science of Fraud" and politicians as "the Professors of that Science." He might sometimes think "that the life of a private Citizen is more desirable than any public character whatever" or that "taking care of a large family" was an "important concern" that could justifiably consume his total attention. But for Lee neither sentiment was a true measure of his deepest feelings. After spending so many years "in the busy scene of politics," he found private life dull and vapid. Within less than a year after he left Congress in 1779, he had returned to politics as a representative from Westmoreland to the Virginia House of Delegates, and on those occasions when illness forced him home he could scarcely wait until he was "in a state to venture on the stormy sea of politics & public business." Whatever his profession, no man could, in fact, have been more eager to surrender "private ease to public service."[25]

Moreover, his years in Congress encouraged a distinct preference for public service on the larger and more conspicuous stage provided by Congress. Even as a young legislator, Lee had shown his ambition for higher office and status by repeatedly seeking appointment to the Virginia Council, and his orientation toward the political world outside Virginia was revealed by his early initiation of correspondence with John Dickinson, Samuel Adams, and other prominent opponents of British policy in the other colonies. That orientation was,

24. Lee to Thomas Jefferson, Nov. 3, 1776, to Patrick Henry, May 13, 1777, to Landon Carter, June 25, 1777, to George Wythe, Oct. 19, 1777, to William Lee, Jan. 25, 1778, to John Adams, May 13, 1778, to Francis Lightfoot Lee, July 27, 1778, to Henry Laurens, Dec. 26, 1778, to John Adams, Oct. 8, 1779, to Samuel Adams, Jan. 18, 1780, to Arthur Lee, Aug. 31, 1780, in *Letters of Richard Henry Lee*, I, 222, 290, 304, 337, 385, 405, 429, 467; II, 155, 170, 197.

25. Lee to John Page, May 26, 1777, to John Adams, Oct. 8, 1779, to William Shippen, Jr., May 7, 1780, to Samuel Adams, Apr. 6, 1783, to James Monroe, Jan. 5, 1784, to Thomas Lee Shippen, Apr. 17, 1787, Sept. 21, 1791, in *Letters of Richard Henry Lee*, I, 296; II, 155, 179, 281, 386–87, 417, 544.

moreover, greatly enhanced by his contacts with his two younger brothers, William and Arthur, who lived in London, the center of the Anglo-American public world, and were deeply involved in British politics in the years prior to independence. Beginning with the First Continental Congress, he identified more and more with the national political scene. He was proud of Virginia's preeminent contribution to the Revolution, of "the spirit, wisdom, and energy of her councils," and, though he once thought of moving to Massachusetts, where he thought the genius of the people might be more consistent with his "ideas of what must constitute social happiness and security," he retained an intense loyalty to "my own country." Furthermore, he occasionally grew sick of "Congress wisdom." But once he had returned to Virginia he missed the "hurry of business" and longed for "the patriotic inhabitants of Liberty Hall" and the "sensible social evenings they pass there."[26] Not rural and remote Virginia, but "Philadelphia or Boston," he wrote his brother Arthur in 1780, "seem to be the only Theatres [in America] for great Actors to play upon." His primary identification was with "those proved Patriots with whom I early toiled in the vineyard of American liberty," with those "original friends to the just rights of America, whose wise and firm perseverance . . . secured to the United States at last the blessings [of freedom], without which there is little difference between men and brutes."[27]

The elegant, dramatic, and persuasive orator, the cogent political analyst, the attentive and hardworking legislator—these were all important ingredients of Lee's political personality. But his most distinctive quality and the one which gained for him the "general confidence" conceded to him by the Virginia political nation, as Edmund Randolph observed, was the "vigor and perseverance of his patriotism." He was the "active" man who "vivified" the politics of restraint practiced by so many of his equally prominent colleagues. Always "earnest for the public," he was "a *scarecrow of violence* to

26. Lee to James Abercromby, Aug. 27, 1762, to William Lee, Dec. 17, 1769, to Landon Carter, Apr. 18, 1771, to George Washington, Nov. 13, 1775, to Patrick Henry, Apr. 20, 1776, to William Whipple, Nov. 29, 1778, to *Pennsylvania General Advertiser*, Dec. 16, 1778, to Francis Lightfoot Lee, Apr. 26, 1779, to John Adams, Oct. 8, 1779, and to George Wythe, Feb. 28, 1783, in *Letters of Richard Henry Lee*, I, 1–2, 40, 52, 156, 176, 454, 457; II, 51, 155, 279.

27. Lee to John Adams, June 20, 1778, to Arthur Lee, Aug. 31, 1780, to William Whipple, July 17, 1782, to Patrick Henry, Feb. 14, 1785, in *Letters of Richard Henry Lee*, I, 417; II, 197, 274, 331.

the gentle warblers of the grove, the moderate Whigs and temperate statesmen."[28] Lee thus found his identity in the public realm as an active cultivator in the "vineyard of Liberty," as one of those "Republican spirits who . . . labored for the liberty of their Country, and whose sole object" was "the security of public happiness." He stood for energy and activity. He was the Virginia epitome of the classic English patriot as exemplified by a long line of heroic figures from Sir John Eliot and Shaftesbury in the seventeenth century to Bolingbroke and Chatham in the eighteenth. Like them, he strove to be the independent and incorruptible man who stood for a strenuous—but responsible—exertion of public spirit, one of those "grave sensible Men" who came to the rescue of his country when liberty was in jeopardy, roused his countrymen to a spirited resistance against tyranny, and never quit the public stage until liberty was secure and virtue ascendant in the public counsels. In "concert with other generous friends to human liberty and the rights of America," he remained adamantly and "uniformly warm for the freedom, happiness, and independence of my Country" and yielded to no one in "zeal for the American cause, and industry to promote its success."[29]

iii.

I opposed and endeavoured to moderate the violent and fiery, who were plunging us into rash measures, and had the happiness to find a majority of all public bodies confirming my sentiments.[30]

Edmund Pendleton brought to the political arena none of the social advantages enjoyed by Richard Henry Lee. Indeed, although he received considerable help from the powerful Robinson family, he was to a large degree a self-made man. The fifth son of a father who died

28. Randolph, *History of Virginia*, p. 184; Grainger, *Character and Style*, pp. 59, 64, 68.

29. Lee to Arthur Lee, Feb. 24, 1775, to Patrick Henry, May 26, 1777, to George Wythe, Oct. 19, 1777, to John Adams, June 20, 1778, to *Pennsylvania General Advertiser*, Dec. 16, 1778, to Silas Deane, Jan. 22, 1779, and to William Whipple, July 1, 1783, in *Letters of Richard Henry Lee*, I, 131, 300, 337, 417, 457; II, 25, 283.

30. Pendleton's "Autobiography," July 20, 1793, in *Letters and Papers of Edmund Pendleton*, II, 607. Portions of this section are adapted from Jack P. Greene, "Virginia Political Culture in the Era of the American Revolution," *Virginia Quarterly Review*, XLIV (1968), 302–10.

before he was born in 1721, a decade earlier than Lee, Pendleton was descended from "a good family, fallen to decay" in England. His grandfather, the immigrant, had been "well educated" and "respectable" for his "piety and moral virtue," but the Pendletons had not made much of a mark upon Virginia society. Thus, Edmund Pendleton, as he later remarked in a brief autobiography, had to make his way "without any classical education—without patrimony—without what is called the influence of Family Connection." But he had natural advantages—in his words, "a docile and unassuming mind, a retentive memory, a fondness for reading, a clear head, and upright heart, with a calm temper, benevolent to all"—that were a sufficient foundation for a spectacular career in law and politics. For a young man of fine parts but small fortune in Virginia during the middle of the eighteenth century, the law provided the readiest access to wealth, status, and fame, and Pendleton, admitted to the bar when he was only nineteen years old, practiced his "profession with [such] great approbation and success . . . at the County Courts" that he moved up to the General Court of the colony when he was barely twenty-four years of age. Within less than two years following his appointment as justice of the peace for Caroline County, he won—in his thirtieth year —election from the same county to the House of Burgesses, in which he served with distinction for the rest of the colonial period. Beginning with the Revolutionary disturbances of 1774–75, Pendleton, as he proudly noted in his autobiography, attained "without solicitation . . . the highest offices in my Country." He was one of the Virginia delegates to the First and Second Continental Congresses in 1774–75, was elected president of the Virginia Committee of Safety in August 1775, succeeded Peyton Randolph as president of the Virginia Convention in December 1775, served as the first speaker of the House of Delegates under the new constitution, and presided over the Virginia ratifying convention in 1788. For a quarter century, from the creation of the state court system in 1778 until his death in 1803, Pendleton served as the "head of the Judiciary Department" of the state, a post to which he was initially elected "by an unanimous vote."[31]

31. "Autobiography," July 20, 1793; Pendleton's Notation, 1801, *Letters and Papers of Edmund Pendleton,* II, 605–7, 700; Greene, "Foundations of Political Power in the Virginia House of Burgesses." The standard biography is Mays, *Edmund Pendleton.*

Superficially, the ingredients of Pendleton's political authority were similar to those of Richard Henry Lee. Like Lee, Pendleton was "a very pretty smoothtongued speaker." Unlike Lee, however, he was "not eloquent" and not histrionic. Though "elegant . . . in style and elocution," he was essentially a debater rather than an orator. "He had not indeed," Jefferson later wrote, "the poetical fancy of Mr. Henry, his sublime imagination, his lofty and overwhelming diction." But, continued Jefferson, Pendleton

was cool, smooth and persuasive, his language flowing, chaste and embellished; his conceptions quick, acute and full of resource; never vanquished: for if he lost the main battle, he returned upon you, and regained so much of it as to make it a drawn one, by dexterous manoeuvres, skirmishes in detail, and by the recovery of small advantages which, little singly, were important all together. You never knew when you were clear of him, but were harassed by his perseverance, until the patience was worn down of all who had less of it than himself.

"Taken all in all," Jefferson thought, Pendleton "was the ablest man in debate I ever met with."[32] Pendleton's ability as a debater was enhanced by his appearance and manner. The Petersburg merchant, Roger Atkinson, compared him "to old Nestor in Homer—in the words of Pope:

> Experienced Nestor, in persuasion skill'd
> Words sweet as honey from his lips distilled."

A man "of easy and cheerful countenance," he was, as Edmund Burke wrote of Sir Robert Walpole, "straightforward, bold, and open, and the least addicted to scheming and cabal." Though by his own testimony he was, like Lee, "particular in friendship with but a few," this openness joined with an "amiableness [that] bordered on familiarity without detracting from personal dignity" gained the trust even of his opponents. Pendleton, said Jefferson, one of his most persistent adversaries, "was one of the most virtuous and benevolent of men, the kindest friend, the most amiable and pleasant of companions, which ensured a favorable reception to whatever came from him." His amiability and honesty guaranteed as well that he would end his

32. Roger Atkinson to Samuel Pleasants, Oct. 1, 1774, in "Letters of Roger Atkinson," p. 357; Jefferson, "Autobiography," in *Writings of Thomas Jefferson*, I, 54–55; Mays, *Pendleton*, I, 283.

life, as another observer noted, with "not only the esteem but the love, the admiration, nay even the veneration of his countrymen."[33]

In his *"capacity for business"* Pendleton matched and probably even exceeded Lee. "Labor," said Edmund Randolph, "was his delight." His life, according to another contemporary, "approached the nearest to constant employment in useful occupations . . . of any I ever knew." This "great industry" in public affairs derived in some large part from an acute awareness of his own limitations, a recognition that he was not a man of broad learning or unusual brilliance: as he phrased it, he was "not equal to Mansfield or Franklin" in mental abilities and not likely to achieve the high "Character of a Statesman." Thus cognizant of his own limitations, Pendleton could and did compensate for them by a constant effort both to "stretch . . . his mental powers" and to apply himself thoroughly to any tasks that came before him. "If I had uncommon merit in public business," he observed in his autobiography, "It was that of superior diligence and attention."[34] Such devoted attention quickly made Pendleton the master of all forms of legislative business. His reputation as a committeeman and draftsman of legislative papers was equal to his stature as a debator. "With a pen which scattered no classical decorations," wrote Edmund Randolph, "he performed the most substantial service by the perspicuity and comprehensiveness of his numerous resolutions, reports, and laws." His chief political tutors and patrons, Speakers John Robinson and Peyton Randolph, who had themselves built their political power on reputations for "great integrity, assiduity and ability in business," had taught him to put "every question so . . . as to be well understood, and free as might be from embarrassment or complexity." He learned his lesson so well that his colleagues sent him as a delegate to the First Continental Congress for the express purpose of being "the penman for business." "With his habits [and extensive knowledge] of business," Pendleton assisted "every burgess who was a stranger to parliamentary forms or unacquainted

33. Mays, *Pendleton*, I, 283, II, 347; Grainger, *Character and Style*, p. 62; Pendleton, "Autobiography," July 20, 1793, in *Letters and Papers of Edmund Pendleton*, II, 607; Randolph, *History of Virginia*, p. 186; Jefferson, "Autobiography," in *Writings of Thomas Jefferson*, I, 55; Grigsby, *Virginia Convention of 1776*, p. 127; Atkinson to Pleasants, Oct. 1, 1774, in "Letters of Roger Atkinson," p. 357.

34. Grainger, *Character and Style*, p. 21; Randolph, *History of Virginia*, p. 186; Pendleton, "Autobiography," July 20, 1793, and Pendleton to George Washington, Sept. 11, 1793, in *Letters and Papers of Edmund Pendleton*, II, 607, 615; Mays, *Pendleton*, I, 122, 261.

with debate." As in the case of Sir Robert Walpole, extensive training and experience in "the craft of politics" and an impressive mastery "of parliamentary business, of ready argument" gave Pendleton "a glare of confidence," an appearance of wisdom, and enormous political authority.[35]

If Lee was the exponent of vigorous and uncompromising patriotism, Pendleton was the voice of moderation. Not that he was in any sense a "quietist." On the contrary, he was an early and firm opponent of parliamentary taxation and, as Edmund Randolph noted, was throughout the period from 1764 to 1776 a "master of the principles of opposition to the ministry." But the politics he found personally so congenial and the politics he had learned from his mentors John Robinson and Peyton Randolph was the politics of the possible, the politics of prudence and restraint, of "circumscribed dissidence" and "political lenity," "of dispute within safe limits with blunted weapons, within the consensus." In the Anglo-American world of the eighteenth century, the primary models for this type of political posture were Sir Robert Walpole, that penultimate master of "humane, civilized and realistic politics," and George Savile, Marquis of Halifax, the "Trimmer." J. H. Grainger has written that Halifax's adversary, Shaftesbury, "stood for violence, emerging causes," while Halifax was the advocate of "poise, some inactivity, consensus, a delimitation of politics, a minimization of rule"—a characterization that, with some softening of the language used to describe Shaftesbury, is equally descriptive of the contrasting political stances of Lee and Pendleton.[36]

Indeed, although there is no evidence that he consciously modeled himself after either Halifax or Walpole or that he thought of himself in terms of the Halifax prescription—for then, as now, the term "trimmer" was one of political opprobrium—Pendleton was, in fact, a classic example of the public-spirited trimmer as originally limned by Halifax. He strove always to keep the political system on an even keel by discouraging dispute over fundamentals and seeking the

35. Grainger, *Character and Style*, pp. 24, 41, 61; Randolph, *History of Virginia*, pp. 185–86, 206; Pendleton to Thomas Jefferson, June 17, 1800, in *Letters and Papers of Edmund Pendleton*, II, 675–76; Fauquier to Board of Trade, May 12, 1761, CO 5/1330, ff. 129–35.

36. Grainger, *Character and Style*, pp. 47–49, 59, 61; Randolph, *History of Virginia*, p. 186; Pendleton to James Madison, Sr., Apr. 17, 1765, in *Letters and Papers of Edmund Pendleton*, I, 20.

pragmatic adjustment of lesser conflicts of interest, personality, and opinion. Realizing, as he put it in an address before the Virginia ratifying convention in 1788, that "perfection in any institute devised by *man*, was as vain as the search for a philosopher's stone," he was willing when—"as in all . . . Political cases"—he could not "get the very best" to "take the best we can get," "to relax in some matters in order to secure those of greater moment," and to work for compromise among "the different Jarring Interests" for the purpose of bringing things "as near the Centre of General good" as possible. The "good of the common cause" could not "be interrupted by Punctilios of no real consequence." Whenever there was a "Variety of Opinions" in politics, "Compromise," the search for "proximate solutions," was the wisest and "most Equitable" course. Prudence dictated that such matters be "as little Agitated as may be, lest differences of Sentiment should be wrought into dissentions, very injurious to the common Cause." It was invariably better for the contestants to "yield, rather than interrupt for a moment the general good."[37] Like Halifax, Pendleton was "a sceptic about political passion," extremely wary of "mere speculative opinions," and distrustful of "the patriot with virtuous politics who would break up the unity of the country." The true patriot should put aside "his zeal and work for prizes within the system." He should also seek to foster unanimity and maintain the "strength and Vigor" of the political system by "watching and breaking the Spirit of Party" and "all Private, dirty, unjust and ingrateful Cabals" and standing up against "Noise," "dissipation," and "dissentions"—those "stated enemies to wisdom and deliberation," to "*social*, as well as *private* happiness." He had to spurn "all Intrigues, Finesse and Stratagems in Government, as well as in Private transactions" and, deeply aware that "Selfish Party regards" were the "bane of all Public Councils," attach himself to "no party" and act under no "influence, but the true interest and real happiness" of the whole society. He should strive to be a man "in Pursuit of *Right* . . . Uninfluenced by anything but the real difference between *that* and *Wrong*," a man

37. Pendleton to William Woodford, May 30, 1775, Dec. 7, 1775, to Thomas Jefferson, Aug. 26, 1776, to James Madison, Sept. 25, 1780, June 17, 1782, Dec. 19, 1786, and Address to the Va. Ratifying Convention, June 12, 1788, in *Letters and Papers of Edmund Pendleton*, I, 103, 136, 201, 309; II, 399, 491, 528; Grainger, *Character and Style*, p. 8. An instance of the popular usage of "trimmer" in a negative sense in Pendleton's Virginia may be found in Isaac Wilkins to David Griffith, July 21, 1771, David Griffith Papers, Va. Historical Society (Richmond). I am grateful to Mr. Rhys Isaac for this reference.

ever on the alert against any ill-considered or "distructive popular measures" that might be a threat to liberty, property, and stability or any tendencies that might lead to the development of "a dangerous aristocracy." In times of uncertainty and stress, when the authority of existing institutions was in doubt, times of possible disruption such as in 1775–76, men like Pendleton had to seize every "opportunity to erect new barriers against folly, fraud, and ambition" and insert themselves between the "Sanguine" politicians, who stood for "rash Measures without consideration," and the "Flegmatic," who, paralyzed by their own fears, were "afraid to move at all." He was the one who took "the middle way" and attempted "by tempering the first sort and bringing the latter into action to draw all together to a Steddy" political course. "He recommended moderation under all circumstances," said Philip Mazzei of Pendleton, "so that [his opponents] . . . called him 'Moderation' instead of Pendleton." Moderation required lenity—not "drawing the reins too tight"—toward political opponents. "I have ever been on the side of lenity," Pendleton wrote in reference to "pretended Neutrals" in 1777.[38]

But moderation and lenity were not appropriate in all cases. Treason or open opposition to the common cause during the War for Independence could not be tolerated. Moreover, Pendleton was an unswerving advocate of a close "Obedience to the Laws" and a strict regard for justice, even for Tories and British creditors. Thus, he opposed closing the courts both in 1765–66 and 1775–76 lest such an action "fix an eternal Stigma on the Country, introduce Anarchy and disorder and render Life and property here precarious." "Laws should be mild and gentle," Pendleton declared in 1782, "but rigidly Executed." A satisfactory government had to have energy. Having spent all of his political life on the inside of Virginia politics, he was far less suspicious of power than was Lee. "I am not overjealous of power," he declared in 1781 in arguing for giving every "public body

---

38. Grainger, *Character and Style*, pp. 47–48; Mays, *Pendleton*, II, 136; Pendleton to Joseph Chew, June 15, 1775, to Va. Convention of 1776, May 6, 1776, to Thomas Jefferson, July 22, Aug. 26, 1776, to Richard Henry Lee, Dec. 6, 1776, Sept. 27, 1777, to William Woodford, Mar. 13, 1778, Nov. 8, 1779, to Joseph Jones, Feb. 10, 1781, to James Madison, Aug. 27, 1781, to Richard Henry Lee, Apr. 18, 1785, to Va. Ratifying Convention, June 12, 1788, to Harry Innes, Nov. 9, 1791, to George Washington, Sept. 11, 1793, to Citizens of Caroline, Nov. 1798; Pendleton's Account of the Case of the Prisoners, Oct. 29, 1782; Pendleton, "The Danger Not Over," Oct. 5, 1801, in *Letters and Papers of Edmund Pendleton*, I, 110, 176, 188, 200–201, 204, 225, 251, 306, 334, 370; II, 422, 478, 519, 580, 615, 651, 695–97.

so much [power] as is necessary to their appointment." A corollary
of this deep veneration for law and belief in vigorous government was
a zealous attachment to "ancient establishments," and during the
Revolution Pendleton was the primary spokesman in Virginia for the
desire for continuity. As Jefferson later recalled, Pendleton was one
of those men who "from their natural temperaments . . . were more
disposed generally to acquiesce in things as they are, than to risk in-
novations." He always preferred, he wrote Jefferson in August 1776,
the "old terms, which custom has made easy and familiar." Yet, his
"habits of mind," a later historian remarked, "insensibly attached
him to the new state of things," and, as Jefferson hastened to point
out, "whenever the public will had once decided," none "was more
faithful or exact" in obeying and carrying out a measure he had opposed. For a man whose only personal ambition in public life was
to be "esteemed by the great and the good of my acquaintance," friend
and foe alike, maintenance of the system was vastly more important
than political victory. "Ever since I had any power," Pendleton declared to the Virginia ratifying convention in 1788, "I was more anxious to discharge my duty than to increase my power." [39]

For Pendleton, this concern with maintaining order, keeping the
political system on an even keel, making sure that justice always prevailed, and preserving the ideal of government by the virtuous, enlightened, and experienced was a means for achieving the larger
objectives of Virginia society, which he defined as securing "substantial and equal liberty to the people" and fostering "Prosperity to
the Community and Security to Individuals." With most Virginia
leaders of his political generation, Pendleton believed that the role
of the people in the polity should be limited, that the suffrage ought
to be confined to "those of fixed Permanent property," and that unqualified and untrustworthy men who in their lust for acclaim used
open demagoguery and irresponsible promises to excite the people's

39. Grigsby, *Virginia Convention of 1776*, p. 47; Jefferson, "Autobiography," in
Writings of Thomas Jefferson, I, 54–55, 59; Pendleton to James Madison, Sr., Feb.
15, 1766, to Ralph Wormely, Jr., July 28, 1774, to William Woodford, June 14,
1775, to Va. Delegates in Congress, Oct. 28, 1775, to Carter Braxton, May 12, 1776,
to Thomas Jefferson, Aug. 10, 26, 1776, to James Madison, July 6, 1781, to Va.
Ratifying Convention, June 20, 1788, to James Madison, Apr. 7, 1789; Pendleton's
Opinion on Fees, May 4, 1774; Pendleton's Account of the Case of the Prisoners,
Oct. 29, 1782, in *Letters and Papers of Edmund Pendleton*, I, 22–23, 82–85, 97, 104,
125, 177, 198, 200, 366; II, 423, 544, 556.

political passion or raise their political pretensions should be firmly opposed. But he had an equally strong commitment to the ideal of preserving an open society in which every free man should have an equal and unrestrained right to acquire property and rise as high in society as he could within the limits imposed upon him by his ability, resources, and opportunities and be secure in the knowledge that he would be protected "in the enjoyment of" his "honestly and industriously acquired property": the people had a fundamental right to be left "at liberty to pursue their labour in peace, and acquire wealth." Thus, as Pendleton argued after Independence, it was important to make future land grants in "small quantities" so as "to give the Poor a chance with the Rich of getting some Lands," to keep "all employments . . . free and open to such as chuse them . . . without clog or restraint," and to accord "equal liberty" to "all [free] men, from the palace to the cottage, without any other [legal] distinction than that between good and bad men."[40]

An outsider who had prospered materially and fulfilled himself personally under the old political and social system, Pendleton had no illusions that his success was attributable entirely to his own efforts. Rather, he understood clearly that it depended as well upon the opportunities available in the American environment and the existence in Virginia of a fluid social and political system that permitted new men such as himself to rise to the highest echelons of wealth, prestige, and leadership. Pleased by his success and appreciative of the "grateful smiles" the Virginia political system had repeatedly bestowed upon him, Pendleton developed a deep veneration for that system and had an especially strong stake in maintaining it, in making sure that the underlying structures and values on which it depended should be transferred intact to the postrevolutionary world. Precisely because other leaders and potential leaders were to varying degrees less well adjusted to the system and for that reason were potentially disruptive influences in a fluid political situation during the Revolution, Pendleton, Robert Carter Nicholas, and others like them had to assume the responsibility for upholding that system, for serv-

40. Resolutions of Va. Convention, May 15, 1776; Pendleton to Thomas Jefferson, May 24, Aug. 3, 10, 1776, to James Madison, May 28, 1781, to Richard Henry Lee, Feb. 21, Mar. 18, 1785, to Va. Ratifying Convention, June 12, 1788, to Harry Innes, Nov. 9, 1791, to ———, Dec. 4, 1792, in *Letters and Papers of Edmund Pendleton*, I, 179, 180, 196, 198, 359; II, 473, 477, 521, 580–81, 593.

ing not merely as its conservators but as its active protagonists against internal as well as external enemies.[41]

In Virginia, as in Britain, rank-and-file politicians seem "on the whole" to have "preferred men of prudence to 'those confounded men of genius.' " Pendleton's prudence and moderation, his dedication to the pragmatic resolution of political problems, his "deeply considered patriotism" and devotion to the Virginia political system—earned for him a degree of trust and responsibility withheld from the more flamboyant, and widely acclaimed, and personally ambitious Richard Henry Lee. Like Lee, Pendleton had found his identity in the public realm. But unlike Lee, he never felt a compulsion to move onto the larger political stage provided by the national government, never experienced any sense of rejection by his peers in politics, and never felt any urge to retire. On rare occasions, he complained about the ardors of politics or hoped for "some leisure to attend . . . private affairs." Once he even remarked that "true pleasure" was "not to be found in a Public bustle." In fact, however, Pendleton was a public man who clearly relished and was devoted to public service. With no children, he took an almost paternal interest in the state of the Virginia political system. Besides, as he wrote Jefferson in 1779, no real friend of his country could retire until he had "taught the rising Generation, the Forms as well as the Substantial principles" of that system.[42]

That Pendleton could write in his autobiography that he had "had the happiness to find a majority of all the public bodies confirming my sentiments" on both the values and objectives of politics throughout his long political career is a testimony to the influence he and others like him had in Virginia politics. "From the experience of nearly sixty years in public life," Pendleton wrote in 1798, "I have been taught to . . . respect this my native country for the decent, peaceable, and orderly behaviour of its inhabitants; justice has been, and is duly and diligently administered—the laws obeyed—the constituted authorities respected, and we have lived in the happy intercourse of private harmony and good will. At the same time by a free

41. Pendleton to William Woodford, Oct. 4, 1778, in *Letters and Papers of Edmund Pendleton*, I, 271.
42. Grainger, *Style and Character*, pp. 46, 58; Pendleton to William Preston, Dec. 18, 1773, to Thomas Jefferson, Nov. 16, 1775, to James Mercer, Mar. 19, 1776, and to Thomas Jefferson, May 11, 1779, in *Letters and Papers of Edmund Pendleton*, I, 80, 130, 160, 284.

communication between those of more information on political subjects, and the classes who have not otherwise an opportunity of acquiring that knowledge, all were instructed in their *rights* and *duties*
as freemen, and taught to respect them." The perpetuation of that
system, Pendleton justifiably liked to think, depended to some significant degree upon the dedication to stability, moderation, and compromise of level-headed and patriotic men such as himself.[43]

iv.

*I recommend it to my sons, from my own Experience
in Life, to prefer the happiness of independence & a
private Station to the troubles and Vexations of Public
Business.*[44]

Among the generation of Virginia political leaders considered in this
essay, only George Washington achieved a greater degree of respect
among his contemporaries than his neighbor George Mason. To later
historians, however, Mason's prominence and authority in the public
realm have remained something of an enigma. Unlike every other
famous Virginian of his generation, he had been only a minor figure
on the provincial political stage prior to the revolutionary crisis. Born
in 1725, four years after Pendleton and seven years before Richard
Henry Lee, he was, like Lee, a fourth-generation Virginian and a
member of a prominent Northern Neck family. But the Masons, unlike the Lees, had not played a major role in provincial politics. For
three generations, George Masons had concerned themselves primarily with building up their estates and had concentrated their political energies in their home county. Each of them served several
terms in the House of Burgesses, George Mason's father representing Stafford County continuously from 1720 to 1735. But each generation seems to have had less impact than the previous one upon that
body. As of 1765 George Mason himself seemed to represent a continuation in this trend. Though he evidenced an early interest in pro-

43. Pendleton, "Autobiography," July 20, 1793; Pendleton to Citizens of Caroline, Nov. 1798, in *Letters and Papers of Edmund Pendleton*, II, 607, 650.
44. George Mason's Will, Mar. 20, 1773, in *The Papers of George Mason 1725–
1792*, ed. Robert A. Rutland (Chapel Hill, N.C., 1970), I, 159. Portions of this
section are adapted from my review essay on the above edition in *South Atlantic
Quarterly*, LXXII (1973), 159–62.

vincial politics by an unsuccessful bid to represent Fairfax County in the Burgesses in 1748 when he was only twenty-three years old, for the next fifteen years he devoted himself largely to his family and estate. He was active on the Truro parish vestry and the Fairfax County Court, was a trustee for the new town of Alexandria, and served one undistinguished three-year term as a member of the House of Burgesses. But his greatest visibility probably derived from his activities as one of the leading spirits in, and treasurer of, the Ohio Company of Virginia, a massive scheme of speculation in western lands.[45]

Only with the prerevolutionary crisis was Mason gradually drawn into a more active involvement in public life, and even that involvement was limited and idiosyncratic. Like most other prominent members of his political generation, he took a strong stand against Parliament's attempt to tax the colonies and other "oppressive" British measures. But his platform was not the House of Burgesses, the main school of Virginia politics, to which he made no effort to return, but the library at his plantation at Gunston Hall. His anonymous letter to the "Committee of Merchants in London," apparently published in the *Public Ledger* in London following the Stamp Act crisis, is one of the best short statements of the American view of the relationship between Britain and the colonies and the American case against parliamentary taxation of the colonies. In 1769 and 1770 Mason worked privately through George Washington and others to help shape the Virginia nonimportation agreements against the Townshend Acts, and in the summer of 1774 he authored the Fairfax Resolves, which in twenty-four resolutions reviewed American grievances against Britain, condemned the Coercive Acts, and advocated a broad program of resistance to secure "Restoration of our just Rights and Privileges." Not until the summer of 1775 did Mason, apparently with extreme reluctance, return to the provincial political arena as a delegate to the Virginia Convention from Fairfax County to replace George Washington, who had gone to Boston to take command of the new American army. Despite his lean and unremarkable political record, Mason exercised an immediate and powerful voice

45. See Robert Rutland, *George Mason: Reluctant Statesman* (Williamsburg, Va., 1961); Kate Mason Rowland, *The Life of George Mason 1725–1792* (New York, 1892); and Greene, "Foundations of Political Power in the Virginia House of Burgesses." For the fullest recent study, see Helen Hill Miller, *George Mason: Gentleman Revolutionary* (Chapel Hill, N.C., 1975).

in the Virginia Convention, which chose him as a member of the committee of safety, and he vaulted into provincial—and international—prominence during the late spring of 1776 as the principal architect of the Virginia Constitution and Declaration of Rights—the first American bill of rights. Subsequently he played a major role in Virginia politics as a representative from Fairfax to the House of Delegates until his retirement in 1781 and, coming out of retirement, was one of the most conspicuous members of the Federal Convention of 1787 and a leader of the opposition to the Federal Constitution at the Virginia ratifying convention in June 1788.[46] What has been so puzzling about Mason's meteoric political ascendance in 1775–76 is that it was the accomplishment of a man who previously had pointedly avoided political responsibility at the provincial level in a political culture that placed extremely heavy and explicit stress upon the obligation of men of ability to serve the public.

Part of the explanation for Mason's sudden political success may be found in a cluster of personal talents and traits that especially fitted him to play a central role in the tense and exigent political circumstances of 1775–76. A man who "concentrated on relatively few endeavors with a patient thoroughness," Mason, as some of his earlier writings reveal, had obviously read deeply in classical and modern English history and, as Edmund Randolph had reported, "was behind none of the sons of Virginia in knowledge of her history and interest." Educated at home by private tutors, Mason had clearly made excellent use of his access to the library of his uncle and neighbor, John Mercer of Marlborough, one of the leading lawyers in Virginia, whose collection of books was among the largest in the colonies. The result was that, although Mason was not a lawyer, he was an avid and learned student of the law. Thus, when "the People of" his "County" "much against" his "Inclination drag'd [him] out of . . . Retirement" to serve in the Conventions of 1775 and 1776, the extensive learning he brought gave him an authority and an expertise that stood out among a group of men who, with the possible exception of the older Richard Bland, were, though politically more experienced and publicly more visible, considerably less learned in such matters.[47]

46. Fairfax Co. Resolves, July 18, 1774, in *Papers of George Mason*, I, 206; Rutland, *George Mason*, pp. 30–110.

47. Mason to Mr. Brent, Oct. 2, 1778, in *Papers of George Mason*, I, cxiii, 434; Randolph, *History of Virginia*, p. 192; Rutland, *George Mason*, pp. 60–67.

Moreover, as his writings and his contemporaries also attest, Mason combined this knowledge with a clear and penetrating intellect. He had few peers as a political analyst: "At a glance," said Randolph, "he saw to the bottom of every proposition." He was a man, avowed Jefferson, "of the first order of wisdom among those who acted on the theatre of the revolution, of expansive mind, profound judgment, cogent in argument, learned in the lore of our former constitution." "Among the many profound statesmen Virginia has produced," said Henry Lee, Mason "was perhaps second to none in wisdom and virtue, and by many of the most renowned of his contemporaries was regarded as the wisest of them all." "The Political Cooks are busy in preparing the dish," wrote Pendleton to Jefferson in May 1776 during the deliberations on the Virginia Constitution, "and as Colonel Mason seems to have the Ascendancy in the great work, I have sanguine hopes it will be framed so as to Answer it's end." So formidable were his learning and his intellectual gifts that "his opinions on a great political question had almost a conclusive authority." As Edmund Randolph put it in reference to Mason's contribution in 1776, Mason's proposals carried such cogency that they simply "swallowed up all the rest."[48]

But the authority of his opinions rested not only upon their cogency but also upon his ability to articulate them with force and persuasion. In the judgment of James Madison, who had ample opportunity to witness Mason's performance, Mason "was the soundest & clearest reasoner that he ever listened to." Unlike Richard Henry Lee, Mason was not a dramatic or polished orator. Preferring a manner of exposition that was "learned & elegant without the Vanity of seeming so," he had no taste for "the florid Ciceronian Style." Rather, his manner of speaking seems to have been modeled upon that of his classical hero, Cato the Younger, whose speech, according to Plutarch, "had nothing about it that was . . . affected, but was straightforward, full of matter, and harsh." Thus, Mason's "elocution," Jefferson testified, "was neither flowing nor smooth; but his language was strong, his manner most impressive, and strengthened by a dash of biting synicism, when provocation made it seasonable."[49]

48. Randolph, *History of Virginia*, pp. 192, 252, 258; Grigsby, *Virginia Convention of 1776*, p. 155; Jefferson, "Autobiography," *Writings of Thomas Jefferson*, I, 60; Rowland, *George Mason*, II, 374; Pendleton to Jefferson, May 24, 1776, in *Letters and Papers of Edmund Pendleton*, I, 180.
49. *Plutarch's Lives*, VIII, 247; Randolph, *History of Virginia*, pp. 192, 252;

Jefferson's description suggests still another source for Mason's political authority: his extreme moral rectitude. He seems to have cultivated—virtually to have personified—the Catonic model. Like Cato, he sought to be—and by his entire bearing to appear as—a man of "unbending character and absolute integrity," who, as his grandson remarked, staked "his life upon the truth." Mason possessed, Edmund Randolph said, "that philosophical spirit which despised the adulterated means of cultivating happiness." In his "habits generally he was severe and strict," displaying extraordinary discipline and self-control as well as a Spartan simplicity and disdain for ostentation. An "inflexible, imperturbable, and altogether steadfast" supporter of his conception of colonial rights prior to 1776, he was a "stern . . . Republican" thereafter, the constant opponent of any measures or social tendencies—including a general "Depravity of Manners and Morals" that seemed to be sweeping the states—that might render the Revolution a "Curse" rather than a "Blessing," an exponent of unpopular measures—such as payment of British debts, security of paper money, and the remedying of defects in the administration of justice—that seemed necessary to fulfill the "Obligations of Morality & Justice" and guarantee "the sacred Rights of . . . Citizens."[50] The cause of liberty and virtue, "the Principles of Justice & Equity," the "Security of private-Property," could never be sacrificed to popularity or exigency. Eager, like Cato, to take "a course directly opposite" to "practices of the time . . . that . . . were bad and in need of great change," he was more alert than most of his contemporaries to the pernicious effects of existing institutions within his own society, as was revealed by his early—for Virginia—condemnation of Negro slavery as a "slow Poison, which is daily contaminating the Minds & Morals of our People" and unjustly debasing "a part of our own Species . . . almost to a Level with the Brute Creation."[51]

Mason to George Brent, Dec. 6, 1770, *Papers of George Mason*, I, 127; Jefferson, "Autobiography," *Writings of Thomas Jefferson*, I, 60; St. George Tucker to William Wirt, Sept. 25, 1815, *William and Mary Quarterly*, 1st ser., XXII, 256.

50. Rowland, *George Mason*, II, 367; Randolph, *History of Virginia*, p. 192; *Plutarch's Lives*, VIII, 245, 253, 259; Mason to George Washington, Apr. 5, 1769, to Arthur Lee, Mar. 25, 1783, to Patrick Henry, May 6, 1783, to Thomas Marshall, Oct. 16, 1789; Petition of Prince William Co. Freeholders, Dec. 10, 1781, Address of Fairfax Co. Freeholders to Delegates, May 30, 1783, and Mason, Speech on Sumptuary Laws, Aug. 20, 1787, in *Papers of George Mason*, I, 99–100; II, 711, 766, 770–72, 779–80, 861–62; III, 962, 1175.

51. Mason, Scheme for Replevying Goods, Dec. 23, 1765, Abstracts from Virginia Charters, July, 1773, and Petition of Prince William Co. Freeholders, Dec.

In the political arena Mason, in sharp contrast to Pendleton, had little patience with anything that smacked either of selfishness or foolishness and no taste for the routine interchange—the hum—of day-to-day politics. The "Partys & Factions" that he encountered at the Virginia Convention in 1775, his first legislative session in over a dozen years, produced so much "Vexation & Disgust" as to throw him "into such an ill state of Health that" he "was sometimes near fainting in the House." Only after weeks of tedious irrelevance were "the Bablers . . . pretty well silenced" so that "a few weighty Members" such as himself could begin "to take the Lead" in fashioning "several wholesome Regulations." By himself or in company with a few peers Mason could accomplish the most demanding legislative tasks. But he was too proud, too persuaded of the rectitude of his own opinions and productions, to accept opposition gracefully. Mason's austere, elevated, and forbidding persona in public might have alienated his colleagues had his "steadfast and zealous" Virginia patriotism been insincere or had he not applied the same high standards to himself that he did to others. But his success, as measured by the positive response of his colleagues, in his strivings to personify those values of "pristine Englishry" that had been so long and so carefully cultivated by the Virginia elite—"justice, moderation, temperance, frugality, and virtue," he called them in the Virginia Declaration of Rights—was instead one of the primary sources of his political appeal and both established him as the conscience—the veritable superego— of Virginia politics and helped to win the respect and admiration of his colleagues in the public arena just as they had earlier impressed his friends and neighbors in private life.[52]

But Mason's spectacular rise and continued exercise of leadership in revolutionary Virginia are also traceable to a still deeper, and probably much more important, source. A persistent and powerful tension ran through the elite culture of eighteenth-century Virginia between the individual's obligation to serve the public and his responsibility to preserve his personal independence.[53] Most men, like Pendleton and Lee, managed to achieve some balance between the

10, 1781, in *Papers of George Mason*, I, 61–62, 173, 275; II, 711; *Plutarch's Lives*, VIII, 249–51.

52. Mason to George Washington, Oct. 14, 1775, Virginia Declaration of Rights, June 12, 1776, in *Papers of George Mason*, I, 255, 289; Grainger, *Character and Style*, p. 63; Jefferson, "Autobiography," *Writings of Thomas Jefferson*, I, 60.

53. See Greene, *Landon Carter*, esp. pp. 70–92.

two, but with Mason the pull of the latter was always infinitely stronger. Unlike Richard Henry Lee, Washington, or younger colleagues such as Jefferson, Madison, or Henry, all of whom found their identities in the public realm, Mason was an intensely private man. His main concerns were overwhelmingly personal: the education of his numerous family, the management of his plantations and the money he had loaned out at interest, and his involvement with western lands. In his own eyes, his most important accomplishment was not the authorship of the Virginia Declaration of Rights but the ample provision he had made for his children: "the Payment of my Daughter's Fortune, the building for, & setling two of my Sons, and raising Capitals in trade for two others." His self-image, as he declared in 1766, was of "a Man, who spends most of his Time in Retirement, and has seldom med[d]led in public Affairs, who enjoys a moderate but independent Fortune, and content with the Blessings of a private Station, equally disregards the Smiles & Frowns of the Great"; and the death of his wife in March 1773 only strengthened his determination to "spend the remainder of my Days in privacy & Retirement with my Children." From his "own Experience in Life," he recommended to his sons in a will written shortly after his wife's death, "to prefer the happiness of independance & a private Station to the troubles and Vexations of Public Business."[54]

Government for Mason was, more than anything else, an instrument to protect men in the peaceful and unfettered pursuit of their own and their posterity's private fortunes and interests and to preserve to them the fruits of their endeavours; and what eventually pulled him out of retirement in 1775—perhaps the only thing that could have done so—was his growing perception that a corrupt government in Britain was bent on denying this invaluable blessing to Americans, a blessing that they had "received from" their "Ancestors" and were obliged "to transmit to" their own "posterity" if America, "the only great nursery of freedom" still "left upon the face of the earth," was not to become "a sink for slaves." "When the Subject is of such Importance as the Liberty & Happiness of a Country," he had written to Richard Henry Lee in 1770, "Every Member of Society is in Duty bound to contribute to the Safety & Good of the

54. Mason to Committee of Merchants in London, June 6, 1766, Will, Mar. 20, 1773, to Mr. Brent, Oct. 2, 1778, and to John Francis Mercer, Aug. 26, 1791, in *Papers of George Mason*, I, 71, 159, 433; III, 1235–36.

Whole" and "every inferior Consideration, as well as the Inconvenience to a few Individuals, must give place to it, nor is this any Hardship upon them; as themselves & their Posterity are to partake of the Benefits resulting from it."[55] When anything less was at stake, however, public service, as Mason petulantly declared in attempting to cut off a movement to elect him to the Virginia House of Delegates in 1784, could only be considered "an oppressive & unjust Invasion of my personal Liberty." Only a dangerous and malevolent threat to that liberty, to the right of every individual to enjoy the "Sweets of domestic Life" at "Ease under the Shade of his own Vine, & his own fig-tree," could justify a society in forcing a man to abandon his "Quiet & Retirement."[56]

For at least a half-century prior to 1775, the Virginia gentry had assiduously cultivated the image of the retired life of virtue, privacy, and independence, free from the bustle and care of public life, at the same time that they were actively participating in that life. For most Virginians, this arcadian image seems to have served as a psychological balm for the pain and anxiety they felt from being so far removed from the really great affairs of state in the metropolis across the Atlantic. For Mason, however, the power of this image in giving coherence to his own identity seems to have depended more upon personal inclination than cultivation: his *genuine* and *deeply rooted* preference was always for "the happiness of independance & a private Station" rather than "the troubles and Vexations of Public Business." This intense commitment to private life, this deep aversion to all public service except that undertaken in behalf of the most fundamental—the deepest—concerns of society, gave Mason a degree of detachment from the concerns of day-to-day politics that most Virginia leaders admired and wanted for themselves, at least in theory, but could never achieve because of their intense devotion to and involvement in public life. Mason's detachment freed him both "from the entanglements, political and personal, of party and passion" and the ambition for office that together circumscribe the independence

55. Mason to Richard Henry Lee, June 7, 1770, Remarks on Election for Fairfax Independent Co., Apr. 17–26, 1775, to George Washington, Apr. 2, 1776, and William Lee to Mason, July 29, 1775, in *Papers of George Mason*, I, 118, 231, 244, 267.

56. Mason to George Washington, Apr. 2, 1776, to Edmund Randolph, Oct. 19, 1782, to Martin Cockburn, Apr. 18, 1784, in *Papers of George Mason*, I, 267; II, 747, 799.

of most political leaders. Just as, much later, Mason would decline appointment to the United States Senate, during the seven years he served in the legislature he was "at different times . . . chosen a Member of the Privy Council, & of the American Congress" but, because of "his indifference for distinction," "constantly declined acting in any other public character than that of an *independent* Representative of the People, in the House of Delegates." Perhaps more than anything else—more than his learning, intelligence, ability in debate, or moral rectitude—this extreme independence—valued by him more highly than "the approbation of any man, or all the men upon earth" —accounted for his rapid ascendancy in 1775–76 and his continuing authority in Virginia political counsels. As in the case of Cato, Mason's carefully nurtured position as "the only man who was [entirely] free" brought him "in greatest measure" that to which he "gave least thought . . . namely, esteem, favour, surpassing honour, and kindness" from his associates in the political arena.[57]

When Mason retired from the legislature in 1781 with the firm intention of spending "the Remnant of my Life in Quiet & Retirement," he did so not only because of the economic costs—"the no small Neglect & Injury of my private Fortune"—of such a heavy commitment of "Time to public Business" but also, and much more importantly, because he had lost some of his authority and, as he saw it, "was no longer able to do any essential Service." "Some of the public Measures have been so contrary to my Notions of Policy and of Justice, that I wished to be no further concern'd with, or answerable for them." In Addison's famous quotation of Cato again: "When vice prevails, and impious men bear sway, The post of honor," for Mason, was indeed "a private station." But Mason was too deeply engaged in the great cause of insuring that "the American Union" would be "firmly fixed, and free Governments well established in our western world" ever to withdraw completely. He wrote to his son in January 1783, "My Anxiety for my Country, in these Times of Danger, makes me sometimes dabble a little in Politicks, & keep up a Correspondence with some Men upon the public stage," and he professed his willingness to "sacrifice my own Ease & domestic Enjoy-

---

57. *Plutarch's Lives*, VIII, 257, 407; Grigsby, *Convention of 1776*, 155; Randolph, *History of Virginia*, p. 192; Mason, Will, Mar. 20, 1773, to Mr. Brent, Oct. 2, 1778, to John Mason, Mar. 13, 1789, and to Beverley Randolph, Mar. 27, 1790, in *Papers of George Mason*, I, 159, 434; III, 1142, 1192. Italics added.

ments to the Public-Good," whenever, as had been the case in 1775–76, some great public business required the exertions of "a few Men of Integrity & Abilitys, whose Countrys Interest lies next their Hearts." He was thus waiting when the call came to go as a Virginia delegate to the Federal Convention in Philadelphia in the summer of 1787. To contrive a workable political system for the "American Union" was indeed a task worthy of Mason's talents: one that was capable, for the first time in his sixty-two years, of drawing him beyond the environs of the Chesapeake Bay. In his own words, it was "an Object of such Magnitude, as absorbs, & in a Manner suspends the Operations of the human Understanding." That this proud man failed to gain support for many of his ideas in Philadelphia probably accounts in large degree for his subsequent opposition to the Constitution: he could not bring himself to support a document that was adopted over his opposition without admitting to himself that he had been unable to live up to his self-image as the virtuous patriot of deep understanding, "*independent* Circumstances and Principles" who, when duty called, could come out of retirement to give fundamental law to his country. It was George Washington's opinion that Mason's pride and "want of manly candour"—to himself—were largely responsible for preventing him from admitting "an error in his opinions" on the Constitution.[58]

Whatever his disappointments in 1787–88—and the narrow margin by which the Virginia Convention ratified the Constitution was in some part a measure of the continuing respect for Mason's opinions—Mason had indeed played an extremely important role and commanded extraordinary authority in the political life of Virginia after 1775. As he wrote his son in 1789, his "conduct as a public man, through the whole of the late glorious Revolution, has been such as . . . will administer comfort to me in those moments when I shall most want it, and smooth the bed of death": insofar as he was aware, he had always "acted from the purest motives of honesty, and love to my country, according to that measure of judgment which God has bestowed on me." But the key ingredient in his political authority was not his moral rectitude, his patriotism, or even his judgment and

58. Mason to R. H. Lee, May 18, 1776, to Mr. Brent, Oct. 2, 1778, to Edmund Randolph, Oct. 19, 1782, to George Mason, Jr., Jan. 8, 1783, to Arthur Lee, Mar. 25, 1783, and to George Mason, Jr., June 1, 1787, in *Papers of George Mason*, I, 271, 434; II, 747, 759–61, 766; III, 892–93; Addison, *Cato*, Act IV, Scene 4, ll. 140–50.

learning. Rather, it was his cherished independence. He was the epitome of the bucolic image—which struck so many positive resonances among the Virginia elite—of the "private man living in the ordered *patria*" of the Virginia countryside who in emergencies could be an effective servant of the public precisely because he was in the political debt of no man. What Mason's remarkable political success would seem to suggest about the larger system of values and patterns of behavior among the extraordinary group of which he was a member is that, however deeply committed the Virginia gentry may have been to the traditional ideals of stewardship and the obligation of public service, a commitment that is well illustrated by the careers of Richard Henry Lee and Edmund Pendleton, they valued individual independence—personal liberty—and the detachment it carried with it even more.[59]

v.

. . . a high sense of personal independence was universal.[60]

Each of the three men analyzed in this essay represented a distinctive mode of political leadership. By focusing on what they had in common, we can delineate more clearly those *essential qualities* demanded of all leaders in the political culture of late colonial and revolutionary Virginia, a political culture in which leaders were selected not by the political community at large but by a small group of peers on the basis of intimate evaluation of day-to-day performance. Those qualities were summarized succinctly in 1761 by Lieutenant Governor Francis Fauquier in his explanation, previously quoted, for the extraordinary popularity of Speaker John Robinson. What gave Robinson such great authority, said Fauquier, were his "great integrity, assiduity, and ability in business," qualities exhibited in substantial measure by all three men here considered. Although Lee was required on more than one occasion to offer public proof of the rectitude of his conduct, each was a man of cultivated and recognized virtue in both the private and the public spheres, a man of genuine independence of mind who was devoted to—and could be

59. Mason to John Mason, Mar. 13, 1789, in *Papers of George Mason*, III, 1142; Grainger, *Character and Style*, p. 26.
60. Randolph, *History of Virginia*, p. 197.

trusted to act in accordance with—what he took to be the best interests of the whole society. Each was also a man of great diligence who performed his duties thoroughly. And each had a remarkable "capacity for business," including an impressive learning (especially in law) that informed his analysis of political issues and an ability to define those issues clearly, devise strategies for coping with them, and elicit support for those strategies from among his peers in the political arena. As the examples of all three men testify, the ability to elicit such support in a political culture like that of Revolutionary Virginia required great skill in speaking and debate. With virtually no infrastructure—with no organized parties, factions, clientage system, or bureaucracy—to serve as a basis for mobilizing opinion, leaders had to depend very heavily upon force of personality and cogency of argument to gain support for their views from within the political community. Finally, the widespread acclaim extended to each of these men was the result not merely of their manifest abilities in these several areas but also of the achievement, in each case, of a remarkable—and demonstrable—congruity between character and persona.

But the divergencies among the three leaders, the particular way each of them gave expression to and utilized the essential qualities of leadership, are perhaps even more revealing of the characteristics, priorities, and responsiveness of eighteenth-century Virginia political culture than the commonalities. Together, the three distinct modes of political leadership represented by Lee, Pendleton, and Mason would seem to cover the complete range of leadership styles available in that culture, at least in the sense that, with relatively minor qualifications, every leader can be fitted into one or the other of them. Throughout the whole period, the persona of the trimmer as characterized by Pendleton was dominant. This role, with its emphasis upon accommodation, moderation, deliberation, and control and its commitment, above all else, to the continuing stability of the polity, had been hammered out and given definition in Virginia by a long line of earlier political leaders, including John Holloway, Governor Sir William Gooch, Sir John Randolph, John Robinson, Charles Carter of Cleve, and Richard Bland. For a polity in which there was virtually no disagreement over the fundamental objectives of society and in which government was expected to do little more than provide maximum scope for individual enterprise by guaranteeing the liberty of its members to pursue their own private interests in a stable and

orderly context and by securing to them the fruits of their enterprise, the authority of this persona rested upon its appropriateness:
the political nation demanded no more of its leaders than that they
maintain a stable political environment. That most leaders among
Pendleton's contemporaries—Peyton Randolph, George Washington, Robert Carter Nicholas, George Wythe, Archibald Cary, Benjamin Harrison V—as well as many of the most prominent members
of the next generation—James Madison, Edmund Randolph, John
Marshall—adopted a similar persona and continued to command
authority throughout the revolutionary era is a testimony both to
the commitment of the political culture to the values it embodied and
was designed to facilitate and to its heightened appropriateness in a
time of political upheaval and change.

As long as none of the fundamental values of the polity were
threatened from either internal or external sources, there was little
room for the emergence of the sort of alternative persona represented
by either Lee or Mason. Hence, there was no precise counterpart to
either Lee or Mason among either of the two previous political generations, albeit during the early stages of the Seven Years' War Landon
Carter seems to have assumed a posture similar to that later exhibited
by Lee. The persona of the vigorous and uncompromising defender
of the basic values and beliefs of the society was thus the creation—
in Virginia—of Richard Henry Lee and some of his young contemporaries, notably Patrick Henry and Thomas Jefferson. Initially its authority was directly dependent upon the exigencies of the mid-1760s,
the internal corruption represented by the Robinson scandals and the
external challenge posed by the Grenville program, and it was given
wide scope for development as the deepening quarrel with Britain
seemed to demand activity, energy, and resolution to prevent the subversion and loss of the most cherished possessions of the community:
liberty, property, and autonomy. That so few of the major leaders
adopted this new persona even in the midst of the revolutionary crisis
is a measure of the extent to which the trimmers, while advocating
different tactics, were committed to the same basic goals and a further
indication of the extraordinary and continuing power of the traditional model of the trimmer in Virginia politics.

The persona represented by George Mason and not shared by
any other Virginia leaders of the revolutionary era reveals even more
emphatically the depth and extent of the Virginia commitment to

those basic goals. The intensely private and talented man who could not tolerate the banalities of politics in ordinary times and would abandon his private station only when his independence and with it the deepest values of his country were in jeopardy, Mason personified the personal independence, the honest and uninterrupted pursuit of private happiness, which Virginians had always—since the very beginning—given the highest possible priority as both personal and social objectives. As the personification of the independence Virginians cherished so deeply, Mason—in the critical moments at the founding of the independent state of Virginia—was accorded the exalted role of giver of fundamental law.

The Ambivalence of Freedom: Whites, Blacks, and the Coming of the American Revolution in the South

W. Robert Higgins   *Baltimore, Maryland*

Because of slavery the rhetoric and actions of revolutionary leaders in the southern colonies were not the same as their compatriots' in the middle and northern colonies. From the Chesapeake to the Saint John's River and the former Spanish Florida, two populations existed side by side: one white and demanding its political freedom founded on cultural and social inheritance; the other black and denied not only its political rights but the totality of its natural rights and human heritage. As the American Revolution unfolded on a national and international stage, the roles of southern whites would alter with freedom; the Indians would be mightily affected by occurrences between the British and English Americans, but the condition of the blacks continued unchanged. They were slaves. The Afro-Americans were unfree before the Revolution; after eight years of war and the Second Treaty of Paris they were no different.

To a great extent the condition of the blacks resulted from the attitudes of whites. Few white Americans advocated freedom for anyone but themselves, and the British fought the war not to promote social change but to restore power. Neither side saw any benefit in giving to the African the freedom and equality possessed by other emigrants to British North America. Instead, each side used the Afro-Americans for its own purposes, fought over ownership and stole Negroes, and even paid soldiers' wages in black flesh.[1] The Negro

1. During the Revolution, both sides seized slaves and used the labor of these people to assist their cause. After the capture of Charleston the South Carolina troops raised by General Thomas Sumter were paid in Negroes; the number a soldier received depended upon his rank and length of service. For this purpose, slaves were theoretically halved and quartered. This method of payment was used

was not a party to the American Revolution in the South; he was a tool,[2] a means to an end for the Americans and for the British.

The attitudes affecting the status of the blacks were rooted deep in the culture and psyche of white Americans and white government. With the exception of British placemen and a few provincial notables loyal to the king in Parliament assembled, the majority of individuals elected to the colonial assemblies and royal councils continued to serve in the transitional and revolutionary governments of the emerging nation.[3] Since the dramatis personae remained constant, change could be engendered only by a shift in the pervasive attitudes of the ruling class. But attitudes did not change. What the political and economic leaders thought about the African slaves had been formed over a very long period of time and would not (and perhaps could not) alter in the relatively brief period between the rupture of imperial relations after the Stamp Act and the end of the American Revolution.

The first factor working against the Negroes in the minds of English Americans was simply color. Long before the English came to America, long before most of them had seen dark-skinned individuals, the people of the British Isles disliked the color black and assigned it evil connotations. Black was bad; therefore black men were marked in the eyes of the white colonists.[4]

The English were terribly egocentric. Their way was better; they

because neither Continental nor South Carolina currency was acceptable to the men, and gold was unavailable. Because of the traditionally high value placed upon blacks by the people of the South, this arrangement prompted ready enlistment in Sumter's corps. S.C. Treasury, *Documents relating to the History of South Carolina During the Revolutionary War*, ed. A. S. Salley, Jr. (Columbia: Historical Commission of S.C., 1909), pp. 51–55, 61–67.

2. The South Carolina Provincial Congress designated male slaves for use by the state military not by name or sex, but categorized them as tools, placing them collectively with shovels, hatchets, etc. S.C. Provincial Congress, *Extracts from the Journals of the Provincial Congressess of South Carolina 1775–1776*, ed. William Edwin Hemphill (Columbia: S.C. Archives Department, 1960), pp. 141, 151. Hereafter cited as *Provincial Congresses of South Carolina*.

3. Eva B. Poythress, "Revolution by Committee: An Administrative History of the Extralegal Committees in South Carolina 1774–1776" (Ph.D. dissertation, Univ. of N.C., Chapel Hill, 1975), Chaps. 1 and 2; and James Kirby Martin, *Men in Rebellion: Higher Governmental Leaders and the Coming of the American Revolution* (New Brunswick, N.J.: Rutgers Univ. Press, 1973) both stress the minimal turnover in local leadership in the South during the Revolution.

4. Frank Tannenbaum, *Slave and Citizen, the Negro in the Americas* (New York: Knopf, 1947), p. 68. Winthrop Jordan, *White over Black: American Attitudes Toward the Negro 1550–1812* (Chapel Hill: Univ. of N.C. Press for the Institute of Early American History and Culture at Williamsburg, Va., 1968).

were civilized. Whoever did not look, act, speak, or think their way was automatically inferior. For this reason the indigenous peoples whom the British encountered in Asia, Africa, and America in the seventeenth century were "uncivilized." Although the English imposed themselves and their ways upon the natives of these regions, only the Africans were removed from their homeland and torn from their base of power, past, and propinquity.

Another factor differentiating black slaves from other settlers of the southern colonies was the profitability of bound labor. From the rice swamps of Georgia and Carolina and the indigo fields of the Carolina interior, to the pine forests with their naval products, and to the tobacco and wheat plantations of the Chesapeake, southern whites invested enormous sums in bound workers and reaped great returns from slave labor. Where land was cheap and readily available, the majority of a man's estate was represented by his African bondsmen.[5] Freedom for blacks would upset the agricultural and economic system developed over the previous one hundred years.

Africans arrived in English North America little more than a decade after successful settlement, and importations continued throughout the colonial period. The actual numbers of slaves landed in Maryland, Virginia, and South Carolina increased over the decades of the eighteenth century. The slave trade peaked in Charleston in 1773 when nearly eight thousand adults and children from Senegal to Angola arrived in one year to meet the labor needs of the settlers. That single forced migration during one year nearly equaled the importations of any biennial period and exceeded total importations of the first fifty years of Carolina.[6]

Such ever-increasing rates of importation resulted in the creation of two separate and disparate populations in the southern colonies. Throughout the eighteenth century before the American Revolution, there was a high level of Africans within the black population, with

5. The author has made surveys of eighteenth-century wills recorded in S.C. Colonial Secretary, "Inventory Books," MSS, S.C. Department of Archives and History, Columbia, S.C., in order to compare the total value of an estate in relation to the value of its slaves. Seldom were the slaves less than 50 percent of the total value, and in many cases they comprised as much as 90 percent of an estate's worth. See also Jack P. Greene, *The Quest for Power: The Lower Houses of Assembly in the Southern Royal Colonies, 1689–1763* (Chapel Hill: Univ. of N.C. Press for the Institute of Early American History and Culture at Williamsburg, Va., 1963), p. 21.

6. See Section Z 303 by the author in Bureau of the Census, *Historical Statistics of the United States* (Washington, D.C.: Government Printing Office, 1975).

even larger numbers of first-generation sons and daughters, and very few acculturated Afro-Americans. Most slaves remained foreign to the English and other European settlers in North America. There was little to bind blacks and whites together; even language isolated most slaves from the white settlers. Their mutually shared history was far too brief to overcome centuries of disparity.[7]

Despite the sense of superiority of the English, bred into them by their culture and associations with non-European peoples and reinforced by the virtually supreme power of the British ruling class in North America, the settlers of the South experienced not only scorn for the Africans in their midst but another and more elemental emotion—fear. A paradox characterized the relations of blacks and whites: the enslavers viewed the enslaved as inferior beings. They learned nothing of the bound people which could change their preconceived opinions, but whites did realize the latent power of the blacks—the power to destroy the entire society built and nurtured in North America. The overriding response of the English Americans was fear.

Since the first mingling of the two peoples at Jamestown, whites had feared the blacks would overthrow their power and destroy the agricultural system of the southern provinces. Sheer fright motivated the governmental response and the attitudes of the ruling class throughout the colonial period; those attitudes continued during the American Revolution.[8]

The views of the English toward their own people upon the eco-

7. In Maryland and Virginia where tobacco was the major crop, the white settlers had learned that it was more beneficial to operate the land as a number of small holdings rather than as one large unified plantation. Therefore the land holdings of the great families were divided into what they called "farms." See Landon Carter, *The Diary of Colonel Landon Carter of Sabine Hall, 1752–1778*, ed. Jack P. Greene (Charlottesville: published for the Va. Historical Society by the Univ. Press of Va., 1965). See also George Washington, *Writings of George Washington*, ed. John C. Fitzpatrick (39 vols.; Washington, D.C.: Government Printing Office, 1931–44). In South Carolina and Georgia the planters lived apart from their lands all or part of the year. For the establishment of a new plantation without any whites, see William Bartram, *The Travels of William Bartram, Naturalist's Edition*, ed. Francis Harper (New Haven, Conn.: Yale Univ. Press, 1958), pp. 298–99.

8. Herbert Aptheker, *American Negro Slave Revolts* (New York: International Publishers, 1963), p. 52; William Gerard DeBrahm, *DeBrahm's Report of the General Survey in the Southern District of North America*, ed. Louis DeVorsey, Jr. (Columbia: Univ. of S.C. Press, 1971), p. 91. Peter H. Wood, *Black Majority; Negroes in Colonial South Carolina from 1670 through the Stono Rebellion* (New York: Knopf, 1974), p. 135.

nomic fringe of society, or beyond the legitimate labor force, was one of contempt. The sturdy beggars were anathema to the established order and objects of scorn. The concepts and planned actions of the British government toward those inferior people is reflected in the act of 1547—the most severe of all servant laws in English history— for the punishing of vagabonds, and for the relief of the poor and impotent persons. This act, authorizing perpetual enslavement of whites, led not illogically to the slave codes of the British island and mainland colonies of America. Even the first Barbadian law for the regulation of slaves was supposedly modeled upon this English precedent. The black code of Barbados was then the progenitor of the slave laws of other islands and South Carolina. The enforcement regulations of Carolina spread to other seaboard plantations and inland states after the Revolution. Thus the English tradition of contempt and physical cruelty to society's unfortunates was continued in America with the enactment of slave codes.[9]

Despite a tradition of cruelty to inferiors which allowed for slavery and the concept of man as property, the system of African enslavement would not have worked in English America if the acquisition and ownership of blacks had been limited to a small economic elite, the great planters of the Chesapeake and the Carolina coastline. Instead, the institution of bound black labor was universally accepted in the South in the eighteenth century, and people in all areas and strata of society looked to the possession of Negroes as a reflection of their own status and an avenue for financial advancement. For this reason the demand for additional black workers increased geometrically. Southern laborers and craftsmen invested their profits in Negroes, taught the slaves their trades, and benefited doubly from the captive blacks, first as simple labor and secondly as noncompetitive skilled workers. The utilization of such assistance increased the range and volume of employment for the slave-owning

9. An Act for the punishing of vagabonds and for the relief of the poor and impotent persons, 1547, in *The Statutes at Large from the Thirty Second Year of King Henry VIII to the Seventh Year of King Edward VI Inclusive* (Cambridge, Eng.: Charles Bathurst, 1763), V, 246–47, 345. Lewis Cecil Gray, *History of Agriculture in the Southern United States to 1860* (2 vols.; Washington, D.C.: The Carnegie Institution of Washington, 1933), I, 343. Elsa Goveia, "The West Indian Slave Laws of the Eighteenth Century," in *Slavery in the New World: A Reader in Comparative History*, comp. Laura Foner (New York: Prentice-Hall, 1969), p. 126.

craftsman. The Charleston house painter Benjamin Hawes claimed that he could "undertake any job as a painter by his use of white apprentices and Negroes." He was not an exception, for nearly half of the Charleston mechanics whose wills were probated during the era of the American Revolution owned blacks.[10]

The new settlers of the piedmont South sought Africans shortly after acquiring land. The great slave merchant Henry Laurens wrote to his London correspondent Richard Oswald in 1763: ". . . a vast number of people seting down upon our frontier Lands . . . will take . . . a Cargo by one or two Blacks in a Lot & it has been from such folks that we have always obtain'd the highest prices & hitherto we have had no reason to be discouraged from dealing with them on Account of bad debts." Georgia's lack of success under the Trustees was blamed on the prohibition of black slavery; after the removal of the ban the southernmost English colony experienced rapid economic growth and large importations of African laborers during the twenty years before the Revolution. The demand of Georgia settlers for Negroes was so great that by 1775 slaves in the colony numbered fifteen thousand, nearly half of the total population.[11]

Whites in the colonial South supported black slavery and sought to acquire Negroes because of the profits available through the labor of subject people. Despite the riches of the land little wealth could be gained without an adequate labor force. This problem confronted not only the English, but all Europeans in the Americas. Only the Spanish solved their labor problem without large-scale importations of workers. Through slavery and serfdom the large American Indian populations within the Spanish sphere were forced to serve Europeans. Elsewhere in America native people attained neither the numbers nor the social development of those under Hispanic control. All other Europeans, therefore, turned to Africa for their labor needs. With imported black workers the land could be put to work and the whites could prosper by their emigration from Europe.

The profitability of black slavery upon southern lands is obvious

10. Richard G. Walsh, *Charleston's Sons of Liberty: The Artisans 1763–1789* (Columbia: Univ. of S.C. Press, 1959), pp. 3, 24, 25.

11. Charleston, Feb. 15, 1763, in Henry Laurens, *The Papers of Henry Laurens*, ed. Philip M. Hamer (4 vols. to date; Columbia: Univ. of S.C. Press, 1968), III, 260. Kenneth Coleman, *The American Revolution in Georgia 1763–1789* (Athens: Univ. of Ga. Press, 1958), p. 145.

to anyone examining the rise of a gentry class from the Englishmen coming to America. Most of these people, or their immediate ancestors, had little money on their arrival from Europe. Their wealth was acquired in the New World through land and labor.

The fact that merchants and mechanics invested in black labor as an outlet for surplus capital attests also to the true value of Africans. The rising merchants and mechanics bought agricultural land and African workers and became planters as well as urban entrepreneurs. It was commonly computed that a Carolina rice or indigo planter could recover his original investment in blacks in four years. Thus the agricultural slave owner expected to support himself, subsist his Negroes, meet interest costs, and clear 25 percent net profit annually.

The net profits of a mechanic are difficult to assess because of the nature of self-employment. The maximum profit range of merchants, however, is determined simply by looking at the commission rates allowed by correspondents. The usual percentage allowed an American merchant for European dry goods was 5 percent. Merchants dealing in slaves from Africa were allowed to charge twice that amount against gross sales, providing 10 percent commission for the trade in humans. Both of these figures were gross income. The colonial factor or merchant then had to guarantee payment for every credit sale, meet local expenses, and secure a return cargo. Additionally, slave merchants had to pay half of the wages of the ship's crew. Most sales were not cash transactions but were secured by credit or a pledge of agricultural produce. In the first part of the eighteenth century the legal interest ceiling in South Carolina was 10 percent. This rate then declined from two shillings on the pound to one and six pence. The maximum gross profits of a southern colonial merchant were thus between 13 and 20 percent, or one-half to four-fifths of the expected *net* of the planter employing blacks in the production of rice or indigo.[12]

12. Liverpool, Jan. 20, 1748 (1749) to Foster Cunliffe; Liverpool, Jan. 20, 1748 (1749) to Edward Trafford; Liverpool, Jan. 20, 1748 (1749) to John Knight; Bristol, Feb. 18, 1748 (1749) to Richard Farr, *The Papers of Henry Laurens*, I, 202–6, 211–12. *Colonial South Carolina: Two Contemporary Descriptions, by Governor James Glen and Doctor George Milligen-Johnston*, ed. Chapman J. Milling (Columbia: Univ. of S.C. Press, 1951), pp. 14–18. Robert Pringle, *The Letterbooks of Robert Pringle*, ed. Walter B. Edgar (Columbia: published for the S.C. Historical Society by the Univ. of S.C. Press, 1972). Levinius Clarkson to David Van Horn, Charleston, Dec. 5, 1772, *Documents Illustrative of the History of the Slave Trade to Amer-*

Still another way to determine the profitability of Negro slavery is to compare values set for white and black labor by probated wills. Thomas Lynch, Sr., a great rice planter in South Carolina, left an estate including 160 blacks and 6 European servants. The slaves ranged from infants to old people, and the values went from a low of £60 currency for an aged woman to £500 for a black man, probably a skilled worker. The highest valuation for the indentured workers was £50 placed on a boy. A husband and wife, with only a year remaining on their indenture, were jointly enumerated at the same sum as the boy. Gilbert Guthries, an adult obligated to the estate for three and a half years, was appraised at only £35 by the trustees of Lynch's property. Despite the fact that all of Thomas Lynch's Europeans were in their prime, none was valued at a sum equal to that of an old slave woman or small black child.[13]

Individuals as geographically and economically disparate as Henry Laurens, George Washington, and Levinius Clarkson all saw the great profits to be derived from slaves. In 1755 Laurens, writing to the firm of William Wells, Jr., and Peter Carew of St. Christopher, complained, "We wish instead of Rum you had sent a few prime Negro Men of any Country but Callabars. Such would have sold immediately at a handsome profit." Washington reflected the same view when he instructed Daniel Jenifer Adams to acquire slaves in exchange for flour which the Virginia planter was sending to the Caribbean by the ship captain. "The Money arising from the Sales I would have laid out in Negroes, if choice ones can be had under Forty pounds Sterling; if not, then in Rum and Sugar from Barbadoes. . . ." Clarkson wrote to his father-in-law in New York, "Had I Purchas'd 10 or 20 Negroes that John Beekman had for sail on my departure for this Place [Charleston] I am Certain I could have cleared 50pc. by them."[14]

---

ica, ed. Elizabeth Donnan (4 vols.; New York: Octagon, 1965), IV, 452; hereafter cited as *Documents of the Slave Trade*. "An Act for reducing of Interest from Ten to Eight by the Hundred," in S.C. Colonial General Assembly, *The Statutes at Large of South Carolina*, ed. Thomas Cooper and David McCord (10 vols.; Columbia: A. S. Johnson, 1936–41), III, 709–12; hereafter cited as *South Carolina Statutes at Large*.

13. Abbot E. Smith, *Colonists in Bondage: White Servitude and Convict Labor in America, 1607–1776* (Gloucester, Mass.: Peter Smith, 1965), pp. 21–22.

14. *The Papers of Henry Laurens*, I, 333; *Writings of George Washington*, III, 98. Levinius Clarkson to David Van Horn, Charleston, Feb. 23, 1773, *Documents of the Slave Trade*, IV, 457.

The English sense of superiority over non-European peoples was transferred to and even expanded in the southern mainland colonies. The racial attitudes of the settlers are easily discerned in several different observations: the preamble of a slave code, the "scientific" examination of an enlightened European, and instructions on plantation management, and then statements by merchants and planters about specific Negroes or blacks in general. In 1712 the South Carolina Commons House of Assembly originated new legislation for the governance of slaves within the province. The preamble of the act was adopted in the succeeding black codes of 1722 and 1735 with minor variations. That portion of the preamble which remained unchanged during a quarter of a century was the white man's analysis of the character of the blacks. A separate body of laws was necessary, the act rationalized, because ". . . the said negroes . . . are of barbarous, wild, savage natures, and such as renders them wholly unqualified to be governed by the laws, customs, and practices of this Province. . . ." Thus the actions taken by the assembly were justified not because the Negroes were slaves, but because their white overlords viewed them as some inferior species incapable of conforming to the laws of "civilized" Englishmen in America.[15]

William Gerard DeBrahm, scientist, philosopher, soldier, and cartographer, migrated from his native Germany to the colony of Georgia. During his lifetime he held a number of royal positions in the southern colonies, including a very important assignment to survey and report on conditions in English America for the king. DeBrahm's report went far beyond the expectations of the British officials who ordered its preparation. He examined all aspects of life and economy. His analysis of plantation life was succinctly phrased: "The tasking of a Negroe and providing Employ . . . is one of a Planters principle Studies, since the preventing of Idleness is the Art, from which depends the whole Discipline of the Negroes and the Planters Success."[16]

---

15. *South Carolina Statutes at Large*, VII, 352–65, 371–84, 85–96. Herndon v. Carr, Jefferson 132, Oct. 1772, *Judicial Cases Concerning American Slavery and the Negro*, ed. Helen Honor Catterall (5 vols.; New York: Octagon, 1968), I, 93. Opinion of Edmund Pendleton, lawyer for the defendants: "Again in their [Negro slaves'] value they are distinguished as lands, the slaves being worth as much as the ground he cultivates. . . . For this reason our laws [Virginia] have put them on a footing with lands. . . ."

16. *DeBrahm's Report*, pp. 7–10, 94.

A native Virginian, Landon Carter,[17] had views similar to those of DeBrahm. Slaves should be kept busy because "they were less honest and more imperfect than white men." Carter also worried about the diligence of his bound people for there was "nothing so certain as spoiling your slaves by allowing them but little to do; so sure are they from thence to learn to do nothing at All." John Ettwein, the spiritual leader of the Moravians at Bethabara in North Carolina wrote about the German settlers in South Carolina whom he had visited, "I wish their Children may turn out a good Race but am afraid the Negroes have too much Influence upon them. . . ." He recorded further, "What I saw & Heard of the Negroes made me very uneasy." Robert Pringle, Charleston merchant and planter, wrote to a commercial correspondent on Antigua, "Your Island has already greatly Suffered by Putting too much trust in Negroes."[18]

If the attitudes of southern colonial whites toward blacks in general was one of superiority and condescension, their views on specific Negroes were much more pointed and derogatory. Thomas Jefferson described one of his mulatto slaves, Sandy, thus: "His behavior is artful and knavish." Henry Laurens, who could speak of the problems of slavery with surprising compassion and objectivity, characterized his trusted black messenger as "the vile Scoundrell of a Negro. . . ." Again, the Carolina merchant complained about others' unwarranted and costly trust in slaves, "But should I be fin'd for the neglect or fraud of their [black] servants [?]" Laurens's colleague in trade, Robert Pringle, chided Nathaniel French about ". . . your Negro who is an Ignorant fellow. . . ."[19]

Some of the most acerbic characterizations of Negroes by any southerner during the colonial period were recorded by Landon Car-

17. Jack P. Greene wrote in the Preface to *Diary of Landon Carter*, p. lx, ". . . it is probably the richest account of the day-to-day life of any single member of the colonial Virginia Gentry," and observed that "it is full of information on . . . slavery. . . ." Carter's views, therefore, give us a better understanding of the white planter class than the more formal writings of other eighteenth-century American leaders.

18. *Diary of Landon Carter*, I, 21–22, 27; *The Papers of Henry Laurens*, III, 356; *Letterbooks of Robert Pringle*, I, 122.

19. Sept. 7, 1769, advertisement for a runaway slave, in *The Papers of Thomas Jefferson*, ed. Julian P. Boyd (17 vols. to date; Princeton, N.J.: Princeton Univ. Press, 1950–), I, 33. Charleston, Dec. 31, 1756, to John Knight; Charleston, Mar. 3, 1756, to Gidney Clarke; Charleston, Dec. 1, 1762, to Joseph Brown, *The Papers of Henry Laurens*, II, 389, 123; III, 178. Charleston, Aug. 20, 1739, to Nathaniel French, *Letterbooks of Robert Pringle*, I, 122.

ter in his diary. On the general moral state of blacks, he stated, "I never rightly saw into the assertion that Negroes are honest only from a religious Principle. They are only through Sobriety, and but few of them." Carter did not soften his attitude with older slaves, "Even the most aged, whilst their lives are made most pleasant to them, are the most ungratefully neglectfull." Basically, slaves could be spurred to greater or better work by two methods, encouragement through rewards or punishment.[20]

Landon Carter did not believe that the former would work. He noted the behavior of his own blacks in the beating of grain sheaves: "They have all encouragement given them but they are such Villains that they will not thresh them cleaner. . . ." Altering his methods of treatment of the same threshers, Carter recorded, ". . . They have been severely whipped day by day." Resorting to a final generalization, Carter tersely declared, "A Negroe can't be honest." The most trenchant of Carter's statements about black slaves was written in August 1778, with the War for American Independence at midpoint. Reflecting inversely on the corporate personality of the blacks as well as the ideals of the Revolution, he propounded, "Indeed, Slaves are devils and to make them otherwise than slaves will be to set devils free."[21]

The idea of the inferiority of non-European peoples held by the English was greatly augmented by the white southern master class of colonial America when considering its African bondsmen, the very foundation of its wealth and livelihood. Blacks were ignorant, deceitful, dishonest, and even nonhuman devils. Obviously such people should not be free and equal to English Americans and could not be free and equal if the logical and proper social structure envisioned for the New World was to be maintained.

Despite their sense of superiority, the freemen of the southern colonies were dreadfully afraid of the blacks whom they held enslaved. Brian Edwards, the Jamaica sugar planter and historian of the West Indies, concluded that slavery could not exist without fear on the part of the master class. He observed, "In countries where

20. *Diary of Landon Carter*, I, 292, 295.
21. Feb. 1757, May 1766, Aug. 1778, *Diary of Landon Carter*, I, 147, 301; II, 1148–49. Despite continued associations with blacks (and aging and mellowing by Carter) over a twenty-one-year period of time, his attitudes did not soften, but hardened and became more acerbic.

slavery is established, the leading principle on which the government is supported is fear. . . ."[22] This apprehension developed quite early in Virginia, when the number of Negroes was small in relation to the total population. During the third Anglo-Dutch war, the House of Burgesses passed a bill legalizing the killing of runaways and providing for indemnification of all slave owners whose fugitive workers were thus killed. The act of 1672 cited the presence of bands of rebellious slaves in different parts of the colony which could not be subdued. As Gerald W. Mullin has shown in his study of slave resistance in colonial Virginia, most new Africans ran away individually and did not flee great distances from the home plantation. Thus the number of Negroes revolting against European enslavement in late seventeenth-century Virginia must have been quite large in order to provide a population base for the formation of gangs or bands of blacks in armed rebellion in 1672.[23]

This fear of slave depredations reappeared in a later colonial conflict. Immediately after the defeat of General Braddock, Governor Dinwiddie explained to his English superiors that he could not commit the total military strength of the colony to attack the European enemy because "I must leave a proper number [of militiamen] in each county to protect it from the combinations of the negro slaves, who

22. Brian Edwards, *The History, Civil and Commercial, of the British Colonies in the West Indies* (3 vols., London: printed for J. Stockdale, 1807), III, 36. See also Converse D. Clowse, *Economic Beginnings in Colonial South Carolina, 1670–1730* (Columbia: published for the S.C. Tricentennial Commission by the Univ. of S.C. Press, 1971), pp. 104, 159; George C. Rogers, *History of Georgetown County, South Carolina* (Columbia: Univ. of S.C. Press, 1970), p. 26. *Colonists in Bondage* shows another side of the fear and a partial solution based upon racial animosity: "The [white] servants were really more important as a defense against possible slave insurrections than as a defense against the enemy from without." Goveia, "West Indian Slave Laws," p. 126.

23. "Act VIII An Act for the apprehension and suppression of runaways, Negroes and Slaves, September 1672–24 Charles II," Virginia House of Burgess, *The Statutes at Large being a Collection of all the Laws of Virginia from the first Session of the Legislature in April 1619,* ed. and comp. William Waller Hennig (13 vols.; Richmond: Samuel Pleasants, 1810), II, 299–300. Philip Alexander Bruce, *Economic History of Virginia in the Seventeenth Century: An Inquiry into the material condition of the people, based upon original and countemporaneous records* (2 vols.; New York: Macmillan and Company, 1895), II, 115; hereafter cited as *Economic History of Virginia.* Philip Alexander Bruce, *Institutional History of Virginia in the Seventeenth Century: an inquiry into the religious, moral, educational, legal, military, and political conditions of the people, based upon original and contemporaneous records* (2 vols.; New York: G. P. Putnam's Sons, 1910), II, 199–200. Gerald W. Mullin, *Flight and Rebellion; Slave Resistance in Eighteenth Century Virginia* (New York: Oxford, 1972).

have been very audacious in the defeat on the Ohio." Dinwiddie later wrote, "We dare not venture to part with any of our white men any distance, as we must have a watchful eye over our negro slaves, who are upwards of one hundred thousand."[24]

When armed conflict was imminent between England and America in 1774, white Virginians again worried about the threat of slave rebellion conjoined with hostilities against the mother country. James Madison wrote to his friend William Bradford in Philadelphia: "If america & Britian should come to an hostile rupture I am afraid an Insurrection among the slaves may & will be promoted. In one of our Counties lately a few of those unhappy wretches met together & chose a leader who was to conduct them when the English Troops should arrive. . . . Their intentions were soon discovered & proper precautions taken to prevent the infection." Evidencing a sound understanding of the psychology of fear, Madison suggested, "It is prudent such attempts should be *concealed* as well as supressed [*sic*]."[25]

Lord Dunmore, the last royal governor of Virginia, made use of the latent hostility of the blacks by calling them to arms against their masters and promising them freedom in exchange for support of the English cause. This he did on November 17, 1775, ten days after he declared martial law. Before Dunmore's actions, Madison again wrote to his friend Bradford on June 19, 1775, about the possibility of such action by the governor and predicting that the British would be striking at the only weakness of the Chesapeake settlers: "It is imagined our Governor has been tampering with the Slaves & that he has it in contemplation to make great Use of them in case of a civil war in this province. To say the truth, that is the only part in which this colony is vulnerable; & if we should be subdued, we shall fall like Achilles by the hand of one that knows that secret."[26]

In South Carolina, where the whites constituted a minority of the population from the early days of the eighteenth century, the fear of an uprising by the black majority was far greater, and more justified. Conditions did not become severe, however, until the third decade of the century when ever-burgeoning importations of bound workers

24. *Writings of George Washington*, I, 151n, 336n.
25. Nov. 26, 1774. Italics by the author. *Papers of James Madison*, ed. William T. Hutchinson and William M. Rachal (8 vols. to date; Chicago: Univ. of Chicago Press, 1962–), I, 129–30.
26. *Papers of James Madison*, I, 153.

displaced the precarious equilibrium and augmented the percentage of African-born slaves. From this time onward, the *South Carolina Gazette* showed a significant increase in the number of advertisements describing non-English- or broken-English-speaking Negroes who had run away.[27] It is quite understandable, therefore, that the largest successful uprising of blacks in colonial North America occurred in South Carolina in the 1730s.

In 1739 the Stono Rebellion rocked South Carolina. Approximately one hundred slaves from James Island and Johns Island southward of Charleston attempted to march from the colony to the Spanish at Saint Augustine and to freedom. With drums beating and horns blowing, the rebellious blacks met the hastily summoned white militia and encountered defeat. The provincial government employed Indians to pursue those slaves escaping into the swamps and set about trying and executing (or executing without trial) the Negroes caught alive.[28]

The problem of rebellious blacks and the fears engendered by such uprisings did not subside in South Carolina after the brutal crushing of the Stono Rebellion.[29] Little more than a year after the insurrection the provincial capital burned and great fear developed among town residents and governmental officials that the blacks would take advantage of the natural disaster to rise and throw off their bonds. Robert Pringle wrote to his brother in London of his fatigue from, first, fighting the fire and, second, serving as a guard to prevent the feared uprising of the Negroes: "It [the fire] Came so suddenly upon us as well as the great risque we Run from an Insurrection of our

27. *South Carolina Gazette* and Daniel E. Meaders, "South Carolina Fugitives as Viewed Through Local Colonial Newspapers with Emphasis on Runaway Notices 1732–1801," *The Journal of Negro History*, LX (Apr. 1975), 288–319.

28. Primary accounts are recorded in *Letterbooks of Robert Pringle*: Charleston, Sept. 26, 1739, to John Richards, I, 135; Charleston, Dec. 27, 1739, to Andrew Pringle, I, 163; Charleston, Oct. 16, 1739, to John Erving, I, 143; and S.C. Colonial Assembly, *The Journals of the Commons House of Assembly Sept. 12, 1739–March 26, 1741*, ed. J. H. Easterby (Columbia: The Historical Commission of S.C., 1952), Nov. 9, 1739, p. 24; Nov. 10, 1739, pp. 25–26; Nov. 21, 1739, p. 37. Eugene Genovese, *Roll, Jordan, Roll: The World the Slaves Made* (New York: Pantheon Books, 1974), p. 588, puts this largest of North American slave rebellions into perspective: "Risings such as those of 25 or so in New York City in 1712 or of 50 to 100 at Stono, South Carolina, in 1739, although impressive in themselves, qualify as minor events in the general history of slave revolts in the Americas."

29. The Carolina government called out the militia, enlisted friendly Indians as trackers, and paid them for black scalps while condoning summary executions in violation of the slave code. *South Carolina Statutes at Large*, Sec. 60, pp. 416–17.

Negroes which we were very apprehensive of, but all as yet Quiet by the strict Guards & watch we are oblig'd to keep constantly night & day."[30]

Within three weeks of the Charleston fire the Carolinians confronted a third direct threat from the African slaves in the interior of the colony at St. John's Parish, Berkeley County. The plan of the blacks was discovered while still a conspiracy and through the seizure of the leaders, the bud of insurrection was cut before it blossomed into a rebellion similar to that at Stono.[31] The result of these three fearful attempts was a new and much more severe slave code law, that of 1740, which remained in effect until 1865 and was copied by most southern states during the nineteenth century.

Despite the new and more stringent Negro governance law, the fears of the Carolinians were not allayed. Actual conspiracy was not necessary to throw the whites into paroxysms of fear. Henry Laurens in London in 1749 wrote that he had received letters from Carolina but there was "no news [,] only confirmation of the Account of a most horrible Insurrection intended by the Negroes there which was providentially discover'd before any mischief done." There was no planned rebellion, but a plot by some slaves to use the whites' fear of such an uprising to rid themselves of hated associates, both white and black, who were quickly seized when a slave member of the conspiracy told his story. The plan by Agrippa and his friends was discovered, however, and they were shipped from the colony and the seven whites who had been arrested were released. What happened to the blacks taken into custody is not recorded.[32]

By the end of the colonial period Georgia was facing the same problems as its neighbors because of the growing slave population and the growing ratio of blacks to whites. As had been and was the case in Virginia and South Carolina, the Georgians were afraid of bands of escaped slaves who threatened the stability of provincial society. In 1772 the Georgia colonial grand jury presented as a grievance "That a Number of fugitive Slaves have Assembled . . . on or

---

30. Charleston, Nov. 22, 1740, to Andrew Pringle, *Letterbooks of Robert Pringle*, I, 273.

31. *Letterbooks of Robert Pringle*, I, 163n; David Duncan Wallace, *The History of South Carolina* (4 vols.; New York: The American Historical Society, 1934), I, 373.

32. Mar. 21, 1749, to James Cowles, *The Papers of Henry Laurens*, I, 299 and n.

near the borders of the River Savannah and are frequently committing Depredations . . . with Impunity." The internal danger, if combined with an external threat, would be calamitous to the slave
economy of the southern province.[33]

The fear of the southern colonial whites assumed two outward
forms, one personal and the other collective through the provincial
governments. The personal reaction to the constant, latent fear was
simple and direct cruelty—the use of power—to vent the owners'
frustration and hostility and cow the people threatening their control.
Two types of cruelty were acted out by the white owners upon their
slaves. The first was simple, direct, brutal physical force implemented by the whip, the knife, and the gun. The master exercised
customary and legal authority given to him by the white society and
government to exact any punishment short of death on his African
bound workers. Physical cruelty normally resulted from the heat of
passion,[34] generated by a single incident, or calculated mistreatment
exerted to break the victim's will and maintain a submissive attitude
within other blacks. For this reason both individual planters and the
governmental officials usually performed their beatings and dismem-
berments before forced gatherings of slaves. In similar fashion Negroes executed by order of freeholder courts were not buried, but
their corpses exposed on gibbets or hung from gates and walls as
mute threats to blacks not submitting meekly to white domination.[35]

The second type of cruelty exhibited by the white master class in
the colonial South against bound black workers was psychological.
The dominant white man used mental cruelty to exact the same re-
sponses from his slaves as he or others hoped to elicit through bodily
torture without physical abuse and consequential damage to the productive capacity of the victim. Perhaps the surest form of psychological punishment was gross mistreatment of one of a group of miscre-

---

33. *Judicial Cases Concerning American Slavery*, III, 6. *The Colonial Records of the State of Georgia*, comp. and ed. Allen D. Chandler (25 vols.; Atlanta:
The Franklin-Turner Co., 1907), XII, 325.

34. "An Act for the better strengthening of this Province . . . ," *South Carolina
Statutes at Large*, III, Sec. 32, 556–68. See also the letter of Lt. Governor William
Bull, Jr., to the Board of Trade, BPRO Transcripts, MSS, XXXIII, 363–64, S.C.
Department of Archives and History, Columbia, S.C.

35. Despite the gory impression caused by such a description, what was done
with blacks was not out of the ordinary in eighteenth-century America or Europe
of the earlier centuries.

ants. The South Carolina slave code from the law of 1690 onward provided for the exemplary execution of only one slave participant if a band of blacks was involved in a crime punishable by death.[36] The survivors would benefit and the owners' property be protected, but all participants experienced the same mental anguish of not knowing who would be selected for death. At the time of execution, the choice was random. During the offenders' brief imprisonment, no one knew his fate and all suffered equally.

Another form of exemplary punishment creating grave anxiety not only for the victim but for all slaves associated with him was transportation. George Washington practiced this punishment in 1766 when he disposed of Tom, a field worker. The Negro was consigned to a ship captain "to sell, in any of the Islands you may go to, for whatever he will fetch. . . ." Washington characterized Tom as "both a Rogue and a Runaway." Because of the black's extreme independence, the future general who secured the freedom of white Americans was obliged to "beg the favour of you . . . to keep him handcuffed till you get to Sea. . . ."[37] Tom was torn from his familiar surroundings, manacled, and sent to a location unknown to him and the other slaves and even unknown to Washington himself.

Several of Landon Carter's female slaves tried to avoid physical labor during pregnancy. Finally, he used psychological means to punish one and set an example for other blacks under his jurisdiction. One woman "pretended to be too heavy to work. . . ." Another, "Criss [,] fell into the same scheme and really carried it to a great length for at last she could not be dragged out. However by carrying a horse with traces the lady took to her feet [and] run away. . . ."[38] Understandably, Carter made no further entries in his diary about black women feigning this problem.

Reading the personal and governmental records of white and black relations in the colonial South inures the individual to the obvious suffering inflicted upon the slaves. Even this mental cushion can be wrenched away by a startling example of cruelty. In September

36. "An Act for the Better Ordering of Slaves," *South Carolina Statutes at Large*, Sec. 8, pp. 345–46.

37. Mount Vernon, July 2, 1766, to Captain Josiah Thompson, *Writings of George Washington*, II, 437.

38. March 1770, *Diary of Landon Carter*, I, 372.

1740 Robert Pringle consigned Esther, a young Negro woman, to his Lisbon correspondents, Edward and John Mayne. His characterization of the girl and his justification for his actions speak for themselves:

She is a Very Likely Young Wench can doe any House work . . . & talks good English being this Province born, & *is not given to any Vice & have always found her honest.* The only Reason of my sending her off the Privince is that she had a practice of goeing frequently to her Father and Mother, who Live at a Plantation I am concern'd in about Twenty Miles from Town from whence there was no Restraining her from Running away there, & Staying ever now & then . . . .[39]

A young child, forcibly separated from her parents, tried occasionally to go by foot the twenty miles to her old home and for that reason was sold not only outside South Carolina, but into a totally foreign country where the language, customs, and government were different from anything she had known, and from which she could never return to her obviously cherished parents.

A second response by whites to the constant threat of black insurrection was governmental regulation and control. Because of the nature of society, what regulated the lives of the slaves also restricted the freedom of nonslaves. Thus in every colony from Maryland to the Saint Johns River, slave patrols were drawn from the militia to maintain constant surveillance of blacks. Membership was not voluntary but required on a rotating basis through the military company. In addition to regulating the bound black workers, the South Carolina patrol law provided that any white unable to identify himself and unknown to the members of a patrol was to be taken into custody and examined to determine that he was not intent upon mischief.[40] The slave codes regulated the lives of the plantation owner and all whites, and even affected the architecture of the owner's dwelling by specifying a special interior room without windows where guns were kept under lock. Homes, businesses, and departing vessels were liable to regular search.

Defendants and apologists of the southern colonial and state slave

39. Charleston, Sept. 19, 1740, to Edward and John Mayne & Co., *Letterbooks of Robert Pringle*, I, 247. Italics by the author.
40. *South Carolina Statutes at Large*, III, 459.

codes offered in mitigation of the generally harsh terms the view that rights and benefits of blacks were also enumerated and guaranteed.[41] By law, if there were violations, the responsible white could be punished. One of the few instances where such actions were implemented in the eighteenth century occurred in North Carolina in which the slave population was significantly smaller and less essential to the economy than in other southern seaboard colonies. In 1719 Benjamin West was fined for making his Negroes work on Sunday in violation of the North Carolina statute allowing slaves a free day on the Sabbath.[42] No such records exist for other colonies with large numbers of slaves and an economy dependent on bound labor.

The maximum length of working days was also specified in the colonial laws regulating blacks. They were violated with impunity. Landon Carter attributed the poor quality of Virginia's processed tobacco to the fact that masters made their slaves work all day in the fields during picking time and then strip the leaves from the stems throughout the night. Carter saw that the discernment needed to avoid torn and damaged leaves was lost from fatigue. He did not, however, suggest that the owners were violating one of the few rights given to the blacks. In South Carolina, where similar laws were codified by the Assembly, the same situation prevailed. DeBrahm reported that after a full day of clearing land, the entire work force of a plantation would be sent to perform nightwork, the burning of purposefully small piles of brush and limbs. This, he wrote, was standard procedure.[43]

Elsa Goveia, in her essay upon the West Indian slave laws, identifies such regulations as one of the many incongruities of the entire legal apparatus erected about the institution of slavery in the Americas. African bound workers were property, and by all definitions property was either inanimate or subhuman. Paradoxically, the giving of rights to Negroes provided them with a legal persona at the same time that the laws were dehumanizing. Slaves could not possess

---

41. Three divergent examples are James Curtis Ballagh, *A History of Slavery in Virginia* (Baltimore: The Johns Hopkins Univ., 1902), pp. 97, 108; Tannenbaum, *Slave and Citizen*, pp. 72–73; *Economic History of Virginia*, II, 117, 121.

42. *Judicial Cases Concerning American Slavery*, II, 9; *The State Records of North Carolina*, coll. and ed. William L. Saunders (26 vols.; Goldsboro: Nash Brothers, 1886–1907), II, 365.

43. Feb. 1770, *Diary of Landon Carter*, I, 357; *DeBrahm's Report*, p. 94.

personal rights and be property at the same time. Such incongruity fostered violation of the few rights allotted to them.[44]

With the onset of the American Revolution and the fighting in Massachusetts, the southern colonies rallied to assist their northern neighbor. They raised troops; they established extralegal governments; and they enumerated grievances against the crown. During this time the omnipresent institution of slavery consistently colored and influenced actions of the provincial leaders. For two colonies the continual fear that blacks might overturn European society seemed to be coming to a most terrible fruition. All of the provinces received copies of the letter from Arthur Lee, informing the Americans that the British ministry was planning to declare "all Slaves & Servants free that would take arms against the Americans." Virginia and South Carolina faced actual uprisings of Negroes in support of the English.

The Revolution engendered the reality of black uprising in the two colonies with the largest slave populations. The black rebellions were put down, but when might others occur? No matter what the rhetoric of the Revolution, freedom had to be clearly defined and understood as a prerogative of whites, not of blacks.[45]

Through a century and more the English and other European settlers had profited from the continually growing numbers of African workers imported to labor in the fields and forests of the South. From the first coexistence of blacks and whites, the whites had worried about the slaves' reaction to their servitude. As the numbers of Negroes increased, the fear of the Whites grew apace. Some day a servile uprising would combine with a natural or human disaster to destroy all that Europeans had built with slave labor. The breach with England came, and the New England and northern colonies called for freedom. Southern leaders echoed the cry, but with qualification—black slavery must remain. In Virginia Madison would

44. "Because he [the slave] was a person, he posed a problem of public order, which the police regulation tended to cover. The law was forced to allow the slave some kind of 'persona' for the purpose of dealing with him under this aspect of his activity as a special kind of property." Goveia, "West Indian Slave Laws," p. 122.

45. Robert Carter Nicholas, Williamsburg, Nov. 25, 1775, to Va. Delegates in Congress, Philadelphia, *Papers of Thomas Jefferson*, I, 266–67. From William Bradford, July 10, 1775, *Papers of James Madison*, I, 156. *Provincial Congresses of South Carolina*, Sunday, June 4, 1775; Wednesday, June 14, 1775; Thursday, June 22, 1775, pp. 37, 51, 66.

read, ". . . but I cannot believe the Spirit of the English would ever allow them publickly to adopt so *slavish* a way of Conquering [as fomenting a Black rebellion]."[46] In the South Carolina Association the provincial meeting would list as reasons for martial action:

The actual commencement of hostilities against this continent, by the British troops, in the bloody scene on the 19th of April last, near Boston— the increase of arbitrary impositions from a wicked and despotic ministry —*and the dread of instigated insurrections in the colonies*—are causes sufficient to drive an oppressed people to the use of Arms. . . .[47]

The British ministry under Lord North not only impinged upon the political rights of the whites in the southern colonies but had driven a black lance into the boil of fear festering in the colonies with the largest slave populations. For this reason Thomas Jefferson included slavery as one of the charges against the king in the Declaration of Independence, but blacks were excluded from the goals of the Revolution. Jefferson and his revolutionary compatriots "could still live with it [the institution of slavery] and off it."[48] Most of the social inequities in the South such as entail, primogeniture, and the established church fell during the American Revolution. But slavery, the most important of all social inequities, was "left untouched by the transforming hand of revolution."[49]

46. From William Bradford, Philadelphia, Jan. 4, 1775, *Papers of James Madison*, I, 132.

47. *Provincial Congresses of South Carolina*, p. 36. Thus South Carolinians considered slave insurrections as one of three coequal reasons for the Revolution. Henry Laurens to John Laurens, Charleston, May 15, 1775, shows the united support of the Association by the members of the General Meeting: "This Association I saw was unanimously approved of in the General Committee 48 members present—it will be recommended to the provincial Congress at their first meeting on the first of June—I have no doubt of a favourable reception there & believe it will be Subscribed to by the Inhabitants throughout this Colony. . . ." *The Papers of Henry Laurens*, S.C. Historical Society, Charleston, microfilm copy, roll 5, pp. 75–76.

48. Peter Gay, *The Enlightenment, an Interpretation: The Science of Freedom* (New York: Knopf, 1969), p. 421. The same castigation was made of Henry Laurens. Frederick Bancroft, *Slave Trading in the Old South* (Baltimore: J. H. Furst Co., 1931), p. 3.

49. *Provincial Congresses of South Carolina*, p. viii.

The South on the Eve of the Revolution: The Native Americans

James H. O'Donnell, III *Marietta College*

Tradd Street in Charleston, South Carolina, may not have been a major thoroughfare or even a principal byway of eighteenth-century Charleston, but to the native Americans of the colonial South, one of its blocks was a focal point in their lives. For in the house at number 146 lived John Stuart, Scottish immigrant turned merchant, soldier, planter, and, from 1762 to 1779, the king's superintendent for the southern Indians. Thus to the rooms and gardens of the white West India dwelling had come numerous visitors during Stuart's years in office.[1]

In the spring of 1775 came a non-Indian caller named William Bartram, the naturalist from Philadelphia who was gathering flora and fauna for his own collections and for those of his correspondents in England.[2] On the spring day that William Bartram called he sought John Stuart's guidance and instruction before departing on a journey westward into the country of the Cherokees and Creeks. Bartram hoped to secure from Stuart letters of introduction to the British deputies among the Cherokees and Creeks, Alexander Cameron and

1. For information on the superintendents and their offices, see John R. Alden, *John Stuart and the Southern Colonial Frontier: A Study of Indian Relations, War, Trade, and Land Problems in the Southern Wilderness, 1754–1775* (Ann Arbor: Univ. of Mich. Press, 1944); Edmond Atkin, *The Appalachian Indian Frontier: the Edmond Atkin Report and Plan of 1755*, ed. Wilbur R. Jacobs (Lincoln: Univ. of Neb. Press, 1966), hereafter cited as Atkin, *Report*; and Arthur Pound, *Johnson of the Mohawks; A Biography of Sir William Johnson, Irish Immigrant, Mohawk War Chief, American Soldier, Empire Builder* (New York: Macmillan, 1930).

2. William Bartram, *The Travels of William Bartram*, ed. Francis Harper (New Haven, Conn.: Yale Univ. Press, 1958).

David Taitt. Also Stuart could provide talks to the several tribal chiefs, explaining Bartram's mission into the interior.

Whether or not John Stuart informed the naturalist of the turbulent state of politics in South Carolina at the time is not known, for there is no reflection of it in Bartram's journals. Indeed, if one used only William Bartram's writings as a source for describing the frontier on the eve of the Revolution, there would be no hint of trouble. Either by nature or by design, the Quaker botanist ignored all signs save idyllic ones. A group of nubile Cherokee maidens may have raised Bartram's natural instincts (which he squelched quickly) but a conversation with Attacullaculla, a venerable Cherokee leader known to the English as the Little Carpenter, brought only brief and dignified comment. Moreover, since the Little Carpenter was on the way to visit John Stuart in Charleston, it is hard to imagine that he did not mention unrest among the Cherokees, for at the same time that he was journeying to Charleston the tribal leader Oconostota wrote to the officials in Virginia about murders of both whites and Indians on the frontier.[3]

In sharp contrast to Bartram's description of quiet forest glades, one may place the report of Colonel William Christian scarcely eighteen months later depicting the successful mission by Virginia troops against the Overhill Cherokee towns. Christian wrote that his army had scattered the people, destroyed villages, and burned thousands of bushels of corn and potatoes.[4]

How are we to comprehend this change of scene? Surely the revolutionary maelstrom was not so fierce as to draw in the southern tribes in so short a span of time! Indeed not. From other accounts may be drawn a picture quite different from Bartram's pastoral scenes. Indeed, had William Bartram been so inclined he might have heard an extremely complex story from John Stuart.

In 1762 Stuart had succeeded to an imperial appointment which was an outgrowth of the British attempt to implement a systematic Indian policy during the Seven Years War. Early in that conflict the appointments of William Johnson in the North and Edmond Atkin in

3. Oconostota to "Dear Friends and Brothers," June 24, 1775, Convention Papers, 1775, Va. State Library.

4. William Christian to Patrick Henry, Oct. 27, 1776, *Virginia Magazine of History and Biography*, XVII (1909), 51–54.

the South had reflected Great Britain's keen awareness of the need for providing imperial structure to Indian relations. During the war Johnson and Atkin, and then Stuart, were responsible for keeping their Indian charges either loyal or so divided that they would not aid the French. In the postwar years their primary concerns would be land and trade.

That the crown was knowledgeable about problems relating to land was reflected in the well-known Proclamation of 1763, which temporarily restricted westward expansion, forbade land sales by the Indians except with the permission of the king (and then only in the presence of the superintendent), and instructed the governors to punish those who trespassed on Indian lands. But if London, the governors, the superintendents, the natives, or the land-hungry settlers seriously were interested in how far west one could go before he became a trespasser, a boundary had to be defined. Precision had to be given the proclamation's vague promise that "land and territories lying to the westward of the sources of the rivers which fall into the sea from the west and northwest . . . [or] any other lands . . . not ceded . . . or purchased . . . [are] still reserved to the said Indians."[5]

Thus during the years 1763–75 the superintendents and their deputies spent much time determining and having surveyed an Indian boundary line that would stretch from Fort Stanwix in New York to the Floridas. But admonitions to the contrary notwithstanding, the settlers crowded against and across this line, incurring the irritation of the colonial officials, the displeasure of the Indian superintendents, and the wrath of the native Americans. The continued encroachments of the "Virginians" (as the southern Indians called all land-hungry frontiersmen) not only would justify complaints and even an occasional raid, but when war came in 1775 would convince the Indians that the best defense of their interests lay in an alliance with the British.

If John Stuart and his counterpart in the North, William Johnson, did not find enough work in settling land and boundary disputes, their involvement in the trade certainly took up the slack. By the

5. The text of the proclamation may be found in any edition of *Documents of American History*, ed. Henry S. Commager (New York: Appleton-Century-Crofts). With regard to the delineation of the boundary in the South, see Louis De Vorsey, Jr., *The Indian Boundary in the Southern Colonies, 1763–1775* (Chapel Hill: Univ. of N.C. Press, 1966); hereafter cited as DeVorsey, *Southern Indian Boundary*.

middle of the eighteenth century, many of the native Americans were almost completely dependent upon the trade for their livelihood. Infants were wrapped in European cloth and adults dressed in manufactured clothing, women cooked in brass kettles, warriors abandoned the bow and spear for the trading musket, and whenever possible they wanted their corn, meat, and rum provided for them. In exchange for these commodities, the natives traded furs and dressed deerskins.

Much of the trouble resulting from the trade was the work of the white or half-breed traders, whose inflated prices, short measures, land schemes, and misuse of rum often created unrest. The superintendents' difficult task was to encourage honesty in dealing with the tribesmen, but their efforts met with little success.[6]

Stuart and Johnson established their influence among the Indians by maintaining resident agents and commissaries in the villages. To further the influence of these representatives, annually the crown sent out gifts for distribution. Often the royal largess was augmented by presents from governors, the assemblies, interested groups such as the traders, and by the superintendents themselves.

Because of this official policy built upon the dispensing of gifts and the control of trade, John Stuart was regarded as a patron by the tribes within his district. In the Southern Indian Department were located four major tribes: the Cherokees, the Chickasaws, the Choctaws, and the Creeks, plus the "domesticated" Catawbas in South Carolina and a few scattered tribal remnants. Stuart was best known by the two Indian nations who lived closest to the frontier, the Cherokees and Creeks. A sojourn among the Cherokees during the Seven Years War had left Stuart many friends there, while frequent contacts with Creeks visiting Charleston or conferring with Stuart at Augusta had won him the title "Alibama King" among the Creeks.

6. Concerning the trade, traders, and common abuses, see Wilbur Jacobs, *Wilderness Politics and Indian Gifts: Anglo-French Rivalry Along the Ohio and Northwest Frontier, 1748–1763* (Lincoln: Univ. of Neb. Press, 1966); Henry Timberlake, *Memoirs . . . 1756–1765*, ed. Samuel C. Williams (Marietta, Ga.: Continental Book Co., 1948); Bartram, *Travels*; David Taitt, "Journal of David Taitt's Travels from Pensacola, West Florida, to and through the country of the Upper and Lower Creeks, 1772," in *Travels in the American Colonies*, ed. Newton D. Mereness (New York: MacMillan, 1916); Alexander Cameron to John Stuart, Sept. 23, 1766, quoted in the Journal of Superintendent's Proceedings, Apr. 21, 1767, to June 6, 1767, "Meetings with traders and Indians concerning Prices and Regulation of the trade," Thomas Gage Papers, William L. Clements Library, Univ. of Michigan; hereafter cited as WLCL.

The several tribes under John Stuart's supervision lived in the area south of the Ohio River and east of the Mississippi River. The Cherokees, whose towns had been classified by the English into four groups (Lower, Valley, Middle, and Overhill), were located in present-day western North Carolina, eastern Tennessee, northwestern Georgia, and northwestern South Carolina. To the south lived the Creeks, a loosely joined confederation containing three divisions (Upper Creeks, Lower Creeks, and Seminoles), whose villages lay in present northwestern Florida, western Georgia, and southeastern Alabama. West of the Creeks would be found the settlements of the Choctaws, located between the Tombigbee river and the upper reaches of the Pearl River in what is today southern Mississippi. Their towns, like those of the Creeks, were grouped into three divisions (the East Party, the West Party, and the Six Towns). North of the Choctaw lived the Chickasaws, whose principal villages were located in the present north Mississippi.

These southern tribes had an estimated population in 1775 of between fifty and sixty thousand.[7] Since the statistics kept by the British Indian officials listed only fighting men per tribe, the totals would depend on whether one accepted a ratio of three, four, or five noncombatants to each warrior. If a four-to-one ratio is assumed to be the most probable, the figures would show: Cherokees, 3,000 warriors, 12,000 total; Chickasaws, 475 warriors, 1,900 total; Choctaws, 3,100 warriors, 12,400 total; and Creeks, 3,500 warriors, 14,000 total. Adding to this figure of 50,300 the few hundred comprising the scattered tribal remnants, and allowing for errors in the estimates, the total Indian population of the South would not exceed 60,000 on the eve of the American Revolution.

Farming was the principal occupation of these southern Indians, and most of them lived in villages located near the streams that pro-

7. For estimates of the Indian population, see James Wright to Lord Dartmouth, Sept. 20, 1773, in "Letters from Governor Sir James Wright to the Earl of Dartmouth and Lord George Germain, Secretaries of State for America, from August 24, 1774, to February 16, 1782," *Collections of the Georgia Historical Society*, ed. G. W. J. De Renne (Savannah, 1873), 169–70; "A New Map of the Southern District of North America. From Surveys Taken by the Compiler and others, from accounts of Travellers and from the best authorities, &ca., &ca., Compiled in 1781 for Lt. Col. Thomas Brown, His Majesty's Superintendent of Indian Affairs by Joseph Purcell," photocopy, North Carolina Department of Archives and History; George Germain Papers, XVII, 11, WLCL; and Atkin, *Report*, pp. 42–44.

vided both water and food.[8] In the towns of the Cherokees the white man would find what to him seemed the most familiar type of Indian housing, because by 1775 the people of that tribe were living in log cabins. Less known would be the lodges of varying construction which housed the other southern tribesmen. The foodstuffs of the Indians would not be totally alien to the white visitor, for game was supplemented by corn, beans, and potatoes grown in the rich river bottoms. Although the natives would eat beef if given a steer, few of the southern tribes were raising cattle by 1775. Most of their animal husbandry was concentrated on the breeding of horses (a skill at which the Chickasaws excelled) and a few hogs. Even at this early date, many of the older craft skills were dying; the Indians still made a few baskets and other utensils but trade provided the majority of their commodities.

The roles played by men and women in Indian society were well defined but by no means rigidly fixed.[9] Usually the man was the hunter and warrior, the partner in propagating the race, sometimes the statesman, and occasionally the priest. Most of the eastern tribes were matrilineal; hence, the boys looked to maternal uncles for fatherly guidance. Because with few exceptions the way to success and status was by prowess in warfare, a man's life would be involved almost completely with war or hunting, which was only a rehearsal for war. The lives of the women were filled with the labors of cultivating foodstuffs, preparing game, making some clothing and household utensils, and childbearing. Yet the Indian woman was not a drudge, for she attended the tribal councils and spoke her mind. A respected woman might be given the title "Beloved Woman."

The warfare which so dominated the life of the warrior was not

8. The discussion of the life and society of the southern Indians is drawn from: Bartram, *Travels*; Timberlake, *Memoirs*; John R. Swanton, *Source Material for the Social and Ceremonial Life of the Choctaw Indians* (Washington, D.C.: Bureau of American Ethnology, 1931), hereafter cited as Swanton, *Choctaw Material*; J. F. D. Smyth, *A Tour in the United States* . . . (2 vols.; Dublin, 1784); Bernard Romans, *A Concise Natural History of East and West Florida*, ed. Rembert W. Patrick (Gainesville: Univ. of Fla. Press, 1962); John R. Swanton, *The Indians of the Southeastern United States* (Washington, D.C.: Bureau of American Ethnology, 1946), hereafter cited as Swanton, *Southeastern Indians*; and James Adair, *The History of the American Indians* (London: Price, Moncriefe etc., 1775).

9. Fred O. Gearing, *Priests and Warriors: Social Structures for Cherokee Politics in the 18th Century*, memoir 93, American Anthropological Association (Oct. 1962); and John P. Reid, *Law of Blood* (New York: N.Y. Univ. Press, 1970).

the total war known to the European but limited raiding—war for status, not war for annihilation. Because of this concept it was unusual for a tribe to sustain hostilities over a long period of time. To native Americans war was a matter of individual accomplishment. According to tribal custom, a male was accepted as an adult and given a man's name when he had proved himself. Most often a "war party" was a band of about a dozen braves, most of them young bloods under the leadership of a war chief. After the proper ceremonies, fastings, and ablutions, the band would start out. Once they had satisfied themselves that the laws of sanguinity had been fulfilled, then they would return home to give a public report of their deeds. Sometimes they brought back prisoners, who in most cases were adopted into the tribe.

If all the gunmen from a given tribe were called together to consider war, much discussion would ensue in both village and tribal councils until the war faction had persuaded the majority to accept the symbolic black wampus, or until the wampus had been rejected. Although for the sake of convenience the English designated one tribal chief as the "emperor" (in the case of the Cherokees it was usually the chief of the "Beloved" town of Chote), he had no real authority in the nation. If he could persuade a majority to follow him, he might deserve his title; otherwise he was little more than a figurehead. Furthermore, even if he and his followers approved a treaty or war, this was no guarantee that all villages of the tribe would agree. More often than not there were rival leaders, as was the case among the Creeks in the 1770s when the Mortar and Emistisiguo sparred for primacy among the Upper Creeks.

Divided loyalties also carried over into relations with the Europeans.[10] Of the four major tribes in the South, only the Chickasaws were consistent and largely unanimous in supporting one European power. They were steadfast in their loyalty to Great Britain. By contrast, among the Cherokees there had at times been Francophiles and Anglophiles, and in the Choctaw and Creek tribes there had been French, British, and Spanish factions at one time or another. Since these alliances depended largely upon the openhandedness of the

10. Smyth, *Tour,* I, 238; Atkin, *Report, p. 62;* Adair, *History,* pp. 277, 296n, 300–301; Bartram, *Travels,* pp. 143–44; John Stuart to David Taitt, quoted in Taitt, "Journal," p. 497.

Europeans, the groupings would change from time to time. As long as the French, British, or Spanish emissaries influenced a few villages within a tribe, it would be hard to get any faction to go to war for fear of reprisal. This factionalism would be used by the Americans after 1775, particularly among the Creeks.

Each of the great southern tribes had reason to be interested in any developing friction between the American colonials and the English government. In North America during past wars Indian auxiliaries had been sought by the belligerents and a new struggle might repeat past practices. Hostilities would interrupt the trade on which the natives had become so dependent. If the colonials should triumph, the Indians would be placed in a disadvantageous trading position as well as face the predicament of losing more lands to victors demanding the spoils of war. To most native Americans in the South the colonials appeared either as treacherous traders or greedy land grabbers, or both, while the British officials represented a source of protection, however temporary it might be.

On the eve of the war the primary pressure on the southern Indians was the colonial desire for land, a desire which seemed to the natives an insatiable lust. The most immediately threatened were the Cherokees, toward whom the tentacles of settlement crept from four directions, grasping first their hunting grounds and then their farming plots. From an axis resting in eastern Tennessee, tribal lands fanned out from Georgia on the south across backcountry South Carolina through western North Carolina (including much of today's middle Tennessee and Kentucky) and over the southwestern tip of Virginia. From the alluvial soil of their creek-bottom fields the Cherokees gathered yearly crops of corn, beans, potatoes, and pumpkins. Villages composed of log dwellings lay near the fields, belying popular European and American assumptions that the Indians lived like deer in herds and wasted the land. To be sure, deer were an integral part of the Cherokee life cycle, since deer brought meat for their diet and skins for the trade.

In exchange for bundles of skins the Cherokees (and other southern tribes as well) received guns and ammunition, cloth, kettles, knives, axes, combs, blankets, and too often, some cheap rum. In the trinity which dispossessed the native Americans, rum was the unholy spirit complementing the father and son of land and trade. The

Cherokees, like their other brethren in the South were in a damned-if-they-did and damned-if-they-did-not relationship with English and colonial traders. If they did not continue ties, their new economic structure based on trade for manufactured goods might collapse; if, on the other hand, they did continue the relationship, the traders cheated them of their pelts, and the speculators (often in alliance with the traders) cheated them of their lands.

Cherokee lands had been eroded steadily in a series of cessions which began in 1721.[11] Through the years millions of acres had been lost, with the last grant before the Revolution occurring in March 1775 when a group of North Carolina speculators headed by Judge Richard Henderson persuaded the Cherokees to grant all of what is today Kentucky and middle Tennessee (an action which the Little Carpenter was hastening to explain to Stuart when he met Bartram on the trail to Charleston).[12] For the Cherokees the so-called Treaty of Sycamore Shoals, or the Transylvania Purchase, signalled more than the loss of tribal lands, for at the gathering of purchasers and chiefs a young tribal leader named the Dragging Canoe had become so incensed at the giveaway that he warned the assembly that the new territories would become "dark and bloody"; he then stalked out of the meeting. This pique was not momentary, however, for the Dragging Canoe became the leader of a strongly anti-American faction of the Cherokees which would ultimately secede from the traditional areas of the nation and withdraw south along the Tennessee river to an area more accessible to British agents coming through the Creek country from Pensacola and St. Augustine.

Those Cherokees who heard the Dragging Canoe's warnings should have suspected the actions of the settlers from Watauga and Nolichucky (settlements well across the mountains and deep in Cherokee territory) who added their smooth words to those of the Transylvanians and wheedled a lease for their lands out of the tribal leaders. These overmountain settlers had begun trickling through

11. Charles Royce, "The Cherokee Nation of Indians," *Fifth Annual Report of the Bureau of Ethnology* (Washington, D.C., 1887).

12. In connection with the Sycamore Shoals negotiations, see Deposition of Charles Robertson, Oct. 3, 1777, in *Calendar of Virginia State Papers and Other Manuscripts, 1652–1781*, ed. William P. Palmer et al. (Richmond: n.p., 1875–83), I, 291; Deposition of Samuel Wilson, Apr. 15, 1777, I, 282–83; Deposition of John Reid, Apr. 16, 1777, I, 284; and William Preston to Governor Dunmore, Jan. 23, 1775, British Public Record Office, Colonial Office, Series 5, Vol. 1553, p. 93 (microfilm), hereafter cited as CO5/vol., p.

the passes as early as 1770 and with each year spread nearer the Cherokee villages. Little did the Cherokees realize in March 1775 that this lease would soon be called a deed and regarded as a bill of sale.

Small wonder then that on the eve of the Revolution the Cherokees looked upon all frontiersmen as cheats, categorizing them all as "Virginians." Whenever the natives needed to color words, the term "Virginia" was used, since a lie, for example, was much worse if it was a "Virginia lie." Little wonder that the tribe looked to John Stuart and his deputies as their protectors, that the warriors were willing to aid the superintendent and in turn the king. Throughout the war and until the British withdrawal from distant St. Augustine, the Cherokees clung to the idea that succor might be afforded them by their British friends.

Nor were the Cherokees alone in their assumption of British support, for it was shared by the other tribe immediately exposed to American pressure, the Creeks. Englishmen spoke freely of the Creeks and the Creek nation when in truth the Creeks consisted of a confederation of a basic Muskoghean stock with accretions of tribal remnants driven west by settlement and war. There were three distinct subgroupings of Creeks: the Upper Creeks of middle Alabama; the Lower Creeks of the Alabama-Georgia boundary; and the Seminollie Creeks (Seminollie is a corruption of the Spanish word *cimmarones*, meaning wild ones) of northern Florida. One could hope for a unified policy by the Creeks in general but this was seldom the case.

The Creeks had been of particular significance during the Seven Years War because of their strategic location.[13] They occupied lands from Apalachicola Bay to near the present Columbus, Georgia, on the Chattahoochee River and then west to the Tombigbee River in today's Alabama. French designs on the "soft underbelly" of British settlement, i.e., the vacant spaces south of Carolina, had brought the Bourbon flag to the Creek country. French forts in Creek country then created a powerful influence which the British attempted to counter through their domination of the trade. These French machi-

13. Alden, *John Stuart*; Verner W. Crane, *The Southern Frontier, 1670–1732* (Ann Arbor: Univ. of Mich. Press, 1956); and two books by David Corkran, *The Cherokee Frontier: Conflict and Survival, 1740–1762* (Norman: Univ. of Okla. Press, 1962); and *The Creek Frontier, 1540–1783* (Norman: Univ. of Okla. Press, 1967).

nations underscored the fact that no one could come against Carolina or later Georgia by the back door save with the cooperation of the Creeks, a point not lost on the American frontiersmen or the Loyalist partisans in the days after 1775.

So lucrative was the Creek trade that many traders from Charleston and Savannah made fortunes sufficient to buy land and thus achieve status and dignity. After the founding of Georgia there had been much activity in the trade as hardy Scots fought established South Carolinians as well as each other for the profits of the peltry trade. Licenses for trading permission in specific towns were contested hotly, with claims and counterclaims, legal actions and counteractions.[14] At times the Creeks had benefited from this competition, but in the end found a system evolving from which they could not escape. As one native American put it so eloquently, "We are so long used to wrap our children in European cloth that we cannot do without the trade."[15]

Intermixed with the difficulties of the trade were matters concerning land. Despite warnings to the contrary by the British officials, trading firms extended credit to individuals in villages throughout the nation. As these debts increased, it was apparent that the balance could never be repaid, so traders sought the next most lucrative commodity possessed by the Indians—land.

Creek land grants to the colonists had come some time after the first Cherokee cessions, but as the Georgians pushed up the Savannah River and westward away from that stream the bounds of the Creek confederation had become more constricted. Like the other tribes, the Creeks found themselves doubly damned in their relations with the whites. There was always some colonial who wanted more land, no matter how much the tribe had ceded already. As indicated above, land had become tied to trade, so that an enterprising trader might turn speculator or join the speculator's interest with his own by agreeing to accept land in order to satisfy debts incurred in the trade.

Such was the case with what has come to be known as the New

14. South Carolina Indian Books, S.C. Department of Archives and History, Columbia, S.C.

15. Journal of Negotiations with the Creeks, Aug., May 1776, Governor's Office, Minutes of the Council, 1777–80, N.C. Department of Archives and History, Raleigh, N.C.

Purchase of 1773.[16] Pressure from yet another wave of English immigrants into Georgia after 1770 coupled with mounting debts to
the traders brought the Creeks to the treaty ground. There followed
an almost classic example of the yen-and-yang relationship between
native Americans and colonists, for some of the Creeks were outraged
by the land "sale" and prepared for war, a conflict almost immediately
terminated when the governor of Georgia forbade continuation of
the trade until hostilities ceased. Hostilities ceased! The trade was
scheduled to be reopened in 1775, but the war came.

War came too to the other southern tribes, although by no means
in the same degree as it would to the Cherokees and the Creeks. For
the Choctaws the new conflict brought some respite from the long
struggle with the Creeks which the British had fomented on the ancient principle of divide and conquer. British Indian officials realized
that no use could be made of either the Choctaw or Creek warriors as
long as they fought each other. But on the eve of the Revolution the
fighting raged on. At the end of 1774 a band of Choctaw raiders
struck into Creek territory and surprised a Creek band which included the Mortar, an influential Upper Creek headman.[17]

Fear of Creek retaliation for this and other raids, however, was not
the only matter which troubled the Choctaws in 1774–75. Their loyalties were being pulled by the wooings of the Spanish and the British
emissaries who came into their towns. The representatives of the
Spanish governor at New Orleans, Bernardo de Galvez, came with
gifts and fair words for those who accepted Spanish commissions,
while the British fought back with the threat of economic sanctions,
no Choctaw support of the English crown, no British trade goods.
Trade was the makeweight, for the Choctaw had recognized long
ago the need, indeed their desperation for English goods. Unless the
Spanish could promise an adequate supply of goods, their influence
was likely to be fleeting.[18]

From these European courtiers the Choctaw coquettes received
one present that was of devastating sociopsychological impact. That
gift was the demonic spirit, rum. Theories about native American

16. De Vorsey, *Southern Indian Boundary*, passim.
17. Corkran, *The Creek Frontier*, p. 287.
18. John W. Caughey, *Bernardo de Galvez in Louisiana, 1776–1783* (Berkeley:
Univ. of Calif. Press, 1934).

drinking patterns aside, the fact remained that the Choctaws drank, and drank too much. Traders and governmental representatives were unmerciful in bringing barrel after barrel of cheap rum into the Choctaw country. When a village received its share, there was no respite from drinking until it was all consumed. Again and again the Choctaw chiefs lamented to the British authorities about the vast quantities of rum being brought into their nation. British visitors found that the reports were not exaggerated; their own observations described entire villages lying in a state of intoxication.[19] Under such circumstances the people could neither care for themselves nor could they deal with those intruders who came into their nations. Although the problem of rum drinking was found among all the southern tribes, it was particularly acute among the Choctaw because of their relative proximity to the coast and the consequent ease with which visitors could come into their country.

Located close to the British posts at Mobile and Pensacola as well as to the Spanish at New Orleans, the Choctaws were more exposed to European power politics than any of their southern neighbors, but in some ways they were less affected by the course of the American Revolution. There were settlers in their country at Natchez, but those colonists were pro-British so at the time they posed no threat to Choctaw integrity and autonomy. There were British overtures for a land cession after the war began, but only for land sufficient to complete the surveying of the so-called Indian Boundary on which so much time and labor had been expended after the Great War for Empire.

There were, however, no fingers of American settlement grasping for the throat of Choctaw lands. Their principal role in the war would be as British scouts on the Mississippi in anticipation of patriot moves southward and as auxiliary forces for the troops at Mobile and Pensacola if they were attacked. The Choctaw would not confront their tribal finitude in the face of American demands until early in the nineteenth century.

Of the Chickasaws, however, the same could not be said.[20] At first appearance it would seem that their position was as removed from

19. Charles Stuart's Report of His Visit to the Choctaw Country, 1 July 1778, CO5/79, 196–202.

20. James H. O'Donnell, III, *Southern Indians in the American Revolution* (Knoxville: Univ. of Tenn. Press, 1973), pp. 136–37.

the scene of battle as was that of the Choctaws, but their lands stretched northward along the Mississippi to its confluence with the Ohio and then eastward to the mouth of the Tennessee. It was on their northern frontier that they stood in the way of frontier expansion, for the Kentuckians were pushing westward while the Virginians, who claimed all of the area to the Mississippi, were interested in a strategic settlement somewhere along the Ohio near the falls of the river. The Chickasaws were pressured on their eastern frontier where the Cumberland settlements had sprung up in the middle of hunting lands long claimed by the tribe. In all these instances, however, the Chickasaws chose the rhetoric of negotiation rather than the reality of war.

Given the appetite for land which drove the colonists, it is little wonder that as hostilities drew near in the spring of 1775, the majority of the Indians leaned toward the British. As far as the royal military officials were concerned, there was no question about calling the warriors into action; they had been used in other wars, and they would be used in this one; it was only a matter of time, place, and degree. Both north and south of the Ohio River, British emissaries would seek to maintain the allegiance of the tribes. As British policy on this matter developed, it was understood that the natives would not be encouraged to raid indiscriminately, but would be used in conjunction with troops. When accumulated grievances drove the Cherokees to war in 1776 and the Iroquois in 1778, British plans were wrecked and the tribes suffered at the hands of the patriots. So severe was the punishment meted out to the Cherokees that the other southern tribes would be reluctant to commit themselves to arms. Although desultory raiding continued all along the frontier throughout the war, the British found it impossible to utilize the manpower potential of their Indian allies.

With the advantage of hindsight one may judge that the Americans really had little cause for worry. But no rational man of the day would take that stance. The threat of Indian attack was a great unknown which had to be considered in defense preparations. Never for a moment could the Patriots assume that the natives would remain passive.

From the Indian point of view, the War for American Independence certainly was another case of choosing the wrong ally, just as many tribes had done during the Seven Years War. The old practice of tribal leaders playing off one suitor against another did not work. What occurred in the long run was a self-inflicted form of the ancient military adage of divide and conquer, with the natives dividing and conquering themselves. Rarely did an entire tribe or confederacy listen to the potential ally of the moment; instead, factionalism prevailed, some villages or factions backing the Americans and others the British. Eventually the entire tribe would suffer, for the patriots would have their way with one group on the grounds of friendship and with another on the premise that to the victors belong the spoils. In any case the tribe would be forced into a land cession, an old story to the Indians. Defeat for the tribes had meant loss of territory since the first clashes in the seventeenth century and would continue to carry the same meaning through the early federal period into the nineteenth century and until the massacre at Wounded Knee in 1890. American Indian policy and the public opinion behind it would change little in nearly three centuries, whether the administrators were British colonials, struggling patriots, citizens of a fledgling republic, ardent expansionsists of nineteenth-century America, or strip-miners in the present century.

James Iredell and the Revolutionary Politics of North Carolina

R. Don Higginbotham   *The University of North Carolina at Chapel Hill*

A single collection of a man's papers may sometimes have a profound impact on the shaping of historical viewpoints toward a whole era. Such a possibility is most likely to exist in the study of a colony or state that is singularly lacking in manuscript holdings of its public figures. So it has been for revolutionary North Carolina, where until recent years the only collection of any note available to scholars has been the writings of James Iredell, a native of Bristol, England, a British customs official at Edenton who cast his lot with the patriots in 1776, and subsequently a distinguished lawyer and jurist.[1] If most of the Iredell material was not deposited in historical libraries until this century, a large part of the Iredell literary treasury was in print, published in the 1850s by Griffith J. McRee as the *Life and Correspondence of James Iredell*.

Historians, almost without exception, have discerned in the Iredell missives evidence to sustain the interpretation of the American Rev-

I wish to acknowledge the assistance of three of my seminar students, Karl Rodabaugh, Charles Waldrup, and Robert Morey, whose statistical data I have occasionally used without—I hope—jeopardizing their opportunity to publish the significant aspects of their own research.

1. Two other major bodies of papers, now available, are worth mentioning. A small portion of the papers of Samuel Johnston at Hayes Plantation near Edenton was copied in the form of typescripts and deposited in the N.C. Historical Commission in the 1920s. In the 1950s the full materials at Hayes were microfilmed; these photoduplicates are in the Southern Historical Collection, the Univ. of North Carolina at Chapel Hill Library. A second group of papers, the Blount correspondence and related items, has lately been published: *The John Gray Blount Papers*, ed. Alice B. Keith and William H. Masterson (3 vols.; Raleigh: State of N.C., 1952–65).

olution advanced by the progressive school of scholarship, which rose to prominence in the first two decades of the twentieth century and which still retains some influence today. They have maintained for North Carolina what Charles H. Lincoln and Carl L. Becker saw in monographs on Pennsylvania and New York respectively: namely, a continuous conflict between western, democratically oriented farmer groups and a handful of liberal, intellectual allies on the one hand and eastern, conservative merchants and planters on the other.

Actually, however, one can find this conflict interpretation of North Carolina's political history in the work of local historians long before the twentieth century, long before the rise of history as a discipline primarily the preserve of professionals who were seminar-trained and based at academic institutions. Class and ideology as the basis of politics appear as early as 1834 with the publication of Joseph Seawell Jones's *A Defence of the Revolutionary History of the State of North Carolina from the Aspersions of Mr. Jefferson.* Jones, who had access to Iredell documents, was followed just a little over twenty years later by Griffith J. McRee, the Iredell collector-editor-author who also stressed the divisions within the Whig ranks in the Revolution.

It is, though, the writings of more recent historians, most of them trained in progressive scholarship, that have perpetuated the conflict analysis of North Carolina's revolutionary past, particularly men such as R. D. W. Conner, Enoch W. Sikes, H. M. Wagstaff, Hugh T. Lefler, and A. R. Newsome. Yet all of them, past and present, have in common an unusually heavy reliance on the pen of James Iredell and his correspondents, which may explain why they have scarcely gone beyond the outlines sketched by Joseph Jones, who described the presence of a "conservative party" which contended for independence, a strong nation, and little more; who also depicted a "radical party" which considered "the establishment of a democracy . . . an object of superior importance to the Independence of this country."[2]

According to the conflict historians, from Jones forward, the conservatives were led by Samuel Johnston, brother-in-law of Iredell, an Edenton planter-lawyer, veteran colonial legislator, and probably

2. Joseph Seawell Jones, *A Defence of the Revolutionary History of the State of North Carolina from the Aspersions of Mr. Jefferson* (Raleigh: Turner and Hodges, 1834), pp. 273–76.

the most influential figure in the revolutionary movement in 1775–76. In view of Johnston's subsequent services in the state legislature, the Continental Congress, and the United States Senate, plus two terms as state governor and other offices, J. G. deRoulhac Hamilton was doubtless correct in ascribing to Johnston "the most notable political career in the history of North Carolina."[3] His principal adversary, the radical chieftain, was said to be Willie Jones of Halifax, who, though a wealthy eastern planter, was a liberal idealist, a champion of the common people.

To be sure, Iredell's correspondence does contain grist for the mill of political controversy. Although Iredell accepted the severing of imperial ties and took pride in his own patriotic contributions, he saw some of the consequences of the Revolution as less than desirable, including certain features of the new state constitution drafted in the fall of 1776. Iredell clearly resented the fact that the planter-merchant-lawyer aristocracy of the Albemarle and Cape Fear regions no longer exercised almost uncontested control in the realm of public affairs. Iredell and his so-called conservative friends wrote critically of "the saints of the Backcountry," "a back-country interest," and "Western men." Iredell and Johnston agreed that "fools and knaves" dominated the first state legislature which convened in 1777. There was no incentive for "gentlemen" to take seats in that body since their wise counsel would be brushed aside, the majority of the elected representatives choosing to "stoop to the common arts of acquiring popularity."

When Johnston declared that he "had an opportunity of seeing an experiment of the new legislature" at firsthand, he wrote as one who temporarily at least was an outsider, "entirely unobstructed with Politicks and Politicians." If he had offered himself to the voters in the previous year to represent his county of Chowan in the fifth provincial congress, which had the task of writing the state's constitution, he was defeated; nor, for whatever the reasons, do we find him in the legislature the following year. It was likely during this time of political change that Iredell, possibly smarting from Johnston's setback (if indeed he suffered one) and probably generally unhappy with the lack of respect shown to old and trusted leaders, dashed off his "Creed of a Rioter" essay, which sarcastically asserted that low men

3. J. G. deRoulhac Hamilton, "Samuel Johnston," *Dictionary of American Biography*, V, 150.

who courted popular favor wished to banish from public life all gentlemen in favor of individuals lacking intelligence or experience.[4]

There were other disconcerting developments to a man such as Iredell in the aftermath of independence. John Penn, a popular Granville County leader, resorted to "the most insidious acts and glaring falsehoods" to oust the able, hard-working Joseph Hewes of Edenton from his position in the Continental Congress. Hewes's defeat, together with his own narrow margin of reelection, prompted William Hooper of Wilmington to step down from his own seat in Congress. To Johnston the year 1777 did indeed seem to be one of internal political revolution, albeit a bloodless one, and this fact scarcely made it easier for him to take. The state naval officer at Port Brunswick, reported Johnston, was summarily dismissed simply because he was a "man of fortune," his station then "filled by a stripling." Simultaneously, the legislature contemplated appointing as judges persons who "scarcely qualified to execute the most inconsiderable Office in the State." The culprits, those whose voices were being heard, were "popular" men, particularly Penn, Griffith Rutherford of Rowan County, and Thomas Person of Granville County, all from the west—all possessed of "narrow and contracted principles, supported by the most comtemptible abilities."[5]

In preparing a modern edition of *The Papers of James Iredell* I have found that some of the materials I have gathered run counter to the progressive interpretation. My intention is to point out examples of this contrary information and to suggest the complexity of North Carolina politics in the revolutionary era.

If in fact two fairly well-defined parties or factions existed, and if the radicals had the upper hand most of the time, why then was it that the legislature (of which Iredell was often so critical) endeavored repeatedly to heap honor and office upon the young Edenton lawyer? After adopting a state constitution the fifth provincial congress had appointed him to a committee to review the North Carolina statutes that had been in force during the last colonial years as well as those

4. Samuel Johnston to Thomas Burke, Apr. 19, June 26, 1777, Thomas Burke Papers, Southern Historical Collection, Univ. of N.C. at Chapel Hill Library; hereafter cited as Burke Papers. Griffith J. McRee, *Life and Correspondence of James Iredell* (2 vols.; New York: D. Appleton, 1857–58), 335–36. Hereafter cited as McRee, *Iredell*.

5. Johnston to Burke, June 26, 1777, Burke Papers.

currently in effect "and to prepare such Bills to be passed into laws as may be consistent with the Genius of a Free People. . . ."[6] In its first two sessions—April and November 1777—under the constitution, the General Assembly implemented most of the proposals of Iredell and his colleagues. In doing so, the legislators did not make a radical departure from the past but instead erected a legal system, with slight modification, based upon their colonial experience. It is true that in December 1777 the legislature chose Waightstill Avery of Mecklenburg County over Iredell for the post of state attorney general because, according to Hooper, of "a back-country interest and Avery's presence" when the lawmakers were in session.[7] But the representatives then picked Iredell to be one of the three associate justices of the superior court (equivalent to the state supreme court today). Later, after Iredell had stepped down from the bench and after Avery had resigned as attorney general, the lawmakers named Iredell attorney general, a position he occupied for more than two years (1779–81), the most critical time of the Revolution in North Carolina when the state faced repeated threats of British invasion. It was while serving as attorney general that Iredell, for personal and financial reasons, declined an opportunity to represent the state in the Continental Congress.

Still another apparent contradiction between the standard historical interpretation and the Iredell manuscripts concerns Willie Jones. Throughout the Revolutionary War years Iredell and Johnston seemed to be on excellent personal and political terms with the wealthy, high-living Halifax planter, supposedly the radical kingpin. On what was probably the most bitter issue in state politics, the confiscation of loyalist property, Iredell contended that it was unfair to seize the lands of persons who were "real British subjects"—that is, those who had never resided in the colony or who had only been there a short time and done nothing inimical to the patriot cause; or, furthermore, to confiscate the estates of people who were not in North Carolina at the time due to circumstances beyond their control. The debate showed Iredell joined not only by conservatives like Johnston,

6. *The State Records of North Carolina*, ed. Walter Clark (16 vols. numbered XI–XXVI; Winston and Goldsboro: State of North Carolina, 1895–1914), XIV, 987.

7. William Hooper to Iredell, Dec. 23, 1777, *The Papers of James Iredell, 1767–1783*, ed. Don Higginbotham (2 vols.; Raleigh: State of North Carolina, 1976), I, 468. Hereafter cited as *Iredell Papers*.

Hooper, and Archibald Maclaine of Wilmington, but also by Thomas Person, for whom Johnston had earlier voiced such contempt, and, most significantly, by Willie Jones, who was harshly critical of the very backcountry elements—on the opposite side of the issue—historians have said were his closest allies.

The conclusion is inescapable that the notion of Willie Jones as "the undisputed leader of the radical party," the political schemer who ardently opposed Samuel Johnston and worked for the latter's defeat at the polls in 1776, is an absolute myth. How therefore did that myth arise? It resulted from an uncritical acceptance of the undocumented story in Joseph Jones's *Defence*, a book marred by the author's aristocratic pretensions and obvious prejudice against Willie Jones; it likewise stemmed from historians having read Willie Jones's later fight with Johnston and Iredell over the Federal Constitution back into an earlier period when serious political friction between the men in question simply did not occur.[8]

Prior to 1787 Jones was evidently closer politically to men of conservative persuasion than to those who represented a radical or western interest. William R. Davie, the Federalist leader, said as much when he confided to James Iredell in 1788 that "Wilie Jones felt some mortification in finding himself in the company of [Timothy] Bloodworth and [Thomas] Persons," both of whom had been on the opposite side of the political fence from Iredell and his friends for years.[9]

The sum total of these disclosures leads to the conclusion that political behavior in North Carolina during the Revolution was not as simplistic as it has customarily been pictured, an opinion already expressed for the events of the year 1776 by Elisha P. Douglass and Robert L. Ganyard. As early as 1955 Douglass observed that, whatever the radical strength in the fifth provincial congress, that body produced a state constitution scarcely fashioned in the pattern of the

8. The only scholarly biographical treatment of Jones is Blackwell P. Robinson, "Willie Jones of Halifax," *North Carolina Historical Review*, (1941), 1–26, 133–70. The author accepts the standard view of Jones as the leader of a radical party, although he offers no evidence from primary sources to support this contention. He does, however, note several inconsistencies in Jones's behavior, especially his breaking ranks with radicals over confiscation.

9. William R. Davie to Iredell, July 9, 1788, McRee, *Iredell*, II, 231. Jones, according to an Edenton resident, "has been heard frequently to declare, that, when he . . . had scrutinized the character of those who were against the Constitution, he blushed to think he was seconded by such a vile herd of infamous fellows." *State Gazette of North Carolina*, Oct. 1, 1789.

radical-inspired Pennsylvania constitution, which contained no property qualification for exercising the franchise, created a unicameral
legislature, and provided for no office of governor—"a Beast without
a Head," exclaimed William Hooper.[10] Douglass further declared
that the new state charter more closely resembled "the views of
Johnston and Hooper than . . . those of the piedmont and frontier
counties."[11] Johnston himself was ambivalent. "As well as I can
Judge," he informed Iredell, "it may do as well as that adopted by
any other Colony."[12]

Even so, Johnston's letters in the Iredell collection show him to
have been soured by much of the proceedings, tedious, rambling, dis-
cursive—in his opinion. He looked with horror upon a proposal that
county justices of the peace be elected rather than appointed. He was
equally agitated by "one of the Members from the back Country"
who called for every future legislator to "swear that he believed in the
holy Trinity and that the Scripture of the old Testament was written by divine inspiration." The latter particularly provoked "very
warm debate" and finally "such a flame" that it threatened to wreck
the congress, although eventually both schemes were beaten back.
Nonetheless, Johnston's most quoted remark leaves the impression
that radicalism reigned triumphant in the constitution-making process: "Every one who has the least pretensions to be a Gentleman is
suspected and born down *Per ignobile Vulgus*, a set of men without
reading, experience or principle to govern them," he complained to
his sister Hannah Iredell.[13]

While Douglass has placed the constitution itself in the perspective of the times, he did not address himself to yet another crucial
question—more recently examined by Robert L. Ganyard—concerning the composition of this fifth provincial congress. In contrast to
the standard picture of the radicals turning to rioting and violence
to elect delegates of their persuasion to that assemblage, Ganyard
unearths no contemporary evidence for that view, which was advanced by Joseph Jones and Griffith McRee. Nor was there "an

10. Hooper to Johnston, Sept. 26, 1776, *The Colonial Records of North Carolina*,
ed. William L. Saunders (10 vols.; Raleigh: State of N.C., 1886–90), 864.
11. Elisha P. Douglass, *Rebels and Democrats: The Struggle for Equal Political
Rights and Majority Rule during the American Revolution* (Chapel Hill: Univ. of
N.C. Press, 1955), p. 129.
12. Johnston to Iredell, Dec. 7, 1776, *Iredell Papers*, I, 423.
13. Johnston to Iredell, Dec. 9, 1776, Johnston to Hannah Iredell, Dec. 13, 1776,
ibid., I, 424, 425.

abnormally large turnover in personnel between the fourth and fifth congresses."[14]

At this point, we must return to post-1776 events. If it was not a radical constitution fashioned by newly elected democratic forces, which henceforth dominated politics in the 1777 legislature and afterward, how do we explain the sentiments of Iredell, Johnston, and like-minded men?

These conservatives were correct, but only to a degree. Changes were occurring, although they had difficulty putting their finger on the precise reasons for them, just as historians have gone astray with their neat, overly simplistic two-party scheme of radicals and conservatives. Assuredly politics did heat up, so to speak, especially in 1776 and 1777. In addition to declaring independence, writing a constitution, and launching a new government, the patriots had laws to enact, a war to be won, and men—many, more than ever—to be elected to office. These developments alone were enough to kindle political fires of a kind that were unprecedented, that went far beyond the interest that politics and public service engendered in the colonial period, when the provincial legislature had comparatively less business, when that body had relatively little to do with the staffing of public offices.

Now the filling of all posts—judges, justices, militia officers, treasurers, customs collectors, and the rest—fell to the legislature. It was virtually inevitable that a lawmaking body with such pervasive authority and responsibility should have been somewhat heady with the wine of power, should have also felt forceful constituent pressures in selecting a virtual horde of officials to run the machinery of the state at every level. Because of its greater power, too, election to that

14. Robert L. Ganyard, "Radicals and Conservatives in Revolutionary North Carolina: A Point at Issue, The October Election, 1776," *William and Mary Quarterly*, 3d ser., XXIV (1967), 568–87. Besides the work of Douglass and Ganyard, the most important studies of North Carolina politics have dealt with the Regulator movement in the decade before independence. While the authors are far from agreement on all points, they do see that movement as a complex phenomenon. Marvin L. Michael Kay, "An Analysis of a British Colony in Late Eighteenth Century America in the Light of American Historiographical Controversy," *Australian Journal of Politics and History*, XI (1965), 170–84; Kay, "The North Carolina Regulation, 1766–1776: A Class Conflict," in *The American Revolution: Explorations in the History of American Radicalism*, ed. Alfred F. Young (De Kalb: Northern Ill. Univ. Press, 1976), 71–123; James P. Whittenburg, "Planters, Merchants, and Lawyers: Social Change and the Origins of the North Carolina Regulation," *William and Mary Quarterly*, 3d ser., XXXIV (1977), 215–38.

representative institution must have become for some men at least a sought-after plum, whereas before the Revolution the colonists were in the main content to allow their "betters" to fill the assembly, gentlemen with wealth and time to perform what was considered to be a public service, an obligation that persons of station were expected to perform for the public good. It should be recalled that the upper house, known as the royal council and appointive in the colonial era, was now an elective senate, a further ingredient to stoke the political fires. Only eighteen men sat on the council in the decade before 1774, a substantial number of them British placemen. After 1776 each county annually chose a senator, thirty-five of whom composed the initial senate.[15]

The consequences of these changes had the greatest impact on the west. Here one can only agree with both contemporaries and historians alike in saying that the interior carried heavier weight in political affairs; that it "waxed very strong," as Willie Jones explained it, "by Division or Subdivision of Counties."[16] In 1775 there were twenty-two eastern counties and thirteen western counties. Of nineteen newly created counties by 1783, all but three were in the interior. This new influence is seen in the election of two western governors: Thomas Burke of Orange County in 1781 and Alexander Martin of Guilford County in 1782. It is also revealed in decisions to shift the meeting places of the state legislature away from the coastal areas during the war—to Hillsborough, Smithfield, and Wake County Court House. If the composition of the council of state, an elected advisory body to the governor, was predominantly eastern in the early years, a majority of its members were from the back parts by 1781. A study of the lower branch of the legislature, the House of Commons, finds that of the forty-nine most influential members between 1777 and 1783— their identities determined by examining service upon important committees—twenty-three came from the western counties.

15. The approach contained in this paragraph owes much to suggestions in James Kirby Martin, *Men in Rebellion: Higher Governmental Leaders and the Coming of the American Revolution* (New Brunswick, N.J.: Rutgers Univ. Press, 1973), passim.

16. Jones to Henry E. McCulloh, ?, 1783, quoted in Robinson, "Willie Jones of Halifax," pp. 144–45. Any east-west line must be somewhat arbitrary; but I have drawn it down through Bute, Edgecombe, Dobbs, Duplin, New Hanover, and Brunswick counties, all of which in same respects seem more aligned with the east than the west. The eastern counties were economically oriented toward the production of naval stores, rice, and tobacco, exporting staples from towns on the coast and the sounds.

One cannot, however, equate a western interest with a well-defined radical party intent on making the Revolution a movement for democracy as well as independence. A reading of the revolutionary laws— contained in volume 24 of the *State Records*—shows there was little in the way of social experimentation, of tinkering with the domestic sector. The abolition of the established church and the severing of all connections between the state and organized religion, a controversial proposition in Virginia until 1786 and in Connecticut and Massachusetts until well into the nineteenth century, produced scarcely a ripple in North Carolina, where Anglicanism had always been a fragile reed, where members of that faith voted to forsake its privileges, which had always existed more in theory than in fact. Entails and primogeniture, legalized practices for holding together the estates of some decedents and thus working to concentrate wealth, were not removed until after the peace—in a series of measures, the effect of which may have been of limited significance since almost all owners of sizable properties appear to have left wills. Neither Tidewater nor Piedmont North Carolinians manifested a disposition to implement meaningfully the provision in the state constitution for public support of education. "No State," as the visitor Elkanah Watson saw it, had "performed so little to promote the cause of education, science, and the arts, as North Carolina."[17]

Had westerners wished to act in unison, to seize control of state affairs, they might have done so when they became numerically stronger than the east in the legislature. But that never happened. Consistent factional groupings were nonexistent, although a recent investigator has discovered that approximately a third of the recorded important votes during the war show a distinct sectional coloration, primarily relating to economic matters (monetary and taxation questions) and the state's relations with the Continental Congress.[18] An examination of roll calls, however, indicates not only that legislative bloc voting was the exception, but that if and when a section stood almost solidly together on an issue, it was more likely the easterners who balloted in likeminded fashion, the westerners who

17. Elkanah Watson, *Men and Times of the Revolution* (New York: Dana and Company, 1856), p. 290.

18. Sheldon F. Kosey, "Continuity and Change in North Carolina" (Ph.D. dissertation, Duke University, 1963), pp. 116, 217–18.

split among themselves, thus enabling eastern interests to maintain the upper hand.

Even so, these cleavages should not be exaggerated. Both the east and the west sent to the general assembly many men of wealth and influence. Samuel Johnston was doubtless accurate in 1777 when he sensed that the legislature contained new men inexperienced in statescraft. Richard Caswell, himself elected governor by the 1777 legislature, conceded privately to Joseph Hewes that most of the representatives, "a very few excepted, seem not [to] have been designed by nature for Legislators."[19] But they were scarcely the have nots of either section. East-west politics, in short, was never the story of the poor and the needy versus the rich and the greedy.

The electorate therefore continued in considerable measure to follow the colonial practice of electing their social and economic betters to office—to practice what has been called the politics of deference. For example, William Hooper, usually regarded as an archconservative easterner, a long-time assemblyman from Wilmington, moved to the west, to Hillsborough in Orange County in the early 1780s. He almost immediately presented himself to the freeholders as a candidate for the House of Commons. He was defeated, only to win in a second attempt a year later in 1784. It was reported that Hooper had unwittingly been done in by his own supporters in the election of 1783; they had offended the common people—"the mechanics"—by saying that a drink of toddy would buy their votes for the transplanted attorney. Hooper's later success suggests he had convinced the electorate that this was not the case. For that matter, western Governors Burke and Martin were men of wealth and refinement. Burke was both a physician and a lawyer. Martin was a graduate of the College of New Jersey, as was another backcountry dignitary, Waightstill Avery, the state's first attorney general; and the so-called radical leader Thomas Person was a man of refinement and large personal holdings.[20]

The deference of the general populace was matched by the deference displayed by the legislators themselves, as one can see from the

19. Caswell to Hewes, Apr. 21, 1778, *State Records*, XIII, 100.

20. In 1782 Person had ninety-eight slaves, and he eventually owned 67,437 acres. Blackwell P. Robinson, *William R. Davie* (Chapel Hill: Univ. of N.C. Press, 1957), p. 155; List of Taxables and Taxable Property for Granville County, 1782, North Carolina State Division of Archives and History.

composition of the influential committees and from the profiles of the speakers of the Senate and the House of Commons. Thirty-eight per-cent of the forty-nine above-mentioned legislative leaders had held elective or appointive office in the royal period, just as 80 percent of the same group belonged to the wealthiest 10 percent of the popula-tion; the remaining 20 percent of the legislative leaders, as far as can be determined, all appear to have fallen into a category of at least better-than-average means.[21]

Possessed of even more wealth, in most cases, were the Speakers of the House of Commons and the Senate, all of whom were planters and most of them lawyers as well. The speakers between 1777 and 1783 were Samuel Ashe of New Hanover, Thomas Benbury of Cho-wan, Richard Caswell of Dobbs, Whitmel Hill of Martin, Allen Jones of Northampton, Alexander Martin of Guilford, Abner Nash of Craven, Edward Starkey of Onslow, and John Williams of Gran-ville. All were easterners except Martin and Williams, both of whom were nominated by easterners and elected unanimously. As for the presiding legislators from the east, most of them were nominated by westerners—two by Thomas Person. And in most cases—the record is absent in a few sessions—the speakers were chosen unanimously.

Deference and lack of clear-cut divisions is further revealed in the selection of governors. Caswell, a veteran legislator, was named gov-ernor three consecutive terms (1777–80), with little opposition on any occasion. So too it was with the election of Abner Nash as chief executive (1780–81), by "a very large majority." Burke, the next governor (1781–82), was popular with conservative easterners such as Archibald Maclaine and Iredell as well as with westerners. The Hillsborough lawyer-physician, who had not sought the office, deemed it a surprise and an "unexpected honor." In 1782 and again in 1783 Alexander Martin was selected as the state's highest officer, although he was scarcely an overwhelming choice.[22]

In the latter year Caswell had made known his willingness to ac-cept the governorship again. He attributed his defeat at Martin's

21. Here I have followed the formula devised by Jackson T. Main, who defines the wealthiest 10 percent as those who owned property valued at £2,000 or more. He defines the better-than-average category as men whose holdings were worth be-tween £500 and £2,000. "Government by the People: The American Revolution and the Democratization of the Legislatures," *William and Mary Quarterly*, 3rd ser., (1966), 393.

22. *State Records*, XV, 227; XVI, 949.

hands to two factors, both generating support in the east for the westerner Martin. First, "the Edenton & Halifax Man with a very few exceptions Voted for Govr. Martin, saying I had cram'd him down their throats last year & they were now determined to keep him there." Second, Martin had adroitly made known his approval for locating permanently the state capital at Fayetteville, formerly called Cross Creek. This prospect won for Martin the ayes of many "Western Men" along with "some Cape Fear Men" since both groups favored that town in part at least because of its importance to both sections as an east-west trade center. Caswell, however, was hardly left out in the cold. He had been picked as Speaker of the Senate in 1782; and perhaps in 1783, after the vote for Martin (66 to 49), his ruffled feelings were soothed when a westerner, Colonel Robert Harris of Granville County, nominated him for a second consecutive term as Senate Speaker, a motion which carried unanimously.[23]

Much remains to be done in the study of the politics of revolutionary North Carolina. If this essay has presented evidence to weaken long-standing assumptions about issues and alliances, it does not purport to replace those older interpretations with a new, overarching one; rather, it seeks to demonstrate—on the basis of the Iredell papers and a limited amount of additional research—that subsequent investigators will have to acknowledge the complexity and diversity of political relationships and considerations.

Unfortunately, a recent provocative book, by Jackson Turner Main, accords only slight treatment to North Carolina (1783–87) in scrutinizing *Political Parties before the Constitution*. And yet it makes a significant point about political alignments that had already become apparent in my examination of the period 1781–83 in North Carolina. There were increasingly identifiable factions or groupings on matters relating to continental or national issues. In fact, Main argues persuasively that approximately two-thirds of the members of the seven state legislatures he studies in detail may be broadly categorized as either cosmopolitans or localists, with the remaining one-third being neutrals or lacking clear identification. Cosmopolitans generally were urban and/or commercial in their world view, often well educated, well traveled, with relationships that transcended state boundaries, possibly the result of revolutionary service in the

23. James Iredell to Hannah Iredell, Apr. 10, 1783, *Iredell Papers*, II, 388; Richard Caswell to William Caswell, May 4, 1783, *State Records*, 948–59.

Continental Congress, the Continental Army, or other broad connections with the war effort.

On the other hand, without any of the above-mentioned factors, men were likely to be localists: rural and agrarian in outlook, their ties insular and their wartime experiences confined to their own states if not their more immediate areas.[24]

Did legislators in the early 1780s recognize these distinctions and acknowledge them to be the basis for the appearance of slowly evolving political alignments? Here Main is inconclusive at best, for he admits that for almost all men "party" as we think of it was still a dirty word.

In North Carolina, at any rate, it is doubtful if the localists—to stay with Main's terminology—saw themselves as an issue-oriented coalition; they may have done so, albeit vaguely, on matters that were strictly speaking of an internal nature—most westerners could predictably be counted on to favor low taxes, payment of war debts in depreciated currency, and new emissions of paper currency. (Even here, however, qualifications are sometimes in order, as, for example, when the House of Commons voted—with both east and west approving the bill by narrow margins—to "repeal such Laws which make paper money a legal tender in the payment of private Debts and Contracts. . . .)[25]

The cosmopolitans, in contrast, were more cohesive in some respects. They were conscious of their similar interests, and they articulated them in their correspondence with one another, although they would have denied, quite correctly, that they were a party or a well-knit faction. Certainly they engaged in no systematic endeavor to create local organizations throughout the state or to work together to take over the legislature. But they did on occasion encourage men of their own thinking to seek elective office, as in the case of Archibald Maclaine's urging Iredell to stand for a seat in the House of Commons in 1783.[26]

24. Jackson Turner Main, *Political Parties before the Constitution* (Chapel Hill: Univ. of N.C. Press, 1973), pp. 311–17, for North Carolina. In another work the same author finds relatively little difference between the two houses of the North Carolina General Assembly. *The Upper House in Revolutionary America, 1763–1788* (Madison: Univ. of Wisc. Press, 1967), 154–61.

25. *State Records*, XVI, 165.

26. Archibald Maclaine to George Hooper, May 29, 1783, *State Records*, XVI, 963. Norman J. Risjord sees in Virginia the formation of a similar "issue-oriented coalition," led by James Madison, which backed, among other things, ratification of

The nucleus of the cosmopolitan group consisted of a cluster of men who long had been critical of much that the legislature did, particularly what they deemed its irresponsibility in fiscal affairs. At the top of the list stood Samuel Johnston, William Hooper, Maclaine, and Iredell. They were joined in sentiment by James Hogg, a Hillsborough merchant, by William R. Davie, a Continental Army hero and a Halifax lawyer, and by several men who had served the state in the Continental Congress, where, as Hamilton viewed it, individuals learned to think "continentally," or as Jefferson described it, they saw affairs "from a high ground." They included Burke and Nash, both of whom had also been governors; Hugh Williamson, versatile physician, clergyman, historian, and merchant of Edenton; Benjamin Hawkins, a former military aide to Washington and Warren County planter; William Blount, one of three mercantile-land speculator brothers, all in the cosmopolitan camp, and a revolutionary officer of Craven County; and Richard Dobbs Spaight, Glasgow-educated, also of Craven County.

The cosmopolitans—"nationalists" may be a better term for them in the 1780s—sought most of all, in the language of the twenty-seven-year-old Davie, "to give strength and permanency to the *common union*." But, he added, that would "be a difficult task with our young republicks whose views are all local and limited, and whose councils cannot yet be illuminated with the truest principles of policy."[27] Localism was assuredly a powerful force as the cosmopolitans found when they sought to get their state to honor fully the terms of the 1783 Treaty of Paris, negotiated by diplomats appointed by Congress, which now had legal status as a result of the final ratification in 1781 of the Articles of Confederation.

The biggest stumbling block to compliance was the already-noted loyalist issue, which saw a strong degree of unity among the cosmopolitans, less agreement among the localists, some of whom at times sought special treatment for their friends or relatives or were concerned about women and children and other dependents of the king's friends. (Not only Willie Jones and Thomas Person, but also Timo-

---

a commerce amendment and compliance with the Treaty of Paris. "The Evolution of Political Parties in Virginia, 1782–1800," *Journal of American History* (1974), 966–67.

27. Davie to Nathanael Greene, Dec. 8, 1783, William R. Davie Papers, No. 2, Southern Historical Collection.

thy Bloodworth, an eastern localist and an outspoken foe of Iredell's group, were in agreement with the cosmopolitans on the Tory question.)

Three articles of the peace settlement were of particular concern. According to Article IV creditors on both sides of the Atlantic were to meet with no lawful impediment to the recovery of their prewar debts in sterling money. Article V stipulated that Congress would "earnestly recommend" to the states the restoration of property confiscated from "real British subjects" and permit people "of any other description" twelve months' residence to settle their business affairs. Article VI declared that there should be no additional confiscations, that there should be no more legal prosecutions, and that those loyalists currently incarcerated should be set free without punitive encumbrances.

In 1783, as well as in subsequent years, the localists in the legislature beat back efforts to repeal all state laws contrary to the Paris agreement. The state further humiliated Congress in 1783 by reversing itself on the Impost of 1781: it rescinded its previous vote for an amendment to the Articles of Confederation that would grant Congress a permanent revenue—the right to levy a 5 percent ad valorem duty on foreign imports. Even previously, under the wartime system of congressional requisitions, the state had not upheld its obligations, lamented Congressmen Hugh Williamson and Benjamin Hawkins. "The pride of every Citizen must be hurt" to find "that North Carolina is one of the few States that has not contributed a farthing." Finally, the delegates to the federal legislature were "not a little embarrassed" by the state's tardiness in ceding her western lands to the Confederation. Since Congress had already accepted the cessions of New York and Virginia, North Carolina would "receive advantages equally with the other states" in those frontier areas and therefore should relinquish its own "extensive Western territory" for the common good of all. If Willie Jones and Timothy Bloodworth lent the cosmopolitans their aid on the cession idea, Samuel Johnston went a step beyond in advocating the enlightened notion that new states should be carved out of the west and given full equality with the original thirteen.[28]

28. *State Records*, XVI, 885, 889; Johnston to ———, July 11, 1784, Hayes Papers, Southern Historical Collection.

The best expression of the North Carolina cosmopolitans' outlook in 1783 is found in several resolutions, composed by James Iredell and adopted by a town meeting in Edenton. Samuel Johnston presided as the Edenton citizens confronted "certain important points" under discussion "throughout the United States," which they then requested their delegation in the assembly to implement as far as possible. North Carolina should "sacredly" fulfill the terms of the peace treaty, "a most solemn engagement of our Government." The former Tories should be dealt with "by motives of Policy, not of Revenge," which was "unbecoming a generous People." The Edentonians regretted the failure of the Impost, "a most wise and judicious measure" of Congress, whose existence was necessary to preserve the American union. Whereas some people spoke with "indecent licence" of Congress, the Edenton citizens felt "a veneration and attachment" for "that august Body." America's destiny rested upon enhancing the authority of the central agency of the Confederation: "The power necessary for its support let us therefore cheerfully give."

Economic considerations were of paramount importance to the cosmopolitans, who feared that North Carolina, a state with a modest quantity of external trade compared to her neighbors, would be bled to death by state-imposed tariffs since many goods would cross its borders, especially from Virginia and South Carolina. This partly explains the cosmopolitans' eagerness for Congress to control external commerce, revenues from which—they explained—should go to paying the public creditors and the army. The townspeople reluctantly went along with still another recent emission of fiat money, which the inhabitants pledged to back only so long as it went toward paying the state's own war debts; as soon as possible thereafter "the present emission" should "be redeemed and burnt."[29]

The North Carolina cosmopolitans of 1783 were not yet ready to scrap the Articles of Confederation. But it seemed to Iredell and his political friends that both the success of the Confederation in dealing with national problems and the willingness of the state to cope with local problems rested, in the last analysis, on the state legislatures. Would they act responsibly by honoring the authority of Congress under the articles, and would they give the Confederacy

29. "Resolutions of the Citizens of Edenton," Aug. 1, 1873, "Instructions to Chowan Representatives," Sept. ———, 1783, *Iredell Papers*, 430–32, 446–51.

new authority in necessary areas such as commerce? Then, too, would they accord equal treatment to all of their own citizens?

Iredell was skeptical. The legislature of North Carolina, as well as the lawmaking bodies in other states, were acting contrary to their own constitutions by passing discriminatory laws that violated contracts and in further ways attacked the rights of property owners. Too much authority rested in the hands of the legislatures, too little in the hands of the governors and the courts. Even so, the people, not legislative organs, were sovereign, an idea Iredell had developed a decade or so earlier in regard to the British Parliament.[30] Legislative supremacy in the state of North Carolina was as illegal as parliamentary supremacy had been earlier in the colony of North Carolina. The legislature, maintained Samuel Johnston, could not act contrary to fundamental law, by which he meant the constitution of the state. But who or what would constrain the legislature, especially when the weight of political authority was so heavily in its favor? Johnston had lamented to Iredell back in 1776 that in all probability "there can be no check on the Representatives of the People in a Democracy but the people themselves, and in order that the check may be the more effectual I would have Annual elections."[31]

Iredell in 1783 proposed another alternative. He believed that "in a Republic . . . the Law is superior to any or all Individuals, and the Constitution superior even to the Legislature, and of which the Judges are the guardians and protectors."[32] Here was one of the first enunciations of the doctrine of judicial review in the revolutionary era, one he was to state more explicitly in 1787 in the case of Bayard v. Singleton, when he helped persuade a North Carolina superior court to strike down an act of the General Assembly.

Once again, as in 1776–77, politics was heating up. Now, as in the earlier years, new issues had come to the fore. But whereas the visceral issues initially were local or state oriented, the matters of great moment to emerge as the war drew to a close were both state and national in nature. They were, furthermore, intertwined, a point clearly recognized by the cosmopolitans; for only by curtailing specific

30. Don Higginbotham, "James Iredell's Efforts to Preserve the First British Empire," *North Carolina Historical Review*, XLIX (1972), 127–45.
31. Johnston to Iredell, Apr. 20, 1776, *Iredell Papers*, I, 350.
32. "Instructions to Chowan County Representatives," Sept. 1783, ibid., II, 449.

powers of the states could the jurisdiction of Congress be increased. These questions provided a continuing forum in which North Carolina politics was to operate in the 1780s. The full story, like that of the politics of the war years, remains to be written. Coupled with the publication of *The Papers of James Iredell*, this essay may at least suggest what the general contours of that story may be.

Part II. The Role of the Individual

American Military Leadership in the Southern Campaign: Benjamin Lincoln

John C. Cavanagh *Suffolk University*

None of the American generals who commanded the Southern Department during the Revolutionary War was so universally admired, yet so unsuccessful in the field, as Benjamin Lincoln of Massachusetts. The amiable, corpulent major general had fought with distinction in the North early in the contest; he was ultimately to play a significant role at Yorktown. Between the successes, however, his record in the southern theater of operations was beset with failure. Nevertheless, not even failure seemed to dim his reputation as a general, for Lincoln was a man of extraordinary resilience.

During the autumn of 1778 the Continental Congress selected Major General Benjamin Lincoln to take command of American military efforts in the South. George Washington had recommended Lincoln for the southern position because the New Englander had used his militia so effectively against Gage at Boston, and against Burgoyne in the Champlain valley. A friendship had developed between Lincoln and Washington during the siege of Boston, when Lincoln participated in the councils of war periodically summoned by his commander in chief. That friendship was to have a decisive effect upon Lincoln's professional fortunes.

The southern command which Lincoln assumed required a man of fortitude and a conciliatory disposition; the civil authorities in the South had been uncooperative with previous Continental commanders. To meet the threat of an anticipated British invasion, the new general would be challenged to assemble an effective fighting force of Continentals, and large numbers of unreliable southern militia. At their best the irregulars made effective light infantry, especially when used alongside regular troops in the field. But the militia were essentially part-time soldiers, and accountable to state, not Continental, authority. The moment their brief terms of service expired, no matter how critical the progress of the war, the militiamen usually shouldered their weapons and went home.[1] Any Continental officer who could manage such troops would prove valuable indeed to the patriots.

As soon as Benjamin Lincoln was appointed to command the South in September 1778, he received disquieting reports that the British might soon launch an attack upon that region. For three years before 1778, the South had been relatively untouched by the Revolutionary War. The British concentrated their efforts in the New England and Middle Atlantic states because these contained the most vital centers of American political and economic activity. Only once before, in 1776, had the British launched a seaborne expedition against the southern provinces; Sir Henry Clinton failed to capture Charleston, however, through tactical blunders and delays. The defeat had been so humiliating that for several years the crown made no further attempts to recover the South. In the summer of 1778, however, Clinton began to make new preparations for a southern campaign. If he could subdue Georgia, it would greatly facilitate an overland invasion into South Carolina and the upper South.

In early October 1778, just before Lincoln left the Hudson highlands for South Carolina, General Washington informed him that "Congress have determined on measures for securing Charles Town, in case the enemy should form an expedition against it."[2] Thus the idea of a vigorous defense of Charleston first came to Lincoln's attention; over a year later, when the idea led to the unfortunate surrender of the city, Lincoln was to seek solace in having obeyed the intentions of Congress.

During his journey southward Lincoln stopped in Philadelphia for discussions with Congressional leaders. Together they explored the vast problem of recruiting sufficient troops for use in the South. Also, Congress urged Lincoln to attempt an invasion of British East Florida, should the enemy delay its rumored expedition. The danger posed

---

1. Robert C. Pugh, "The Revolutionary Militia in the Southern Campaign, 1780–81," *The William and Mary Quarterly*, XIV, No. 2 (Apr. 1957), 168.

2. George Washington to Benjamin Lincoln, Oct. 3, 1778, Benjamin Lincoln MSS., Houghton Library. Hereafter cited as Houghton Library Lincoln MSS.

by General Augustine Prevost and his enemy garrison at St. Augustine might thereby be eliminated before they could seriously threaten the southern states.

The discussions at Philadelphia disturbed Lincoln. For over a year he had been relatively inactive, convalescing from a severe leg wound he received at Saratoga; he found the prospect of formidable new responsibilities somewhat unnerving. He confided in a letter to General Washington that "I wish the Congress had fixed their minds on some other officer for the Southern department, as well from a consciousness that many others would render . . . more important services to the public, as from an apprehension that I may suffer in the journey from my wound which is not yet healed. . . ." Lincoln added that he had not objected to his congressional appointment "because to make excuses is painful."[3]

After resuming his journey, Lincoln held scheduled conferences with the governors of Virginia and North Carolina; he needed to consult with Patrick Henry and Richard Caswell about obtaining reinforcements from their respective states. In this business Lincoln could claim the backing of Congress. That body had already decided on the wisdom of strengthening Charleston; it had also urged the governors "to afford every necessary assistance to Major Gen. Lincoln for enabling him to subdue the province of East Florida," were any such offensive to be launched.[4] During his Williamsburg interview with Governor Henry, Lincoln welcomed the prospect of obtaining a thousand Virginia reinforcements, as soon as they could be paid their long overdue wages. Later in Kinston, North Carolina, Governor Caswell assured Lincoln that in several days he could expect eleven hundred Continentals and state militia to start out for Charleston. But the troops were slow to materialize; Lincoln soon learned that he could not rely on even the best-intentioned promises of reinforcements.

Soon after reaching Charleston on December 4, the new commander discovered that the British were moving against Georgia by both land and sea. Governor William Houstoun of that state reported that Prevost and about three thousand redcoats were gradually

3. Benjamin Lincoln to George Washington, Oct. 24, 1778, George Washington Papers, Manuscripts Division, Library of Congress.
4. Henry Laurens to Richard Caswell, Nov. 14, 1778, Richard Caswell Papers, Southern Historical Collection., Univ. of N.C. Library.

advancing up the coast from East Florida. An enemy deserter also revealed that a British fleet carrying several thousand troops was "expected every moment" at the mouth of the Savannah River.[5] The unwelcome news convinced Lincoln that, for the time being at least, his plans of taking the offensive against East Florida would have to be shelved; it was far more important that he concentrate immediately on the problem of southern defense.

Lincoln faced the extremely difficult task of assembling a large Continental army, of enlisting the effective cooperation of southern militia forces, and of ensuring that all these men were adequately provisioned. To make matters worse, Congress had been able to furnish Lincoln with little more than his personal expenses. He would be obliged to appeal for financial assistance from the four state governors in his department. However, he first discovered from the returns of his Continentals in South Carolina and Georgia that very few men were fit for duty. Lincoln wondered why the promised troops from Virginia and North Carolina were slow to arrive. Sobering reports had reached him that very few stores were to be had in the lower South; of the six Continental fieldpieces at Charleston, for instance, none was usable.

Lincoln knew it would be difficult to find solutions for his problems. His predecessor, Major General Robert Howe, had become involved in considerable altercations between the civil and military authorities in South Carolina. Lincoln, however, wanted no part of the jealousies and intrigues he observed at Charleston. The stolid New Englander assured General Washington of a strong desire "never [to] be drawn to the hard necessity of altercating with the civil power."[6] Lincoln was confronted with that hard necessity on December 20, however. He asked President Lowndes of South Carolina to furnish supplies and arms to General Rutherford and eight hundred North Carolina militiamen, who were approaching Charleston. When the president emphatically refused to offer stores to anyone but South Carolinians, Lincoln used diplomacy to soften Lowndes' position. He presented the executive with an elaborate plan

5. Benjamin Lincoln to John Ashe, Dec. 8, 1778, Benjamin Lincoln Letter Book, Massachusetts Historical Society. Hereafter cited as M.H.S. Lincoln Letter Book.

6. Benjamin Lincoln to George Washington, Dec. 19, 1778, M.H.S. Lincoln Letter Book.

for the defense of Charleston. The president was reassured. He responded immediately with promises of increased cooperation, and assurances that Lincoln's "Advice and Council will ever have a due Weight and Influence with [me]."[7] The promises were kept; the North Carolina militia were issued supplies when they subsequently reached Charleston. It was apparent the president had learned to appreciate Lincoln for his industry, pluck, and patient good humor. The New Englander had shown he could deal persuasively with individuals. Many problems, nevertheless, still ranged beyond his particular talents.

During the final week in December Benjamin Lincoln faced the tough challenge of an enemy attack from the sea. The long-expected British fleet had appeared near Savannah, bringing 3,500 seaborne invaders from New York under Lieutenant Colonel Archibald Campbell. Lincoln also had General Prevost to contend with; the advancing expedition from East Florida might soon combine forces with Campbell. The nearest rebel army which could offer resistance was an 850-man detachment under General Robert Howe, thirty miles south of Savannah. Lincoln knew it was undoubtedly his duty to march to the assistance of Georgia.[8]

On December 27 General Lincoln left Charleston with 1,250 men. President Lowndes had permitted him to take only two regiments of Charleston militia, so Lincoln depended primarily upon the newly arrived North Carolina Continentals. Lincoln was fairly realistic about his military objectives. If he could not save Savannah, nor dislodge the British from their main centers of concentration, he hoped at least to prevent them from extending their influence into the interior of the lower South. When Lincoln was within thirty miles of Savannah, he learned that Campbell had taken possession of the city on December 29 after a fruitless though brave defense by Howe and a thousand troops. It was a serious blow to the Americans, but Lincoln accepted the result as virtually inevitable; he wrote dejectedly to the governor of North Carolina that "all [the troops] I can collect amounts to [only] . . . a small force to act against an Enemy so much superior."[9]

7. Rawlins Lowndes to Benjamin Lincoln, Dec. 24, 1778, Benjamin Lincoln Papers, Massachusetts Historical Society. Hereafter cited as M.H.S. Lincoln Papers.
8. Benjamin Lincoln to Rawlins Lowndes, Dec. 26, 1778, M.H.S. Lincoln Letter Book.
9. *The State Records of North Carolina, Published under the Supervision of*

Lincoln had faith he could eventually frustrate the British designs upon the South. He decided to station his force as close to the enemy as he could with safety. In early January 1779 he made camp on the Savannah River at Purysburg, fifteen miles above the recently captured city. Although reinforced by the remnants of Howe's army, Lincoln's total force had been so depleted by militia desertions that it amounted to only fourteen hundred men. Most of these were militiamen who were inadequately disciplined for combat. Lincoln had attempted, without success, to extend regular army discipline over the irregulars; if they served under his overall general direction, he reasoned, they would be "of no service without being subject to the [Continental] articles of war." Each state so jealously guarded its own prerogatives, however, that Lincoln's proposal got nowhere.[10]

Lincoln jousted with the British through the winter and spring of 1779, primarily along the Savannah River, which separated the opposing forces. By mid-January General Prevost had distracted Lincoln at Purysburg by stationing a thousand troops on the shore opposite the American camp. Meanwhile, Campbell and fifteen hundred others marched on Augusta, which they captured with virtually no opposition on January 29. The victorious Scotsman had discovered, to Lincoln's particular chagrin, that the Georgia Loyalists were flocking "by hundreds to the King's officers," and were making "their peace at the expense of their patriotism."[11] Prevost hoped that his troops would receive the same kind of reception in South Carolina. He ordered two hundred men to march on Beaufort, situated about thirty miles in Lincoln's rear, halfway to Charleston.

By the end of January Lincoln had been sufficiently reinforced by General John Ashe and some North Carolina Continentals, plus a few South Carolina militia brigades, to bring his troop strength above thirty-six hundred. When Lincoln heard about the British incursion to the east he detached three hundred South Carolina militiamen under General William Moultrie to challenge the enemy. Lincoln might have sent a larger force, but he felt "little was to be ap-

the Trustees of the Public Libraries, ed. Walter Clark (Vols. XI–XXVI; Winston, N.C., 1895–1906), XIII, 342.

10. William Moultrie, *Memoirs of the American Revolution So Far As It Is Related to the States of North and South Carolina, and Georgia* (2 vols.; New York, 1802), I, 286–87.

11. Henry B. Dawson, *Battles of the United States* (2 vols.; New York, 1858), I, 476.

prehended" from the enemy's turning action.[12] He was proved correct; after a brief but hotly contested engagement at Beaufort on February 3, the small British expedition was forced to flee to Savannah by sea. Lincoln was particularly happy that Moultrie had handled the militia so effectively against enemy regulars.

Meanwhile Lincoln had been concentrating on the "necessity & importance" of keeping the patriots in control of the southern interior. The enemy penetration to Augusta had distressed him, for Lincoln obtained most of his supplies from the upcountry. He also needed to prevent the loyalists there from further aiding the British. Lincoln decided he could best achieve his objectives by an "endeavor to regain as much of Georgia as possible."[13] His resolution to take the offensive was considerably strengthened when hundreds of militiamen gathered at his Purysburg camp in early February; the victory at Beaufort had filled them with new hope for the patriot cause in the South.

By the second week of February, Lincoln had stationed sixteen hundred men on the northern shore of the Savannah River opposite Augusta. General John Ashe commanded the expedition, which only slightly exceeded Campbell's force in Augusta. Ashe was under no orders to attack the British; Lincoln had urged caution because the Americans would soon lose four hundred militia from expiring enlistments. On February 13 Campbell unexpectedly evacuated Augusta and retreated toward Savannah. By the time Lincoln could order Ashe in pursuit, the British were well in advance. On March 3, at a place where Briar Creek empties into the Savannah River, the redcoats turned and struck the Americans a severe blow. More than 150 of the rebels were killed, 173 captured, and of the 800 who escaped nearly half deserted; Lincoln had lost one-third of his southern forces. For the time being at least, he abandoned all hope of recovering Georgia.[14]

On March 9 Lincoln assembled a court-martial to investigate Ashe for his conduct at Briar Creek. The examiners concluded that Ashe had been neglectful about guarding against surprise, but that he certainly showed no lack of personal courage. Lincoln observed that Ashe possessed "the character of a good man" and had been pri-

12. Benjamin Lincoln to Rawlins Lowndes, Feb. 4, 1779, M.H.S. Lincoln Letter Book.

13. Benjamin Lincoln to John Jay, Feb. 6, 1779, M.H.S. Lincoln Letter Book.

14. Moultrie, *Memoirs*, I, 322–26; Christopher Ward, *The War of the Revolution*, ed. John Richard Alden (2 vols.; New York, 1952), II, 684.

marily an unwitting victim of circumstances.[15] Later in the war Lincoln was to employ a similar rationale in explaining some of his own difficulties in the field. In justice to Ashe, probably few patriot generals could have done better in the face of such an able and daring enemy attack. Nevertheless the experience so humiliated Ashe that he retired to private life in North Carolina. General Lincoln shared in the embarrassment and frustration; by mid-March he had informed President Jay of Congress that he would be willing to resign his southern command.[16] Meanwhile, however, Lincoln turned his attention to the pressing matters at hand.

Since arriving at Purysburg, Lincoln had been wrestling with problems which seemed to defy solution. He had raised only a fraction of the seven thousand Continentals he thought were needed in his department. The South Carolina militia presented him with his greatest challenge. The state assembly in Charleston finally directed its militia "to act in conjunction with the regular forces," but some of the militia commanders did not cooperate with Lincoln. General Andrew Williamson, for instance, consulted so infrequently with Lincoln that the commander could not rely on his subordinate. It was because of these problems that Lincoln turned for help to the recently installed chief executive of South Carolina, Governor John Rutledge. The Charleston aristocrat assured Lincoln of his complete cooperation, and then began fulfilling his promise. Two emissaries were dispatched from Charleston to plead with the governors of North Carolina and Virginia and with the Congress to supply the lower South with more troops. Rutledge meanwhile set a good example; he transferred sixteen hundred South Carolina militia from the coast to reinforce Generals Lincoln and Williamson in the interior. Furthermore, the state militiamen, including the recalcitrant Andrew Williamson, were ordered to cooperate more fully with Lincoln.[17]

As a result of the Briar Creek disaster in early March, however, Governor Rutledge began to doubt that Lincoln could successfully defend South Carolina from the British. While having taken some steps to assist Lincoln, the chief executive also embarked on his

15. Benjamin Lincoln to John Rutledge, Mar. 4, 1779, M.H.S. Lincoln Letter Book.
16. John Jay to Benjamin Lincoln, Apr. 15, 1779, M.H.S. Lincoln Papers.
17. John Rutledge to Benjamin Lincoln, Feb. 15, 1779, Division of Manuscripts, Henry E. Huntington Library.

own course of action to strengthen his state. He began distributing most of the new militia recruits among his Charleston, Augusta, and Orangeburg garrisons. By early April Rutledge personally commanded three thousand militia at Orangeburg in the center of the state. Lincoln meanwhile transferred most of his men up the river to Black Swamp; he hoped that, by establishing an additional post on the Savannah River, he would more effectively deter the British from crossing into South Carolina.

General Prevost learned in mid-April that the rebel forces were distributed across South Carolina; with five thousand men at his disposal, he felt confident that his army could overrun the state. His decision to attack was precipitated by some fresh activity from Lincoln's quarter. In a council of war held at Black Swamp on April 19, Lincoln and his officers decided he should lead an expedition across the Savannah River to Augusta, and establish a strong post in Georgia. Lincoln also arranged for a thousand of his men to remain behind at Purysburg and Black Swamp under General Moultrie; the coastal region of South Carolina might thereby be secured from attack. Considering the vast superiority of British forces near the coast, however, Lincoln's plan for Moultrie was unrealistic.

Any advantage Lincoln may have gained from the Augusta expedition hardly justified the risks. Although he promised to reinforce Moultrie if the need arose, Lincoln practically invited a British counterattack. "If the enemy should discover any inclination to attempt you in force & to move on towards Charles-Town," Lincoln told his subordinate, "you will please as soon as possible to . . . delay [the enemy] as much as it is in your power and give time for us to come up."[18] Lincoln was jeopardizing the city he had been particularly charged to defend. It was the sort of plan General Washington would not have risked. Only weeks before in New Jersey, the commander-in-chief had confided to Lafayette that "General Lincoln is assembling a force to dispossess . . . [the British], and my only fear is, that he will precipitate the attempt before he is fully prepared for the execution."[19] Regrettably, Washington shared no hint of these apprehensions with Lincoln; instead, Washington wrote his southern com-

18. Benjamin Lincoln to William Moultrie, Apr. 22, 1779, M.H.S. Lincoln Letter Book.

19. *The Writings of George Washington from the Original Manuscript Sources, 1745–1799*, ed. John C. Fitzpatrick (39 vols.; Washington, D.C., 1931–44), XIV, 219; hereafter cited as *The Writings of George Washington*.

mander that, being "so utter a Stranger to the Country in which you are . . . I cannot pretend to offer my opinion upon the measures that ought or ought not be pursued." Washington added that he was "confident, that your Abilities and activity will accomplish whatever can be done."[20]

Lincoln found his abilities put to the severest possible test in late April. General Prevost, in an attempt to counter Lincoln's move toward the Georgia frontier, crossed the river at Purysburg on April 29 with twenty-five hundred men. Lincoln remained calm when he first learned the news, for he assumed the enemy only intended "to distract and divert us from our present intentions."[21] But when he learned that Moultrie had been unable to halt the invaders and was retreating toward Charleston, Lincoln awakened to the danger. Prevost had entered the state without specific plans to attack the city; when he encountered almost no rebel opposition, he decided to advance up the coast behind Moultrie. On April 30 Governor Rutledge rushed east from Orangeburg to strengthen the defenses of his capital. Two days later Lincoln ordered his forces to join the race for Charleston.

While General Lincoln advanced across the state, Governor Rutledge and General Moultrie entered Charleston with their troops on May 4 and 9, respectively. Since Lincoln's army was expected momentarily to reinforce them, the leaders within the garrison had reason to hope for a successful defense. Prevost even delayed his advance for about three days while his forces looted the coastal plantations. By the time the British stood before Charleston on May 11 and demanded its immediate surrender, the mood in the city was changing. The leading merchants and planters despaired for the safety of themselves and their property. General Lincoln had not yet arrived, and no one knew certainly when to expect him. Influential citizens therefore exerted pressure upon Governor Rutledge and his council to pledge the neutrality of South Carolina for the duration of the war if the British would spare the city. Prevost rejected the compromise offer; he had learned from his scouts that a large force under Lincoln was approaching the British rear. Prevost had little alterna-

20. George Washington to Benjamin Lincoln, Mar. 15, 1779, Houghton Library Lincoln MSS.
21. Benjamin Lincoln to Andrew Williamson, May 1, 1779, M.H.S. Lincoln Letter Book.

tive but to withdraw his outflanked and outnumbered troops to the coastal islands, preparatory to an evacuation by sea. Lincoln finally reached the Charleston peninsula on May 14. It may have taken him two long weeks to cross the state, but he at least had removed the present threat to the city. The question remains whether Lincoln, by arriving earlier, might have trapped the British in a tightening American vise.[22]

Lincoln encamped with his army at Ashley Ferry, about nine miles northwest of Charleston; while affording protection to his allies in the city, he was also within easy striking distance of the enemy troops to his south. But Lincoln appeared in no hurry to attack the British while they still remained on the coast. He hesitated primarily for lack of reinforcements from Charleston. Governor Rutledge and his council refused to detach any of the three thousand troops within the city, for fear of making it vulnerable to another enemy attack. The only thing the governor did send Lincoln was a message of encouragement, containing the somewhat gratuitous wish "that the Inhabitants of this State . . . will, at your hands, have full and ample revenge" on the British. Rutledge probably hoped to soften the unfavorable impression Lincoln had received from the Charlestonians' negotiations with Prevost.[23]

By early June Lincoln was experiencing a personal crisis which had been several months in the making; both his health and his morale were on the decline. He had during March, and again in April, let it be known in Congress that he feared his leg wound would "prove fatal" if he remained in the South during the hot summer season; without asking directly to be recalled from his southern command, Lincoln had hinted that any such order from Congress "would be agreeable" to him.[24] His leg was apparently not much worse than it had been the previous year, but he was particularly discouraged about affairs in his department. He wrote to General Washington on June 5 that "our situation . . . *I do assure you*, wear[s] a very serious aspect here." Lincoln complained that the few available militia were much inferior to the enemy troops, and unless his southern army were quickly reinforced, South Carolina would be in "great danger" of

22. Edward McCrady, *The History of South Carolina in the Revolution, 1775–1780* (New York, 1902), pp. 376–77.
23. John Rutledge to Benjamin Lincoln, May 19, 1779, M.H.S. Lincoln Papers.
24. Everard Meade to Benjamin Lincoln, May 6, 1779, M.H.S. Lincoln Papers.

being overrun.[25] The Briar Creek rout, the abortive Augusta expedition, the subsequent loss of Georgia, and the British attempt on Charleston—all had taken a heavy toll on Lincoln. To General Moultrie, Lincoln expressed his discouragement over the "unkind declarations" about him in the Charleston press, and for having resultingly "Lost that confidence of the people . . . without which I can render little service to the public."[26] His detractors charged that his recent activities had opened the South Carolina low country to the enemy and needlessly endangered Charleston. Moultrie may have surmised from Lincoln's message that the commander himself did not wholly discount the charges. On June 9, in this frame of mind, Lincoln received some welcome news from Philadelphia. Six weeks before Congress had voted that Lincoln could resign his command in the Southern Department; Moultrie was to be designated his successor.

Upon learning that Lincoln intended to step down, General Moultrie, Governor Rutledge, and the South Carolina Council implored the New Englander to reconsider the matter. Their action may have surprised Lincoln, but it also assuaged his wounded pride; he agreed to remain in the South, his health permitting. Perhaps he was reassured when Moultrie defended him as "a brave, active, and very vigilant officer." Rutledge told Lincoln that his "Character, and knowledge and Experience in the Art of War are such . . . that your remaining here will ensure great good to this, and the Neighboring State." As if to emphasize that he was not conveying the usual platitudes, Rutledge pledged his increased support to Lincoln, so that together they would be "soon enabled, to compleat . . . the restoration of . . . Tranquility to Georgia, & this Country."[27]

It is interesting to attempt to fathom why the southerners acted as they did. From the moment he had arrived in the department, the squat, rotund Yankee farmer had been something of a curiosity to his genteel southern hosts. He was afflicted with a painful wound and a conspicuous limp, as well as a "Pickwickian syndrome" which caused him to lapse into brief sleeps, sometimes in public. His unclear diction, rich with New England colloquialisms, fell strangely on Caro-

25. Benjamin Lincoln to George Washington, June 5, 1779, M.H.S. Lincoln Papers.
26. Benjamin Lincoln to William Moultrie, June 10, 1779, M.H.S. Lincoln Letter Book.
27. Moultrie, *Memoirs*, I, 476; John Rutledge to Benjamin Lincoln, June 13, 1779, M.H.S. Lincoln Papers.

lina ears. When in his usual good humor, few men were any kinder or more engaging than Lincoln. However, his personal feelings for friends and associates blinded him occasionally to their shortcomings. As an officer he was vigilant, but also overcautious; he made few important decisions without prior deliberation with his officers in council. He may not have excelled as a strategist, but the southern patriots were in far greater need of his organizational skills, especially for the raising of militia. He had already earned the highest respect as a scrupulously honest and tireless administrator. In a worsening southern war, Lincoln had encountered his inevitable share of difficulties, and perhaps a few more. Yet he persevered in working as conscientiously for the revolutionary cause as any leader in the South. Rutledge, Moultrie, and the others obviously concluded that in June 1779 there were plenty of good reasons to continue the services of Benjamin Lincoln.

On June 15 Lincoln went to Charleston to confer with the civil and military authorities there. He sought help in arranging a plan of attack against the British force at Stono Ferry. Lincoln hoped to deliver a crippling blow while his enemy still lingered on the coast. General Prevost had established a strong post at the ferry in late May, on the mainland side of Stono Inlet opposite Johns Island. Lieutenant Colonel John Maitland and nine hundred British regulars had been stationed at the new camp, which secured Prevost's main avenue of retreat. About six hundred additional men—a mixed force of British, Hessians, and Loyalists—remained on Johns Island, directly across from the British post. The enemy fort made an inviting target; it lay separated by water from the nearest reinforcements. Lincoln secured twelve hundred militiamen from Charleston before deciding to spring the attack. In early June he transferred his base camp to 13-Mile House, about six miles north of Stono Ferry. He next stationed eight hundred South Carolina militia on James Island under General Moultrie, for use in diverting the adjacent enemy forces on Johns Island. It was imperative that Moultrie prevent the British from transporting reinforcements across Stono Inlet to the fort. Lincoln then led his own fourteen hundred troops southward from 13-Mile House during the early morning hours of June 20.[28]

28. Francis Bowen, "Life of Benjamin Lincoln, Major-General in the Army of the Revolution," *The Library of American Biography*, 2nd Series, ed. Jared Sparks (15 vols.; Boston, 1847), XIII, 287–88.

General Lincoln arrived before Stono Ferry shortly after daybreak and positioned his forces in the pine woods opposite the enemy fort. Once the battle erupted into furious hand-to-hand combat, the Americans began driving the enemy back against the fort. Just as victory seemed almost within Lincoln's grasp, the North and South Carolina militia suddenly retreated before a combined force of Hessians and Highlanders. Moreover, Moultrie failed in his mission to divert the British. As soon as Lincoln discovered that Maitland was being strongly reinforced from Johns Island, he withdrew his men into the pine woods. Among his casualties were 179 killed and wounded, most of them Continentals; in addition, 155 militia were lost through desertion.

Soon after Lincoln and his army had returned north to their base camp, Prevost began withdrawing his troops from the coast. In a dispatch to Governor Rutledge on June 21, Lincoln admitted that "though we had not the wished-for success, yet, I think, good will arise from the attempt." He explained that "our men now see that little is to be feared either from musquetry of field pieces; they are full of Spirits, & are sure they can beat the enemy on equal grounds at any time."[29] If patriot morale had been heightened, it was transitory; with the coming of the hot season neither the Americans nor the British had any interest in resuming campaigning until autumn. In fact, Lincoln's entire attitude following the Stono Ferry engagement became one of increased caution. As the British forces withdrew, Lincoln issued only the most perfunctory orders for harassing them.[30] General Prevost returned to Savannah in late June with half of his force, leaving Lieutenant Colonel Maitland with the remainder on Port Royal Island, to keep a foothold in South Carolina. Lincoln re-established his headquarters in Charleston, and stationed his dwindling forces at strategic places in the lower South.

During much of the summer the Charleston heat and humidity confined Lincoln to bed, where he attended to military affairs without notable success. Although he obtained a few supplies from the French West Indies, the shortages persisted. To help attract new recruits, Lincoln put pressure on the Georgia Council to raise the pay levels of the militia serving that state. The salaries offered to the

29. Benjamin Lincoln to John Rutledge, June 21, 1779, M.H.S. Lincoln Letter Book.
30. Moultrie, *Memoirs*, I, 499–506, passim.

South Carolina militia were, at his insistence, made comparable to rates paid the regulars. Still the recruits did not come, nor could Lincoln obtain enough funds to satisfy the men already under arms; for lack of pay, a militia regiment at Sheldon mutinied in July, though the attempt was quickly put down.[31]

To halt the worst abuses among militiamen, Lincoln did not hesitate to take unpopular actions, even at the risk of alienating the irregulars. In August, for instance, he learned that several militia officers serving under General McIntosh had been conducting raids from Augusta into the interior of Georgia, plundering the loyalist inhabitants as they went. Lincoln had long deplored the fact that the southern war was becoming increasingly fratricidal, that the patriots and loyalists steadily looted and destroyed the others' property. For several months he had been making special efforts to restrain the patriots from such activity. Whenever an offender was caught, he was punished and the booty forfeited so it could enrich the southern military chest. When Lincoln was informed of the offenses committed in Georgia, he displayed one of his rare flashes of anger and rebuked General McIntosh for having tolerated such "reprehensible" practices.[32]

As the summer waned Lincoln felt increasing apprehension as to what the autumn campaigning might bring. To Governor Rutledge he wrote that "slaughter and desolation will early mark . . . [the enemy's] progress in these . . . States—unless the greatest exertions are made to check them in their wicked and barbarous career."[33] He pressed Rutledge to furnish four thousand men for the approaching campaign. The preparations lagged, however, and Lincoln once again offered to resign and return North "the first moment it can be done with propriety."[34]

During the last week of August Lincoln received several pieces of information which raised his lagging spirits. A vessel arrived in Charleston from Cuba, bearing news that Spain had declared war

31. Benjamin Lincoln to the Georgia Council, Aug. 14, 1779, Benjamin Lincoln Letter Book, Rare Book Department, Boston Public Library. Hereafter cited as B.P.L. Lincoln Letter Book.

32. Benjamin Lincoln to Lachlan McIntosh, Aug. 2, 1779, M.H.S. Lincoln Letter Book.

33. Benjamin Lincoln to John Rutledge, Aug. 23, 1779, M. H. S. Lincoln Letter Book.

34. Benjamin Lincoln to Horatio Gates, Aug. 20, 1779, Horatio Gates Papers, New York Historical Society.

against Britain the previous June. Lincoln learned also that Major Jameson and some Virginia light dragoons had crushed a party of twenty-five loyalists near Briar Creek, Georgia, on August 14. It was a relatively minor skirmish, but atoned somewhat for Ashe's defeat at the same location five months before. From the North came word of a victorious rebel stroke against Stony Point, a British outpost on the Hudson River. Furthermore, there were persistent rumors that Admiral d'Estaing and his large French fleet were enroute toward the Georgia coast to assist Lincoln against the British.

Lincoln had known since the preceding spring that efforts were being made from several quarters in America to enlist d'Estaing's help. Whereas General Washington had given some thought to a combined land and sea operation in the North, Lincoln and Rutledge had appealed to the admiral for assistance in the South.[35] Lincoln devoted little additional attention to the matter, however, until he heard the rumors of d'Estaing's approach in August. The previous month d'Estaing had defeated a British fleet in the West Indies, giving France a brief superiority in American waters. It was at this juncture that d'Estaing heeded the appeals from Charleston and sailed to Lincoln's aid; his decision to leave the Caribbean was hastened by the fact that the hurricane season threatened soon to suspend all naval operations there. Upon nearing the American coast in late August, d'Estaing sent General Fontanges ahead to Charleston, to help arrange a plan of operations between the French and American forces. The obvious target of any such cooperative venture was to be Savannah, the principal British base in the South.

Benjamin Lincoln was the chief architect of the strategic plan which he, Governor Rutledge, and General Fontanges discussed at length on September 4 and adopted the following day. When he framed the proposals, however, Lincoln had been considerably influenced by d'Estaing's insistence upon a brief campaign.[36] The admiral's emissary explained that d'Estaing preferred not to keep his three thousand troops ashore for more than ten days, for he needed to be back in the Caribbean by late October for a new campaign. The

35. Bowen, "The Life of Benjamin Lincoln," p. 299.
36. Benjamin Lincoln, MS Journal of the Siege of Savannah, Sept. 3 and 4, 1779, Journals and Diaries, Manuscripts Division, Library of Congress. Hereafter cited as Journal of the Siege of Savannah.

allied strategy, therefore, was predicated upon the swift reduction of Savannah. Lincoln directed d'Estaing to land his troops at Beaulieu plantation, fourteen miles south of Savannah. The American troops under Lincoln would be gathered at Ebenezer, so that a juncture between the armies could easily be made. The enemy would thereby be cut off from the coast, as well as from its reinforcements and supplies. Lincoln did not think the British garrison on Port Royal Island would interfere seriously with these plans. He also predicted that, considering the inadequacy of the defensive works around Savannah and the relatively small garrison within, the British would be forced into an immediate surrender of the town. To his orderly, methodical mind, the plan on paper appeared quite feasible; Lincoln never seemed to doubt it would succeed.[37]

The American preparations for the expedition began promisingly. Lincoln ordered General McIntosh to march his 350 militia from Augusta to Ebenezer; Lincoln hoped that by September 11 he could collect all his available forces at that small Georgia community, sixteen miles northwest of Savannah. Governor Rutledge proved helpful by supplying Lincoln with a quantity of hastily raised militia and by sending boats down the coast to assist d'Estaing in ferrying his soldiers, stores, and cannon ashore. The patriots were so certain of success that General Moultrie observed, "No one doubted but that we had nothing more to do, than to march up to Savannah, and demand a surrender."[38]

Soon after Benjamin Lincoln and his troops departed Charleston on September 8 his campaign began to encounter difficulties. His forces were delayed by broken bridges at nearly every stream and river they passed. Lincoln arrived with 650 men at Ebenezer on September 12, but became anxious and virtually immobilized because he could learn nothing about d'Estaing's situation. On the fifteenth the French commander reported that his landing had been delayed by heavy rains but that he was nearing Savannah. Once he had reconnoitered the enemy's works the following morning, he hoped to confer personally with Lincoln at a designated site near the town.

37. "Plan of Operations between Count d'Estaing and Genl. Lincoln," Sept. 5, 1779, The Thomas Addis Emmet Collection of Manuscripts, Manuscripts Division, New York Public Library; hereafter cited as Emmet Collection.
38. Moultrie, *Memoirs*, II, 33.

The American commander left camp early on the morning of September 16 to meet with d'Estaing, but was delayed by several hours when a guide led the party by a wrong route. Once he had joined d'Estaing around noon Lincoln became angered by what he discovered. During the morning the count had learned that the enemy's works in front of Savannah did not appear formidable enough to withstand an attack. Because he was impatient by temperament, and because Lincoln was late in arriving, he had acted alone in summoning Prevost to surrender to the forces of France. Lincoln roundly lectured d'Estaing for having ignored the American interests, and the Frenchman perfunctorily agreed that all future negotiations with Prevost should be conducted jointly by the allies. Privately, however, d'Estaing seemed to have regarded Georgia as a British possession, and therefore legitimate prey for French conquest. Moreover, d'Estaing felt that his forces were far superior to Lincoln's in military ability as well as in numbers; during the weeks that followed, the French nobleman often patronized the onetime Massachusetts farmer, despite their alliance.[39]

Inside Savannah General Prevost handled his predicament with cunning. By arranging a twenty-four-hour truce on September 17, ostensibly to negotiate a surrender, Prevost stalled Lincoln and d'Estaing long enough to smuggle in eight hundred reinforcements from Port Royal Island. That evening the allied commanders received word from Prevost that his officers were unanimously decided to defend Savannah at all costs. But it soon became apparent to Prevost that his announcement had elicited no immediate military response from the French and American armies; for a week they engaged in little more than worrisome preparations, establishing their camps south of the town.[40]

By September 23 d'Estaing felt that his army was ready to begin the reduction of Savannah. He and Lincoln agreed that they should not risk a direct frontal assault; the French and American commanders began to lay siege to the town. By October 1 Lincoln had begun to doubt seriously that the siege was a wise course of action, instead arguing "that a more determined mode of attack must be adopted

39. Franklin B. Hough, *The Siege of Savannah, by the Combined American and French Forces, Under the Command of Gen. Lincoln, and the Count d'Estaing, in the Autumn of 1779* (Albany, N.Y., 1866), pp. 89–90, 129; Kenneth Coleman, *The American Revolution in Georgia* (Athens, Ga., 1958), p. 129.
40. Journal of the Siege of Savannah, Sept. 18–24, 1779, passim.

. . . before Savannah is ours."[41] D'Estaing concurred in the matter. Once he finished mounting his heavy guns on October 3, he opened a heavy fire upon the British lines. The cannonade proved so damaging that Prevost begged permission to evacuate the women and children from Savannah. At this juncture Lincoln displayed a firmness and dispatch that were somewhat uncharacteristic; after insisting he speak for the allies, he flatly rejected the enemy request. He accused Prevost of stalling for time, and reminded him that during the truce in mid-September the British commander had no other object than that of being reinforced. Lincoln sternly warned him to make no further delays.[42] Meanwhile d'Estaing received dispatches from several captains in his fleet urging him to abandon the expedition. He summoned a council of the French and American officers, and there told Lincoln he felt obliged either to raise the siege altogether or to make an effort to storm the town. The American commander accepted the latter alternative without hesitation, and the two leaders devised a plan to launch their attack early on the morning of October 9. Unfortunately an American deserter forewarned Prevost of the allied plan, and he was better enabled to meet the emergency.

The ill-fated attack lasted for three hours, during which time the British guns systematically slaughtered the French and American soldiers. Count d'Estaing was wounded, and the allies suffered over 800 casualties, of which 650 were French. The British defenders sustained 150 losses. The fury of Prevost's resistance had seldom been equaled during the war; not since Bunker Hill, in fact, had a battle been fought more furiously. During the late morning, the allies had little alternative but to withdraw and call for a truce. Lincoln protested in the strongest terms when d'Estaing revealed his plans to evacuate his army from the coast, but the Frenchman could not be dissuaded. There remained no alternative for the crestfallen Lincoln than to return with his troops to South Carolina.[43]

General Lincoln arrived back in Charleston on October 21; the next day he sent a full report to Congress on the Savannah campaign. For the record, Lincoln was full of praise for d'Estaing, whom he suggested "has undoubtedly the interest of America very much at

41. Benjamin Lincoln to John Rutledge, Oct. 1, 1779, B.P.L. Lincoln Letter Book.

42. Benjamin Lincoln to Augustine Prevost, Oct. 6, 1779, B.P.L. Lincoln Letter Book.

43. Journal of the Siege of Savannah, 1779.

heart." He assured the Congress that "in our service . . . [d'Estaing] has freely bled," and that "we regard with high approbation his intentions to serve us. . . ." Lincoln offered no hint that occasional altercations and wounded feelings had also characterized his relationship with the Frenchman. Neither did he make any excuses for his own role in the disastrous joint operation.[44] In fact he displayed an admirable fairness in his remarks; whether by design or not, they undoubtedly elicited sympathy for their author and his predicament. Privately, however, Lincoln did not reveal such a forbearing attitude. He complained to an aide, Major Everard Meade, that nothing should have prevented the success of the Savannah expedition; it had failed only because of "the necessity the count was under to leave the coast."[45] Lincoln oversimplified the matter. From the beginning of the operations allied prospects were all but wrecked by mutual discord, missed opportunities, and fatal delays. It is not surprising that a wave of discouragement swept America once Congress learned the news of Savannah.

In New York Sir Henry Clinton rejoiced over the latest intelligence from Georgia. With the British now in firm control of that province, Clinton planned a major new offensive against the South. He wanted first to establish a base of operations at Charleston, from which he would command the seacoast, and then to penetrate the Carolinas. Meanwhile, in South Carolina, General Lincoln had become increasingly anxious over reports of an impending enemy invasion. A dispatch from General Washington urged Lincoln to "make every exertion in . . . [his] power" to repel the invaders, but warned him not to expect any Northern reinforcements, for none could be spared. He would have to rely solely for assistance on the southern state governments.[46]

The message could not have reached Lincoln at a more inopportune time; since returning from Savannah he had found it increasingly difficult to obtain the cooperation of the civil authorities in the Carolinas and Virginia. The events at Savannah had further undermined their confidence in Lincoln and his Continental army, and had encouraged the officials to rely more heavily upon the militia of

44. Benjamin Lincoln to Samuel Huntington, Oct. 22, 1779, B.P.L. Lincoln Letter Book.
45. Benjamin Lincoln to Everard Meade, Nov. 1, 1779, Emmet Collection.
46. *The Writings of George Washington*, XVI, 351–53.

their respective states. In late October the South Carolina assembly passed a law which forbade using the militia to fill the Continental battalions. At the time, Lincoln had fewer than a thousand regulars fit for duty, distributed among the Carolina upcountry, Sheldon, and Charleston. He immediately warned Congress that unless it could give him assistance, the southern states "must fall a sacrifice, if the enemy mean seriously to attempt them." Lincoln was certain the British planned such a move.[47]

During November and December Lincoln worked feverishly to prepare for an attack which did not come. Clinton had been delayed, but the growing fears of his imminent arrival at Charleston began to work in Lincoln's favor. During the first week of November, the assemblymen of North Carolina resolved to send Lincoln three thousand militia, yet offered no assurances that Lincoln could expect the men anytime soon. During the succeeding weeks he became painfully aware that resolutions made poor substitutes for troops; only a fraction of the promised North Carolinians were ever dispatched to Lincoln's aid. The South Carolinians, too, rankled Lincoln. In his attempts to ensure the safety of Charleston he had repeatedly urged the need for leveling the woods and houses which lay outside the defensive works; the enemy would thereby be denied valuable cover in the event of a siege. Among the Charlestonians who owned the threatened property were some state councillors, and for a time they succeeded in denying Lincoln permission to clear the land.[48] These influential citizens revealed once again that expediency dictated their attitude toward the patriot cause. Their motives had been similar during the previous May when they attempted to compromise with General Prevost to prevent his entering the city.

In spite of the disheartening delays which Lincoln encountered, he began to estimate his chances of defending Charleston against attack "if all was done for its' security, which ought to be done." He made the assumption that the enemy would approach from the western, or land, side of the city. He played down the danger of an assault by sea, believing that Fort Moultrie, on Sullivan's Island, could adequately defend the harbor entrance. The fort had served that pur-

47. Benjamin Lincoln to Henry Laurens, Oct. 22, 1779, B.P.L. Lincoln Letter Book.
48. John Rutledge to Benjamin Lincoln, Dec. 6, 1779, M.H.S. Lincoln Papers; Bowen, "The Life of Benjamin Lincoln," p. 325.

pose during the abortive British campaign of 1776. If he could only obtain enough troops to man his fortifications across Charleston Neck, Lincoln felt his defensive works "should not be easily insulted" by the enemy.[49]

Lincoln kept appealing so persuasively to Congress for reinforcements that the delegates pressed General Washington for assistance. In early December the commander in chief ordered General William Woodford and 750 Continentals to join Lincoln. Congress meanwhile ordered Commodore Abraham Whipple and five armed frigates to sail from Philadelphia to Charleston. By the third week in December the ships had reached their destination, and the promised reinforcements were beginning to move southward.

Benjamin Lincoln was elated by his support from General Washington and the Congress; he resolved to attempt a firm stand at Charleston, come what may. Not only was he acknowledging the political pressures to defend Charleston, but also he thought that such a defense "was right . . . when it is considered that . . . in abandoning it we . . . [would give] up the Continl. ships of war, and all our stores, while there . . . is yet a prospect of succour."[50] His expectation that quantities of reinforcements would rescue the city from danger was unrealistic; since arriving in the South the previous year, he had encountered nothing but difficulty in obtaining troops. Moreover, through his plans for a static defense, Lincoln appeared willing to expose his entire army to the threat of capture. It was an unnecessary risk for him to take. He should more wisely have considered the advantages of abandoning Charleston, as Washington had evacuated New York in 1776; past experience throughout most of the war had shown the patriots the folly of attempting to hold their seaports against British attack.

On December 26, 1779, Sir Henry Clinton finally embarked for the South with his formidable armada. He and his second in command, General Earl Cornwallis, sailed with eighty-five hundred troops aboard ninety transports, escorted by Admiral Arbuthnot and a fleet of fourteen warships. From the very beginning the voyage was a nightmare; rough seas and violent winds delayed its progress by many weeks. Not until February did the British disembark on the

49. Benjamin Lincoln to George Washington, Nov. 7, 1779, B.P.L. Lincoln Letter Book.
50. Benjamin Lincoln to George Washington, July 17, 1780, Emmet Collection.

sea islands, thirty miles southwest of Charleston. Clinton then began his gradual advance toward the American stronghold.[51]

Meanwhile, in Charleston, Lincoln was sending urgent messages to all the patriot governors in the South, warning them that only through their increased assistance could he ever hope to succeed. The growing reluctance of the South Carolinians to cooperate frustrated Lincoln; by February 1780 only a fraction of the twenty-four hundred defenders in Charleston were South Carolina irregulars. To make matters worse, Lincoln despaired whether he could even use the militia effectively "until all of them are really influenced by those principles of patriotism, that love of their Country, and concern for their own freedom and independence, [necessary] to oppose the tyranny of Britain."[52] Considering his past experience with southern militia, such expectations were unreasonable. Lincoln was in effect denying the usefulness of his irregulars while still seeking desperately to enlist their aid. The commander was obviously wearing under the strain of the gathering crisis.

As his problems mounted, Lincoln began harboring serious doubts about his ability to defend Charleston. In late January he advised Governor Rutledge that nothing could force the surrender of the town "more early than the distress brought on the Troops should make it necessary."[53] Nevertheless Lincoln resolved by mid-February that his decision to remain in the city was final, and that "no consideration could induce me to adopt a new mode of conduct." He still clung to his stubborn belief that if he were only "supported by the people of the Country," the reinforcements would somehow ensure his success.[54] Not long afterward, when Rutledge pledged to supply two thousand more militia, the general considered using them as a special covering force to "render an evacuation practicable" if the necessity arose. But if Lincoln did not rule out the possibility of a retreat, neither did he devote much further thought to such an alternative.[55]

51. Henry Clinton, *The American Rebellion: Sir Henry Clinton's Narrative of His Campaigns, 1775–1782, with an Appendix of Original Documents*, ed. William Willcox (New Haven, Conn., 1954), pp. 160–63.

52. Benjamin Lincoln to Richard Caswell, Jan. 3, 1780, B.P.L. Lincoln Letter Book.

53. Benjamin Lincoln to John Rutledge, Jan. 28, 1780, B.P.L. Lincoln Letter Book.

54. Benjamin Lincoln to John Rutledge, Feb. 14, 1780, B.P.L. Lincoln Letter Book.

55. Benjamin Lincoln to George Washington, July 17, 1780, Emmet Collection.

He may well have decided that he would face serious risks if he retreated. The British were capable of navigating the southern rivers
into the interior and might thereby intercept the Americans in their
flight. Furthermore, had Lincoln ordered his South Carolinian forces
to abandon their state capital and major seaport, he might not have
been obeyed.

By the final week of February some of the British invaders had
advanced as far as James Island, which lay just south of Charleston
Harbor. Lincoln, however, made no attempts to detach troops and
challenge the enemy's progress; he feared that Clinton might completely elude any such force, and then attack the weakened city. As
it was, Charleston seemed anything but secure to Lincoln; on February 25 he ordered the public records of South Carolina and Georgia
to be removed from the city and transported to the safety of Monck's
Corner, thirty miles to the north. Yet within a few days Lincoln took
steps which further eroded the security of his garrison. Commodore
Whipple reported that at low tide the water was too shallow at the
channel entrance for his vessels to guard the mouth of the harbor.[56]
After becoming satisfied at first hand that Whipple was correct, Lincoln ordered the fleet to withdraw to the vicinity of Fort Moultrie.
Although he suggested that the channel near the fort be obstructed
with a sunken vessel, the attempt was abandoned because of deep
water and swift tides. Thus in an almost perfunctory manner, Lincoln gave up his option to challenge the British fleets attempt to
enter Charleston harbor. On March 20 Arbuthnot got more than
twenty vessels through the unguarded harbor entrance, forcing Commodore Whipple to withdraw his eight ships up the Cooper River.
Sir Henry Clinton and his army subsequently crossed the Ashley
River to Charleston Neck during the night of March 28 at a point
three miles above Ashley Ferry. Lincoln had mistakenly thought the
redcoats would attempt the operation at the ferry itself, where he had
concentrated his defenses to no avail.[57]

Once the British army was situated on Charleston Neck, about

56. Abraham Whipple to Benjamin Lincoln, Feb. 27, 1780, Chamberlain Collection, Rare Book Department, Boston Public Library; Bowen, "The Life of Benjamin Lincoln," p. 333.

57. *The Siege of Charleston, with an Account of the Province of South Carolina:
Diaries and Letters of Hessian Officers from the von Jungkenn Papers in the William L. Clements Library*, ed. Bernhard A. Uhlendorf, Vol. XII of the Univ. of
Mich. Publications on History and Political Science (Ann Arbor, Mich., 1938), pp.
31–33.

twelve miles north of the American lines, Lincoln withdrew his men toward the city. He had been outmaneuvered by superior forces. Lincoln did, however, order that the Cooper River channel be obstructed with eleven sunken vessels, including most of his Continental frigates. With the British fleet thus denied access to the river, Lincoln could more easily keep open his line of communications with the north. As a special measure of security, he ordered General Isaac Huger and a force of five hundred cavalry to guard Monck's Corner; that outpost was Lincoln's only remaining escape route from the city.

Clinton gradually advanced his army toward the American lines. On April 8 he summoned General Lincoln either to surrender Charleston and its entire garrison, or risk the destruction of them both. At the time Lincoln received the summons he had 5,150 Continentals and militiamen at his disposal. Approximately 1,950 of that total had been obtained since early winter; in contrast the southern governors, Congress, and General Washington had between them promised to supply Lincoln with over 9,000 troops during the same period. It was largely because of these official assurances that Lincoln had determined to defend Charleston, and he still hoped more troops would arrive.[58] Without consulting anyone, therefore, Lincoln flatly rejected the British demands. In his reply he emphasized that "duty and inclination point to the propriety of supporting . . . [the city] to the last extremity."[59] The tension in Charleston rose sharply as the British closed in with their heavy artillery. In mid-April Lincoln made an extraordinary effort to lift the morale of his troops. Despite his conspicuous limp and excessive weight, the general went to the front lines, obtained a pick and shovel, and worked alongside a fatigue detail for an entire day. It was one of the more heroic acts of his military career.[60]

On the morning of April 13 the British batteries opened fire upon the city with a damaging barrage of round shot and incendiary bombs. Lincoln summoned a council of his officers and gave them a discouraging report. Besides the acute shortages of supplies and weapons, his engineers had advised him that the fortifications could

58. Benjamin Lincoln to George Washington, July 17, 1780, Emmet Collection; William G. Simms, *South Carolina in the Revolutionary War* (Charleston, 1853), p. 119.

59. Benjamin Lincoln to Henry Clinton and Marriot Arbuthnot, Apr. 10, 1780, B.P.L. Lincoln Letter Book.

60. Deposition of James Cannon, June 28, 1780, enclosed in Benjamin Lincoln to George Washington, July 17, 1780, Emmet Collection.

hold only a few days more. Moreover, he had received almost no reinforcements during the previous week, and was beginning to doubt
that more would arrive. For the first time Lincoln gave serious consideration to the evacuation of Charleston. His officers, however,
agreed only that Governor Rutledge be urged to leave the city as
soon as possible; by seeking help in the northern part of the state,
he might expedite any possible rebel retreat in that direction. Before the council could deliberate further, a heavy enemy cannonade
abruptly ended the meeting. Rutledge and several of his councillors
departed from Charleston shortly thereafter, leaving Lieutenant Governor Christopher Gadsden to serve as the ranking civilian authority
in the city.

Lincoln hesitated too long in deciding whether to evacuate Charleston; during the early morning hours of April 14 the British suddenly
closed his one remaining escape from the city. The bold young Lieutenant Colonel Banastre Tarleton and his legion, reinforced by Major
Patrick Ferguson's loyalist volunteers, completely routed General
Huger's forces at Monck's Corner. Lincoln, now surrounded, described the hopelessness of the situation in his private journal: with
a scarcity of provisions, no hope of reopening an escape route, and an
inability to defend his fortifications much longer, he concluded that it
"became necessary in this embarrassed state of affairs to . . . [do]
what was most expedient to . . . the good of the Service."[61] The expedient thing, he realized, was capitulation.

At a council of officers which Lincoln assembled on April 19 the
major general revealed his decision but assured them he hoped to
obtain the honors of war for his Continental troops. Although a majority of the generals agreed with Lincoln, Lieutenant Governor
Gadsden did not; he had been allowed to sit in on the council and
now showed considerable distress at the thought of a surrender. The
resulting clash between the civil and military authorities was sharper
than any Lincoln had ever encountered in the South. Gadsden demanded a postponement of the deliberations until evening, when
he returned with four of his state councillors. The South Carolinians
angrily threatened to "open the gates for the enemy" should Lincoln
attempt to abandon Charleston. As he had done on previous occasions,

61. Benjamin Lincoln, MS Journal of the Siege of Charleston, Apr. 19, 1780,
Rare Book Department, Boston Public Library.

Lincoln postponed making any decision. The effect was salutary: tempers were cooled, and an intolerable crisis avoided. The following morning he and his generals met privately and decided that, despite civilian opposition, they would seek honorable terms of capitulation.[62]

On April 21 Lincoln informed Clinton that he could occupy Charleston if the rebel garrison were given ten days in which to withdraw all its equipment and supplies. The proposal was hardly realistic under the circumstances, and the British lost no time in turning it down. When Clinton reiterated his demands that Charleston be surrendered intact, Lincoln made no immediate reply. For the ensuing two weeks Clinton tightened his grip on the city with methodical restraint, as if savoring the event. Meanwhile, Lincoln refused to accept the enemy terms, for he reasoned that to delay the enemy "as long as possible" was "an object worthy [of] our attention." At this late hour he still held to the remote possibility of being reinforced or rescued, of somehow escaping capture. He also felt it was a matter of honor to resist to the last extremity.[63]

On May 2 the British made one last effort to negotiate an unconditional surrender before forcing their way into Charleston. Clinton stressed in his final summons that Lincoln would be held personally responsible for the horrors of an assault if he persisted in his stubbornness. Lincoln immediately assembled a council of war; all but five of the sixty officers who attended agreed that further opposition was useless. They insisted, though, that Lincoln should attempt to obtain more honorable terms than the ones Clinton proposed. When Lieutenant Governor Gadsden was informed, he demanded to know why he had not been consulted on so momentous a decision. Lincoln attempted to accommodate the ruffled executive, and included three of his proposals among those newly submitted to Clinton. When the British commander turned them down, it was largely because Gadsden demanded special treatment for the South Carolina citizens and militia.[64]

62. Lachlan McIntosh, "Original Journal of the Siege of Charleston, S.C. in 1780," *The Magnolia; or Southern Apalachian*, I, No. 6 (Dec. 1842), 369.
63. Benjamin Lincoln to George Washington, July 17, 1780, Emmet Collection; Franklin B. Hough, *The Siege of Charleston, by the British Fleet and Army under the Command of Admiral Arbuthnot and Sir Henry Clinton, which Terminated with the Surrender of That Place on the 12th of May, 1780* (Albany, N.Y., 1867), pp. 95, 86.
64. Hough, *The Siege of Charleston*, pp. 100–101, 106.

Since the beginning of the Charleston campaign Lincoln had allowed civilian pressures to influence his military decisions unduly. He had sometimes been intimidated by such pressures, but he generally welcomed them. It had long been his democratic, if unmilitary, belief that it "is well not only to pay *some* but great attention to the advice of the Citizen and especially to those who have evidenced . . . unshaken attachment to the cause of their Country. . . ." Lincoln even admitted to feeling "unhappy when I differ from these [civilians] in opinion, and am led to suspect my own judgment," as well as to act "with great precaution."[65]

The breakdown of negotiations between Lincoln and Clinton on May 9 signaled the beginning of a heavy and unremitting bombardment of the city. By the following night the spirit of resistance in Charleston had been completely broken. Lieutenant Governor Gadsden, his councillors, the South Carolina militia officers, and a number of leading citizens presented Lincoln with signed petitions, demanding that he accept the British surrender terms as soon as possible. Most of these individuals had been distressing Lincoln for weeks with their insistence that he neither evacuate nor surrender the city; now they shifted positions, once their self-interests were no longer served by further resistance. On the tenth Lincoln offered unconditionally to capitulate. Both military circumstances and civilian pressures had finally forced his decision. He told Clinton simply that he acted from "a wish on my part to lessen as much as may be the distresses of war to [the] Individuals" in Charleston.[66]

At eleven o'clock on the morning of May 12 General Lincoln formally turned Charleston over to his enemies. A British officer who witnessed the event recorded that "Lincoln lim'p out at the Head of the most ragged Rabble I ever beheld. . . ."[67] Clinton arranged for the Continental forces to be confined in a camp north of the city until exchanged. The militia returned to their homes as prisoners on parole, after guaranteeing that they would not again bear arms during the conflict. An approximate total of 5,400 men were thereby lost to the patriot cause, along with a sizable quantity of weapons and military stores. At a cost to the British of only 76 killed and 189 wounded,

65. Benjamin Lincoln to Colonel Walton, Jan. 28, 1780, P.B.L. Lincoln Letter Book.
66. Minutes of a Council of War, May 11, 1780, M. H. S. Lincoln Papers; Benjamin Lincoln to Henry Clinton, May 11, 1780, B.P.L. Lincoln Letter Book.
67. Hough, *The Siege of Charleston*, p. 129.

Clinton, Arbuthnot, and Cornwallis had maneuvered the Americans into their greatest defeat of the war.[68]

Sir Henry Clinton permitted General Lincoln, accompanied by his aides and their servants, to go to Philadelphia on parole. Lincoln pledged to reside with his family at Hingham, Massachusetts, until such time as he could be exchanged. During his stopover at the capital in late June Lincoln asked that Congress make an immediate investigation into his conduct at Charleston. Equally at stake, he contended, were his own reputation and the honor of Congress.[69] The delegates at Philadelphia agreed to comply with Lincoln's petition on condition that General Washington convene the court of inquiry. The commander in chief protested, however; he said that a satisfactory investigation would be impossible because so many necessary witnesses, including Lincoln himself, were still prisoners of war.[70] For these reasons the inquiry was postponed indefinitely.

Practically all the leading patriot generals rallied to defend Lincoln for his recent conduct in the South. On May 15, before Washington even knew about the fall of Charleston, he had encouraged Lincoln in a letter "to persevere in your determination of defending the Town to the last extremity." Probably because Lincoln had done precisely that, the commander in chief felt disinclined to complain. When Henry Knox wrote to Lincoln on June 24, he did not commiserate with his friend; instead, Knox remarked that "the great defense made by you and your Garrison in field fortifications, will confer on you and them the esteem and admiration of every sensible military man." Horatio Gates, whom Congress had named to succeed Lincoln as Southern Commander, offered him some sympathy but more praise. Gates lauded his predecessor for having shown "Dignity . . . Virtues, and . . . perseverance" in his attempt to defend Charleston. At this critical hour of the war, the niceties of how Lincoln had handled his duties became secondary to a far more pressing need. The patriot leaders felt they must close ranks solidly behind their imperiled cause.[71]

68. Banastre Tarleton, *A History of the Campaigns of 1780 and 1781, in the Southern Provinces of North Carolina* (Dublin, 1787), pp. 64, 22.
69. Benjamin Lincoln to Samuel Huntington, June 23, 1780, B.P.L. Lincoln Letter Book.
70. *The Writings of George Washington*, XIX, 147–48.
71. *The Writings of George Washington*, XVIII, 363; Henry Knox to Benjamin Lincoln, June 24, 1780, Henry Knox Papers, Massachusetts Historical Society;

In the summer of 1780 Lincoln returned to Massachusetts as a prisoner on parole. He was greeted enthusiastically, and commended for his courage during the late campaign. After his exchange was negotiated in November, he spent the winter and spring months in his native state. When Washington resumed campaigning in the summer of 1781, it was Lincoln he selected as his second in command for the Virginia expedition against Cornwallis. In October, when the allies surrounded their enemies at Yorktown, Washington designated Lincoln to accept the ceremonial British surrender on behalf of the Continental army. The terms imposed on Cornwallis were not appreciably different from those which had been dictated to Lincoln at Charleston; the American general had evened an old score, and his reputation was enhanced once again.

Lincoln represented something of a paradox during his tenure of command in the South. Although he was constantly frustrated by problems which either resisted his efforts at solution, or which he unwittingly brought on himself, the man elicited surprisingly little criticism. Even at the nadir of his military fortunes following the surrender of Charleston, few of his associates wavered in their respect and affection for the man. Lincoln was an immensely sympathetic figure, and so generally good-natured that even his enormous bulk and pronounced lameness became definite assets. Although he could be somewhat ingratiating about it all, he personified such traditional New England virtues as integrity, honesty, common sense, and reliability. He was also a methodical, hardworking individual, if sometimes ponderously so. He believed ardently in the revolutionary cause, and unflaggingly gave the best that was in him to the war effort in the South. Unfortunately, his best was none too adequate.

The former agriculturalist and Congregational deacon was generally overwhelmed by large-scale military responsibilities. His reputation as an administrator, one who could skillfully recruit and train the militia, had been made in the North early in the war. But at that time there had been much less scope to his authority, and he contended with far fewer troops. In his enlarged southern command he found the responsibilities taxing. Lincoln was especially frustrated by his endeavors with the militia, for he periodically met with unco-

Horatio Gates to Benjamin Lincoln, June 24, 1780, Horatio Gates Papers, N.Y. Historical Society.

operative resistance from southern officials and citizens. As the rebel military position deteriorated, so did the local peoples' inclination to put Continental interests above self and state. It is doubtful that anyone else could have dealt with the problem much more effectively than Lincoln did between late 1778 and mid-1780.

Like so many other revolutionary officers, Lincoln was essentially an amateur at strategic planning and tactics. Otherwise he would not have left Charleston vulnerable to attack in early 1779, when he marched his army toward Augusta. Later that year he devised an expeditious scheme for the reduction of Savannah, and then he and d'Estaing frittered away their opportunity with endless preparations. Lincoln's decision to defend Charleston in 1780 needlessly subjected an entire army to capture for the dubious sake of a city. One fatal flaw in all of these matters was his belief that, if he could only assemble enough Continentals and militia, his men would be able to stand up to seasoned British regulars. He consequently took grave risks, such as making a stand at Charleston, on the mere hope of being heavily reinforced. Circumstances during the war suggested, however, that he should not have risked any direct confrontation with an enemy so superior.

At times during his southern sojourn Lincoln simply bowed to the inevitable; he seemed swept along by events, neither controlling nor comprehending them fully. Small wonder that he was often cautious and indecisive under pressure, as happened at both Savannah and Charleston. In the report he sent General Washington following the surrender of Charleston, Lincoln portrayed himself basically as an unwilling victim of circumstances. Ironically enough, he may have been close to the truth. Lincoln had never really welcomed the southern command, with its responsibility for thousands of men in a sizable part of the continent. He had come South largely because he felt it his duty. Later he tried several times without success to resign his post, concealing his emotional frustrations behind a painful leg wound and the rigors of humidity and heat. Nevertheless, he stayed and suffered and earned widespread esteem for his indefatigable efforts in the South.

Major General Horatio Gates as a Military Leader: The Southern Experience

Paul David Nelson   *Berea College*

As military commander of the Southern Department in 1780, Major General Horatio Gates experienced both the agonies of defeat and the pleasures of at least a partial victory. Called upon to lead an army against Charles, Earl Cornwallis, he suffered at Camden one of the worst trouncings received by an American officer during the Revolutionary War. But after being compelled to withdraw the remains of his army from South Carolina, he quickly reorganized patriot forces and yielded to Generals Nathanael Greene and Daniel Morgan the puny, yet tenacious army that these officers would employ with such effectiveness in the following year. Many American military leaders who were familiar with the general's abilities as a tactician were not surprised to learn that he had met defeat at Camden, for despite Gates's success at Saratoga in 1777 (and it was *his* success, not that of his subordinate officers),[1] he was at best only an average field commander.

On the other hand, few people with knowledge of his talents were surprised when Gates employed his gifts as a military organizer, administrator, and disciplinarian to restore his army's strength and morale. On three occasions prior to 1780—at Boston in 1775, at Ticonderoga in 1776, and during the Saratoga campaign of 1777—Gates had wrought near miracles in reforming shattered or disorganized armies. Interestingly, historians who have commented upon Gates's activities in the South have been prone to emphasize his failures and to forget his successes. While they have said a great deal about the

---

1. Paul David Nelson, "Legacy of Controversy: Gates, Schuyler, and Arnold at Saratoga, 1777," *Military Affairs*, XXXVII (Apr. 1973), 41–47.

disastrous battle of Camden, they have written little about the mundane but nonetheless important details of troop reorganization that he emphasized after the battle. For a clear understanding of Gates's military role in the South, due weight must be given both the negative and positive aspects of his leadership.

In a sense the two roles that Gates played as commander of the Southern Department illuminated his weaknesses and strengths as a military officer during his entire career. Born of humble English parents, Gates entered the Royal Army at an early age, rose through the ranks while serving in America during the Seven Years' War, and learned much about how to run an army. By 1762 he had achieved the rank of major, an advancement that was due as much to the patronage of his commanding officers as to his own merits or exploits. After the war Gates discovered that he had reached a dead end in his career, for as the British army reverted to a peacetime footing he could not secure higher rank; hence he resigned his commission and settled with his family in America. The beginning of the Revolutionary War found him living in obscurity upon a small plantation in the lower Shenandoah Valley of Virginia. At the outbreak of hostilities he was called quickly to service by the Continental Congress and spent a year as adjutant general under George Washington at Boston and New York. Then in 1776 he was appointed a major general and sent to command the patriot army that had invaded Canada the year before but had recently retreated into upstate New York. In both these positions Gates gave signal service to the patriot cause as a capable army administrator and organizer. He reached the peak of his fame after defeating Lieutenant General John Burgoyne at Saratoga in an uninspiring but tactically sound campaign. During the two following years he served as chairman of the Board of War and as commandant of Boston and Rhode Island. At the end of 1779 he received permission from Washington to go into semiretirement at his home in northern Virginia; it was from here that he would be called back to service in the southern theater.

As a man Gates did not inspire his subordinates, either by his activities or his intellect; but by all reports he was an easy officer under whom to serve. His associates described him as a genial, mild mannered, convivial, extroverted, and garrulous person. Rarely did he lose his temper, but when he did his language, according to some accounts, became foul beyond description. It has been charged by some of his friends that Gates was gullible, and seemingly he often was too trusting of cunning and calculating men. At the same time, however, he had a remarkably penetrating mind, best seen in his discussions of grand strategy, where more than once he almost exactly described what the British planned for America in subsequent campaigns. He was not, then, a simple-witted man but possessed considerable native intelligence. When he made up his mind to follow a course of action, he could be tenacious to the point of stubbornness, even refusing the wise counsel of his advisers. Perhaps his greatest fault, both before and during his tenure in the South, was his inability to determine when he should heed advice and when he should cling to his own ideas.

On June 12, 1780, Congress voted to place Gates in command of the Southern Department.[2] By the time this action was taken, the patriot cause in Georgia and South Carolina was in desperate trouble, and North Carolina revolutionaries seemed threatened by British forces upon their borders. Two years earlier strategists in London had begun to pay attention to possible English opportunities in the southern states, and as a consequence Lord George Germain instructed Sir Henry Clinton, commander in chief of royal troops in America, to carry out offensive operations against Georgia. To expedite his orders, Clinton sent Lieutenant Colonel Archibald Campbell with a force to attack Savannah; the town fell to the British in late 1778. America's commander in the South, Major General Benjamin Lincoln, attempted in the following year to recover this loss but was forced to withdraw toward Charleston. In the spring of 1780 Sir Henry Clinton mounted a full-scale attack against Charleston, with the result that on May 12 Lincoln surrendered the city and an army of fifty-five hundred men to his opponent. The command of the remaining American forces in North Carolina then devolved upon General Johann, Baron de Kalb, who had been sent by Washington with about fourteen hundred Delaware and Maryland Continental troops to assist Lincoln, but who had only reached Fredericksburg, Virginia, when he heard news of the debacle at Charleston. Marching into North Carolina, de Kalb took up a position near the center of the state upon Deep River at a place called Coxe's Mill and awaited

2. *Journals of the Continental Congress, 1774–1789*, ed. Worthington C. Ford (34 vols.; Washington, D.C.: Library of Congress, 1904–37), XVII, 508.

the arrival of his replacement before attempting any action against the enemy.[3]

Riding into the village of Hillsborough, North Carolina, on the thirteenth of July, Gates was appalled by conditions prevailing in his department. Even when he received news of his selection by Congress to take charge in the South, the general had not expressed much enthusiasm for his new position.[4] But what he found at Hillsborough certainly did nothing to bolster his flagging spirits. To Governor Thomas Jefferson of Virginia, Governor Abner Nash of North Carolina, and to the president of Congress he wrote plaintive letters complaining of an almost total lack of muskets, cannon, powder, shot, shells, tents, clothing, and food for his army.[5] Seeing nothing more that he could accomplish by remaining at Hillsborough, he marched with 1,438 Virginia militia that he had found in the town toward de Kalb's bivouac at Coxe's Mill. He reached his destination on July 25 and discovered that conditions in the camp upon Deep River and among other military units throughout North Carolina were as wretched as any that he had seen until that time. The army, a hodge-podge of forces that had been collected since May or had somehow evaded the British dragnet at Charleston, was stationed at numerous places in the state. This dispersal of troops was made necessary by the fact that magazines of stores did not exist, and patriot soldiers were having to steal flour, corn meal, meat, and forage from a sullen citizenry that refused to accept American currency or due bills. Gates found that he had under his command a considerable army of about forty-two hundred men, counting the Continentals that had marched with de Kalb from Washington's army, a few patriot cavalrymen at Halifax, some artillerymen and sixty dragoons under Colonel Charles Armand at Coxe's Mill, the Virginia militia unit that had collected

3. John Richard Alden, *The American Revolution, 1775–1783*, New American Nation Series (New York: Harper & Row, 1954), pp. 227–31; de Kalb to Board of War, June 6, 1780, Horatio Gates Papers, Box 14, New York Historical Society, New York City; hereafter cited as Gates Papers, NYHS; de Kalb to Gates, June 6, 1780, *State Records of North Carolina, 1777–1790*, ed. Walter Clark (16 vols.; Winston and Goldsboro: State of N.C., 1895–1905), XIV, 499–500.

4. Gates to Congress, June 21, 1780, Papers of the Continental Congress, No. 154, Vol. 2, 206–7, Library of Congress, Washington, D.C., hereafter cited as PCC, 154; Gates to General Lincoln, July 4, 1780, Maine Historical Society, Portland.

5. Gates to Jefferson, July 19, 1780, and to Nash, July 19, 1780, Gates Papers, Box 19, NYHS; Gates to Congress, July 20, 1780, PCC, 154, Vol. 2, 214–15.

at Hillsborough, and a force of North Carolina militia commanded by Major General Richard Caswell at Moore's Ferry on the Yadkin River.[6] But the effectiveness of his troops was curtailed drastically by monumental problems of organization and supply. If ever an army was in need of Gates's recognized talents as an administrator, this one was.

To restore his command to fighting capability, the general needed time—but time, for some reason, he felt he did not have. Hence, instead of remaining stationary at Coxe's Mill, Gates immediately decided to march toward the enemy in South Carolina.[7] Why he felt compelled to mobilize half-starved, ill-trained soldiers under such conditions is hard to fathom. It appears that he was under little pressure from the British to act with haste. After Charleston fell in May, Sir Henry Clinton departed the South, leaving Lord Cornwallis in command of the Royal Army. The latter had dispersed his troops into South Carolina and Georgia, attempting to reduce patriot resistance, and by the middle of July British and loyalist forces had penetrated as far north as Camden. But the small garrison of that town (only about fifteen hundred men), under the command of Lieutenant Colonel Francis, Lord Rawdon, showed no inclination to begin a thrust into North Carolina. In fact, Cornwallis, for the time being, had his hands full in securing America's two southernmost states. Seemingly Gates would have been well advised to take advantage of this respite to rebuild his army. In addition to the foregoing circumstances, Gates had learned from General Thomas Sumter, who was in camp near the Catawba River with a band of 3,200 patriot guerillas, that the enemy's total strength in South Carolina was only about 3,482 men, considerably less than the American total and dispersed throughout the state in various small detachments.[8]

Once Gates had made the decision to march southward, he would let nothing stand in the way of arriving at his destination in the shortest possible time. Most of his officers, opposed to any movement by the impoverished American troops, encouraged him at least to march

    6. Information upon troop dispositions and numbers is found in de Kalb to Gates, July 16, 1780, *State Records*, XIV, 503, and Otho Holland Williams, "Narrative of the Campaigns of 1780," in William Johnson, *Sketches of the Life and Correspondence of Nathanael Greene* (2 vols.; Charleston: A. E. Miller, 1822), Appendix B, I, 486.
    7. Williams, "Narrative," p. 486.
    8. Sumter to Gates, July 17, 1780, Gates Papers, Box 14, NYHS.

towards Camden by a western route through Charlotte, where food was plentiful and the citizens favored the Revolution. Gates decided instead to direct his army southward through wild pine barrens which were devoid of food and forage and contained many loyalist guerillas. For him the advantage of the southerly route was that it saved eighty miles of marching. But, as his officers counseled, this asset was overriden by two points in favor of the other route: a certain food supply for the marching army and a secure line of retreat in case it became necessary to withdraw from South Carolina.[9] So adamant, however, was the general about marching by the shorter route that he ignored every argument of his subordinates.

Moreover, so anxious was he to proceed that he almost overlooked his main cavalry forces under Colonel Anthony White, which were attempting to reorganize at Halifax after suffering blows two months earlier in the battle for Charleston. He seemed totally to disregard the vital services of this group of troops as gatherers of intelligence and as a shock force upon the battlefields of the southern Piedmont, an area that was generally covered with trees but devoid of the underbrush that hampered the activities of horsemen. The American cavalry unit, reduced from five hundred dragoons before clashes with Lieutenant Colonel Banastre Tarleton's Tory Legion at Monck's Corner and Lenew's Ferry, now possessed only fifty effectives. But Gates made no effort to hide his opinion that cavalry forces were inconsequential in his plans, a view which led Colonel Otho Holland Williams to observe later that the general's neglect of patriot horsemen was a great mistake. Gates's lack of concern about his cavalry seems all the more incomprehensible, given his full knowledge that the British army possessed the famous Tory Legion of more than four hundred horsemen under the capable leadership of Tarleton. When General Greene assumed command in the South, he would not make the same error as his predecessor; indeed, he realized all too well the danger of sending an army of foot soldiers without the support of horsemen against an enemy force that contained a strong contingent of cavalry.[10]

For all that can be said against his decision to march with such

9. Williams, "Narrative," pp. 487, 498.
10. Ibid., p. 506. For Greene's views upon the use of cavalry in the Southern Department, see Greene to Alexander Hamilton, Jan. 10, 1781, Alexander Hamilton, *Papers of Alexander Hamilton*, ed. Harold C. Syrett and Jacob E. Cooke (15 vols. to date; New York: Columbia Univ. Press, 1961–), II, 421.

alacrity into South Carolina, the general's reasons for stubbornly adhering to his scheme made some sense. First, he had learned from General Sumter, in the letter informing him of enemy numbers, that the British seemed to be using Camden as a staging area for an invasion of North Carolina. A quick thrust by the American army, said Sumter, would forestall the intention of Cornwallis to use the town as a base of operations and would pose no threat even to the weak patriot forces.[11] Sumter's intelligence was faulty, for the instructions of Cornwallis from London were to secure South Carolina by concentrating his forces within the state. It was after Gates arrived with his army near Camden that the British commander realized he could carry out his orders only by an offensive to the northward. Thus, ironically, Gates's rapid march toward South Carolina, instead of hindering the enemy's invasion plans, actually did much to trigger them. But at the time General Gates made his decision, he was unaware of his opponent's orders and could not foresee this unfortunate result.

The second, and probably most important, reason for Gates's haste was the enormous pressure he was under from local civil and military leaders to take the offensive against the enemy in order to bolster quickly the sagging morale of the patriots. One soldier of the southern army, in defending General Gates against his detractors a week after the battle of Camden, maintained that many local chieftains had collaborated to force the American commandant into activity against his will. Two of Gates's officers in particular, William Smallwood and Richard Caswell, were cajoling him to proceed with haste. The latter, in fact, at great risk to his men and in direct violation of the commander's orders marched independently with his North Carolina militia against Lord Rawdon before Gates could reach his encampment. Forced to rush his exhausted men "with the utmost Expedition" to Caswell's aid, Gates was furious at his recalcitrant subordinate and fumed to him on August 3, "This is a Mode of conducting War, I am a stranger to. The Whole should support and sustain the Whole, or the Parts will soon go to decay."[12] Of course, Gates did not have

11. Sumter to Gates, July 17, 1780, Gates Papers, Box 14, NYHS.

12. "Extracts of a letter from Salisbury," Aug. 23, 1780, printed in *Maryland Gazette*, Sept. 15, 1780, cited in Don Higginbotham, *The War of American Independence: Military Attitudes, Policies, and Practices, 1763–1789*, The Macmillan Wars of the United States (New York: Macmillan, 1971), pp. 359 and 384, n. 11; Gates to Caswell, Aug. 3, 1780, "Copy Book of Major Gen. Gates, June 21, 1780–

to yield to pressure from Caswell or anyone if he were convinced that yielding would endanger his army; hence he must ultimately bear the responsibility for acting with unseemly haste. However, his errors in judgment may be partially explained by the conditions under which he was forced to make decisions in late July.

As the American army marched southward through the enervating heat of a Piedmont summer, it suffered tremendously from lack of food and rum. Some days the troops had nothing to eat except green corn and green peaches. On other days they were lucky enough to seize a cow or a little flour to provide themselves with a few morsels of bread and meat. In an attempt to keep up morale Gates and his officers suffered privations with their troops; in addition the commander made numerous promises that food and drink soon would be found upon the line of march.[13] Although the supplies never materialized (Gates, in fact, knew they did not exist), the army at least remained upon its feet. And the American commander never gave up trying to find succor for his weary troops. On August 3 he implored Governor Jefferson to send flour, beef, and rum to the southern army; to Governor Nash he made the same desperate request.[14] Neither message brought results, and Gates should not have expected that they would. Had the general remained at Hillsborough or Coxe's Mill until the civilian governments of the southern states had supplied him with the necessities of war, he might have avoided the suffering that his army now experienced. With his army lying quietly in bivouac, he could have pointed out to Governors Jefferson and Nash that, since they had not equipped the American army for combat, they could take the blame for enemy successes. As the situation now stood, he alone had to assume ultimate responsibility for supplying his troops, and if he failed civilians need not share much of the guilt.

By the first week of August Gates's half-starved army was poised upon the border of South Carolina and seemed prepared to do battle with Lord Rawdon's forces. The American commander was kept fully aware of enemy activities by Colonel Francis Marion of South Carolina, who had joined him upon the march and who had been sent

---

October 7, 1781," No. 27, Thomas Addis Emmet Collection, New York Public Library, New York City.

13. Williams, "Narrative," p. 486.
14. Gates Papers, Box 19, NYHS.

forward upon the east side of the Black River to provide news of British activities. General Thomas Sumter, whom Gates ordered with his guerrilla force of thirty-two hundred men to swing west of Camden and march upon enemy supply lines from the Catawba River area, also provided intelligence.[15] In addition, from Generals Griffith Rutherford and Richard Caswell the American commander received word that Rawdon had posted the Camden garrison of about fifteen hundred men upon Little Lynch's Creek in preparation for a battle with the Americans as they entered the state.[16] Responding to this news, Gates concentrated his own army by joining with Caswell's force of North Carolina militia and allowing the Virginians under General Edward Stevens to join him upon the march. The American army under Gates's immediate command now numbered about thirty-five hundred, some seven hundred fewer than two weeks before, because during the advance from Coxe's Mill more than four hundred of the Virginia militia had gone home and upon order of the commander another two hundred had been left by Stevens to guard Masque's Ferry across the Peedee River. Additionally, the decimated cavalry unit under Colonel White had been left behind at Halifax. After joining Caswell's troops Gates must have been relieved to discover food stores enough to relieve the most pressing demands of his army. Given a few days to rest and eat, the American soldiers, while not completely revived from their enervating march, presented a better appearance to their anxious chieftain.

Even though they outnumbered their opponents, the patriots were by no means ready to take on the British in a pitched battle, and Gates never intended that they would. Instead of attacking Rawdon's strong position, the American commander marched around the enemy's left in the direction of Hanging Rock. Rawdon responded by hurrying his own army toward Camden and urgently ordering all British and loyalist garrisons in the vicinity to concentrate in that town. Of more importance, the British officer notified Cornwallis of the danger that Gates's army presented to upstate South Carolina, and the latter hurried northward with reinforcements to assume com-

15. Williams, "Narrative," p. 488; Sumter to Gates, Aug. 15, 1780, cited in Banastre Tarleton, *A History of the Campaigns of 1781, in the Southern Province of North America* (London: T. Cadell, 1787), pp. 147–48; hereafter cited as Tarleton, *Southern Campaign*.

16. Rutherford to Gates, July 30, 1780, *State Records*, 14:514–15; Caswell to Gates, Aug. 4, 1780, Gates Papers, Box 14, NYHS.

mand at Camden.[17] Although Gates was not yet aware of the fact, at the moment Cornwallis superseded Rawdon on August 13, the Americans had lost the desperate race to endanger Camden before the British could collect forces there. Continuing his march, Gates swung his army southward from Hanging Rock and on August 14 arrived at Rugeley's Mill, only thirteen miles from the increasingly powerful position of the enemy.

With almost seven thousand men now under his immediate or indirect command, General Gates put into operation at this moment a twofold strategy that had been crystallizing in his mind perhaps since he had taken command of the Southern Department in July. First, he would put great pressure upon enemy supply lines from Charleston to Camden and, he hoped, force the British to abandon Camden without a fight. Already Gates had begun a potential pincer movement against Rawdon by sending Sumter far to the west of Camden while Marion marched to the east. If these two forces could swing behind the British troops at Camden, Rawdon would be isolated from the rest of the royal army and be obliged to retreat. On August 12 Sumter was encouraging Gates to attempt precisely this kind of maneuver, but the American commander needed no encouragement.[18] It was because of this plan that General Gates made the otherwise curious decision on August 15 to send from his own force, which lay almost face to face with the enemy, a contingent of four hundred troops (one-fourth of them Continentals) to march to Sumter's assistance. Since neither man knew at this time that Cornwallis had reached Camden with reinforcements and had no intention of withdrawing peacefully, they believed that their scheme would succeed.

The second part of Gates's plan dovetailed with the first. It called for him to post his own troops only a few thousand feet from the British outer works at Camden in a well-protected, defensive site on Granny Creek, similar to the one he had employed at Saratoga in 1777. Many years later Thomas Pinckney, an aide to Gates during the campaign, maintained that the American commander was attempting to carry out this movement, and Gates himself in a letter to Congress after the battle of Camden wrote that his intention just

17. *Correspondence of Charles, First Marquis Cornwallis*, ed. Charles Ross (3 vols.; London: John Murray, 1859), I, 54–55; Franklin and Mary Wickwire, *Cornwallis: The American Adventure* (Boston: Houghton Mifflin, 1970), p. 157.
18. Sumter to Gates, Aug. 12, 1780, *State Records*, XIV, 553–54.

prior to the action was "to take Post in a very advantageous Situation, with a Deep Creek in Front seven miles from Camden."[19] It was asserted by another source that the site Gates intended to occupy had been chosen by Colonel Christian Senff, an engineer whom the general had sent to reconnoiter for a defensive position.[20] Probably because he needed to reach this place quickly, Gates decided on August 15 to put his army in motion during the coming darkness, even though he realized that such a plan was fraught with risk.

The twofold strategy outlined by Gates makes sense and helps to explain a number of his otherwise unorthodox activities during the campaign. In light of this plan his neglect of cavalry is more understandable, for horsemen would be of no particular use to him behind breastworks. His almost brutal punishment of the patriot army in its march from Coxe's Mill does not seem so harsh if one believes that he intended no battle upon reaching South Carolina and expected only that his troops would rest and recuperate in a fortified position. His weakening of the army on August 15 appears not nearly so absurd as his critics made it seem after the fact if he believed Sumter needed the four hundred detached soldiers more than he did. Finally, his reasons for launching his undisciplined army upon a night march toward Camden can be understood if one considers the turmoil into which the British at that post would have been thrown by the sudden appearance of nearby enemy breastworks.

For all that can be said in defense of Gates's plan, however, it contained a fatal flaw, one which the American commander should not have overlooked under any circumstances. Early in the war, when discussing the basic premises he felt should guide a military leader in making decisions, Gates had declared, "It is a Rule with me, to conclude the Enemy will allways attempt to do that, which is most for their Interests."[21] In mid-August of 1780 the general ignored his own sound observation. Not only was he circumscribing his flexibility by placing reliance wholly upon one plan, but he was doing so on the assumption that his opponent would act exactly as expected, even

19. Thomas Pinckney to William Johnson, July 27, 1822, *Magazine of American History*, V (Dec., 1880), 524–26; Gates to Congress, Aug. 28, 1780, PCC, 154, Vol. 2, 234–37.

20. Alexander Garden, *Anecdotes of the Revolutionary War in America* (Charleston: A. E. Miller, 1822), p. 346.

21. Gates to John Adams, Apr. 23, 1776, Bernhard Knollenberg, "Correspondence of John Adams and Horatio Gates," *Proceedings of the Massachusetts Historical Society*, LXVII (1945), 140–41.

though such action would not be in the best interests of the British army. Certainly Cornwallis perceived, upon hearing of Gates's approach toward Camden with an army, that he must not allow himself to be pushed back into South Carolina and lose his hard-earned gains of the previous three months. It ought to have been just as obvious to the American commander that control of Camden and the surrounding countryside must be decided by a decisive battlefield confrontation. For the Americans to fritter away their energy with other strategies, while the British concentrated upon this primary task, was to invite disaster.

Even as late as August 15 Gates might have retrieved the American position by shrewd tactical judgments. But within the next twenty-four hours he committed other military blunders that left him in an almost impossible position. Putting his army in motion toward Granny Creek at ten o'clock on the night of August 15, Gates groped blindly forward with unseemly optimism against a powerful enemy force. Before marching he detached his baggage wagons and sent them toward the Waxhaw settlements, about thirty miles north of Camden. By sheer coincidence Cornwallis set his army in motion northward at nearly the same time. About midnight, much to the surprise of both commanders, the two armies blundered into each other at Saunders Creek, halfway between Camden and Rugeley's Mill. After a brief but sharp encounter, both sides drew back to await daylight. Gates was now concerned to learn that the enemy before him had been reinforced quite recently and was under the orders of Cornwallis. He quickly called a council of war to determine a course of action, but it soon became apparent that no alternative the patriots might choose would be satisfactory. Discussing the feasibility of a retreat, the council decided that the patriot army would invite disaster if it turned its back upon the enemy; for in any case Cornwallis would surely harass the Americans into eventual action. Finally General Stevens glumly observed that it was "too late now to do any thing but fight"; at least, he said, the patriots occupied ground that seemed favorable for a battle. With these observations Gates reluctantly concurred and decided to fight where he was. All things considered, he seemed to have no other choice in his present uncomfortable situation.[22]

On the morning of August 16 the opposing armies marched into

22. Williams, "Narrative," pp. 494–95.

their positions. The Americans quickly found themselves better disposed than their enemies, but the British possessed other advantages.
Cornwallis had under his command about 2,239 men (of whom only
1,900 were effectives) as compared to Gates's 3,100 under his immediate command; hence the patriots had a definite numerical prepon-
derance. However, the well-supplied army of Cornwallis was made
up of more than two-thirds regulars and also included Tarleton's
dreaded Tory Legion, while Gates's force was almost two-thirds
militia, untrained, unrested, unfed, unhealthy, and low in morale.
The Delaware and Maryland Continentals presented a somewhat better picture, but they were severely handicapped by the size of Cornwallis's regular force. Because of their advantage in numbers, the
Americans were favored by the terrain they occupied, for on the
flanks of both armies were impenetrable swamps and behind the
British ran Saunders Creek. If Gates could make use of his larger
army to drive Cornwallis against these natural barriers, he might
yet have the better of an unhappy situation. But to exploit his advantages, he must take the offensive in battle—an unpropitious prospect with so few trained regulars. It must have crossed Gates's mind
at some time during the hours before battle that he now could make
good use of Sumter's thirty-six hundred men, who because of his
own aborted plans were idly whiling away their time on the far-
removed banks of the Catawba River.

Having already made numerous miscalculations since joining the
southern army, Gates was about to make another that was perhaps
more critical than all the others combined. As the American commander observed the maneuvers of Cornwallis on the morning of battle, he noticed that the right side of the British line was to be composed of the Twenty-third and Thirty-third Regiments and a strong
force of loyalists called the Volunteers of Ireland. The enemy left,
on the other hand, was to be manned by inferior militia forces that
were no better trained or disciplined than Gates's own citizen soldiers. In reserve Cornwallis was placing part of the Seventy-first
Regiment and the Tory Legion under Tarleton. Viewing these arrangements (and remembering that the patriots probably would
have to charge the enemy line), Gates ought to have disposed his
soldiers to take advantage of British weaknesses. The Delaware and
Maryland Continentals needed to be placed opposite the Twenty-
third and Thirty-third Regiments and patriot militia opposite the

weak Loyalist units. But in forming his line Gates reversed this order, posting the Continentals on the right wing and the inexperienced militia on the left. Hence the general's poorest troops were left facing the strongest ones of Lord Cornwallis. In final dispositions, Gates planted six cannons along the front lines and sent some Maryland Continentals to the rear as a reserve force.[23]

As a result of the American commander's latest decisions, the patriot army was in imminent peril at the opening of battle. Cornwallis quickly took advantage of his opportunity by stealing a march upon his foe and ordering his regulars to charge the American left. Gates, sitting astride his horse immediately to the rear of his center, noted this British activity but mistook it for some slight troop rearrangements. To benefit from what appeared to be a tactical blunder by his opponent, he ordered General Stevens to advance with the Virginia militia. The American commander had made egregious errors in assuming that Cornwallis would adjust his line in the face of an enemy upon the battlefield or that militia could move forward advantageously against enemy veterans under even the most ideal conditions. As the Virginia troops began their ragged charge they were surprised to discover that the British regulars, instead of presenting a confused mass, were attacking them with precision, firing and shouting as they came on. Thrown into utter panic, the Virginia militia fled through the American lines and also terrified the North Carolinians into confused flight. As the American left disintegrated, Cornwallis ordered Tarleton's cavalry to plunge into the melee and strike the flank of the Maryland Continentals.[24]

Gates was swept from the field by the retreat of the militia, struggling vainly to restore order as he went. Three times he endeavored to rally the militia, each time in vain. Compounding his distress, some of the Tory Legionnaires were hot upon his heels attempting to capture him. Finally the citizen soldiers simply disappeared into the woods, and Gates, alone except for a few aides, found himself about three miles from the battlefield. He gave some thought to returning

23. Ibid., pp. 495–97; General Edward Stevens to Jefferson, Aug. 20, 1780, and Jefferson to Washington, enclosing "A Narrative of the late disaster in South Carolina . . . ," Sept. 3, 1780, Thomas Jefferson, *Papers of Thomas Jefferson*, ed. Julian P. Boyd et al. (17 vols. to date; Princeton, N.J.: Princeton University Press, 1950–), III, 558–59, 593–97.

24. Evidence upon the battle of Camden is taken from the sources listed above, plus Gates to Congress, Aug. 28, 1780, PCC, 154, Vol. 2, 234–37.

to de Kalb's embattled position, but two factors weighed against such a decision. First, if he turned south he might be captured by one of the enemy cavalry patrols which were striving to ensnare him. Second, there seemed no possibility that the Continentals could prevail against the entire British army, and the patriot forces would have to be reorganized somewhere to the north. Hence Gates decided to "retire towards Charlotte," as he told Congress later, and there attempt to rebuild the shattered American army.[25]

When he reached Charlotte on the night of August 16, Gates began to receive bad news concerning the fate of his command. As he had earlier feared, the Continentals who remained in battle were doomed to defeat; but for about an hour after he departed they had made a valiant stand against overwhelming odds. De Kalb, as senior officer upon the field, had thrown the Maryland reserves into the line on the left and had even ordered one bayonet charge. However, the American line could not long withstand the onslaught of Lord Cornwallis's combined forces, and it finally disintegrated. In the struggle General de Kalb went down with a fatal bullet wound and was captured by the enemy before he died. As the patriots fled from the battlefield, they were harassed for many miles by Tarleton's cavalrymen. Even the baggage wagons that Gates had detached from his army just before the engagement fell prey to the Tory Legion. Moreover, American strength and morale suffered another blow two days after the royal army's victory at Camden when Sumter's considerable body of troops was taken unaware by a much smaller force under Tarleton and dispersed to all points of the compass with a loss of more than four hundred killed and captured.[26] When statistics on American casualties began to reach Gates, he was dismayed, for aside from Sumter's losses, his army had suffered at least six hundred killed, captured, or wounded as compared to about three hundred for the British. With a fifth of his army completely destroyed and the rest dispersed through miles of countryside, the American commander's prospects in the days following the debacle at Camden seemingly could have been no gloomier.

General Gates realized immediately that his new post at Charlotte

25. "Plan of Camden by Colonel Senff," Friedrich Wilhelm, Baron von Steuben Papers, New-York Historical Society, New York City; Gates to Congress, Aug. 28, 1780, PCC, 154, Vol. 2, 234–37.
26. Tarleton, *Southern Campaign*, pp. 111–14.

was too near the victorious British army for use in reorganizing the decimated patriot forces. Therefore he continued on to Hillsborough and arrived on August 19, after riding 180 miles since leaving half his army engaged upon the battlefield at Camden. His critics now had a field day with his discomfiture, mocking his "ineptitude" and making sarcastic remarks about his ride. Commented Philip Schuyler to Alexander Hamilton in September, "I am informed Gates is to have the thanks of the Senate for not despairing of the Commonwealth. . . . He is to have a potent army and to drive Cornwallis . . . into the Sea with more rapidity than he flew to Hillsborough."[27] Despite Schuyler's observation, Gates could hardly be faulted in terms of immediate military necessity for fleeing from the battlefield. By returning to Camden, he would not have altered the military situation, for de Kalb and the Continentals were doomed to defeat, and he definitely would have been liable to capture by the Tory Legion. Perhaps it would have been noble of him to expose himself to physical danger at this time, but it would have served little purpose militarily. Of more overriding concern to him, as he wrote Washington on August 20, was to put his army back together, and that task, he felt, could only be accomplished in the safety of a position far removed from Cornwallis's forces, behind the physical barriers of North Carolina's many rivers.[28] For Gates time was crucial, because he fully expected that the British would drive immediately northward from Camden. He must reach Hillsborough with the utmost expedition, regardless of how his precipitious ride might appear to his opponents. Hence, while his hasty departure from Camden did not cover him with a mantle of glory, still the general's enemies might have heeded the example of Colonel Williams when discussing the outcome of battle. Said Williams to Alexander Hamilton on August 30, "I think it ungenerous to oppress dejected Spirits in a premature Censure."[29]

However, in criticizing Gates's use of citizen soldiers against British regulars, the general's enemies had valid arguments. Why he aligned untrained militia to oppose combat veterans remains even to this day a seemingly impenetrable mystery, and no possible explanation for his decision is satisfactory. Some writers have suggested that by 1780 he had come to have too high a regard for militia because of

27. Hamilton, *Papers of Hamilton*, II, 385–87.
28. Gates Papers, Box 19, NYHS.
29. Hamilton, *Papers of Hamilton*, II, 385–87.

his positive experiences with such troops at Saratoga. Others place the blame for his mishandling of militia at Camden upon his subordinate officers, who supposedly were not giving him the forcible advice he received in earlier campaigns. Still others suggest that political pressure from southerners for a hasty battlefield decision against the enemy may have stampeded him into a misuse of his forces. None of these explanations are adequate, for they do not conform to evidence regarding either Gates's past military record or his strategy for dealing with the British in South Carolina. At Saratoga he never overestimated the capabilities of the New England militia, and he accepted from his field commanders only those suggestions that supported his own generally sound opinions. And while he doubtless was under strong pressure from civilian and military leaders in the South to achieve a quick victory, he could have secured that goal by no better remedy than making wise use of his Continental regulars. Gates himself seemingly never wrote a word, either of justification or self-criticism, regarding his curious decision to make such prominent use of militia at the battle of Camden.

For a time after the rout of American forces by Cornwallis's army, General Gates suffered tremendously from fears of enemy intentions. How, the American commandant asked himself, could the patriots counter even the weakest thrust from the enemy into North Carolina when the defending force simply had ceased to exist? Fortunately, he was not required to answer this question. After the British army's decisive strokes of August 16 and 18 Cornwallis paused to take stock of his situation and, despite his renown as an unremitting fighter, rested his army for three weeks by the placid waters of Waxhaw Creek. As he wrote Sir Henry Clinton in September, sickness among his troops, the almost unbearable heat of a summer in South Carolina, and partisan warfare against his lines of supply temporarily had halted the progress of the royal army. Hoping soon to recommence his advance against the patriots, however, he requested that Clinton give him assistance by mounting a diversionary expedition in the Chesapeake region of Virginia.[30]

The British general was not exaggerating his difficulties, because even after accounting for the fantastic battle losses of the Americans

30. Lord Cornwallis to Sir Henry Clinton, Sept. 19, 1780, *State Records*, XIV, 278–82; Piers Mackesy, *The War for America, 1775–1783* (Cambridge, Mass.: Harvard Univ. Press, 1965), p. 345.

he realized that his own were severe and irreplacable. By all odds the worst problem he now faced was the general uprising of patriot irregulars that Gates's advance had created in South Carolina, against which he could do little. Partisan warfare between opposing civilian guerrillas raged about him for miles, hindering loyalists from augmenting his army and endangering his lines of communication. General Gates, of course, was pleased with this turn of events, because the activities of patriot irregulars such as Sumter and Marion were buying time for the American army. Sumter's corps especially gave the American commander pride, for although scattered by the Tory Legion on August 18 it had been restored within a few days to a total strength of one thousand men. To General Washington near the end of August Gates cogently observed that Cornwallis would be constrained from marching northward while this force hovered upon his left flank.[31]

Taking advantage of his slight reprieve, General Gates worked with the utmost expedition to reorganize his main army. The retreating patriots, suffering from "care, anxiety, rain, poverty, hurry, confusion, humiliation, and dejection," to use Colonel Williams's words, were drifting into camp at Hillsborough. During their withdrawal from Camden Gates had given them all the support he could, but, as he admitted, the assistance was slight.[32] On September 3 he wrote Washington a long letter explaining that his troops had been dispersed across North Carolina, in order both to cover the country and to expedite the collection of supplies (North Carolina officials still had made no effort to establish magazines of food for the army). Virginia and North Carolina militia, drafted since Camden and numbering about thirty-three hundred men, were posed at Salisbury to guard strategic Yadkin River fords. Another militia force under the command of General Stevens lay quietly at Guilford Court House, and Colonel White's cavalry nursed its strength on the Cape Fear River at Cross Creek. The Continental regulars, of whom only eight hundred remained, were consolidated into one regiment at Hillsborough and placed under orders of Colonel Williams. All the other Maryland officers were ordered home by Congress to recruit new

31. Higginbotham, *War of American Independence*, pp. 360–63; Mackesy, *War for America*, pp. 343–44; Gates to Washington, Aug. 30, 1780, Gates Papers, Box 19, NYHS.

32. Williams, "Narrative," p. 501; Gates to Caswell, Aug. 22, 1780, Gates Papers, Box 19, NYHS.

soldiers. Another body of men Gates had been promised by Governor Jefferson and had expected to arrive shortly was a regiment of Virginia Continentals led by Peter Muhlenberg. In addition to these troops, the Americans had in the field the many bands of irregulars already mentioned.[33]

With his army continuing to suffer from an almost total lack of equipment or food stores, Gates spent much time during September and October trying to alleviate these problems by writing letters to civilians. From officials in Virginia, North Carolina, and Philadelphia he demanded to know how he was expected to keep an army in the field, fend off the enemy, and prepare for the coming winter without assistance from them. He never received satisfactory answers to any of his queries, and soon he was utterly disgusted with most of the men upon whom he must depend for support. His only cause for optimism during these dark days was the unfailing fortitude of his army, which, despite its many wants, remained loyal to its officers and refused to heed the advice of a very few to mutiny. Even the American officers were amazed at the cheerful manner of the troops, since there seemed little for them to be happy about.[34] It must have been more difficult for the British to fathom the reasons for the high morale among Gates's soldiers.

Another problem with which General Gates had to contend during these months was attacks upon his authority by a few of his officers and by some civilians within the government of North Carolina. Offending subordinates he either removed from their commands or placed in less responsible positions, but for the remainder of the campaign he continued to receive intimations of hostility from a minority of his officers.[35] Trouble came from the government of North Carolina in the form of a civilian Board of War, organized within the legislature to direct operations of the state's citizen soldiers. Seemingly the board believed that it exercised absolute authority within this sphere, for it even went so far as to countermand certain orders of Gates respecting the North Carolina militia. Not until he threatened arrest of any officer who obeyed the Board of War instead of himself did Gates reestablish his authority over civilians

33. Gates to Washington, Sept. 3, 1780, Gates Papers, Box 19, NYHS.
34. Williams, "Narrative," p. 506.
35. Thomas Rodney to Caesar Rodney, Oct. 7, 1780, Rodney Collection, Historical Society of Del., Wilmington.

who would infringe upon his prerogatives. Regarding the merits of this body of men, Gates's assessment was probably the same as that of Major John Mazaret, who asserted to the commander, "It's my Opinion they be caled the useless bord."[36]

In addition to all his other difficulties after Camden, Gates was worried about the intentions of Congress toward his position as commander of the Southern Department. On August 31 Congress received a letter that Gates had written eleven days earlier, outlining the tragedy that had struck the Ameircan army in South Carolina. The legislators were horrified at this bad news, but they would not act immediately in regard to the general's tenure in the South; on September 3 John Armstrong, Jr., wrote Gates that Congress had no immediate plan to censure him. Yet Congress was not immune from public opinion, and when a number of southerners began to demand that Gates be removed from his command, the legislators were forced to take heed of criticism directed against the general. The North Carolina legislature even went so far as to send a delegate to Congress with instructions to lobby against Gates. Governor Nash did his part by writing letters to friends in Philadelphia, and Congressman John Mathews of South Carolina finally raised the issue upon the floor. Bowing to these pressures, Congress voted on October 5 to remove Gates from command and to order a court of inquiry into his conduct at Camden.[37] By late October the American commandant had received official notification from President Samuel Huntington that he was soon to be replaced by Nathanael Greene.[38]

Working desperately against overwhelming odds, General Gates tried to make the best of the limited time that remained to him to restore his military reputation. However, his options were few and the pressures upon him were enormous. By early September Cornwallis seemed prepared to strike Charlotte, and Gates was being urged from all sides to hasten all his forces in that direction. "Certain persons here," he wrote Jefferson on September 9, "have been extreamly Anxious that I should remove the whole Force, and take post with them immediately in Mecklinbourg, and Roan Countys,

36. Board of War to Gates, Oct. 30, 1780, and Gates to Board of War, Oct. 30, 1780, Horatio Gates Papers, N.C. State Archives, Raleigh; Mazaret to Gates, Nov. 7, 1780, *State Records*, XIV, 724.

37. John Armstrong, Jr., to Gates, Sept. 3, 1780, *State Records*, XIV, 587–89; *Journals of the Continental Congress*, XVIII, 906.

38. President Huntington to Gates, Oct. 15, 1780, *State Records*, XIV, 699.

on the Western Border of this State." Two weeks later Congressman George Measom was writing Gates that it was the mood of the central government that the Southern army should "Push on again without delay."[39] But the American commander had no intention of budging from his present position until conditions within his command improved. He remembered only too well the dearth of support that he had received from civilians a few weeks before during his advance toward Camden, and he was not about to advance against the enemy until his army had been supplied with the necessities of war, not the least of which was a certain food supply. To Jefferson he wrote on September 20, "I will not risque a Second Defeat, by marching through Famine, and encountering every distress . . . Slow, and I hope sure, will be our next attempt."[40] Even after Cornwallis had put his army in motion and seemed to be threatening all of western North Carolina, Gates would not change his plans. In early October he informed Congress that his only intention, "until I am properly reinforced," was to harass and delay the enemy by using some light infantry and a few militia units upon the Yadkin River. "With these," he said, "I hope to retard, and confine Lord Cornwallis's Army, until I am in Strength to play a different Game." "The Enemy," he wrote Smallwood on October 23, "are Sly and Desperate, therefore it is our business to be slow and sure. Cornwallis will be governed by his expectations from Sir H. Clinton, & of these we know nothing."[41]

The strategy upon which Gates now placed his hopes for defeating Cornwallis and recovering the American position in the South contained one essential element: the arrival of a French fleet upon the coast of South Carolina. As early as August 9 he had been informed by President Huntington that a joint effort between the French navy and the American Southern Army was planned to expel the enemy from Charleston. If by some miracle America's Bourbon allies were to arrive in southern waters during September or October, Gates believed that his major problems would be over. Hence he hoped, al-

39. Gates to Jefferson, Sept. 9, 1780, Jefferson, *Papers of Jefferson*, III, 620–21; Measom to Gates, Sept. 21, 1780, *State Records*, XIV, 634–35. See Richard Hawley to Gates, Sept. 22, 1780, Gates Papers, Box 18, NYHS.

40. Gates Papers, Box 19, NYHS.

41. Gates to Congress, Oct. 5, 1780, PCC, 154, Vol. 2, 267–68; Gates to Smallwood, Oct. 23, 1780, "Copy Book of Major Gen. Gates," No. 134, New York Public Library.

most beyond hope, that the French navy would appear. On September 5 he informed Congress that a fleet of "our High Allies" had arrived. His intelligence proved faulty. Twelve days later, he wrote Sumter, "I hourly expect the arrival of a large fleet of our allies upon the coast." The ships did not materialize. To Jefferson he mused on October 3, "This is a Bon Momment, for a Squadron of our Allies, to make their Appearance at Chas. Town. In this Case, I think it would be easy to carry the place, before the Earl could arrive to save it. But without a naval Armament, nothing can be done here." No squadron appeared. Finally, in the middle of October Gates ordered Colonel Senff to the coast, with instructions to notify him immediately if the French should come to his assistance. But he now despaired of that possibility. At best, his hope for support from a French fleet had been only a fond dream and hardly to be expected as a solution to his problems.[42]

While Gates awaited the appearance of the Bourbon navy, events in western North Carolina were greatly improving the American stance in the Southern Department. Lord Cornwallis led an army of one thousand men out of his encampment at Waxhaw Creek and two weeks later, on September 21, crushed a token resistance by patriot militia and occupied Charlotte. It now seemed to Gates that the Yadkin River fords at Salisbury were threatened, and that the British army might be approaching Hillsborough within a week. To delay this inauspicious prospect, he reinforced the main body of militia at the Yadkin with an infantry unit commanded by newly commissioned Brigadier General Daniel Morgan, who had just arrived upon the scene.[43] Had Gates been aware of the problems which Cornwallis was encountering, his anxiety would have been considerably reduced. The British commander, who had been led to believe that hordes of loyalists would join him in Charlotte, was greatly disappointed with his reception in the town. "The number of our friends in [this] province," he grumbled to Lord George Germain, "are not so great as had been represented, and their friendship is only passive. . . ."[44]

42. President Huntington to Gates, Aug. 9, 1780, Gates Papers, Box 14, NYHS; Gates to Congress, Sept. 5, 1780, PCC, 154, Vol. 2, 243–44; Gates to Sumter, Sept. 17, 1780, State Records, XIV, 772; Gates to Jefferson, Oct. 3, 1780, Jefferson, Papers of Jefferson, IV, 5–6; Gates to Senff, Oct. 13, 1780, Alderman Library, University of Va., Charlottesville.

43. Gates to Jefferson Oct. 3, 1780, Jefferson, Papers of Jefferson, IV, 5–6.

44. Diary of the American Revolution, ed. Frank Moore . . . (2 vols.; New York: Scribner, 1860), II, 352; Mackesy, War for America, pp. 252–54, 341–45.

Without support from loyalists, his small army could not achieve much in the coming weeks.

The troubles of Cornwallis were only beginning, for events on both flanks of his main position soon would force him to revise all plans for an offensive during the present campaign. Major Patrick Ferguson, whom Cornwallis had ordered to march with a detachment of loyalist militia (eleven hundred strong) through the Carolina backwoods and protect the left flank of the main British army, fell into great difficulties while executing his orders. With alacrity about fourteen hundred American frontiersmen collected at the Holston River settlements under Colonel William Campbell and other patriot leaders to oppose Ferguson's contingent. Soon Ferguson realized his peril and attempted to retreat to Ninety-Six, but his foes compelled him to take a defensive position at Kings Mountain. On October 7 he was attacked and his force was annihilated.[45] Cornwallis could do nothing to avert this debacle, for another problem had arisen on his eastern flank. Francis Marion, who was raiding against loyalists with great success upon the Peedee River, wrote Gates on October 4 that his "little Excursions" had frightened the Tories out of their wits. Marion expressed his intention of marching farther into South Carolina and declared, "If I could raise one hundred men [he had only sixty], I Shou'd Certainly pay a Visit to Georgetown." This possibility frightened Cornwallis, for the British commander dared not lose Georgetown and expose his supply lines even more than they already were. Hence on October 7 he was compelled by "This damned Geo. Town Business" to send the Sixty-third Regiment, commanded by Major James Wemyss and originally intended for Ferguson's relief, to counter the threat from Marion. Nothing came of Wemyss's mission, however, for he and his regiment had to be recalled when news of Ferguson's defeat reached British headquarters.[46]

It was now apparent to Lord Cornwallis that for the moment he could no longer pursue an invasion of North Carolina. His only alternatives seemed to be a withdrawal from Charlotte and limited raids against patriot irregulars who continued to harass his supply lines in South Carolina. On October 12 he retired with his army from

45. General William Davidson to General Jethro Sumner, Oct. 10, 1780, *State Records*, XIV, 685. See John Richard Alden, *The South in the Revolution, 1763–1789* (Baton Rouge: La. State Univ. Press, 1957), pp. 249–50.

46. Information from a packet of enemy letters captured by Davidson's men, sent to Gates by Sumner on Oct. 9, 1780, *State Records*, XIV, 679–80.

North Carolina and without opposition from the Americans marched to Winnsborough, a town to the west of Camden. There he posted his troops and remained for the rest of the year. At the same time he ordered Tarleton to continue his molestation of American guerrillas in the field. But this overzealous cavalry officer, who seemed to make little distinction between friend and foe, soon had acquired a reputation for attacking with equal fervor both loyalists and patriots. Noting the effect of Tarleton's activities upon the morale of sympathizers to the crown, Marion commented happily, "He spares neither Whig nor Tory."[47]

General Gates, after experiencing almost two months of reverses and ill tidings, was pleased with the American victories at Kings Mountain and the withdrawal of Wemyss from the South Carolina low country. On October 12 he informed Governor Jefferson that as soon as his army received an expected supply of shoes, he would begin to shift patriot strength toward the Salisbury-Charlotte area. A day later he sent the same information to Congress. However, before he could begin his march from Hillsborough, he learned from Jefferson that an enemy invasion was beginning at Portsmouth. Sir Henry Clinton had responded to Cornwallis's request for a diversion in the Chesapeake by sending to Virginia an army of twenty-five hundred men under the command of Major General Alexander Leslie. But by late October Jefferson was informing Gates that Virginia militia and Peter Muhlenberg's Continentals (who had never reached the Southern Army) could stave off Leslie's forces. Thus on November 6 Gates began moving his center of power toward the west, carrying with him from Hillsborough all stores of clothing, food, and ammunition, plus the cavalry of Colonel Anthony White.[48]

When he reached Salisbury five days later Gates went into a series of councils with the American officers to determine the strength and disposition of his army. In a message to Congress on November 25 he reported his findings. General Morgan, he learned, was encamped with 404 men about ten miles below Charlotte, shadowing the enemy at Winnsborough. Sumter was still in the field with a thousand troops on the west side of the Catawba River. On the other side of the

47. Marion to Gates, Nov. 9, 1780, copy in PCC, 154, Vol. 2, 334.
48. Gates to Jefferson, Oct. 12, Nov. 8, 1780, Gates Papers, Box 19, NYHS; Gates to Congress, Oct. 13, 1780, PCC, 154, Vol. 2, 299–300; Mackesy, *War for America*, p. 352.

state Colonel Marion and an indeterminable number of irregulars retained firm control of the headwaters of the Peedee River. The Continental regiment contained 1,053 soldiers under Colonel Williams, and the militia forces (including North Carolinians already at Salisbury plus the Virginians which Gates had recently ordered to join him) totaled 1,147 men. Added to these numbers was Colonel White's reorganized cavalry unit of two hundred dragoons. Deducting the troops of Sumter and Marion, over whom Gates had no direct control, the American army in mid-November possessed a total strength of 2,804 effectives and presented, according to Tarleton, "a tolerable appearance." With this band of ragged and half-starved troops, Gates marched on November 20 toward Charlotte and a few days later, after choosing a site for winter quarters, set his men to work constructing huts for protection from the elements.[49]

The general was now at the end of his tenure as commander of the Southern Army. Near the end of November he issued his last orders of the campaign, sending General Morgan upon an abortive raid against the Waxhaw settlements in quest of food stores.[50] A few days later, on December 2, Nathanael Greene arrived to supersede Gates, and the latter prepared to depart for Virginia. Despite the resolution of Congress calling for an examination into Gates's performance at Camden, Greene refused to conduct such an investigation; this requisition he felt to be both unfair and unnecessary.[51] So the deposed general was forced into retirement with a cloud of suspicion hanging over his head, one that would linger for almost two years while his congressional opponents allowed him to suffer. Not until August 14, 1782, months after fighting had ceased in America, did Congress rescind its resolution for a hearing and allow Gates to join Washington's army in its encampment at Newburgh.[52] At the end of the Revo-

49. "Return of the Southern Army," Nov. 25, 1780, PCC, 154, Vol. 2, 335; Tarleton, *Southern Campaign*, p. 181.
50. Morgan to Gates, Nov. 27, 1780, Gates Papers, Box 15, NYHS; Tarleton, *Southern Campaign*, p. 182; Don Higginbotham, *Daniel Morgan: Revolutionary Rifleman* (Chapel Hill: Univ. of N.C. Press, 1961), p. 113.
51. Greene to Gates, Dec. 4, 6, 1780, Nathanael Greene Papers, Henry E. Huntington Library, San Marino, Calif.; Gates to Greene, Dec. 4, 1780, Preston Davie Collection, Univ. of N.C. Library, Chapel Hill; Greene to Washington, Dec. 7, 1780, *Correspondence of the American Revolution: Being Letters of Eminent Men to George Washington*, ed. Jared Sparks (4 vols.; Boston: Little, Brown, 1853), III, 165–68; Theodore Thayer, *Nathanael Greene: Strategist of the American Revolution* (New York: Twayne 1960), pp. 291–92.
52. *Journals of the Continental Congress*, XXIII, 466.

lutionary War the general retired into obscurity, lived for twenty-three more years in peace and prosperity, and died at the age of seventy-eight.

It has been said that Gates was warned by Charles Lee upon assuming command of the southern army to "take care lest your Northern laurels turn to Southern willows." Probably this remark was apocryphal, but if Lee actually made it his foreboding about the future of his colleague was not groundless. For General Gates, as commandant of the Southern Department in 1780, plumbed the depths of military disaster at Camden, largely as a result of his own mistakes. Earlier in the campaign, at Hillsborough in late July, he had been too sanguine in assessing the abilities of his weak force and the intentions of his enemies. He simply had assumed too much in believing that the troops of the southern army could accomplish much without securing the supplies that only civilian authorities such as Governors Jefferson and Nash could furnish. Later on he had not taken into account the strategic reality that his plans to secure control of Camden, and consequently the rest of northern South Carolina, would necessitate a decisive victory upon the field of battle rather than a dispersed and piecemeal effort such as he envisioned. Once he had been forced against his better judgment into action at Camden, he made an incomprehensible tactical blunder in placing untrained militia in line of battle against British regulars.

But Gates learned from his mistakes, and while his remaining months of command were anything but a time of unbroken good fortune, conditions within his army definitely improved. Taking advantage of Cornwallis's difficulties, the American general wisely overrode civilian and military opposition to his strategy of defense and worked mightily to restore his shattered army. Hoping against hope that a French fleet would appear off Charleston to assist him in autumn, he patiently awaited at his headquarters the arrival of reinforcements and supplies which had been promised him by Congress and the states of Maryland, Virginia, and North Carolina. Not even the threat of Cornwallis to western North Carolina in September could deter him from his plan. Gambling that militia forces, Morgan's light troops, and South Carolina irregulars could delay the enemy near Charlotte, he was rewarded with news of the engagement at Kings Mountain. Only after Cornwallis was required in mid-October to withdraw from Charlotte, and only after Gates had received some long-awaited provisions from Governor Jefferson, did the American commander transfer his major operations into the western part of the state. Even then, his motley army hardly presented a picture of regularity and military bearing. General Greene, after viewing his new command in December, declared that "the appearance of the troops was wretched beyond description, and their distress, on account of provisions, was little less than their sufferings for want of clothing and other necessities."[53]

Appearances, however, could be deceiving. Of these same soldiers Morgan was to write on January 19, 1781, two days after his brilliant victory at the Cowpens, "Our success must be attributed to the justice of our cause and the bravery of our troops." In March General Greene himself commented about his men's performance at Guilford Court House, "Never did an army labour under so many disadvantages as this; but the fortitude and patience of the officers and soldiery rise superior to all difficulties."[54] It is no detraction from the merits of the brave and loyal soldiers who served in the southern army, or the abilities of Greene and Morgan, to say that General Gates had played a part in preparing the troops for the rigors of 1781. During the previous autumn he had applied his superior administrative and organizational skills to the massive problems that deluged him, had restored the fighting ability of his men, and had held his force together until Greene arrived to take command. Rarely are such inglorious exploits listed among the great achievements of military men, and few have been the historians who give Gates credit for these accomplishments. But with justification the general looked upon them as a victory of sorts, even if they never eradicated the memory of his defeat at Camden.

53. *The Spirit of 'Seventy-Six: The Story of the American Revolution as Told by Participants*, ed. Henry Steele Commager and Richard B. Morris (2 vols.; Indianapolis and New York: The Bobbs-Merrill Company, 1953), II, 1150.
    54. Ibid., II, 1159, 1164.

Arthur Lee, Autonomy, and Diplomacy in the American Revolution

Louis W. Potts *University of Missouri, Kansas City*

The three Commissioners who assembled in Paris in late 1776 were a disparate lot. As representatives of the rebellion in America their upbringings, careers, and perspectives illustrated the diversity of the movement. Noting the divergence of the delegation a loyalist wag, Jonathan Odell, quipped

> When it became the high United States
> To send their envoys to Versailles' proud gates
> Were not three ministers, produced at once?
> Delicious group, fanatic, deist, dunce! [1]

The "fanatic" was Arthur Lee, at thirty-six the youngest of the group. Although Virginia born and bred, he had been educated at Eton, Edinburgh, and the Inns of Court. His prominence as an Anglo-American physician, polemicist, and agent was perhaps undercut by the transatlantic course of his life. Not so for the "deist," seventy-year-old Benjamin Franklin, the foremost cosmopolite in the British realm. He had augmented his conspicuousness as a wealthy provincial printer with European renown from his studies of electricity. Silas Deane, the "dunce" of the trio, was a former Connecticut school-teacher. His penchant for commercial dealings cast him into the orbit of Robert Morris at Philadelphia and led him subsequently to the French Court to seek foreign aid for the American cause and personal profit for himself and his enterprising associates. For the next three years the American diplomatic effort would be hampered, rather

1. From *The Loyalist Poetry*, quoted in Moses C. Tyler, *The Literary History of the American Revolution 1763–1783* (2 vols.; New York: Barnes & Noble, 1941), II, 112.

than advanced, by the lack of unity in the Commission; it was "an unequal troika, each of the three pulling in different directions, marching each to the sound of his own drummer."[2] The chief source of disagreement, according to his colleagues, was the petulant, paranoid Lee.

The impression that the choice of American emissaries to the French Court was wholly rooted in regional bargaining in the Continental Congress is illusory. Although the South differed from the East (or North) in terms of economic interests, social structure, and racial composition, the divisive tendencies of sectionalism, apparent in the debates on the Continental Association during the First Continental Congress and deliberations in the Second over Jefferson's diatribe against slavery, were usually transcended by nationalism in the early stages of the Revolution.[3] Indeed, so pervasive has been the impact of nationalism on American historiography that, according to one analyst, "a modern reader could almost go through the whole corpus of southern writings about the Revolution without finding any evidence that a southern sectional consciousness ever existed or that a sectional war ever took place."[4]

A welter of factors—cultural, economic, ideological, and political —affected the American frame of reference in both the formulation of foreign policy and in the conduct of diplomacy. In the first years of resistance and rebellion the name Lee was synonymous with both Virginia and radical patriotism but was not always in harmony with southern interests. In 1779, for example, when discussion of a peace proposal engrossed Congress, Arthur's older brother and mentor,

2. Cecil B. Currey, "Ben Franklin in France: A Maker of American Diplomacy," in *From Benjamin Franklin to Alfred Thayer Mahan*, Vol. I in *Makers of American Diplomacy*, ed. Frank J. Merli and Theodore A. Wilson (New York: Scribner's, 1974), p. 7.

3. John Richard Alden, *The First South* (Baton Rouge: La. State Univ. Press, 1961), pp. 4–7, 14, 22, 33; Alden, *The South in the Revolution 1763–1789*, Vol. III in *A History of the South*, ed. Wendell C. Stephenson and E. Merton Coulter (Baton Rouge: La. State Univ. Press, 1957), pp. 208–11; Marc Egnal and Joseph A. Ernst, "An Economic Interpretation of the American Revolution," *William and Mary Quarterly*, 3rd series, XXIX (Jan. 1972), 12 n.

4. Charles G. Sellers, "The American Revolution: Southern Founders of a National Tradition," in *Writing Southern History: Essays in Historiography in Honor of Fletcher Green*, ed. Arthur S. Link and Rembert W. Patrick (Baton Rouge: La. State Univ. Press, 1965), p. 59. That the idea of the South might be more subjective than objective is the thesis of *Myth and Southern History*, ed. Patrick Gerster and Nicholas Cords (Chicago: Rand McNally College Publishing, 1974).

Richard Henry Lee, evinced his personal and persistent radicalism by allying himself with kindred spirits from New England and voting against the desires of southerners.[5] Lees—Richard Henry in Congress and Arthur in Europe—joined the Adamses in endorsing the virtue-conscious constellation of values subsequently labeled the puritan ethic.[6] Such individuality proved costly. In the later years of the war the Lees were at the periphery rather than the center of power in America.

Selection of the Commission in 1776 illustrated the abilities of rival factions within the political schemata of Congress. Silas Deane, failing reelection by Connecticut, had attached himself to the fortunes of Robert Morris, the Pennsylvania merchant prince and early conservative leader in Congress. Morris's position on the Committee of Correspondence, the largely autonomous body which formulated and executed foreign policy for Congress, led to Deane's appointment as an emissary.[7] In March 1776 he had been dispatched to France on a dual mission. In a public capacity he was to solicit arms, aid, and a commercial pact with France for the rebellious Americans. In a private role he was operating on commission from Morris, in quest for goods to funnel into speculative trade with the Indians.[8] Benjamin Franklin, a member of the Committee of Correspondence, was the

5. Herbert James Henderson, *Party Politics in the Continental Congress* (New York: McGraw-Hill, 1974), pp. 46, 72, 103, 165, 168.

6. This convoluted credo "called for diligence in a productive calling, beneficial both to society and to the individual. It encouraged frugality and frowned on extravagence. It viewed the merchant with suspicion and speculation with horror. It distrusted prosperity and gathered strength from adversity. It prevailed widely among Americans of different times and places, but those who urged it most vigorously always believed it to be on the point of expiring and in need of renewal." Edmund S. Morgan, "The Puritan Ethic and the American Revolution," *William and Mary Quarterly*, 3rd series, XXIV (Jan. 1967), 7.

7. Edmund C. Burnett, *The Continental Congress* (New York: Norton, 1964), p. 118, explains, "As at first constituted, the committee consisted of Benjamin Harrison, Benjamin Franklin, Thomas Jefferson, John Dickinson, John Jay; but two months later (January 30, 1776) Robert Morris was added. Called at first the Committee of Correspondence, the committee itself soon added the word 'secret,' and as the Committee of Secret Correspondence it was hereafter designated until, on April 17, 1777, Congress resolved that 'for the future it shall be styled the Committee for Foreign Afairs.' Such was the beginning of what is now known as the Department of State." See also George C. Wood, *Congressional Control of Foreign Relations During the American Revolution 1774–1789* (Allentown, Pa.: H. R. Haas & Co., 1919), pp. 42–48.

8. Silas Deane to Elizabeth Deane, March 1776, *The Deane Papers: Correspondence Between Silas Deane, His Brothers and their Business and Political Associates, 1771–1795*, Connecticut Historical Society *Collections* (2 vols.; Hartford, 1870, 1930), II, 360–64.

most experienced of Americans in the ways and byways of European negotiations. In September, when Congress decided to create a polygonal Commission to treat with the French, he was not unwilling to return to Europe.[9]

The original nominee as third member of the negotiating team had been Thomas Jefferson. However, when the young Virginian refused the appointment in order to remain close to his own affairs, both domestic and political, Arthur Lee was selected. This choice may be credited to the Adams-Lee axis in Congress, an affiliation of radicals which had been spawned in Arthur Lee's transatlantic correspondence before hostilities erupted.[10] Also a consideration was the fact that Arthur was already in Britain as an agent for Congress. The *Journals* of the Congress, however, give no clues as to the extent and nature of debate over Lee's selection. Morris, writing on behalf of the Secret Committee to inform him of his appointment, politely observed that the Congress "flatter ourselves from assurances of your friends here, that you will cheerfully undertake the important business and that our country will greatly benefit from those abilities and that detachment you have already manifested" as a secret agent.[11]

Arthur Lee coveted a conspicuous role in the diplomacy of the American War for Independence. His career previous to the appointment seemingly primed him for such a task. Yet, paradoxically, development of his character tended to undermine this ambition. Analysis of his contributions to the diplomacy of the American Revolution indicates three paradoxes. Although he was a patriot, and thus technically a victor in the war, he found himself feeling that his side had

9. For a discussion of the distinction between foreign aid and foreign alliances, see Richard B. Morris, "The Diplomats and the Myth-makers," in *The American Revolution Reconsidered* (New York: Harper & Row, 1967), pp. 92–126.

10. Oliver Perry Chitwood, *Richard Henry Lee: Statesman of the Revolution* (Morgantown: W. Va. Univ. Library, 1967), 104–5; Samuel Adams to Richard Henry Lee, July 15, 1776, *The Writings of Samuel Adams*, ed. Harry A. Cushing (4 vols.; New York: G. P. Putnam's Sons, 1904–8), III, 298; Henderson, *Party Politics*, pp. 12–18. Commenting on the quality of this correspondence, Bernard Bailyn, *The Ordeal of Thomas Hutchinson* (Boston: Belknap Press of Harvard Univ. Press, 1973), p. 193, claims Arthur Lee's letter to Samuel Adams of April 10, 1771, was "perhaps the most paranoid letter in the entire literature of the American Revolution."

11. *Journals of the Continental Congress*, ed. Worthington C. Ford (34 vols.; Washington, D.C.: Government Printing Office, 1904–37), VI, 879; Robert Morris to Arthur Lee and Benjamin Franklin, Oct. 23, 1776, *The Lee Family Papers*, ed. Paul R. Hoffman and John L. Molyneaux (Charlottesville, Va.: Microfilm Publications—Univ. of Va. Library, 1966), microfilm edition, reel II, frame 0704.

miscarried. Although he strove zealously for a successful foreign policy, he was destined to fail as a diplomat. Although a Virginian, he found his approach and his outlook on foreign affairs continually attacked by southerners throughout the war.

Malignant discord and controversy continuously disrupted Lee's life. Two prevalent characteristics of Arthur's personality could be traced to his early childhood experiences: his personal sense of independence or autonomy and his distrust of his fellow men. These quirks combined with Lee family traits: the ambition of his father, Thomas, who had amassed thirty thousand acres in the Northern Neck of Virginia; the haughty, aristocratic mien of his mother, Hannah Ludwell Lee; and the propensity of his siblings to gravitate to the arena of political conflict. The prestige and prominence gained by Arthur and his five older brothers was later limned in patriotic hues by John Adams: "that band of brothers intrepid and unchangeable, who like the Greeks at Thermopylae, stood in the gap, in defense of their country from the first glimmering of the Revolution in the horizon through all its rising light, to its perfect day." Although Adams had found Arthur to be bitter and sour, he later reflected that Lee had been: "a man too early in the service of his country to avoid making a multiplicity of enemies; too honest, upright, faithful and intrepid to be popular; too often obliged by his principles and feelings to oppose Machiavelian intrigues, to avoid the destiny he suffered. This man never had justice done him by his country in his lifetime, and I fear he never will by posterity."[12]

Clues to Arthur's mature personality may be found in his experiences as a child. Little testimony on the Lee child-rearing practices exists; only in his will did Arthur record a brief comment concerning his parents. It may be surmised that his father's involvement in colonial politics on the Virginia Council, speculations in land along the Ohio River, and management of the baronial holdings at Stratford left little time for family affairs. According to legend Arthur's mother contented herself with raising her daughters and eldest son "and gave up her younger sons, when boys, to be fed, in a great measure, by their own enterprise and exertions."[13] The Lee family biographer,

12. John Adams to Richard Bland Lee, Aug. 11, 1819, *The Works of John Adams, Second President of the United States with a Life of the Author,* ed. Charles Francis Adams (10 vols; Boston: Little, Brown, 1856), X, 382; Page Smith, *John Adams* (Garden City, N.Y.: Doubleday, 1962), pp. 374–89; 425–26.

13. Photocopy of Arthur Lee's will, dated July 27, 1792, from Middlesex County

writing before the era of psychoanalysis, claimed Arthur "was left, until an advanced period of boyhood, with the children of his father's slaves: to partake of their fare, and to participate in their hardy sports and toils. Hence his body was early inured to hardship, and his mind was accustomed to unrestrained exercise and bold adventure."[14] This sense of autonomy, with perhaps a whiff of apprehension, was reinforced when, following the death of both parents within a year, Arthur was dispatched to England in 1751 to be educated at Eton. Cut away from the familiar confines of Stratford, Arthur was forced to rely upon his self-reliance to see himself through adolescence in a British school. Like many children in eighteenth-century America where parents apparently were not sure whether to protect or to reject their children, he learned to fend for himself.[15] The independence which he experienced as a child and exhibited as an adolescent became ingrained in his style as an adult. To his role of diplomat Arthur Lee brought his idiosyncracy. In the decade before 1776 his stance and manner placed him in the vanguard of American independence from Britain. In the following decade he denied the fledgling American republic need be dependent on European allies.

A sense of distrust, if not the roots of the persecution complex which would later haunt Lee, was gained from another episode in Arthur's youth. Although his father's will granted the two youngest sons (William and Arthur) £1000 at their maturity, £200 for building a home, and additional sources of revenue, the boys were not satisfied. It seems their father had designated Arthur to be trained as a clergyman or physician, while William was destined to be the family's commercial agent in Europe.[16] Soon after the will was pro-

---

Wills, G, 1787–93, found in Jessie M. Fraser Transcripts of Arthur Lee Papers, Alderman Library, Univ. of Va., Box 20; hereafter cited as Fraser–box number; Richard H. Lee, *Memoir of the Life of Richard Henry Lee and his Correspondence* . . . (2 vols.; Philadelphia: H. C. Carey & I. Lea, 1825), I, 244.

14. Richard Henry Lee, *Life of Arthur Lee* . . . (2 vols.; Boston: Wells & Lilly, 1829), I, 11–12. A twentieth-century Lee believed Arthur was consigned by his mother to be nursed by an old slave. Marguerite duPont Lee, *Arthur Lee, M.D., LL.D., F.R.S.* (Richmond: n.p., 1936), pp. 3–4.

15. John F. Walzer, "A Period of Ambivalence: Eighteenth Century American Childhood," in *The History of Childhood*, ed. Lloyd de Mause (New York: Psychohistory Press, 1974), p. 374, asserts, "By the eighteenth century it would seem that the shift in parents' attitudes toward their children and the shift in children's attitudes toward dependence and independence had surfacd and probably had a great deal to do with the Atlantic revolutions which occurred at the end of the century."

16. Burton J. Hendrick, *The Lees of Virginia: Biography of a Family* (Boston: Little, Brown, 1935), p. 85; Lee, *Life of Arthur Lee*, I, 12; Ethel Armes, *Stratford*

bated in July 1751 strife arose within the family over the handling of the estate. By 1754 the two boys successfully petitioned to have their eldest brother, Philip Ludwell, replaced as legal guardian by their cousin, Henry Lee. It was not until 1764 that a series of intra-family suits were drawn to a close. This litigation—nakedly reveal-ing contentiousness, anger, and aggression—primed both William and Arthur for the politics of confrontation which they practiced as adults. Such behavior may be interpreted as a ploy to overcome a sense of vulnerability such as memories of shame and doubt.[17] Arthur learned from this experience that the world was inhabited by avari-cious and cunning men, such as his own brother, who sought to de-prive the virtuous of their just deserts. This experience, compounded by the unsettling almost-simultaneous deaths of both parents, proved congruent to both Arthur's British education in the classics and his immersion in contemporary Whig political theory.

From his early years Arthur not only gained an outlook on life which would affect his role as diplomat, but he also developed an arsenal of tactical weapons. First at Stratford, where the family pro-vided a Scotch Presbyterian minister as tutor, and then at Eton Arthur struggled to surpass his siblings and peers in recitations and writing assignments.[18] From his schooling he learned to rely on his powers of argumentative discourse. As he had won applause as a child, so as an adult he continually resorted to writing petitions as a diplomatic tactic. From schoolboy debates Arthur developed the aggressive contentiousness characteristic of his later diplomatic practice.

Chief among the few warm relationships Arthur formed in his lifetime was the intimacy and reverence he felt for Richard Henry, eight years his senior. The early years of these two brothers found them geographically distant from each other; the elder returned from schooling in England soon before the younger was dispatched there. Nonetheless, Richard Henry served as a goal of emulation, the voice of authority, and a mentor for his younger brother. Arthur relied heavily on this source in planning his career, sought praise

Hall, *The Great House of the Lees* (Richmond: Garrett & Massie, 1936), pp. 534–38.

17. Armes, *Stratford Hall*, pp. 534, 91–101; Arthur Lee to Richard Henry Lee, Sept. 1–2, 1764, Fraser–1; John Demos, *Little Commonwealth: Family Life in Plymouth Colony* (New York: Oxford Univ. Press, 1970), pp. 49–50, 136–139.

18. Chitwood, *Richard Henry Lee*, pp. 7–11.

and encouragement from him, gloried in his brother's rapid rise in Virginia political circles, and shared with him the Whiggish or "country" perspective on government. From Richard Henry, Arthur learned to serve selflessly in public life, to contend against ubiquitous corruption in politics, and to cherish republicanism. Arthur particularly applauded his brother's "patriot spirit and love of liberty which have hitherto influenced your resolve uninjured by public corruption or party zeal."[19] Both brothers shared with other American radicals a deep respect for the concept of virtue, a tenet which propelled them to take an idealistic and moralistic stance in the development of foreign policy and self-righteously to condemn the diplomatic aims of other nations and other Americans.[20] For both Richard Henry and Arthur the movement to gain and sustain independence was a compound of personal drives and political desires.

Arthur's formal education was the best available in the Anglo-American world. After Eton he chose to study medicine at Edinburgh, where courses were less expensive, more vigorous, and less oppressive for American students than at Cambridge. Numerous experiences in Scotland reflect his developing personality. First, his brilliant record in classes and association with the galaxy of genius on the faculty resulted in a prize awarded to his M.D. dissertation and a heightened sense of self-esteem. Second, in the somewhat alien world of Scotland, Arthur sought to maintain his identity with his homeland. His sense of loyalty prompted him to participate in the Virginia Club, an organization of students from the Old Dominion which sought to raise the standards of medical practitioners in the colony.[21]

19. Arthur Lee to Richard Henry Lee, Dec. 24, 25, 28, 1760; Fraser-1; Arthur Lee to Richard Henry Lee, Dec. 22, 1763, *Lee Family Papers*, I/0305–0306; Arthur Lee to Richard Henry Lee, Aug. 19, 1761, Fraser-1.

20. Paul A. Varg, *Foreign Policies of the Founding Fathers* (East Lansing: Mich. State Univ. Press, 1963), p. 4; J. G. A. Pocock, "Virtue and Commerce in the Eighteenth Century," *Journal of Interdisciplinary History*, III (Summer 1972), 121. Describing this mindset Pocock notes, "the moral health of the civic individual consisted in his independence from governmental or social superiors, the precondition of his ability to concern himself with the public good, *res publica*, or commonweal. Should he lose the economic foundations of this ability (i.e., independent property), or be demoralized by an exclusive concern with private or group satisfactions, a comparable imbalance or disturbance in the civic and social foundations of moral personality would set in which would also prove irreversible. The name most tellingly used for balance, health, and civic personality was 'virtue'; the name for its loss was 'corruption.' "

21. Arthur Lee to Richard Henry Lee, (1764?), Fraser–1; Arthur Lee to

In 1764 Arthur exhibited attachment to his homeland and utilized his pen to engage in public debate. The occasion was a pamphlet he published which took exception to Adam Smith's comments about slavery in America.[22] This effort should be considered Lee's initial foray into the field of diplomacy as it focused on relations between the colonies and the mother country. It illustrated characteristics of his later torrent of writings between 1768 and 1776: reliance on publication of petitions as a diplomatic tool, utilization of a melange of sources to buttress his argument, and fervid attachment to liberty.[23] The two main points of the pamphlet were that slavery should be abolished as it was harmful to slaves and masters alike and that the root cause of the practice lay in the scheme of empire. From Lee's perspective slavery was an example of "confined and puny" policy which treated Americans "not as fellow-subjects, but as the servants of Britain." From this point forward in his career Lee believed the goal of the British was to secure the chains of bondage on the colonists. To him, as to other ideologically charged Americans, the British ministry appeared bent on subverting Anglo-American liberties. Lee's cherishing liberty might be traced to his firsthand observations of the severities of slavery. His aggressive attacks on British policy could be interpreted as releases of personal anxiety.[24]

The either-slavery-or-liberty Manichean prism through which such men as Lee viewed reality led ultimately to the Revolution.[25] The

Richard Henry Lee, Mar. 20, 1765, *Lee Family Papers*, I/0327; Wyndham B. Blanton, *Medicine in Virginia in the Eighteenth Century* (Richmond: Garrett & Massie, 1931), pp. 20, 90–91, 226, 401–2.

22. [Arthur Lee], *An Essay in Vindication of the Continental Colonies of America, from a Censure of Mr. Adam Smith, in His Theory of Moral Sentiments. With Some Reflections on Slavery in General* (London: T. Becket & P. A. DeHondt, 1764), pp. 9–10, 13–15, 20; Winthrop D. Jordan, *White Over Black—American Attitudes Toward the Negro 1550–1812* (Chapel Hill: Univ. of N.C. Press, 1968), pp. 310–11; Richard K. MacMaster, "Arthur Lee's 'Address of Slavery': An Aspect of Virginia's Struggle to End the Slave Trade, 1765–1774," *Virginia Magazine of History and Biography*, LXXX (Apr. 1972), 141–57.

23. A. R. Riggs, "Arthur Lee, A Radical Virginian in London, 1768–1776," *Virginia Magazine of History and Biography*, LXXVIII (July 1970), 268–69, estimates that between 1768 and 1776 Lee published, under at least ten different pen names, 170 essays, 17 petitions, and 9 pamphlets, plus at least 50 anonymous personal letters which friends submitted to the colonial press.

24. Peter Loewenberg, "The Psychology of Racism," in *The Great Fear: Race in the Mind of America*, ed. Gary B. Nash and Richard Weiss (New York: Holt, Rinehart & Winston, 1970), pp. 186–201.

25. Jack P. Greene, "Changing Interpretations in Early American Politics," in *The Reinterpretation of Early American Politics—Essays in Honor of John Edwin Pomfret*, ed. Ray A. Billington (San Marino, Calif.: Huntington Library, 1966),

synergistic reaction between Lee's heightened sense of Americanism, gained from frequent correspondence with radical patriot leaders and his Whiggish concern for freedom, drove the fledgling physician into the polemical center of the dispute between Britain and the American colonies. In 1765 he apparently wrote a poem entitled *Oppression*, and three years later combined with John Dickinson to produce lyrics for "The Liberty Song," which pleaded:

> Then join hand in hand brave Americans all
> By uniting, we stand, by dividing we fall;
> *In so righteous a cause*, we must surely succeed,
> For heaven approves of each generous deed.
> In freedom we're born, and in freedom we'll live
>   Our money is ready
>   Steady, boys, steady
> Let's give it as Freemen, but never as Slaves.[26]

The contentiousness and suspiciousness which Arthur later manifested in his relations with fellow American diplomats was also evident in his years at Edinburgh. For example, Lee's attempts to gain loans to finance his education were undermined by a London merchant who publicized that the Virginian was a gambler and a bankrupt. In justifying himself to his brother, Arthur self-righteously thundered:

Foes are not wanting to the best on earth. God forbid that I should ever be deaf to the complaints of the oppressed and injured; but the scandalous whispering of malice, the weak insinuations, and malevolent operations of untruth I shall always despise; Nor shall I have regarded the present defamation so much as to answer it, had you not desired it, it can only operate to the conviction of the weak and unjust and of such I neither de-

---

p. 175, notes, "Ideas, then, in all their several forms, operate to impede men's perspectives of reality at the same time that they give it shape and meaning." Pocock, "Virtue and Commerce," p. 122, contends, "The Country ideology did not cause the Revolution; it characterized it. Men cannot do what they have no means of saying they have done; and what they do must in part be what they can say and conceive that it is."

26. John W. Blassingame, "American Nationalism and Other Loyalties in the Southern Colonies, 1763–1775," *Journal of Southern History*, XXXIV (Feb. 1968), 55, 63; H. Trevor Colburn, *The Lamp of Experience: Whig History and the Intellectual Origins of the American Revolution* (Chapel Hill: Univ. of N.C. Press, 1965), pp. 136–38; Arthur M. Schlesinger, "A Note on Songs as Patriot Propaganda 1765–1776," *William and Mary Quarterly*, 3rd series, XI (Jan. 1954), 79–88 (emphasis in original).

sire the favor nor regard the ill opinion, as long as I shall be conscious to myself of its being merited.[27]

From this episode emerged a characteristic pattern of behavior for Lee. He would enter a situation with an immense sense of self-confidence and an equal amount of suspicion toward those he encountered. When he became thwarted he would accuse these associates of faithlessness or selfish ambition, believe himself to be solely in the right, pen his grievances to a small circle of confidants, and await justice. Such a pattern, most pronounced in his relationships with Franklin and Deane in France, led to the characterization of Lee as "a marplot" and as a man "cursed with a persecution complex."[28]

By September 1764 Lee's personality traits were distinguishable; not so with his career. He returned to Virginia to practice medicine but soon became involved in the turmoil of the Stamp Act and Townshend crises. Finding himself ill-suited for the rigorous life of a physician in Williamsburg, Lee devoted himself to writing polemical pieces for the newspapers and engaging in public agitation. He contributed a series of "Monitor" letters to the *Virginia Gazette* in 1768 exhorting readers to resist subversion of their rights, sided with Richard Henry in disputes with local supporters of British policy, and determined "to form a correspondence with leading patriotic men in each colony."[29] In the summer of 1768 he journeyed to England to establish himself as the hub of a communications network which would link men on both sides of the Atlantic who feared for their rights. This primary role would be supported by a secondary one—that of British physician. He could always rely on Richard Henry to offer financial assistance as well as intangible support.

The critical period of 1768 to 1774 found Arthur Lee in the center of the mounting storm within the British Empire. Situated in London, he immersed himself in the metropolitan radicalism which swirled around the person of John Wilkes. Simultaneously he cultivated the friendship of the Earl of Shelburne, Lord Chatham, and other politicians seemingly partial to the colonial cause. By 1770 he turned

27. Arthur Lee to Richard Henry Lee, Oct. 14, 1761, Fraser–1.
28. Mark A. Boatner, III, ed., *Encyclopedia of the American Revolution* (New York: D. McKay Co., 1966), pp. 603–5; John R. Alden, *History of the American Revolution* (New York: Knopf, 1969), p. 378.
29. "Arthur Lee's Memoir of the American Revolution," in Lee, *Life of Arthur Lee*, I, 224.

away from the healing profession toward more contentious pursuits: those of polemicist and lawyer. As he worked his way through law training at Lincoln's Inn and the Middle Temple, Lee continuously criticized British policymakers in numerous pseudonymous articles printed on both sides of the Atlantic.[30] His fire-breathing private correspondence with kindred spirits in the colonies, such as Samuel Adams in Massachusetts, played a crucial role in contorting information that passed across the Atlantic. It also resulted in Lee's appointment as associate agent in England for the Massachusetts House of Assembly. By 1773 Arthur believed himself to be "the most obnoxious Supporter of the Cause of America" then residing in England.[31] He gloried in such prominence.

Whatever Lee's self-image, to most of his contemporaries he was overshadowed by Benjamin Franklin. The relationship between the two men was never warm; a combination of factors led to differences between them. Franklin was thirty-four years older than Lee. Although both were multifaceted, the Pennsylvanian was self-taught and practical-minded while the Virginian considered himself a member of the intelligentsia. In England Lee and Franklin represented competing colonial companies in quest of grants of land in the Ohio River Valley. They also reacted differently to the use of violence in politics, Lee embracing and Franklin rejecting the tactics of mobs in both London and Boston.[32] Lastly, the men disagreed over the relationship of colonial turmoil to the international scene. Where Franklin counseled conciliation, Lee sought to aggravate the crisis and to

30. Pauline Maier, *From Resistance to Revolution: Colonial Radicals and the Development of American Opposition to Britain 1765–1776* (New York: Vintage Books, 1974), pp. 222–23; Alvin R. Riggs, "Arthur Lee and the Radical Whigs 1768–1776" (Ph.D. dissertation, Yale Univ., 1967) is the best coverage of Lee's public actions and writings. The personal side is covered in Louis W. Potts, "Arthur Lee—American Revolutionary" (Ph.D. dissertation, Duke University, 1970).

31. Arthur Lee to Richard Henry Lee, Feb. 14, 1773, Fraser–2.

32. Verner W. Crane, *Benjamin Franklin and a Rising People* (Boston: Little Brown, 1954), pp. 134–35; Michael G. Kammen, *A Rope of Sand* (Ithaca, N.Y.: Cornell Univ. Press, 1968), p. 129; Thomas P. Abernethy, "The Origins of the Franklin-Lee Imbroglio," *North Carolina Historical Review*, XV (Jan. 1938), 1–12; Maier, *From Resistance to Revolution*, pp. 253–54. H. James Henderson, Jr., "Political Factions in the Continental Congress, 1774–1783" (Ph.D. dissertation, Columbia University, 1962), pp. 30–32, notes, "The urbane and cordial tactics of Franklin in Parliament and at Court as well as his attitude toward the Wilkes affair present a stark contrast to the belligerent activism of Arthur Lee, a man who demanded a great deal by way of patriotism and accepted very little of the gentler art of compromise. He was a radical who could not come to terms with the traditional ways of doing business in the colonial agencies."

solicit European support for the American cause.[33] Such an attitude would later divide the men in their roles as Commissioners. Lee advocated militia diplomacy wherein the Americans would force themselves upon foreign courts and disregard the delicacies of diplomatic protocol. Such an impetuous approach, as practiced by Lee, proved fruitless. Franklin, a more cautious and successful practitioner, did not wish to go suitoring over Europe.[34]

The zealous Virginian coveted Franklin's conspicuity. Frustrated in his own ambitions, Lee came to perceive his competitor as both selfish and cunning, the opposite of his self-image. In 1773 he whined to Samuel Adams, "Dr. Franklin frequently assures me that he shall sail for Philadelphia in a few weeks; but I believe he will not quit until he is gathered to his fathers."[35] Ultimately both men found themselves incapable of effecting change in British policy as the imperial breach approached. Ironically Lee did gain his wish for prominence in 1775 when, following Franklin's departure for America, he became the most significant colonial agent in England, an impotent post, however. Though unfulfilled in his personal ambitions, Lee could look forward to opportunities presented by the American War for Independence for he was the "last of the colonial agents and the first national diplomat."[36] Soon he sought to influence foreign-policy decision-making by demanding of the Committee of Secret Correspondence that Franklin and John Jay "must be left out, and L's

33. Wonyung Hyun Oh, "Opinions of Continental American Leaders on International Relations, 1763–1775" (Ph.D. dissertation, Univ. of Wash., 1963), p. 39.
34. Gerald Stourzh, *Benjamin Franklin and American Foreign Policy* (Chicago: Univ. of Chicago Press, 1954), p. 126. David M. Griffiths, "American Commercial Diplomacy in Russia, 1780 to 1783," *William and Mary Quarterly*, 3rd series, XXVII (July 1970), 391, observes, "The notion that it was beneath the dignity of the United States to resort to traditional diplomatic measures to obtain a hearing from the European courts was a fundamental principle of the anti-Gallicans. American diplomats were simply to appear at selected courts, outline the commercial advantages to be reaped from relations with the United States, and enter into negotiations for treaties of alliance and commerce . . . this pattern of thinking was usually termed 'militia diplomacy.' "
35. Arthur Lee to Richard Henry Lee, Oct. 20, 1773, Fraser–14; Arthur Lee to Samuel Adams, June 11, 1773, Lee, *Life of Arthur Lee*, I, 229–32; Benjamin Franklin to Thomas Cushing, July 7, 1773, *The Writings of Benjamin Franklin*, ed. Albert H. Smyth (New York: Macmillan, 1905–7), VI, 81–85; Kammen, *Rope of Sand*, pp. 148–51.
36. Kammen, *Rope of Sand*, p. 318. Richard L. Bushman has perceived that "eventually, when relations with Britain became too strained, Franklin, it is proper to say, withdrew rather than revolted." "On the Uses of Psychology: Conflict and Conciliation in Benjamin Franklin," *History and Theory*, III (1966), 238.

[Lee] and A's [Adams] put into their places." He also confided that he considered "the New England men are fittest to be trusted in any dangerous or important enterprise."[37] Thus did he hope to swing foreign policy into the radicals' hands.

In the era of the American Revolution, as in our own, men made diplomacy. As two analysts of American foreign policy have recently remarked, "Elements of personality (even idiosyncratic behavior and personal foibles) have affected events. Issues of foreign policy and the forces that produce them transcend the purposes and preoccupations of individual statesmen; nevertheless, they can only find expression through the marvelously unpredictable, chaotic realm of human motivations and the decisions of fallible men."[38] Difficulties which Lee, Deane, and Franklin encountered as Commissioners in France may be credited to personal differences as well as to the inadequacies of the Continental Congress where policy making by committee was hamstrung by "factionalism, inefficiency, and lack of direction." This led to "the lamentable spectacle of the triad of American diplomats in France and later others wandering all over Europe uncertain of their assignments and jealous of their colleagues."[39]

The infamous Lee-Deane dispute which ultimately flamed on both sides of the Atlantic and threatened to engulf Franco-American harmony can be traced to Lee's initial maneuverings as agent for Congress in England in 1775. Through London's Lord Mayor, John Wilkes, Lee came in contact with Pierre Caron de Beaumarchais, an agent of the French foreign ministry. Together the two zealots intrigued to commit France to covert support for the American cause. What Beaumarchais said and what Lee heard in these conversations became controversial. The Frenchman later claimed that the proffered assistance, funneled through the bogus firm of Roderique Hortalez and Company, had been in the nature of a loan and that he should be reimbursed. The American, in reply, asserted he had understood the assistance to be a royal gift. Lee came to imagine that Beau-

---

37. Arthur Lee to Lt. Gov. Colden, Feb. 13, 1776; Arthur Lee to ———, Feb. 13, 1776, *The Revolutionary Diplomatic Correspondence of the United States*, ed. Francis Wharton (6 vols.; Washington, D.C.: Government Printing Office, 1889), II, 71–74; hereafter cited as *Correspondence*.

38. *Makers of American Diplomacy*, p. xv.

39. Lawrence S. Kaplan, *Colonies into Nation: American Diplomacy 1763–1801* (New York: Macmillan, 1972), p. 101; Jennings B. Sanders, *Evolution of Executive Departments of the Continental Congress 1774–1789* (Gloucester, Mass.: Peter Smith, 1971), pp. 38–49.

marchais, in collusion with Silas Deane, sought to reap windfall profits for himself.[40] The Virginian's assertions were anchored in the distrust he immediately showed Deane. When the New England man arrived in France he became a favorite of Beaumarchais and displaced Lee in the secret conferences. His pride hurt after being cut off from promising negotiations, Lee ventured to Paris in August 1776 to reassert himself but was rebuffed by both Deane and the French playwright. He returned to London. Arthur's piqued pride thus lay the foundation for a momentous feud with Deane. Beaumarchais, in turn, convinced his superiors that Lee was anti-Gallic at heart. Such an impression led French agents in America to press Congress to deprive Lee of both diplomatic and policy-making roles in foreign affairs. In truth, Arthur Lee was not so much anti-French initially as he was adamant on American autonomy. He warned his brother in early 1777, "Two things, however, I wish to impress on your minds: to look forward and prepare for the worst event, and to search for every resource within ourselves, so as to have as little external dependence as possible."[41]

Lee returned to France in December 1776 to assume his position as a coequal Commissioner with Deane and Franklin, who had recently arrived. The Pennsylvanian apparently wished to rid himself of the pesky Virginian, first trying to convince Lee to return to England, then persuading him to venture to Spain. The Virginian acceded to the latter request in early 1777. Though the Spaniards did not grant him access to their capital, Lee doggedly negotiated promises of assistance from the callous and wary agents of Charles III. Lee, "having achieved the first major American diplomatic breakthrough of the war," returned to Paris only to be shunned by his colleagues. According to the reports of spies employed by the British, Lee's presence made Franklin and Deane ill at ease for it interfered with their various private schemes. Two symptoms of the fissure in the Commission were the facts that Deane and Franklin had taken up residence in Passy, while Lee was forced to find lodging three miles

40. Samuel F. Bemis, *The Diplomacy of the American Revolution* (Bloomington: Ind. Univ. Press, 1957), pp. 35–36, and Kaplan, *Colonies into Nation*, p. 92, claim Lee's detailed reports of his early dealings with Beaumarchais were lost at sea and that the oral report of Lee's messenger added to the confusion about the nature of French assistance.

41. Ralph L. Ketcham, "France and American Politics, 1763–1793," *Political Science Quarterly*, LXXVIII (June 1963), 201–7; Arthur Lee to Richard Henry Lee, Jan. 4, 1777, *Lee Family Papers*, III/0001–0002.

away at Chaillot, and that Lee was not permitted a key to the files of the American mission.[42] British agents were convinced that "Lee is upon very bad terms with Franklin and Deane," that the French so distrusted him due to his friendship with various Englishmen that they "deal only in generals" in his presence, and that Lee's absence meant "a clear stage" for spies who had infiltrated the American embassy.[43]

Before his suspicions could swell, Lee was persuaded to engage in another foray of militia diplomacy; this time to the Court of Frederick the Great. There in the summer of 1777 Lee encountered frustration and humiliation. The Prussians refused to enter into any form of commercial alliance with the Americans no matter how persistent and pleading Arthur Lee might be. Furthermore the American became the center of public ridicule when it was discovered that the English representative in Berlin had pilfered Lee's daily journal and portfolio of diplomatic correspondence. Such a brazen venture aided the British intelligence system, aggrevated Lee's embarrassment over his failures, and cast him into a despondent and irritable mood.[44]

Lee's disputes with his associates pivoted on his image of the ideal diplomat; to him Deane and Franklin lacked both system and patriotism. Deane wrapped himself up in private speculative ventures with cohorts in France, Britain, and America. Ultimately this would lead to treachery.[45] Franklin, on the other hand, took too causal an approach to his mission. Lee believed the Pennsylvanian's cultivation of French opinion was both fruitless and fawning. With an eye on posterity, Lee kept record of the lack of cooperation within the Com-

42. Cecil Currey, *Code Number 72/Ben Franklin: Patriot or Spy?* (Englewood Cliffs, N.J.: Prentice-Hall, 1972), pp. 113–19.

43. Lord Stormont to Earl Weymouth, Apr. 16, 1777; Dr. B[ancroft] to Mr. W[entworth], Apr. 24, 1777, *Facsimiles of Manuscripts in European Archives Relating to America, 1773–1783*, ed. Benjamin F. Stevens (25 vols.; London, Malby & Sons, 1889–98), No. 1518, no. 65.

44. William Eden, "Narrative of the Abstraction of Arthur Lee's Papers at Berlin," July 11, 1777, *Facsimiles*, No. 1468; "Account of the Robbery of the Papers of (Arthur) Lee, American Agent, at Berlin 26 June 1777," *Lee Family Papers*, VIII/0039–0061.

45. Julian P. Boyd, "Silas Deane: Death by a Kindly Teacher of Treason?," *William and Mary Quarterly*, 3rd series, XVI (Apr.–Oct., 1959), 165–87; 319–42; 515–50; E. James Ferguson, "Business, Government, and Congressional Investigation in the Revolution," *William and Mary Quarterly*, 3rd series, XVI (July 1959), 293–318.

mission in the autumn of 1777. Once he carped, "A great deal of money has been expended in my absence, and almost all without consulting me. In consequence I am utterly incapable of giving any account of expenditures." Later he indignantly noted the failure of a joint consultation: "In this determination Mr. L. had no part, but in this, as in many other things, they seemed to like Dr. F.'s idea, that the majority formed the Commissioners . . . and that therefore it was not necessary to ask my opinion."[46]

On October 4 Arthur Lee could no longer restrain his bitterness. In two nearly identical letters to Richard Henry Lee and Samuel Adams he unleashed his anger.[47] Both messages evinced Lee's equation of his personal prominence with the patriotic cause. To Adams he reiterated his view that American independence would be more honorably gained "by our own efforts without Allies." Having encountered equivocacy at three European courts within the past year, he rationalized that "perhaps the liberties established by labor and endurance will be more prized and durable than those acquired by foreign interposition." This was a revision of militia diplomacy. To both politicians, Arthur proposed a revamping of the American foreign service: "Dr. Franklin to Vienna as the first, most respectable, and quiet," Deane to Vienna, William Lee to Berlin as commercial agent, cousin Edmund Jenings to Spain, and crony Ralph Izard to Tuscany. He allotted for himself the sole post in France, "the great wheel that moves them all." Thus he outlined "adapting characters and places."

Lee's pronouncements and proposals were linked with reports of dissension within the American Commission. The Virginian pointed to Deane, the mercantile dealer, and his henchmen, Edward Bancroft and William Carmichael, as men "who have been practicing against me." He whined to his brother: "I have borne patiently a thousand

46. Arthur Lee's Journal, entries of Nov. 2, 20, 1777, Lee, *Life of Arthur Lee*, I, 346–52. The London *Public Ledger* published an anonymous letter dated July 12, 1777, which asserted, "Dr. Lee is certainly joined in the Commission, but he understands the business of courts so ill, that not one of the ministers, will negotiate with him. He is the straight-laced image of awkward formality. To the preciseness of a Presbyterian he endeavours to add the Jesuitism of a Quaker. The one renders him ridiculous, the other suspected. When he thinks he is imposing on mankind, they are laughing at him." Quoted in *Letters of William Lee*, ed. Worthington C. Ford (3 vols.; New York: Burt Franklin, 1968), I, 208n.

47. Arthur Lee to Samuel Adams, Oct. 4, 1777; Arthur Lee to Richard Henry Lee, Oct. 4, 1777, *Facsimiles*, No. 1713, no. 267. Both letters fell into British hands.

causes of resentment and dispute to prevent an appearance of dispute
which I well knew must injure the public. . . . Yet in truth however I
have been disgusted and offended, I have taken care never to let it
break into a quarrel. . . . The object of one of them I believe was to
get me from Paris where I am a disagreeable check upon him, of the
others a vain idea that their importance would recommend them to
my place."

Lee's pleas failed. Neither of his correspondents could carry out
his desires. Rather these letters plus one Arthur dispatched two days
later to the Committee of Foreign Affairs caused an explosion on
both sides of the Atlantic. The spark was Lee's adamant opposition
to Deane's claims that Congress should reimburse Beaumarchais.[48]
A contributing factor was the presence in Paris of Arthur's brother,
William, who sought to displace Jonathan Williams, Deane's and
Franklin's choice as chief agent at the port of Nantes for American
commerce.

The climax of the Lee-Deane feud and a major turn in diplomatic
affairs coincided. On November 29 the Virginian told his allies in
America that Deane was a disgrace to the American mission; he had
mixed private and public affairs to the extent that "three millions of
livres have been expended, and near another million of debt incurred," without Congress yet receiving "a livre's worth."[49] Five
days later the Commissioners received word of Burgoyne's capitulation at Saratoga and Washington's ambitious assault at Germantown, tidings that hastened Foreign Minister Vergennes to fulfill the
Commissioners' dream of a Franco-American alliance. The American goal was to be consummated as the mission disintegrated.

Diplomatic maneuverings sped apace in December and January.
While Gérard, Vergennes's first secretary, opened full-scale negoti-
ations with the Americans, French messengers were sent over the
Pyrenees to entice the Spanish to enter the discussions. Meanwhile

48. Arthur Lee to Committee of Foreign Affairs, Oct. 6, 1777, *Correspondence*,
II, 402–3; Charles J. Stille, "Beaumarchais and 'The Lost Million,' A Chapter on
the Secret History of the American Revolution," *Pennsylvania Magazine of History
and Biography*, XI (1887), 1-36.

49. Arthur Lee to Samuel Adams, Nov. 29, 1777, Fraser–3. Arthur apparently
overlooked brother William's private speculations. See *Letters of William Lee*, I,
284–86, 295–98, 300. Arthur himself acted simultaneously as agent for Congress
and for Virginia in seeking weapons for the war effort. Lee, *Life of Arthur Lee*, I,
413–25.

the trembling North ministry dispatched undercover agents to Paris to feel out Deane and Franklin concerning the terms of an Anglo-American reconciliation. Lee, the British discovered, was unapproachable on this topic and incorruptible. To one inquirer the Virginian proclaimed that the British seemed "determined to make us a great people, by continuing a contest which forces us to frugality, industry and economy, and calls forth resources which without that necessity would never have been cultivated."[50] Thus he recited the regenerative creed of the American radicals.

Beaumarchais, meanwhile, tried his hand at court intrigue in an effort to pare "the insidious politician Lee" from the negotiations. Vergennes approached the Spanish ambassador in Paris, Count d'Aranda, with the proposal that the Virginian be enticed to resume his mission to Madrid. The Spaniard observed that such a ploy was dangerous: "If he is to be put out of the way simply because he is troublesome, it seems to me that we must reflect whether a worse result would not follow in case he should perceive this distrust with regard to him." Perhaps mindful of Lee's following in Congress, the Bourbon statesmen abandoned the scheme. Beaumarchais shifted tactics; in an effort to discredit his American antagonist he circulated rumors of the Virginian's enduring friendship with Shelburne and other English politicians.[51]

Periodic negotiations began December 12 between Vergennes and Gérard for the French and the three American Commissioners. The "Plan of 1776," the model commercial pact developed by John Adams for Congress, served as the framework for discussions. On December 17 Gérard promised French recognition of American independence and overt material assistance for the American cause. Such a commitment perplexed Lee. He feared that French intervention would cause the British to redouble their war efforts and might lead to a relaxation on the part of American patriots. Nonetheless, he envisioned, "The last ray of British splendor is passing away, and the

50. Bemis, *Diplomacy of the American Revolution*, p. 59; Arthur Lee to Dr. [John] Berkenhout, Aug. 1, Nov. 19, Dec. 3, 1777, Lee, *Life of Arthur Lee*, I, 145–46, *Lee Family Papers*, III/0618; III/0667–0669.

51. Beaumarchais to Vergennes, Dec. 7, 12, 1777; Jan. 3, 1778, *Facsimiles*, No. 1763, 1776, 1829; Henri Doniol, *Histoire de la participation de la France à l'etablissement des Etats-Unis d'Amerique* (5 vols.; Paris, Imprimerie Nationale, 1884–92), II, 683, III, 167–75; Aranda to Vergennes, Dec. 11, 1777, *Facsimiles*, No. 1767 (Stevens' translation).

American sun is emerging in full glory from the clouds which obscured it."[52]

Negotiations on the Franco-American alliance did not move smoothly. Gérard procrastinated as he awaited Spanish commitment. Meanwhile the Lees let loose volleys which shook the American Commission. The attack on Deane's handling of affairs at Nantes caused him to second Franklin's diagnosis that their colleague wavered on the edge of insanity. A duel appeared imminent but Deane, instead, turned his attention to the temptations offered by the British agent Paul Wentworth.[53] The Virginians turned their bilious thrusts at Edward Bancroft, the secretary to the Commission. They demanded that Bancroft, who was actually a British spy, be expelled from his post. Bancroft demanded a face-to-face confrontation but Lee backed off. He wailed to Richard Henry, "Things are going worse and worse, every day among ourselves, and my situation is more painful. I see in every department, neglect, dissipation and private schemes." He feared he would be blamed for the "misdeeds" of his colleagues.[54]

Lee's suspicious nature made an impact on the bargainings with Gérard. In late December he convinced Franklin to keep the Commission's instructions secret and to demand that France renounce claims to retake Canada. He was satisfied on January 8, when Gérard confided that the French king sought to guarantee American independence despite hesitation on the part of the Spanish. In the next ten days the twin pacts, a commercial alliance and an offensive-defensive treaty in case France and Britain went to war, were produced by the negotiators. More experienced than either Franklin or Deane in legal technicalities, Lee studied the French proposals cau-

52. Lee, *Life of Arthur Lee*, I, 357–64; Arthur Lee to Samuel Adams, Dec. 18, 1774, Fraser–3.

53. Silas Deane to Arthur Lee, Dec. 13, 1777, Silas Deane to Dr. Edward Bancroft, Jan. 8, 1778, Silas Deane to Jonathan Williams, Jan. 13, 1778, *The Deane Papers*, ed. Charles Isham, New-York Historical Society *Collections*, XIX–XXIII (5 vols.; New York, 1887–91), XX, 272–73, 310, 327. William Lee to Silas Deane, Dec. 17, 1777, *Letters of William Lee*, I, 288–95; Lee, *Life of Arthur Lee*, I, 366–67.

54. Edward Bancroft to Arthur Lee, Jan. 22, 1778, *Lee Family Papers*, IV/0088; Arthur Lee to Richard Henry Lee, Jan. 9, 1778, Lee, *Life of Arthur Lee*, II, 127–28; I, 367. Wentworth offered the following caricatures of the Americans: "Dr. Franklin is taciturn, deliberate and cautious—Mr. Deane vain, desultory and subtle, —Mr. A. Lee suspicious and insolent—Alderman [William] Lee peevish and ignorant . . . all of them insidious, & Edwards [Bancroft] vibrating between hope and fear, interest and attachment." Paul Wentworth to William Eden, Jan. 4, 1778, *Facsimiles*, No. 769.

tiously to be certain the Americans did not bargain themselves into an inferior position. Thus on January 25 following detailed analysis he raised an objection to two articles in the commercial pact, apparently out of regard for the southern tobacco trade.[55]

Arthur proposed that William Lee and Ralph Izard, a fellow militia diplomat, be brought into negotiations. When Deane and Franklin vetoed this maneuver, the Virginian discussed the proposals with his friends anyway. In the original "Plan of 1776," the Americans proposed they be exempted from all duties on molasses purchased from the French West Indies, a boon to New England merchants. Gérard countered with the demand that no duties be placed on merchandise exported from America to the French islands. Lee, backed by Izard, felt this to be "mischievous," as one French product was equated with all American exports. He warned, "We are . . . really tying both our hands with the expectation of binding one of her fingers." He also feared the effect would be "the encouragement of commerce at the expense of agriculture." He thus moved for deletion of both articles but was overruled. His associates, persuaded by Gérard that the King had approved the draft, let the disputed articles stand. Lee acquiesced, for the sake of a unified stance for the Commission. However, he soon dispatched copies of his argument to Congress which ultimately, in the process of ratification, expunged the controversial section.[56]

The moment of exhilaration came on February 6, 1778, for the Americans. At the office of the Ministry for Foreign Affairs in the Hôtel de Lautrec in Paris, their mission was consummated. Following the official exchange of credentials Gérard and the three Americans moved to affix their signatures to the Treaty of Amity and Commerce, a Treaty of Alliance, and an Act Separate and Secret. No sooner had the Frenchman and Franklin signed than Deane and Lee broke into a quarrel. Lee, because he held Congressional Commissions to both France and Spain, wished to sign twice. Deane objected. Gérard intervened. Ultimately the Virginian, styled "Councellor at Law" in the alliance, signed once as "Deputy, Plenipotentiary for France and Spain."[57]

55. Arthur Lee's Journal, Dec. 24, 1777, Jan. 18, 1778, Lee, *Life of Arthur Lee*, I, 124–30, 368–78.

56. *Correspondence*, I, 477–85; Lee, *Life of Arthur Lee*, I, 379–91.

57. *Despatches and Instructions of Conrad Alexandre Gérard 1778–1780*, ed.

Their task accomplished, the Commissioners soon lost all sense of unified mission. Within a month Deane was notified he had been recalled by Congress and replaced by John Adams. Lee then turned to snap acrimoniously at Franklin. Finally in the spring of 1779 Congress reorganized its foreign service, abolished diplomacy by committee and designated Franklin as sole ambassador to the Court of Louis XVI. Lee was assigned the mission to Madrid if the Spaniards would permit it. They did not. Congressional factionalism stirred in Philadelphia by Deane and Gérard, the first French ambassador to the United States, discredited and unseated the Virginian in the autumn. The movement for Lee's recall had been spearheaded by William Paca of Maryland, Meriwether Smith of Virginia, and William Henry Drayton of South Carolina. Support was mustered from the ranks of all southern delegations plus New York. The Lee-Adams axis at the center of the eastern or radical faction was split as Arthur Lee lost his Madrid assignment to John Jay while John Adams was selected as peace commissioner.[58] The Virginian eventually returned to America and gained one of his state's seats in Congress. He continually voiced criticisms of both the foreign and financial policies of Congress, but as the fervor of the Revolution moderated, he was castigated as a malignant crank.[59]

In appraising the work of the American Commission it has been fashionable to condemn Arthur Lee, to laud Benjamin Franklin, and

---

John J. Meng (Baltimore: The Johns Hopkins Press, 1939), pp. 84–87; Lee, *Life of Arthur Lee*, I, 393–94; Edward S. Corwin, *French Policy and the American Alliance of 1778* (Hamden, Conn: Archon Books, 1962), pp. 385–91.

58. H. James Henderson, "Congressional Factionalism and the Attempt to Recall Benjamin Franklin," *William and Mary Quarterly*, 3rd series, XXVII (Apr. 1970), 247–55; Henderson, *Party Politics*, pp. 198–210; Potts, "Arthur Lee," pp. 363–72. Lee's support rested in the eastern faction, which "could be expected to seek New England objectives such as rights to the fisheries, and to insist upon a pure —even puritan—commitment to the integrity of a republican revolution. Thus American aims should not be contaminated by the alliance with France; the people's revolution should not be jeopardized by the establishment of a continental military elite; public virtue should not be corroded by private profit." Henderson, "Recall," 247–48.

59. Lee came to believe that Franklin "sold us in the negociation with France" in 1778 and sought to do so again in the peace parleys. He believed that under Robert Morris's schemes "the public money is lavished away, the soldiery defrauded and the public plundered." Arthur Lee to James Warren [ca. July 23], 1782; Arthur Lee to James Warren, Sept. 13, 1783, *Letters of the Members of the Continental Congress*, ed. Edmund C. Burnett (8 vols.; Washington, D.C.: The Carnegie Institution of Washington, 1921–34), VI, 389–90; *Warren-Adams Letters*, The Massachusetts Historical Society *Collections* (2 vols.; Cambridge, 1917, 1925), II, 224–26.

to grudgingly admit Silas Deane's perfidy. It now appears Deane sold out to the British as early as 1778 and had prior knowledge of Bancroft's duplicity. Franklin, it is evident, also looked out for himself in commercial ventures, possibly at the expense of public interests. As Lee charged, both men were careless to the extreme in their failure to keep records of transactions and to maintain secrecy at Passy. Arthur Lee, it seems, "was on the mark when he stated that his colleagues carried on activities that would not bear the scrutiny of honest men."[60] Yet despite his disclaimers, the Virginian was not blameless. By judging his associates by his own high ideals—those of a virtuous or ascetic revolutionary—he had roiled his American colleagues, earned the eternal enmity of Beaumarchais, and toiled largely in vain as a militia diplomat in Prussia and Spain.

Arthur Lee's personality feasted on controversy and failure. Both before and after the Declaration of Independence he served in diplomatic roles wherein his idiosyncratic outlook and style influenced the formulation of policy and the conduct of diplomacy. He lacked the tact, delicacy, and discretion so frequently cited as the necessary attributes for such a position. Rather he utilized tactics he had found successful in his own interpersonal relationships: moralistic petitions and face-to-face confrontations. He sought to impose the salient features of his own personality—distrust and autonomy—upon the Americans' revolutionary movement. His influence climaxed in 1774–76 in the thrust for independence. As the war front shifted in 1778–79 his power base in America—the Adams-Lee axis in Congress—lost out to the southern faction, which heavily depended on French aid. Opposition to such reliance ultimately cost Lee his post and prestige.

60. Currey, *Code Number 72*, pp. 141–42, 281.

Portrait of a Southern Patriot: The Life and Death of John Laurens

Richard J. Hargrove   *Western Illinois University*

i.

Historians, in their search for the causes of events, have often focused their attention on great men. The events of Watergate have reminded us of the importance of the men and women upon whom a leader depends for advice and for carrying out the business of state. Although George Washington, the great man of the American Revolution, has been praised for many virtues, his wisdom in surrounding himself with remarkably able subordinates has been perhaps too little noticed. Alexander Hamilton, for example, began his notable career as an aide to Washington. Others less prominent but equally talented served the renowned leader.

One of the most appealing and dedicated (though largely unsung) young men of the Revolution was John Laurens. Scholars have devoted more time and attention to the life of his father, Henry Laurens, and in fact publication of the elder Laurens's papers continues to proceed.[1] Furthermore, an earlier biography will be replaced soon.[2] John Laurens as yet has no definitive biography nor is an up-to-date complete edition of his papers available. A sketch, essentially a short synopsis of John Laurens's life, was written by W. Gilmore Simms and appended to a selection of Laurens papers which he edited for

The writer wishes to thank the Research Council of Western Illinois University for subsidizing part of the expense incurred while he was engaged in research for this paper.

1. *The Papers of Henry Laurens*, ed. Philip M. Hamer, et al. (4 vols. to date; Columbia, S.C.: Univ. of S.C. Press, 1968–).

2. David D. Wallace, *Life of Henry Laurens* (New York: Putnam's, 1915, and Russell and Russell, 1967).

publication in the nineteenth century.[3] A generation later David D. Wallace presented a brief account, which he introduced rather apologetically: "In view of the lack of any life of John Laurens save a few inadequate sketches, I shall throw together . . . information gathered concerning him . . ."[4] More recently, in 1958, Sara Townsend published a biography of Laurens which is interesting but not definitive.[5] Finally, in 1976 Robert M. Weir contributed a psychoanalytical account of Laurens, one which raised questions about his personality and motivation, the meaning of his life, and, especially, the significance of his death.[6]

John Laurens has been described as charming, radical, generous, candid, bold, warm, a crusader for the equalization of wealth, a stout defender of freedom for black slaves, and a pleader for leniency toward loyalists. He was all of these and more, and when he died at the age of twenty-seven, his father was prostrate with grief. Yet mixed with the mourning one can find criticism. Washington considered him rash, and Nathaniel Greene called him a glory seeker. Weir noted that Laurens's letters were "crammed" with references to his death, that he actually courted death.[7] Was this evidence part of a personal order of priorities? An examination of John Laurens's background, education, relationship to his father, attitude toward his wife, and involvement in the American Revolution will provide an opportunity to test Weir's hypothesis, and to draw conclusions concerning its validity or lack thereof.

John Laurens was born on October 28, 1754, in Mepkin, the Laurens plantation house near Charleston, South Carolina. The family of John's mother, Elizabeth Ball, came from England. His father, who was to become a president of the Second Continental Congress, was reputed to be one of the richest men in America. The Laurens family were devout French Huguenots who, after generations of hard work, became wealthy and well known throughout the South. That Henry Laurens did not count his wealth in purely monetary terms may be gathered from a letter to his friend Monkhouse David-

3. *The Army Correspondence of Colonel John Laurens*, ed. W. Gilmore Simms (New York: Bradford Club, 1867).

4. Wallace, *Laurens*, Appendix I.

5. Sara Townsend, *An American Soldier: The Life of John Laurens* (Raleigh, N.C.: Edwards and Broughton, 1958).

6. Robert M. Weir, "Portrait of a Hero," *American Heritage*, XXVII, No. 3 (Apr., 1976), 16–19, 86–88.

7. Weir, "Portrait of a Hero," p. 19.

son in 1762. He had fathered by that time "more than a [half] dozen children of one sort and another . . ." of whom he was "blessed with one boy [John] eight years old and two girls."[8] Henry Laurens, who virtually retired from business in order to educate his children when his wife died in 1770, displayed his parental affection in the same letter to Davidson: "I believe if anything tempts me to cross the Atlantic Ocean it will be to put the boy to school in England. He is very forward in his books and behaves so well in general as to gain at least the approbation of a partial father."[9] Late in September 1771 John's father made good his promise, escorting both his seventeen-year-old son and his six-year-old son James to Great Britain to complete their education.[10] Eight-year-old Henry had been sent ahead in April. Elizabeth Laurens had died the previous May, and it seems possible that her death brought father and son very close during the month-long Atlantic crossing.[11] In any case the letters between Henry and John in the years they were separated show clearly the affection they had for each other.

Whatever sadness John might have felt over the loss of his mother may have been alleviated by the time and distance separating him from Charleston and by the sights and sounds of bustling metropolitan London. It is ironic to find the eventual patriot writing to his uncle in a burst of enthusiasm that he had had the honor "of seeing the King in all his glory on the throne in the House of Peers."[12] Far from being inspired by what he witnessed in England, Henry Laurens was appalled by the corruption he saw. British society appeared to him far more decadent than he had suspected; like many of his American contemporaries, Henry was to view the forthcoming revolutionary struggle as a battle for supremacy between a dissolute society in England and a relatively moral culture in the new world.[13]

Henry Laurens's shock at the state of English society and education might be written off as that of a perhaps too scrupulous provincial Huguenot. His opinion was shared, however, by the sophisticated

8. Wallace, *Laurens*, pp. 59–60. By "one sort and another" Henry meant both living children and those deceased.
9. Ibid., p. 60.
10. Local tutors had been employed for the boys' education in South Carolina.
11. Wallace, *Laurens*, genealogy, ff. p. 502.
12. John Laurens to James Laurens, 1771, Townsend, *Soldier*, p. 23.
13. Jack P. Greene, "Search for Identity: An Interpretation of the Meaning of Selected Patterns of Social Response in Eighteenth-Century America." *Journal of Social History*, III, No. 3 (Spring 1970), 189–219.

historian Edward Gibbon, who "lamented the fourteen months which he spent [at Oxford] as 'the most idle and unprofitable of his whole life' and records that discipline, examinations, and systematic instruction were practically non-existent, while 'the dull and deep potations of the fellows excused the brisk temperance of youth, and the velvet cap of a Gentleman Commoner was the cap of liberty.' "[14] For a time, the three boys studied in London with a tutor, the Reverend Richard Clark, but Henry's dissatisfaction with both the tutor and London caused the sons and their father to move on to Geneva early in the summer of 1772.

ii.

The moral and intellectual climate of Geneva was different from that of London. Geneva was where young scholars went to study if they were serious about their studies. The Duke of Hamilton, Lord Stanhope, and Chesterfield and other aristocratic youths studied there at the same time as the Laurens boys. Sons of wealthy American colonials also studied in Geneva. Among them were fellow South Carolinians John Rutledge, William Henry Drayton, Charles C. Pickney, and Arthur Middleton.[15]

John Laurens's course of study seems to have been a standard though rigorous classical program, including Latin, Greek, Italian, belles lettres, physics, chemistry, history, geography, mathematics, and civil law. Fencing, riding, and drawing were also a part of his curriculum. It is evident that John was studying to be a gentleman. His father, although he approved of Laurens's course of study,[16] (and obviously was interested that he receive a sound education) cautioned him to "be careful . . . not to crowd too much upon your mind, lest it should have an ill effect upon your health, your temper, or your manners."[17] The elder Laurens also warned his son to "avoid gaming and all approaches to it" and worried that as John's friends increased, so would his temptations.[18] Henry, orthodox Huguenot that

14. Wallace, *Laurens*, p. 188.
15. John R. Alden, *The South in the Revolution* (Baton Rouge: La. State Univ. Press, 1957), p. 35.
16. Wallace, *Laurens*, p. 190.
17. Henry Laurens to John Laurens, Dec. 15, 1772, Laurens Papers, Library of Congress.
18. Ibid.

he was, may have feared that the religious skepticism made fashionable by Voltaire and Rousseau might influence his son.[19] He need not have been alarmed. John and his friends remained theologically orthodox and indeed were so studious that they agreed to visit each other only in the afternoon.[20]

Perhaps because his father was both a gentleman and a businessman, John, although only seventeen years old and in his first year of study, felt the need to choose a profession. Writing to his Uncle James in 1772, he demonstrated not only concern for his own plans, but the idealistic concern for others which characterized him throughout his life, a trait he shared with his father. The letter is worth quoting at length:

... For my own part, I find it exceedingly difficult, even at this time, to determine in which of the learned professions I shall list myself. When I hear a man of an improved education, speak from the goodness of heart divine truths with a persuasive eloquence which commands the most solemn silence and serious attention from all his audience, my soul burns to be in his place. When I hear of one who shines at the bar, and overpowers chicanery and oppression, who pleads the cause of helpless widows and injured orphans, who, at the same time that he gains lasting fame to himself, disperses benefits to multitudes, the same emulous ardor rises in my heart. When I hear of another who has done eminent service to mankind, by discovering remedies for the numerous train of disorders to which our frail bodies are continually subject, and has given relief to numbers whose lives, without his assistance, would have been insupportable burdens, I cannot refrain from wishing to be an equal dispenser of good.

Thus I am agitated. Tis beyond, far beyond the power of one man to shine conspicuous in all these characters; one must be determined upon; and I am almost persuaded that it would be that of the divine, if this did not preclude me from bearing arms in defense of my country—for I cannot read with indifference the valiant acts of those, whose prudent conduct and admirable bravery have rescued the liberties of their countrymen, and deprived their enemies of power to do them hurt.

No particular profession is in itself disagreeable to me. Each promises some share of fame. I never loved merchandise, nor can I now. There are but three considerations that can reconcile it to me, first, that the universal correspondence which it establishes, gives one a knowledge of mankind;

19. Although Voltaire did not live in Geneva, he lived only four miles outside the city in Ferney, France. Rousseau was a regular visitor to Geneva.
20. Wallace, *Laurens*, p. 189.

then the continual flow of money peculiar to this employment, enables a man to do extensive good to individuals of distressed fortunes, without injuring himself, as well as to promote works of public utility, under the most beneficial terms. . . .[21]

The concern for others expressed in the letter above was later exemplified in John Laurens's plan to free the slaves and in his attempts to persuade the South Carolina legislature to raise black troops.

John's letter to his uncle displayed that *amor patriae* which Washington later attributed to him. In addition, John's desire to defend his country may have further proved the growing disaffection of even conservative-minded colonists. This letter was written by the same young man who just a year before told his uncle of "seeing the King in all his glory on the throne." John's letter is also interesting because it clearly portrayed him as a patriot unmotivated by economic self-interest or egotistical craving for personal glory. One might object that Laurens was only seventeen and that such idealism is often the folly of youth. At twenty-seven, however, he died enacting those high ideals.

John Laurens spent two years studying in Geneva, all the while maintaining an affectionate correspondence with his father, who approved of his son's activities. Writing from Paris late in 1772, Henry thanked John for "such respectful attention" (presumably to some piece of advice), adding, "You know how to please your Papa and at the same time that you love to please him."[22] This, despite the enormous bills Henry was often required to pay! The elder Laurens vastly preferred Geneva to London as a place to educate his two sons. After John and young Henry had been in Geneva a year Henry senior praised the Swiss city for its "moral atmosphere" and wrote in glowing terms of the "progress, better discipline . . . and better teaching" it provided his sons. He visited them often, partly from a sense of filial affection, partly because he himself loved the city. For these reasons, perhaps, the father did not balk at the more than £200 his son John required to meet his educational and social expenses.[23]

Although John had expressed himself in a quandary early in 1772 over which profession to choose, sometime during that year he told

21. John Laurens to James Laurens, Apr. 17, 1772, *Army Correspondence*, pp. 13–15.
22. Henry Laurens to John Laurens, Dec. 15, 1772, Laurens Papers, Library of Congress.
23. Wallace, *Laurens*, p. 190.

his father he wished to become a barrister. Henry, apparently approving the choice, sent him a set of Blackstone "for private reading."[24] Not deterred by those weighty tomes, "le Voltaire de votre Province" (as one of his boyhood teachers, hearing of his progress, fondly called him)[25] determined to return to London for his legal training. Despite protestations from the senior Laurens, who wished his son to complete his baccalaureate studies before beginning professional training,[26] John left Geneva in September 1774 and began to read law at the Middle Temple or at a private accommodation "under the eyes of an honest lawyer."[27] John pondered the ethical dilemma implicit in pursuing the law as a career: "But a horrible prospect it is, that I am to get my bread by the quarrels and disputes of others, so that I can't pray for success in my occupation without praying at the same time that a great part of mankind may be in error through either ignorance or design . . . ."[28] At the same time Laurens was attracted by the morally uplifting tasks of his chosen field: "The defence of the weak and oppressed" which he determined "never to neglect" was foremost on his list of obligations. Aware that such endeavors would not enrich him monetarily, he declared that they could "make a man happy": "What can be equal to the heartfelt satisfaction which abounds in him who pleads the cause of the fatherless and the widow, and sees right done to him that suffers wrong . . . ? Law is the knotty subject which I must endeavor to render pleasant."[29] In November 1774 John made good his intent to study law by entering a bond and paying his fees.[30]

iii.

Throughout his youth John's letters showed him anxious to please his father and there can be no doubt that Henry Laurens's values were reflected in his son's idealism. It is perhaps significant, however,

24. Ibid.
25. B. Henri Himeli to John Laurens, Dec. 2, 1773, cited by Wallace, *Laurens*, p. 464.
26. Henry Laurens to John Laurens, Oct. 26, 1773, Laurens Papers, S.C. Historical Society.
27. Wallace, *Laurens*, pp. 188 and n. 4 and 470.
28. John Laurens to James Laurens, Sept. 15, 1774, *Army Correspondence*, p. 16.
29. Ibid.
30. John Laurens to James Laurens, Nov. 1774, *Army Correspondence*, p. 16.

that much of the youth's soul-searching is found in letters to his uncle, a man to whom John did not mind showing himself as less than perfect.

Several historians have suggested that, were it not for his untimely death, John might have become another Jefferson or Hamilton. These were men, however, motivated by principle as much as by zeal, while John Laurens was clearly a zealot. Wallace, for example, patterned the son after the father, although the two men were clearly very different personalities. Henry, in word and deed, showed himself a careful and self-disciplined man who recommended his way of life to his sons not out of a narrow or prudish morality but because that sort of life created whole men. Writing to John in 1773, he declared himself pleased with his son's "Temperance and Regularity—an example worthy the Imitation of your Father."[31] Continuing, he wrote that the ". . . benefits which will result from your Moderation cannot be described by anybody but yourself . . . you will possess the Command of your whole time & preserve your Life in Health to a good old Age."[32]

Who would not wish to please such a father? The desire to please, however, was no equal to self-discipline. John, although he tried and often succeeded in pleasing his father, had an impetuous temperament which he apparently could not control. Instilled with his father's idealism, young Laurens's recklessness was rarely harmful to others but the fact remains that he was from an early age reckless. Wallace recounted John's leaving his sickbed as a boy to help extinguish a fire.[33] His impulsive and romantically motivated choice of law as a profession foreshadowed later impulsiveness. This is not to suggest that Laurens was irresponsible. He was intelligent enough to understand, for instance, the moral dilemma facing a man who chose law as a profession. But, having recognized the problem, he decided to emphasize the good he might do (just as he emphasized the good done by ministers and physicians) and plunged headlong into the study of law rather than waiting to complete his bachelor's degree.

As a law student he studied hard[34] at first but failed to keep to a

31. Henry Laurens to John Laurens, Mar. 22, 1773, Laurens Papers, S.C. Historical Society.
32. Ibid.
33. Wallace, *Laurens*, p. 463.
34. John Laurens to Francis Kinlock, Nov. 6, 1774, Laurens Miscellaneous

budget—much to his father's displeasure.[35] In Geneva John had also run through his allowance too speedily, causing his father to caution him of the evils of prodigality—not only of money but also of time.[36] Barely a year later the senior Laurens found it necessary to sound the same note: "In the ordinary course of affairs I should plead strongly *only* for the saving & improvement of Time, but in our present unhappy circumstances it would be neglect in me if I did not again sound the alarm of *frugality* in your Ears, it would be Criminal in you if you were to delay one hour to pay a becoming attention. . . ."[37] In the same letter Henry Laurens expressed chagrin and disappointment in his son's companions, finding a party to Cambridge which John had joined especially obnoxious. "Alas," wrote Henry:

how far have you diverged from the line marked out by yourself & highly approved of by your Father in the short space between the 29th October and 5th December! I pray this paper may have a quick passage & be blessed with the success of uniting with your own endeavours to bring you back again to that state of mind in which I left you.

Consider a Moment your voluntary proposition [,] your determined Resolution to keep close to study & to avoid a certain set of Company . . . Consider & compare your reasons for declining the proposed modest Journey to Bristol, with the projected & I suppose accomplished plan for a Romp to Cambridge & the party of whom no doubt the Chief Engineer is the same whose principles you so readily penetrated & marked with so much Justice & severity. . . .[38]

The tone of this letter forces one to wonder if John Laurens ever had the chance to mark out a line for himself, if any of his endeavors were really his own and if the "voluntary proposition" attributed to him by his father was not simply one more example of pleasing papa. Henry's further expostulations in the same letter lend credence to this interpretation: ". . . were you under any restraint while your Father was in England? No! You were his companion his bosom friend—whence then these retrograde notions immediately after his departure

---

Manuscripts, New York Public Library; see also John Laurens to Henry Laurens, Dec. 3–4, 1774, Edes Manuscripts, Mass. Historical Society.

35. Henry Laurens to John Laurens, Feb. 6, 1775, *South Carolina Historical Magazine*, IV (1903), 273–77.

36. Henry Laurens to John Laurens, Mar. 8, 1774, *SCHM*, III, No. 4 (1902), 213–15.

37. Henry Laurens to John Laurens, Feb. 6, 1775, *SCHM* (1903) (additional note on "our present unhappy circumstances").

38. Ibid.

like a Bird after long confinement fled from her Cage?"[39] Henry, obviously hurt by his son's inexplicable behavior, sensed John's feeling of restraint (though he denied playing any part in the restraining). The young Laurens must indeed have felt like a "Bird after long confinement [fleeing] from her Cage." The external restraint of the father exercised over the son, however well intentioned, may be seen as the cause of John's failure to develop self-control. So long as Henry was there to tighten the reins, John had no need to tighten them himself. Ironically, the benevolence of the paternal dictator and his real affection for his son must have aggravated the son's dependence. Such a companionable father would have been hard to declare one's independence against. As a boy, Henry's best friend was Christopher Gadsden, with whom he "formed a league of virtue," vowing "to support and encourage each other in every virtuous pursuit, to shun every path of vice or folly, to leave company whenever it tended to licentiousness, and by acting in concert, to parry the charge of singularity so grating to young persons."[40] Henry followed these ideals all his life, and, not surprisingly, wanted his son to follow them, too. But whereas ideals voluntarily accepted and pursued caused Henry Laurens not only to prosper but to influence the course of history, those same ideals, imposed by another, were, for John, primarily a reminder of how far short of them he fell. In the letter he wrote back to Henry responding to his father's chastisement, he expressed deep and doubtless sincere regret for disappointing the senior Laurens:

your foolish Son . . . cannot call you Friend and Father without being confounded at his own excessive Weakness in abusing your Confidence and betraying himself. It grieves me that ever I mixed so much in the Carolina Set against which I have been forwarned . . . for drawing [funds] so far beyond your Expectation—I will immure myself all the Summer in London, and draw for no more money during my stay in this house. . . . I am persuaded that however greatly I have offended, you would pity me could you conceive the Torture of Mind that I have undergone this day— I have experienced the same distressful Sensation in putting Pen to paper to address you, that an offender does in lifting his Eyes, which Shame had cast down; [sic] to meet those of his injured Friend—Oh such a Letter from you my Father—and I . . . to have given occasion for it. . . .[41]

39. Ibid.
40. Wallace, *Laurens*, pp. 14 and 106.
41. John Laurens to Henry Laurens, Mar. 29, 1775, Berol Manuscripts, Columbia Univ. Library.

John's letter continued in the same vein, thanking his father for pointing out his error, bewailing the fact that he had become "such a Man as I almost hate" through his despicable conduct and supplicating the pardon and pity of the elder Laurens. Asking to be restored to his father's esteem, he signed himself "your Unworthy, tho much afflicted and penitant Son."[42]

In the latter part of April he was still holding his resolution,[43] but early in May (perhaps sooner) he was paying regular visits to Elizabeth Manning, the daughter of his father's London business associate. John wrote of these visits to his sister, but did not mention them to his father at all.[44] A year and five months later he was writing to his uncle that "Pity has obliged me to marry" but that he chose a "clandestine celebration lest the father insist upon my stay in this country as a condition of the marriage": ". . . the matter has proceeded too far to be longer concealed, and I have this morning disclosed the affair to Mr. Manning in plain terms—reserving to myself the right of fulfilling the more important engagements to my country."[45] John concluded the letter by requesting that James keep "the matter" a secret. The next day he wrote to his father asking pardon for making him a father-in-law without his permission and telling him that he might expect soon to be even a grandfather.[46] Without awaiting Henry's reaction to the news of his marriage, John, who had badly wanted to return home because of the impending war, set sail for America in January, leaving his wife and child behind.[47] It is clear that Laurens behaved as well as he could, given the circumstances. It is equally clear, however, that he created those circumstances, giving little thought to the future. The result in this

42. Ibid.

43. John Laurens to Henry Laurens, Apr. 20, 1775, Berol Manuscripts, Columbia Univ. Library.

44. John Laurens to Martha Laurens, May 5, 1775, *Army Correspondence*, pp. 18–20.

45. John Laurens to James Laurens, Oct. 25, 1776, Laurens Papers, cited by Wallace, *Laurens*, p. 465.

46. John Laurens to Henry Laurens, Oct. 26, 1776; Henry Laurens to James Laurens, Mar. 24, 1777, cited by Wallace, *Laurens*, p. 465.

47. Wallace says Laurens finally did receive his father's permission in November 1776 (Wallace, *Laurens*, p. 471). Although Wallace devoted considerable space defending the honor of Miss Manning, he speculated that Laurens stayed in England some months after receiving permission to leave in order "to see his wife safely a mother." Since only three months elapsed from the marriage in October to Laurens's departure in January, Elizabeth must have been pregnant when they married.

case was a birth. The exercise of similar rashness six short years later resulted in his own death.

Henry Laurens did not want his son to abandon his studies. The two had eagerly exchanged information about the struggle between America and England, Henry sending the latest from the colonies and John, who attended Parliament regularly, reporting on the response of His Majesty's government. John's letters, written between 1774 and 1776, are characterized by patriotic fervor. Discussing the possibility of "Civil War" between Britain and America, an event which "many sensible & serious Men" predicted, Laurens tried to persuade his American but pro-British friend Charles Kinlock of the evils of monarchy. He enclosed in letters to his former classmate in Geneva copies of George III's speech from the throne in which the king severely criticized the colonies. He also sent reactions from the House of Lords "reechoing the King's speech," and noted that the Commons was about to follow suit. Laurens declared his determination to return to America should war break out. "I have a Father, I have Sisters, I have the tenderest ties there," he expostulated, adding, "I have a country which claims the small Assistance I can give —O my friend, shall I see Our Fertile Plains laid waste, parcel'd out to new masters? No, we can die but once, and when more gloriously than in defence of our Liberties. . . ."[48] Writing to his father in November 1774 he hoped that ". . . we shall have patriots enough to keep the faint hearts from sinking and false brethren in awe."[49]

As Anglo-American political relations continued to deteriorate, John informed Henry that he had had "the mortification" to hear the king's anti-American speech from the throne "pronounced in a distinct and firm Voice. . . ." The address from the Lords was "no more than the accustomed Echo of the Royal Voice." Lord Hillsborough, he reported, was "most remarkable for Virulence and Rancour. . . .": ". . . we have cherished a Viper [,] said he [Hillsborough] in our bosom, which is now stinging us to Death—and in [the House of Commons] there are dangerous Persons, at this very time secretly going about and poisoning the Minds of his Majesty's Subjects. . . ."[50] Despite John's zeal for the American cause, he continued his respect for the

48. John Laurens to Francis Kinlock, Nov. 6, 1774, Manuscripts Division, New York Public Library.
49. John Laurens to Henry Laurens, Nov. 15, 1774.
50. John Laurens to Henry Laurens, Dec. 3, 1774, Edes Collection, Mass. Historical Society.

king, who, though he might speak against the Americans, spoke in "a distinct & firm Voice." There seems to be some implication, too, in the passage above that not only the minds of his Majesty's subjects were being poisoned but also perhaps the mind of his Majesty himself. And when Laurens wrote to his father of his willingness to fight against the British, it was "the Pride and Obstinacy of the Ministry" he blamed, not that of the king.[51] A few months later John reported George III's delight in the seemingly reformed personality of John Wilkes, the well-known British libertine and crusader for American rights. He told his father that the king's happiness with the "Decency and Propriety" of Wilkes's behavior gave John "a favorable Opinion of the King's generosity," considering "how much he must have suffer'd *as a man of great filial Piety*, for the scandalous Abuse thrown out [by Wilkes] against his Mother."[52] John's feelings about the king, although apparently inconsistent with the cause he espoused, were not at all inconsistent with the character of a young man whose father had bred in him perhaps an excess of filial piety.

Henry appreciated hearing news from England, but he was adamant in not wanting that to be John's sole preoccupation. "Why confine youself wholly to America[?]," he wrote in February 1775. "Why read of nothing but America?"

Your spirited declarations of readiness to bleed in your Country's cause may sound well enough late at night in the Falcon . . . yet my Dear Son, I should be extremely deficient in my Duty if I forbore to tell you freely, that talking and writing of the "cheapness" of ones Life, bear no mark of either. . . . Life is the Gift of God & we are accountable to him not only for, but for the improvement of, it. Reserve your life for your Country's call, but wait the Call—mind your chosen business [,] study to be quiet & do not neglect the proper means which lie before you for serving your Country—or rather for qualifying you in *due time* to serve it. . . .[53]

In August of the same year John wrote his father nevertheless that "every Intelligence [he received]" made him wish to return to America: "What have I to do here in the present Circumstances of my

51. Ibid.
52. John Laurens to Henry Laurens, Apr. 20, 1775, Berol Collection, Columbia Univ. Library; emphasis added.
53. Henry Laurens to John Laurens, Feb. 6, 1775, *SCHM*, IV, no. 4 (1903), pp. 273–77.

Country? What have I not to do at home?"[54] His accurate reading of British politics caused him to warn Henry that the additional protest documents being prepared by Congress would be to no purpose. Even John Hancock's congressional address, he said, would have "no favorable Result . . . no one in British government recognized the Congress."[55] The hope of accommodation was remote: "I see nothing but a promise of continued Bloodshed—till Victory be declared for one or the other party . . . they will therefore make further attempts, God grant us all equally fruitless, to humble us. . . ."[56] By November 1775 Laurens despaired of anything but a protracted armed conflict, writing that the "pleasing hopes which we once entertained of a Reconciliation are vanished."[57]

The young law student showed some political expertise in his assessment of Britain's attempt to sign separate treaties (which would undermine American unity) with each colony. He also foresaw the possibility of a complete break between England and America.[58] He did not, however, dwell on that prospect with any particular enthusiasm. But then such a dutiful son would not easily have cut his ties with the mother country. The letter to Henry written in November 1775 demonstrated an almost hysterical sense of duty in John as he defended himself from his father's charge that he was defying him and begged forgiveness:

. . . if in my zeal I have inadvertently gone too far or have said any thing which implied a Design or Desire of Independence on you or your Counsels, I sincerely ask pardon—and earnestly entreat you to erase those Cruel Lines—No my Dearest Friend and Father, I feel the same Obligation to you, the same unbounded Love at this period of my Life that I have ever hitherto acknowledged and as I am attached to you by firmer ties than any Laws can make—no legal privilege will ever tempt me in the remotest Degree to violate them. . . .[59]

54. John Laurens to Henry Laurens, Aug. 20, 1775, Ford Collection, New York Public Library.
55. Ibid.
56. Ibid.
57. John Laurens to Henry Laurens, Nov. 24, 1775, Feinstone Collection, American Philosophical Society.
58. John Laurens to Francis Kinlock, Apr. 12, 1776, Ford Collection, New York Public Library.
59. John Laurens to Henry Laurens, Nov. 24, 1775, Feinstone Collection, American Philosophical Society.

He concluded by promising to obey in all that his father might require of him.

Although he yearned to return to America and take an active part in the struggle for liberty, Laurens resigned himself to his father's will and continued his study of the law: "the noblest employment of the Mind, and what our Country particularly requires of her Sons at this juncture. . . ."[60] John, who so willingly sacrificed himself to his father's will, thought self-sacrifice on the part of the Americans essential if they were to win the struggle with Britain. The men of property seemed "firm," "resolute," but Laurens worried about support from the "lower class." "Britain," he wrote Kinlock "may destroy our Riches, but what are these to Americans, when set in competition with that Liberty for which they nobly sacrifice their Lives. . . ."[61] Laurens sized up the difficulties Britain was to encounter in her attempt to subdue the colonies. He accurately predicted not only the physical problems British troops would discover in America but also the expense to England of fighting the Americans. Laurens doubted that Britain was really prepared to pay the cost of a war that would enormously increase the national debt. "How long," he queried, "[would] they be able to continue it[?]" Americans, on the other hand, "have already sacrificed their Luxuries and many of them have gone farther, the longer they live in a frugal, temperate manner & the longer they are accustomed to Arms—the more will they despise Affluence and it's [sic] Incidents, the more will they prize Liberty and the better able will they be to repulse their Enemies. . . ."[62] The influence of the father's principles on the son is evident in this letter although also evident is the younger Laurens's desire to make a name for himself: "If this Struggle continues," he observed to Kinlock, "America will abound with great Characters. . . ."[63] The letter leaves no doubt that John wanted to be one of these great characters.

Two months later, in another letter to Kinlock, Laurens took his strongest stand heretofore in favor of republican government. "I hate the name of King," he told his friend and then proceeded to demolish Kinlock's arguments against democracy. The letter contains a

60. Ibid.
61. John Laurens to Francis Kinlock, Apr. 12, 1776, Ford Collection, New York Public Library.
62. Ibid.
63. Ibid.

startling denunciation of monarchy. If his argument was laden with emotion and put perhaps too much faith in government as a way to make men virtuous, it was also, given the premises, well argued. Laurens may have been studying hard, but it seems evident from his letters of the period that he was also reading many pamphlets concerning the Anglo-American struggle. He undoubtedly spent time arguing his beliefs with other students in London coffee houses.

To Americans today some of Laurens's words may well seem prophetic. Citizens of a healthy state, he argued, must not concern themselves with the acquisition of private fortunes or become too dependent upon "Riches" and "Luxuries." The public good should be put foremost and the "Ambition of acquiring greater Riches than the rest of ones fellow Citizens, the establishing that odious Inequality of Fortunes" must be curbed, by law if necessary.[64] (One can hardly fail to think of monopolies and oil companies.) Laurens predicted that if the new republic did not live up to its ideals it would advance "from Infancy, to the Corruption of an old and Ruin'd State, without ever having had any intermediate Maturity. . . ."[65] He also decried the use of slaves in a country of free men:

I think we Americans at least in the Southern Colonies, cannot contend with a good Grace, for liberty, until we shall have enfranchised our Slaves—how can we whose jealously has been alarm'd more at the name of oppression sometimes than at the Reality, reconcile to our spirited Assertions of the Rights of Mankind, the [   ] abject Slavery of our Negroes. . . .[66]

He did not believe that slavery was necessary to the South, but, he wrote Kinlock, even if it were, generous souls would "sacrifice Interest to establish the Happiness of so large a part of the Inhabitants of our Soil. . . . Let us try it [farming without slave labor] as a country—and *ubi libertas Patria* (where there is a fatherland, let there be liberty.)"[67] Henry Laurens held a similar position on the question of slavery as had his father before him.[68] It was the intrepid

64. John Laurens to Francis Kinlock, June 16, 1776, Laurens MSS., Boston Public Library.

65. John Laurens to Francis Kinlock, Apr. 12, 1776, Ford Collection, New York Public Library.

66. Ibid.

67. Ibid.

68. Wallace, *Laurens*, pp. 65–68; 445–55.

John Laurens, though, who tried to put his principles into practice in his efforts to raise and command a black regiment.[69]

Laurens returned to America early in 1777[70] and joined the army; he was taken onto Washington's staff perhaps through the influence of his father.[71] At the age of twenty-two he became an aide-de-camp of Washington, who greatly valued his service. During 1777 John fought at Germantown, Monmouth, and Rhode Island. He quickly gained a reputation for taking grave risks and again he displayed his propensity for courting death during 1779 at the siege of Savannah and the defense of Charleston.[72] He did not exactly cover himself with glory on the latter occasion. Moving his troops without authority to engage the enemy he was badly wounded and nearly lost one-fourth of General Moultrie's army.

His rashness on the battlefield is, perhaps, reflected in his admirable attempt to form a black regiment. Earlier his idea had been opposed even by his egalitarian father as a notion for which the world was not yet ready.[73] But raising such a regiment had become an *idée fixe*: "It will be my duty and my pride to transform the timid slave into a firm defender of liberty & render him worthy to enjoy it himself . . . As a soldier, as a citizen, as a man, I am interested to engage in this work, and I would chearfully [*sic*] sacrifice the largest portion of my future expectations to its success."[74] At first a voice crying in the wilderness, Laurens eventually found favor with the Congress which, on March 29, 1777, recommended, because of the desperate state of the war in the South, that South Carolina and Georgia raise three thousand black troops. According to the congressional plan, the blacks were to serve under white commanders and were to be freed at the end of the war. Congress would recompense their former masters. John's proposal failed in the state legislature, where it was "blown up with contemptuous huzzas."[75] Three years later Laurens reintroduced his proposal for a regiment of

69. Ibid., pp. 448–55.
70. Ibid., p. 471.
71. Ibid., p. 472.
72. Ibid., p. 477.
73. Ibid., p. 488.
74. John Laurens to Henry Laurens, Feb. 17 and Mar. 10, 1779, *SCHM*, IV (1903), 138, 139.
75. Wallace, *Laurens*, p. 450.

black troops. The South Carolina legislature turned it down again, although it received twice as many votes the second time.[76]

On September 29, 1779, John Laurens was appointed by the Continental Congress secretary to the minister plenipotentiary at the Court of Versailles. Laurens, however, declined the appointment, feeling that he had more to offer on the battlefield. He was again honored by Congress in 1780, when he was elected unanimously special minister for procuring a loan from the French.[77] There is evidence that he did not want this appointment either, but, being convinced that he was the most able man for the job, he dutifully accepted.

Arriving in Paris in the middle of March, Laurens found himself put off by "fair promises and no performance."[78] Realizing the importance of obtaining French assistance, Laurens apparently threw protocol to the winds, upsetting Franklin, amazing the French minister Vergennes, but succeeding in his mission. Captain William Jackson, Laurens's secretary at the time, recounted forty-one years later that Laurens spoke so sharply to Vergennes that the latter "in a manner at once smiling and sarcastic, observed—Colonel Laurens, you are so recently from the Head Quarters of the American Army that you forget that you are no longer delivering the orders of the Commander-in-Chief, but that you are addressing the minister of a monarch, who has every disposition to favour your country." To this veiled threat Laurens is said to have replied, "Unless the succour I solicit is immediately accorded, I may be compelled, to draw against France, as a British subject."[79] Laurens returned triumphantly home on August 25, 1781, bringing with him 2,500,000 livres ($500,000) in cash and two cargoes of military supplies. The mission had taken Laurens only six months and twelve days.

Colonel Laurens, after reporting to Congress, joined Washington at Yorktown where he again triumphed and was allowed to negotiate the terms of surrender. In January 1782 he attended the South Carolina legislature and then rejoined the forces fighting in the South. On August 27, with the war virtually at an end, he arose from his

76. Ibid., p. 452.
77. Continental Congress to John Laurens, Dec. 23, 1780, American Philosophical Society.
78. Wallace, *Laurens*, p. 483.
79. Ibid.

sickbed to lead troops against a British expedition in search of provisions. In disregard of his orders, he pursued the enemy and was shot to death by the British, who lay in ambush for him. "No man," wrote Washington of him, "possessed more of the *amor patriae*. In a word, he had not a fault, that I could ever discover, unless intrepidity bordering on rashness could come under that denomination; and to this he was excited by the purest motives."[80] John Adams wrote to Laurens's father that the country had lost its most promising character in the young Laurens.[81] Benjamin Franklin, who had hoped that Laurens would succeed him in Paris, considered no one better qualified for the position.[82]

What, then, is the meaning of John Laurens's life and death? Certainly his early experiences were significant. The death of Elizabeth Laurens left Henry a very prominent place in John's young life. The unfolding developments noted above can perhaps best be interpreted within the context of Henry's and John's relationship. The elder Laurens disliked London and sent John to Geneva, where he obtained a classical education. Did he internalize classical values, as Weir suggests, and thus seek death in battle as an appropriate end to a life modeled on the literature of Cicero and Horace? Many young men were similarly educated without later courting death recklessly. Other factors must also have been at work. And it may be worth noting that John eventually threw over his studies in Geneva and returned to decadent London, a decision his father strenuously opposed. Furthermore, it was in London that John impregnated a girl whom he felt compelled to marry.

Weir has postulated, too, that the puritan ethic was a major factor in the development of John's character. It seems unlikely, however, that the puritan ethic could have had much influence on John, a southern aristocrat far removed from middle-class New England. As Carl Bridenbaugh has emphasized, southern culture in general lacked the compulsive drive of transplanted Calvinism. John, a descendant of immigrants, doubtless identified with his southern peers and their values rather than the Huguenot tradition of his ancestors.

In other important respects John diverged from family tradition.

80. George Washington, *The Writings of George Washington*, ed. John C. Fitzpatrick (Washington, D.C., 1921–44), IX, 100, cited by Wallace, *Laurens*, p. 489.

81. John Adams to Henry Laurens, Nov. 6, 1782, ibid.

82. Benjamin Franklin to John Laurens, May 17, 1781, ibid.

Through the generations the Laurens family emphasized frugality; as has been demonstrated above, he was practically a spendthrift. His letters, filled with guilt, are unconvincing testimonials, for John continued in debt throughout his residence in Europe.

In bright contrast to his family tradition of almost single-minded devotion to the accumulation of wealth, John Laurens demonstrated remarkable concern for others. Whether considering careers in law, medicine, or the ministry, the younger Laurens always focused upon service to humanity. Hence it is not surprising to find him campaigning to free slaves or supporting the use of black troops.

Since John developed his own ideas concerning his education, a career, the handling of money, and other matters, his decision to abandon London and cross the ocean to join the Revolution in express contradiction to his father's wish should not have been unexpected. If Henry was prudent in his approach to the war, John was reckless. Time and again he narrowly escaped death. Despite or perhaps because of cautions from his father, Alexander Hamilton, and others, Laurens almost defiantly threw himself against the fates. Weir has suggested that John was responding to his father's impossible demands by deliberately courting death. Indeed, Laurens's impetuosity can be glimpsed at almost every juncture of his life.

Looking back in summary at the events of John's life, I concur in the view that he unconsciously searched for death as a way out of an impossible situation. But it is also worth noting that John's death was the culmination of a pattern which developed early. Henry moved John from London to Geneva; John moved himself back to London, and in the event discontinued the studies his father wanted him to complete. Cautioning John to be prudent in his relationships with others, Henry was dismayed to discover that he had gotten a girl pregnant and was forced to marry her. Urging his son to be financially responsible, Henry was required frequently to send him large sums of money. Despite parental advice to remain in London and finish his legal studies, John defiantly crossed the ocean and joined the American cause. Ignoring pleas from family and friends, John recklessly and frequently risked his life in battle.

While John said he wished to please his father, he in fact did just the opposite, as the events of his life demonstrate. Such a pattern of behavior is typical of adolescence; John continued it to age twenty-seven. It would appear that Henry Laurens's attempt to superimpose upon John his own system of values left John a zealot without standards, a puppet who acted only in response to his father's wishes. Had he emerged a man with internalized values of his own, he might have lived to join Hamilton in Washington's first cabinet.

Part III. The Framework of Military Conflict in the South

Britain's Southern Strategy

Ira D. Gruber   *Rice University*

During the War for American Independence engagements were often fought on ground chosen by the rebels. American officers decided to fortify Breed's Hill; to defend New York and Charleston; to stand at White Plains, Fort Washington, Brandywine, and Guilford Court House; and to attack Trenton, Savannah, and Yorktown. But with few exceptions the British determined where campaigns would take place, where the center of fighting would be from one season to the next. Weighing political and military considerations against geography, topography, and climate, British leaders ever sought the right place and the right plans for ending the rebellion. They gathered their forces first at Boston, then in the middle colonies and along the periphery of New England, and finally at New York and in the South. And they pursued a variety of strategies: isolating and crushing resistance in the most disloyal provinces, combining an overwhelming display of force with conciliatory gestures, destroying the Continental Army in a climactic battle, and raising loyalist forces to help recover the colonies piecemeal. This essay examines British strategy in one theatre of the war—in the colonies lying south of the Potomac River. It asks why the British decided to send forces to the southern colonies, what strategies they employed there, and how those strategies were related to their overall plans for restoring royal government in America.

When in January of 1775 the British government first decided to use troops to enforce its authority in America, it gave little thought to the South or to the middle colonies. Massachusetts had long been considered the center of colonial unrest, and by early 1775 nearly two-thirds of all British troops in North America were assembled at

Boston. Thus a desire to punish Massachusetts and the disposition of available forces led the ministry to act first in New England, to see whether crushing the spirit of resistance in the most disloyal of colonies would not have a therapeutic effect throughout America. The ministry sent reinforcements to Boston and ordered General Thomas Gage, the commander in chief, "to take a more active and determined Part": to gather any additional troops he might need from other garrisons in America, arrest and imprison leaders of the provincial congress, and, if necessary, impose martial law in Massachusetts.[1] When Gage reported a cooling of revolutionary feeling, the ministry merely urged him to be more aggressive. Sending three major generals to Boston and four regiments to New York, it instructed him to employ the four regiments either along the Hudson (to cut off supplies flowing from the middle colonies to New England) or at Boston (to augment his own forces). He was also to continue arresting leading rebels and to begin dismantling or occupying fortifications and seizing magazines. The ministry hoped that these firm measures would restore order throughout America without starting a war. It was, however, prepared to fight to preserve the empire.[2]

The ministry did not rely on force alone. Its strategy of ending the rebellion by isolating and punishing New England depended on political and economic as well as military measures. In February Lord North, the king's principal minister, asked the House of Commons to declare Massachusetts in rebellion and to endorse the use of troops. He then sought permission to introduce a bill restraining the trade of New England to Great Britain and the British West Indies and prohibiting New Englanders from fishing the Banks of Newfoundland. Having made clear the penalties for rebellion, he offered a conciliatory resolution: whenever a colony agreed to support its own government and to contribute its share toward imperial defense, Parliament would lay taxes in that colony only for the regulation of trade and would return any revenue from such taxes for the use of the colony in which it was collected. By encouraging each colony to treat separately with the mother country, he hoped to undermine the authority of Congress, weaken the colonies' capacity to support New

1. William Legge, Earl of Dartmouth, to Gage, Jan. 27, 1775, Colonial Office Papers, 5/92, Public Record Office, London. Hereafter cited as C.O. 5/92.
2. Gage to Dartmouth, Jan. 18, 1775, and Dartmouth to Gage, Apr. 15, 1775, C.O. 5/92.

England, and satisfy those ministers and members of Parliament who favored a peaceful settlement of the imperial crisis. Although North was subsequently forced to place restrictions on the trade of other colonies and to acknowledge that his conciliatory resolution made no genuine concessions, he would continue for several years to insist that persuasion be a part of British strategy.[3]

So it was that the ministry adopted a comprehensive plan for ending the rebellion by subduing New England. But during the spring of 1775 the ministry also began drifting toward another, separate strategy. It did so in response to the little good news then arriving from America. Indeed, with one exception, royal governors from New Hampshire to South Carolina declared themselves powerless. Colonists everywhere were establishing revolutionary governments, choosing delegates for the second Continental Congress, raising armed forces, supporting economic sanctions against Britain, and offering material as well as moral support for Massachusetts. Parliamentary resolutions that called upon the king to use force and offered to let the colonists tax themselves neither intimidated nor attracted the rebels.[4] Only in North Carolina were the loyalists still said to be in a majority; only there did a royal governor believe he had sufficient popular support "to maintain the sovereignty of this country to [his] royal master in all Events."[5] Desperately eager for such news, the ministry did all that it could to encourage Governor Josiah Martin and to enlist the support of loyal North Carolinians. It authorized Lieutenant Colonel Allan Maclean to recruit a provincial regiment in North Carolina for service in New England; and it urged Governor Martin to organize loyal associations, consider arming them, and apply to General Gage, if necessary, for the assistance of a regular army officer.[6] In these instructions the ministry first approached a strategy of employing loyal colonists to preserve royal government.

Thus the British had adopted one strategy and anticipated another before war began in Massachusetts. Although their forces fared

3. Ira D. Gruber, *The Howe Brothers and the American Revolution* (Chapel Hill, N.C., 1974), pp. 16–19.

4. John Murray, Earl of Dunmore, to Dartmouth, Mar. 14, 1775, C.O. 5/1353; Josiah Martin to Dartmouth, Jan. 26, March 10 and 23, Apr. 7, 1775, C.O. 5/318; Thomas Gage to Dartmouth, Feb. 17 and 20, March 4, 1775, C.O. 5/92; William Bull to Dartmouth, Jan. 20, Feb. 22, Mar. 28, May 1, 1775, C.O. 5/396.

5. Josiah Martin to Dartmouth, Mar. 10, Apr. 20, 1775, C.O. 5/318.

6. Dartmouth to Gage, Apr. 15, May 3, 1775, C.O. 5/92; Dartmouth to Martin, May 3, 1775, C.O. 5/318.

badly in the initial fighting at Lexington and Concord and were subsequently besieged in Boston, the British did not begin to revise their
strategies until after the Battle of Bunker Hill. Gage and his generals
then agreed that the rebels were a formidable enemy and that further
efforts to break the siege of Boston or invade eastern Massachusetts
would be foolish. None as yet doubted that the rebellion could be put
down provided there were at least twenty thousand troops to do it,
and none seems to have questioned the ministry's strategy of isolating and punishing New England. But all, having misgivings about
starting a campaign from Boston, recommended that the offensive
against New England be launched from New York where popular
feeling as well as geography would be more favorable to the British.[7]
The ministry readily agreed to nearly all of these suggestions. It decided to provide an army of twenty thousand by spring, to increase
the North American squadron from thirty to fifty ships, to recall the
"mild" General Gage, and to tell his successor, General William
Howe, that it favored shifting the war to New York.[8]

The ministry remained preoccupied with news of Bunker Hill and
plans for reducing New England until September 10 when it received fresh dispatches from Governor Martin of North Carolina.
Although Martin had been forced to take refuge on a British warship, he remained confident that he could raise loyalists enough in
the Piedmont to recover the Carolinas and to awe Virginia; indeed,
if supported by loyalists and Negroes in other colonies, he would
restore royal government throughout the South. All that he asked
of the ministry was ten thousand stand of arms, six field pieces,
ammunition, money, and authority to proceed.[9] The ministry was

7. Gage to Dartmouth, June 25, July 24, Aug. 20, 1775, C.O. 5/92; abstracts of
letters from John Burgoyne, [June 25, 1775], Aug. 10, 1775, George III, *The Correspondence of King George the Third from 1760 to December 1783*, ed. Sir John
Fortescue (6 vols.; London, 1927–28), III, 224–27, 242–45; Henry Clinton to Henry
Fiennes Clinton, Duke of Newcastle, June 20, July 13, 1775, Newcastle Papers,
University of Nottingham Library, Nottingham; William Howe to Richard Lord
Howe, June 12, 1775, Dartmouth Papers, Staffordshire County Library, Stafford.
8. George III to Frederick Lord North, July 26, 28, Aug. 1, 1775, and memo-
randum of George III, Aug. 5, 1775, George III, *Correspondence*, III, 235–38, 240;
Dartmouth to Thomas Gage, Aug. 2, 1775 (two letters), and Dartmouth to William
Howe, Sept. 5, 1775, C.O. 5/92; Philip Stephens to Samuel Graves, Aug. 3, 1775,
Admiralty Papers, 2/550, Public Record Office, London; hereafter cited as Adm.
2/550.
9. Martin to Dartmouth, June 30, July 16, 1775, C.O. 5/318.

skeptical of Martin's claims, but it was so eager to exploit potential loyalist support that it approved his proposal at once. It subsequently decided to send the arms via General Howe and ordered Howe, in turn, to detach a regiment of regulars to assist Martin.[10] These measures represented a modest increase in the ministry's commitment to a southern strategy. During the spring and early summer the ministry had authorized recruiting in North Carolina, sent three thousand stand of arms to Virginia, and approved Gage's having assigned several companies of regulars to Governor Dunmore.[11] Now it was ordering ten thousand stand of arms together with artillery and a full regiment to North Carolina. The investment and the risks remained small, but the returns might well be large. As Dartmouth told Howe, "there is no doubt that if what Mr. Martin suggests can be effected, it would be an advantage of the greatest Importance next to the regaining our Ground in New York."[12]

Soon after deciding to send troops and arms to North Carolina, the ministry received intelligence that made its southern strategy seem even more promising. In late September it learned from a British officer at Charleston that "a very considerable part of the People" of South Carolina, suffering under the rebels, was prepared to defy its new masters and support royal authority.[13] Governor Dunmore said much the same of Virginia. The rebels had alienated many inhabitants of the Tidewater by imposing arbitrary restrictions on their trade; and even though Dunmore, like Martin, had been forced to flee to a British warship, he remained persuaded as late as August that with "a few hundred" regular troops, a supply of arms and ammunition for loyalists, and authority to exercise command he "could in a few months reduce this colony to perfect submission."[14] Until these dispatches arrived, the ministry had been skeptical of Martin's glowing reports of potential loyalist strength in Piedmont North

10. John Pownall to George III, Sept. 12, 1775 (two letters), George III, *Correspondence*, III, 259–60; Dartmouth to Howe, Sept. 15, 1775, C.O. 5/92; Dartmouth to Martin, Sept. 15, 1775, C.O. 5/318. In October the ministry would decide to send the arms directly to North Carolina: Eric Robson, "The Expedition to the Southern Colonies, 1775–1776," *English Historical Review*, LXVI (1951), 542–43.

11. Dartmouth to John Murray, Earl of Dunmore, July 12, 1775, C.O. 5/1353; Dartmouth to Thomas Gage, July 1, 1775, C.O. 5/92.

12. Dartmouth to William Howe, Sept. 15, 1775, C.O. 5/92.

13. John Pownall to William Howe, Sept. 25, 1775, C.O. 5/92.

14. Dunmore to Dartmouth, Aug. 2, 1775, C.O. 5/1353.

Carolina. Now, the prospect of employing loyalists to help recover the South seemed more plausible and more appealing than ever.

The prospect was particularly appealing to Lord North. Since July he had been trying to raise twenty thousand troops for the ensuing campaign. Having had little success, he was beginning to fear that British forces would not be ready to take the offensive in the spring of 1776 and that the rebellion might drag on disastrously: the rebels tightening their grasp on the colonies, Parliament and the English people losing their patience with the war, and foreign powers finding intervention ever more tempting.[15] In an effort to make use of the slender resources at hand—to "alarm the Americans & raise the spirits of *our friends* who are . . . dissatisfied that we are not acting with sufficient spirit"—North proposed an immediate expedition to the southern colonies. On October 15 he recommended that the king order four or five regiments to sail from Britain for the Carolinas before Christmas. If what the governors said was true, this force would be able to restore loyalists to power throughout the South and still have time to join Howe at New York for a summer offensive against New England. If not, it would at least be able to punish the rebels and establish loyalist enclaves before the campaign began at New York.[16] In short, North enthusiastically embraced a strategy of raising loyalists to recover the South. With a relatively small number of regular troops he would strike a swift, telling blow at the rebellion. He would also complement his efforts to promote a negotiated peace. By demonstrating his commitment to vigorous measures, he would not only persuade Parliament to authorize a peace commission but also encourage the colonists to receive it favorably.[17]

However complex North's motives, his proposal for an expedition to the southern colonies—for a further commitment to a strategy of raising loyalist troops to recover the South—was quickly adopted. By October 16 the king had decided to order five regiments of infantry together with artillery and ten thousand stand of arms to be embarked for North Carolina by December 1. The whole would proceed to the Cape Fear River, which seemed to offer both a safe port

15. Frederick Lord North to George III, Aug. 25, Nov. 12, 1775, George III, *Correspondence*, III, 249, 289–90.

16. North to George III, Oct. 15, 1775, ibid., pp. 265–68; Dartmouth to Howe, Oct. 22, 1775, C.O. 5/92.

17. Gruber, *Howe Brothers*, pp. 5–38.

and a direct approach to the loyal Scottish Highlanders living in the interior.[18] When, subsequently, two regiments were added to the five already preparing to sail, the ministry modified its plans but not its strategy. Seven regiments required more transports and a more powerful escort than five, and there was no assurance that more and larger ships could safely land troops in the Cape Fear River. If, therefore, the river proved unsuitable or if the loyalists of North Carolina did not come forward as expected, the expedition would go on to another colony, preferably South Carolina or Georgia. The governors of the Carolinas would make every effort to see that the loyalists were organized and ready to join the regular forces as soon as they arrived. The commander of the expedition would, in turn, not only take further steps to enlist the loyalists and employ them in restoring royal government but also establish such garrisons, including regular troops, as were necessary to keep order. If he failed to raise loyalists, he would then be free to adopt a different strategy: to establish a base, devote the remainder of the winter to carrying out raids in the South, and take the whole of his force to join Howe early in the spring. But the ministry left no doubt that the "Object & purpose of this Expedition is to endeavour, with the Assistance of the well affected Inhabitants in the Southern Colonies, to effect the Restoration of legal government."[19]

Although North and the king were determined to pursue their southern strategy as expeditiously as possible, they did not have a realistic idea of the time required to do what they wished. In mid-October they decided that their expeditionary force should sail from Cork by December 1, go directly to North Carolina, restore royal

18. George III to North, Oct. 16 [16–17], 1775, George III, *Correspondence*, III, 270–72; Dartmouth to William Howe, Oct. 22, 1775, C.O. 5/92.

19. Quoting Lord George Germain to Henry Clinton, Dec. 6, 1775, C.O. 5/92. Dartmouth to Josiah Martin, Oct. 27, Nov. 7, 1775, C.O. 5/318; Dartmouth to William Howe, Nov. 8, 1775, C.O. 5/92; Dartmouth to Lord William Campbell, Nov. 7, 1775, C.O. 5/396. Paul H. Smith, *Loyalists and Redcoats: A Study in British Revolutionary Policy* (Chapel Hill, N.C., 1964), pp. 24–25, believes that changing the destination of the expedition represented a fundamental alteration in British strategy. If so, it was certainly not intentional. Throughout the autumn the ministry consistently maintained that wherever the expedition went, its purpose was to engage loyalists to help recover the South. Although I differ with Smith on several specific questions, I find his research sound and his broad interpretations nearly always reliable. In assessing the role of loyalists in British strategy he comes closer than anyone to a comprehensive study of Britain's southern strategy in the American war.

government, and join Howe "as early in the Spring as possible."[20] Their plans reflected a desire to act decisively and a fear that any delays would jeopardize their prospects of raising loyalists and of recovering the South. But their plans allowed no room for error.[21] If the expedition had sailed from Cork on December 1 as scheduled, it is unlikely that it could have reached Cape Fear before the first week in February or that it would have had much more than eight weeks to subdue the southern colonies. As it was, administrative inefficiencies, accidents, and foul weather kept the fleet from reaching North Carolina until early May.[22] By then British prospects in the South were so altered and the season so far advanced as to require a complete reappraisal of the strategy which North had proposed in October.

Just as delays would affect Britain's southern strategy so too would the personalities of the commanding officers. Major General Henry Clinton, who in October 1775 was serving as second in command to General Howe, would proceed from Boston to Cape Fear to take command of the land forces as soon as they arrived from Ireland. Major General Charles, Earl Cornwallis, would embark at Cork and serve as Clinton's second.[23] The two generals were friends and had much in common. Both enjoyed the advantages of powerful families and friends; both were considered highly competent and courageous officers; both had served primarily in Germany during the Seven Years War; and both, favoring a negotiated settlement with the colonies, were serving in the American war—in part, at least, out of a sense of duty. However similar their opportunities, training, and achievements, their personalities were fundamentally different. Clinton, for all of his ability, was unsure of himself—comfortable with only a few close friends, reluctant to press his views on superiors, and greatly inhibited by the responsibilities of command. Cornwallis,

20. Dartmouth to William Howe, Oct. 22, 1775, and, quoting, Lord George Germain to Henry Clinton, Dec. 6, 1775, C.O. 5/92.

21. As a single ship usually took ten weeks to sail from Portsmouth to New York, a convoy was sure to take longer to reach North Carolina. Gruber, *Howe Brothers*, p. 357.

22. David Syrett, *Shipping and the American War 1775–83: A Study of British Transport Organization* (London, 1970), pp. 194–95; Robson, "Expedition to Southern Colonies," pp. 539–48; John Montagu, Earl of Sandwich, to George III, Jan. 11, 1776, George III, *Correspondence*, III, 328–31.

23. Lord George Germain to Clinton, Dec. 6, 1775, and Germain to Cornwallis, Dec. 6, 1775, C.O. 5/92; Frederick Lord North to George III, [Nov. 26, 1775], George III, *Correspondence*, 294–95.

by contrast, was a confident, gregarious man, filled with energy, and capable of acting decisively—even rashly. Such divergent personalities did not promise to complement each other. Clinton understood the rebellion and Britain's strategic prospects better than Cornwallis. Yet lacking the capacity to act, he was almost sure to frustrate and to be frustrated by his energetic, ambitious lieutenant.[24] Their mutual frustrations would in time have an important influence on Britain's southern strategy. For the present—for the campaign of 1776—Clinton would find other officers more trying than Cornwallis.

On January 6, 1776, Clinton learned that he was to command the expedition to the southern colonies. Two weeks later he sailed south from Boston. At New York City and at Hampton Roads he heard encouraging reports from North Carolina; indeed he would not have been surprised to find both loyalists and redcoats awaiting his orders at Cape Fear. When at last he arrived on March 12, he found neither. The Loyalists, having risen prematurely in North and South Carolina, had been defeated, disarmed, and dispersed. The redcoats were unaccountably overdue.[25] These circumstances forced Clinton to consider alternative ways of carrying out the ministry's strategy. It was clear that he would not have time to advance to the loyalist settlements in the interior or to undertake an attack on the formidable rebel defenses at Charleston. He decided, therefore, to recommend establishing posts on Perquimans River off Albemarle Sound and on Elizabeth River adjacent to Norfolk. These posts together with the Great Dismal Swamp would secure a tract of fertile land along the coast of North Carolina as a refuge and a base. There he would gather loyalists, and thence he would employ them with small detachments of regulars in attacking Virginia and the Carolinas, making accommodation more attractive to the rebels in the South.[26]

24. William B. Willcox, *Portrait of a General: Sir Henry Clinton in the War of Independence* (New York, 1964), pp. 3–93; Franklin and Mary Wickwire, *Cornwallis: The American Adventure* (Boston, 1970), pp. 7–46, 74–80.
25. Henry Clinton, *The American Rebellion: Sir Henry Clinton's Narrative of His Campaigns, 1775–1782, with an Appendix of Original Documents*, ed. William B. Willcox (New Haven, Conn., 1954), pp. 23–26; Willcox, *Portrait of a General*, 68–77; Lord William Campbell to Dartmouth, Jan. 1, 1776, C.O. 5/396; Josiah Martin to Dartmouth, Jan. 12, 1776, and Martin to Lord George Germain, Mar. 21, 1776, C.O. 5/318.
26. Josiah Martin to Lord George Germain, July 5, 1776, C.O. 5/318; Henry Clinton to Hugh Lord Percy, March 24, [1776], Vol. LI, Percy Papers, Alnwick Castle, Alnwick, Northumberland; Clinton, *American Rebellion*, pp. 26–28; Willcox, *Portrait of a General*, pp. 82–84.

On March 23 Clinton wrote Howe asking permission to pursue this plan. Before he received a reply much of the spring had slipped away, and he had decided to postpone further efforts to carry out the ministry's southern strategy. As early as April 21 he conceded that his prospects of accomplishing anything in the South before summer were very poor: the loyalists had been suppressed, the rebels were thoroughly aroused, and the main British force from Cork had not arrived. By the time that force reached Cape Fear on May 3 Clinton thought mainly of joining Howe. Not that he had lost confidence in the loyalists or in the strategy of employing them to recover the South, but he doubted he could create secure loyalist communities before summer, and he feared that doing less would expose the loyalists to retaliation and destroy their willingness to serve in the future. By May 18 Clinton was ready to leave the South, but not knowing where to go—where to join Howe—he decided to embark his forces for Virginia and wait there for further orders.[27]

He was soon persuaded to change his plans—indeed, to depart sharply from the ministry's southern strategy. He did so at the request of Commodore Sir Peter Parker, who was reluctant to leave the South without making some effort to cripple the rebellion. Shortly after reaching Cape Fear Parker had sent two officers to reconnoiter Charleston, which was considered by Governor Lord William Campbell and the ministry to be the center of rebellion in the southern colonies as well as an important base for privateers.[28] The two officers returned on May 26 to report that although the town was strongly fortified, the works on Sullivan's Island commanding the entrance to the harbor were as yet unfinished and vulnerable to attack. Parker thereupon urged Clinton to join forces in capturing Sullivan's Island. At almost the same time Clinton received a letter from Howe expressing a preference for taking Charleston and giving him leave to stay in the South somewhat longer. Lacking the confidence to refuse both Parker and Howe, Clinton put aside his own plans for quitting the South. He did not

27. Clinton, *American Rebellion*, p. 28; Clinton to Hugh Lord Percy, Apr. 21, [1776], Vol. L, Percy Papers; Clinton to Henry Fiennes Clinton, Duke of Newcastle, May 18, [1776] and "Out Lines of General Clinton's plan for a Winter Expedition" [c. May 18, 1776], Newcastle Papers.

28. Lord William Campbell to William Legge, Earl of Dartmouth, Oct. 19, 1775, C.O. 5/396; Lord George Germain to Henry Clinton, Dec. 6, 1775, C.O. 5/92; Francis Rawdon-Hastings, Lord Rawdon, to Francis Hastings, Earl of Huntingdon, July 3, 1776, Hastings Papers, Henry E. Huntington Library, San Marino.

expect to be able to take Charleston or to restore the loyalists to power in South Carolina. He did manage to persuade himself that occupying Sullivan's Island would not merely close the harbor and prepare the way for a future attack on the town but would also let the loyalists know that they had not been abandoned. However flimsy the connection between taking Sullivan's Island and pursuing the ministry's strategy, Clinton persisted in going to Charleston even after learning that he was "to proceed immediately to join Major General Howe . . . if . . . nothing could be soon effected that would be of great and essential service." Such persistence led only to an abortive attack on Sullivan's Island and further delays. Clinton did not join Howe at New York until August 1.[29] It would be more than two and one-half years before the British returned in force to the southern colonies.

In the interim the British would concentrate on ending the rebellion in New England and the middle colonies. Ministers and general officers had agreed soon after the Battle of Bunker Hill to withdraw from Boston, assemble their forces at New York, and devote the campaign of 1776 to an offensive against New England. But they did not agree on how that offensive was to be conducted. The king and a majority of his advisors expected that General Howe and his brother, Admiral Richard Lord Howe, would take New York, occupy the Hudson River Valley, and join forces with an army from Canada in destroying the Continental army and conquering New England. Once the rebellion had been broken and royal government restored, the Howes would discuss a reconciliation. Neither the Howes nor General Guy Carleton, commanding British forces in Canada, shared the ministry's preference for crushing the rebellion. The three senior British officers in America were too deeply concerned with pacifying the colonists and preserving their own armies and fleet to favor a devastating offensive. All hoped to end the resistance with a combination of force and persuasion, to apply just enough military pressure to make an accommodation attractive. Relying primarily on flanking maneuvers and limited engagements, they drove the rebels from New York, Rhode Island, portions of New Jersey, and Lake Champlain. Although they did not succeed in destroying the Continental army or in isolating New England, and although they had

29. Willcox, *Portrait of a General*, pp. 84–85; Clinton, *American Rebellion*, pp. 29–30; Robson, "Expedition to Southern Colonies," pp. 554–56.

no genuine concessions to make, they did force many colonists to think seriously of a negotiated settlement. Indeed the rebellion might well have collapsed during the winter of 1776–77 had not Washington won brilliant victories at Trenton and Princeton, victories that restored American morale and revealed the weaknesses of a strategy that was neither wholly coercive nor effectively conciliatory.[30]

British strategy for 1777, like that for 1776, suffered for want of coordination and cooperation. The ministry believed that it had approved plans for securing the middle colonies and conquering New England. It expected that Sir William Howe would open the campaign by capturing Philadelphia and restoring the loyalists to power in Pennsylvania and that he would then return to New York, proceed up the Hudson, and join an army from Canada in attacking Massachusetts. The ministry also urged the Howes to send detachments of ships and men to scour the coasts of New England. General Burgoyne, who had been appointed to take Carleton's place at the head of the troops advancing south from Canada, shared the ministry's understanding of the plans for 1777. The Howes did not. General Howe talked initially of cooperating with the Canadian army along the Hudson. But once he began planning an expedition to Philadelphia—once he became obsessed with raising loyalist troops in Pennsylvania—he promised no more than a corps to act defensively upon the lower Hudson, to cover New Jersey and to "facilitate in some Degree the Approach of the army from Canada."[31] Having warned Burgoyne, he left New York in July and proceeded to Philadelphia by way of Chesapeake Bay. By the time he received explicit instructions to "cooperate with the Army ordered to proceed from Canada and put itself under your command," he was in the Chesapeake and incapable of doing what the ministry wished. Howe went on to capture Philadelphia while Burgoyne, without support from New York, was trapped at Saratoga. His surrender was the result primarily of uncoordinated efforts—of the ministry's having failed to ensure that what Howe planned was compatible with an offensive from Canada and of Howe's having willfully ignored what he knew to be the ministry's intentions.[32]

30. Gruber, *Howe Brothers*, pp. 77–157; A. G. Bradley, *Lord Dorchester* (New York, 1926), Chaps. 6–7.

31. Sir William Howe to Lord George Germain, Dec. 20, 1776, C.O. 5/94.

32. Quoting Lord George Germain to Sir William Howe, May 18, 1777, C.O. 5/94. Gruber, *Howe Brothers*, pp. 158–267.

Burgoyne's surrender produced sharp changes in British strategy for 1778. The loss of his army not only left Canada vulnerable to attack but also reduced dramatically the number of troops available for an offensive against the rebels. For once experts on both sides of the Atlantic agreed that huge reinforcements would be required to destroy the Continental army and recover New England,[33] The ministry was by no means willing to abandon the war or concede American independence. But it did not have the resources to reinforce Canada, garrison the middle colonies, and provide all of the additional troops that would be required for a conquest of New England. It decided, therefore, to adopt a strategy consistent with its limited means. It would reinforce Canada (as well as Nova Scotia, Newfoundland, and the Floridas); add a few thousand troops to those in the middle colonies; abandon Philadelphia if necessary to release men for active service; and rely more than ever on British warships and loyal colonists. It would also recall General Howe, who was not aggressive enough to satisfy a majority of the ministry, and offer terms of conciliation to keep the European powers from intervening openly on the side of the rebels. On March 8 it ordered the new commander in chief, Sir Henry Clinton, to combine raiding warfare and a blockade in the North with further efforts to employ loyalists in recovering the South. If Clinton were unable to bring the Continental army to action at the beginning of the campaign, he was to send detachments to destroy American ports from New York to Nova Scotia. When these operations were completed and while other detachments created a diversion in Chesapeake Bay, he would embark seven thousand troops for Georgia. The ministry assumed that such a force, supported by regular units from East Florida and by loyalists, would soon be able to restore royal government in Georgia and the Carolinas; that Virginia would then fall; and that without the support of the South the rebellion in the North would collapse under a blockade.[34]

Here for the first time in the War for American Independence operations in the southern colonies had come to have a principal place in British strategy. North's expedition to the Carolinas in 1776 had

33. Sir William Howe to Lord George Germain, Nov. 30, 1777, C.O. 5/95; J. C. Long, *Lord Jeffery Amherst: A Soldier of the King* (New York, 1933), p. 238.
34. Lord George Germain to Sir Henry Clinton, Mar. 8, 1778, most secret, C.O. 5/95; Gruber, *Howe Brothers*, pp. 278–79.

been a speculative adventure involving less than a tenth of the regular forces in the colonies. Although some members of the government believed the expedition to be potentially important, none seems to have regarded it as more than complementary to the primary objective of the campaign: the conquest of New England. Similarly, although Sir William Howe did include expeditions to Virginia, South Carolina, and Georgia in his first plans for the campaign of 1777, those expeditions were to be undertaken only after operations along the Hudson were completed and only if there were then troops to spare. In revising his plans Howe omitted any mention of operations in the South; and by January of 1778 he was so discouraged by his failure to enlist loyalists in Pennsylvania and so eager to resign his command that he rejected flatly a ministerial proposal for a winter expedition to Georgia and South Carolina.[35] Now, however, on March 8, 1778, the ministry was ordering Clinton to include the South in his plans for the ensuing campaign. It still held faint hopes that he would be able to lure Washington into a decisive battle, and it intended to devote a considerable number of ships and men to a maritime war on New England, to a series of raids and a blockade. But the primary effort ashore in 1778 was to be made in Georgia and the Carolinas. Britain's southern strategy had become an integral part of British strategy.

It had become so because the ministry, desperate for a quick and inexpensive way to end the rebellion, was swayed by the reports of refugees from the southern colonies. The former governors of Georgia and the Carolinas were particularly skillful in emphasizing the advantages of campaigning in the South. Attributing the failure of the expedition of 1776 to chance, and ignoring the obstacles that climate, topography, and geography would present to any extended operations south of the Chesapeake, they argued not merely that a majority of southerners remained loyal and would gladly help restore royal government but also that recovering the South would weaken the rebels elsewhere by depriving them of a principal source of raw materials.[36] These arguments became even more effective after Burgoyne's surrender diminished support for the war in England and

35. Sir William Howe to Lord George Germain, Nov. 30, 1776, C.O. 5/93; Germain to Howe, Sept. 3, 1777, C.O. 5/94; Howe to Germain, Jan. 16, 1778, C.O. 5/95.
36. Smith, *Loyalists and Redcoats*, pp. 29–31, 89–90.

encouraged France to take an overt part in behalf of the rebels. The ministry had not then the time or the money to raise substantial regular forces and mount a new offensive against New England. It had to rely primarily on the regular forces that were already available in the colonies and on the one source of popular support that had not as yet been fully tried—the loyalists of the southern colonies. If the governors of Georgia and the Carolinas were right, the British would have at once and at little expense all of the troops they needed to secure the South. The ministry would also have evidence to justify continuing the war, to support its contention that a majority of the colonists were basically loyal and sought only an opportunity to escape the tyranny of the rebels. Necessity, in short, led the ministry to follow the dreams of exiled governors and give the South a prominent place in British strategy for 1778.

Although this strategy was set forth in instructions of March 8, 1778, it was not carried out for nearly eight months. In the interim the ministry and the commanders in chief were forced to adopt very different measures. On March 13 the French government announced that it had concluded a treaty of amity and commerce with the United States, an announcement that was tantamount to a declaration of war. The ministry was, of course, angered by this blatant interference in its imperial affairs and eager to have revenge—to strike a blow against the French West Indies. Although it also wished to continue the war against its rebellious subjects, it had to put aside temporarily the strategy of March 8. There simply were not forces enough to carry out extensive operations in North America and to wage war with a major European power simultaneously. On March 21 the ministry ordered Clinton and Admiral Howe to prepare at once for a war with France. They were to detach five thousand troops and eleven warships to capture the French island of St. Lucia and three thousand men with a suitable naval escort to reinforce the Floridas. They were then to evacuate Philadelphia, go to New York, and await the issue of new peace overtures. If the overtures failed or if they found themselves in jeopardy, they were to abandon New York for Halifax, making sure that Rhode Island, Canada, and Newfoundland were secure. If they were able to stay at New York, they were to consider raiding rebel ports. But once they had settled at New York or Halifax Howe was to send home fourteen frigates and six sloops.[37] These complicated instructions were considerably simplified by events in America. Before Clinton and Howe could do more than evacuate Philadelphia, their efforts were interrupted by the arrival of a French fleet. For the remainder of the summer they were far too busy with the French to carry out their secret instructions of March 21, and by the time Clinton saw his way clear to send troops to St. Lucia and the Floridas, he was once again considering the ministry's instructions of March 8.[38]

On October 10 he received orders for resuming the war in North America. He was not to interrupt the departure of ships and men for the West Indies, the Floridas, and other scattered posts. But if the rebellion continued, he was to do more than hold New York and Rhode Island. He was to pursue the ministry's strategy of March 8 as far as limited resources and altered circumstances would allow. The ministry urged him specifically to attack colonial ports and to consider a winter expedition to Georgia and South Carolina.[39] When these orders reached New York, the season for raiding warfare had passed, and Clinton had neither the inclination nor the resources for a major offensive in the southern colonies. Believing that the American War had been subordinated to the war with France, that his forces were inadequate for ending the rebellion, and that his reputation was in jeopardy, he had already asked permission to resign his command. He also knew that once he sent detachments to St. Lucia, the Floridas, the Bahamas, Bermuda, Nova Scotia, and the British Isles, there would be few men or ships to spare from the defense of the middle colonies.[40] Hence, to satisfy the ministry without committing himself to extended or hazardous operations and without risking his posts at New York or Rhode Island, he decided to add a thousand men to the two thousand that were being sent to reinforce East Florida and to order the whole to attack Georgia. He doubted

37. Lord George Germain to Sir Henry Clinton, most secret, Mar. 21, 1778, and secret instructions for Sir Henry Clinton, Mar. 21, 1778, C.O. 5/95; Gruber, *Howe Brothers*, pp. 280–81.

38. Gruber, *Howe Brothers*, pp. 297–324.

39. Lord George Germain to Sir Henry Clinton, Aug. 5, 1778, C.O. 5/96; Smith, *Loyalists and Redcoats*, p. 92. Clinton, *American Rebellion*, pp. 116, 118, is misleading: it confuses the ministry's instructions of Aug. 5, 1778, with those of Dec. 3, 1778, and Jan. 23, 1779.

40. Sir Henry Clinton to Henry Fiennes Clinton, Duke of Newcastle, Sept. 21, 1778, Newcastle Papers; extract, Clinton to Lord George Germain, Oct. 8, 1778, Clinton, *American Rebellion*, pp. 392–93; Clinton to Germain, Nov. 8, 1778, C.O. 5/96.

that such an expedition would yield any "permanent advantage."
But he thought this a relatively safe and inexpensive way of testing
the disposition of the colonists in the South and of seeing whether
the restoration of royal government in one colony would weaken the
rebellion elsewhere. At the very least recovering Georgia promised
to deprive the rebels of some of their staples, to protect East Florida,
and to provide bases for a future offensive in the Carolinas.[41] Of necessity the British had once again reverted to a southern strategy.

The expedition to Georgia proved far more successful than anyone had anticipated. On November 24, 1778, Lieutenant Colonel
Archibald Campbell sailed from New York for Savannah. Arriving
on December 23, he promptly engaged the rebels, captured the town,
and began raising loyalist units. At almost the same time Brigadier
General Augustine Prevost marched north from St. Augustine to attack Sunbury and to assist Campbell in recovering the remainder of
Georgia. By the end of January they had driven most of the rebel
units across the Savannah River and had sent a detachment to Augusta not merely to secure the hinterlands of Georgia but also to
support the loyalists living in the Piedmont of the Carolinas.[42] Although they subsequently decided to abandon Augusta—because
their communications were threatened and because the inhabitants
were not so loyal as expected—they remained confident that with
reinforcements they would be able to capture Charleston, conquer
the Carolinas, and, of course, secure the interior of Georgia. Indeed, during April and May, Prevost tried unsuccessfully to capture Charleston with no more than the forces that could be spared
from the defense of Georgia.[43]

Reports from Georgia so impressed Clinton that he began con-

41. Clinton's memorandum, Oct. 11, [1778], quoted in Smith, *Loyalists and
Redcoats*, p. 93; Clinton to Lord George Germain, Nov. 8, 1778, No. 26, C.O. 5/96;
Clinton, *American Rebellion*, pp. 116–17. The ministry also believed that Georgia
could supply provisions and lumber for the British islands in the West Indies as
well as a port for cruisers on the southern coasts.

42. Sir Henry Clinton to Lord George Germain, Nov. 24, 1778, C.O. 5/96;
Campbell to Clinton, Jan. 16, 1779, and Prevost to Clinton, Jan. 19, 1779 (both en-
closed in Clinton to Germain, Feb. 3, 1779), C.O. 5/97; Campbell to Frederick
Howard, Earl of Carlisle, Jan. 18, 1779, *Facsimiles of Manuscripts in European
Archives Relating to America 1773–1783*, ed. B. F. Stevens (25 vols.; London, 1889–
98), I, No. 113.

43. Prevost to Sir Henry Clinton, Mar. 6, 1779 (enclosed in Clinton to Lord
George Germain, Apr. 3, 1779), C.O. 5/97; Prevost to Clinton, Mar. 1, 15, 28, Apr.
16, May 21, 1779 (enclosed in Clinton to Germain, July 26, 1779), C.O. 5/98.

sidering a full-scale offensive in South Carolina. As early as March 2 he proposed an attack on Charleston. Assuming that the troops sent to St. Lucia would be free to return to North America in the spring, he urged that they be ordered to Port Royal and promised to reinforce them from New York. Such a force would, he believed, be able to capture Charleston and, perhaps, recover the remainder of the province.[44] By April 4 he had begun to change his mind. No longer confident that he could depend on help from the troops at St. Lucia or from the people of South Carolina, he doubted that he would be able to send a sufficient force from New York to take and hold Charleston. To take any post without the assurance of being able to keep it was, he thought, to risk misleading the loyalists—to risk encouraging their premature declarations of allegiance. Moreover, detaching troops enough from New York to capture Charleston would destroy any prospect of a summer campaign in the middle colonies and seriously impair his ability to reinforce other British outposts that might come under attack. So it was that he decided to defer any major offensive in South Carolina until autumn, until he had finished his operations along the Hudson and until he had the force and the time to be sure of success in the southern colonies.[45]

During the spring and summer of 1779 Clinton did no more to prosecute the war in the South than undertake a brief expedition to the Chesapeake, an expedition that was designed as much to prepare the way for operations at New York as to take pressure from British forces in Georgia. Sir George Collier, who was temporarily in command of the North American Squadron, and Lord George Germain, the secretary of state for America, both urged Clinton to consider raiding rebel posts in the Chesapeake; both stressed the importance of disrupting the overseas trade of Virginia and Maryland as well as the more immediate advantages of combating privateers, destroying magazines, and discouraging Virginians from serving elsewhere against the British.[46] Clinton agreed that a raid in the Chesapeake

44. Clinton to Duncan Drummond, Mar. 2, 10, 1779, Clinton Papers, William L. Clements Library, Univ. of Mich.; Clinton, *American Rebellion*, p. 120.
45. Clinton to Lord George Germain, Apr. 4, 1779, C.O. 5/97.
46. Collier to John Montagu, Earl of Sandwich, Apr. 19, 1779, John Montagu, Earl of Sandwich, *The Private Papers of John, Earl of Sandwich First Lord of the Admiralty, 1771–1782*, ed., G. R. Barnes and J. H. Owen (Publications of the Navy Records Society, Vols. LXIX, LXXI, LXXV, LXXVIII; London, 1932–38), III, 127–28; Collier to Germain, Apr. 19, 1779, *Report on the Manuscripts of Mrs. Stopford-Sackville of Drayton House, Northamptonshire*, Historical Manuscripts

would keep supplies and men from reaching rebel armies in the middle colonies and Georgia; he also hoped that it would mask his plans for an offensive on the Hudson. On April 29 he instructed Major General Edward Mathew to take command of twenty-five hundred men and join Commodore Collier in an attack on Virginia. Mathew and Collier were to destroy ships, supplies, and naval stores and create panic throughout the Tidewater. But they were not to call forth the loyalists or attempt to establish a permanent base; and unless some extraordinary opportunity offered, they were to return to New York by the end of May.[47] Mathew and Collier did just as they were told. They departed on May 5, took Portsmouth and Norfolk without opposition, sent detachments to scour the bay for rebel shipping, destroyed vast quantities of supplies, ammunition, and naval stores in Suffolk and Norfolk counties, and returned to New York on May 29. Collier, impressed with the friendliness of the inhabitants and the advantages of Norfolk as a naval base, had tried to persuade Mathew to delay his return. Mathew insisted on following orders, and the two reached New York before learning that Clinton had authorized their staying longer in the Chesapeake.[48]

For three months after Collier and Mathew returned from the Chesapeake, Clinton concentrated on the war in the middle colonies. Even though he still wished to be relieved of his command and complained bitterly of being given too much advice and too few troops, he did try to carry out the ministry's plans for the summer of 1779.[49] Those plans were designed to end the rebellion in the middle colonies with only a modest additional investment of regular forces and without diverting any troops from Georgia. Clinton was to begin the campaign by trying to engage Washington in a decisive battle. That

Commission Reports (2 vols.; London, 1904–10), II, 125–26; hereafter cited as *Manuscripts of Stopford-Sackville*; Germain to Clinton, Jan. 23, 1779, secret and confidential (received by Apr. 29 and acknowledged in Clinton to Germain, 3 May 1779), C.O. 5/97.

47. Clinton, *American Rebellion*, pp. 122–24; instructions for Major General Mathew, Apr. 29, 1779 (enclosed in Clinton to Germain, May 5, 1779), C.O. 5/97.

48. Collier to Clinton, n.d. (enclosed in Clinton to Germain, May 19, 1779), Mathew to Clinton, May 16, 1779 (enclosed in Clinton to Germain, May 21, 1779), and Clinton to Germain, May 21, 1779, C.O. 5/97; Clinton to Germain, June 18, 1779 (enclosing additional correspondence with Mathew and Collier, May 20–24, 1779), C.O. 5/98; Clinton, *American Rebellion*, pp. 123–24; Collier to John Montagu, Earl of Sandwich, June 15, 1779, Sandwich, *Private Papers*, III, 131–33.

49. Clinton to Henry Fiennes Clinton, Duke of Newcastle, May 21, 1779, Newcastle Papers; Clinton to Germain, May 22, 1779, private, C.O. 5/97.

failing, he was to drive the Continental army into the Highlands of the Hudson so that royal government might be reestablished in New York and New Jersey—that those colonies might become models of secure, prosperous communities under the crown. To complement his operations along the Hudson, he was to send substantial detachments to attack rebel shipping in the Chesapeake and on the coasts of New England. The ministry would provide Clinton with some reinforcements—sixty-six hundred recruits, four ships of the line, and all of the men that could be spared from the five thousand that had gone to St. Lucia. But it expected him to raise large numbers of loyalists in the middle colonies, to borrow troops from Nova Scotia, and to benefit from Indian attacks on the frontiers of New York.[50] By the time he received these instructions—by late April—Clinton was already considering an expedition to the Chesapeake as well as a summer campaign along the Hudson, and he had little trouble adjusting his plans to those of the ministry. As soon as Collier and Mathew returned to New York, Sir Henry proceeded to capture Stoney and Verplanks Points on the Hudson, forty miles north of New York City. He did so not merely to sever a principal route across the river but also to tempt Washington to risk a general action on unfavorable terms.[51] When Washington refused to fight, Clinton decided to send detachments to raid the coasts of Connecticut and to defer any further efforts against the Continental army until reinforced.[52]

On August 21, after learning that he would receive no troops from St. Lucia, that he would have to send two thousand of his own men to Canada, and that British forces in Georgia were threatened, he decided to wait no longer for reinforcements from England. He would abandon the campaign in the middle colonies and proceed as soon as possible to attack Charleston.[53] Clinton made this decision primarily, he said, to protect Georgia. But it is also clear that he believed his

50. Lord George Germain to Clinton, Jan. 23, 1779, secret and confidential, C.O. 5/97.

51. Clinton to Lord George Germain, May 3, 1779, C.O. 5/97; Clinton to Germain, June 18, 1779, Nos. 57 and 58, C.O. 5/98; Clinton to Duke of Newcastle, June 18, 1779, Newcastle Papers.

52. Clinton to Lord George Germain, June 18 and July 25, 1779 (two of latter date, Nos. 60 and 61), C.O. 5/98; Clinton to Henry Fiennes Clinton, Duke of Newcastle, Aug. 14, 1779, Newcastle Papers.

53. Clinton to Lord George Germain, Aug. 20, 21, 1779, C.O. 5/98; Clinton to Henry Fiennes Clinton, Duke of Newcastle, Aug. 14, 1779, Newcastle Papers.

best prospects for combating the rebellion lay temporarily in the South. Since April he had been planning an autumn offensive in South Carolina—a sustained effort to enlist the support of loyalists in overturning the rebels and in restoring royal government. Such an offensive now seemed as necessary as it was desirable. In their dispatches of late July and early August General Augustine Prevost and Governor James Wright agreed that Georgia was not then and would never be secure until the rebels had been driven from South Carolina. Although neither seemed to think Georgia in immediate danger of being overrun, Wright repeatedly urged Clinton to come south in October; and Prevost suggested that with four thousand troops Clinton would be able to capture Charleston, recover South Carolina, and provide for the permanent security of Georgia. These dispatches reached New York just when Clinton was coming to realize that he had neither the forces nor the time to do what he wished in the middle colonies—to destroy the Continental army or restore royal government in New York and New Jersey before winter. Knowing that the ministry thought "the Recovery of South Carolina . . . an object of . . . great Importance" and that there still were said to be many loyal colonists in that province, he did not hesitate to cut short his operations along the Hudson and to prepare for an attack on Charleston.[54] He would improve the defenses of New York, send a detachment to raid the Chesapeake, and sail for South Carolina. If all went well, South Carolina and Georgia soon would be firmly in his grasp.[55]

All did not go well. Admiral Arbuthnot arrived on August 25 with reinforcements from England—with about half of the sixty-six hundred men that Germain had promised for the campaign of 1779. As most of the new men were too ill for active duty and as they soon in-

54. Clinton to Newcastle, Aug. 14, 1779, Newcastle Papers; Prevost to Clinton, July 30, 1779, and Wright to Clinton, July 30, Aug. 7, 1779 (enclosed in Clinton to Lord George Germain, Aug. 21, 1779), C.O. 5/98; quoting Germain to Clinton, Mar. 31, 1779, C.O. 5/97 (received July 28 and acknowledged in Clinton to Germain, July 29, 1779, C.O. 5/98); James Simpson to Germain, Aug. 28, 1779, *Manuscripts of Stopford-Sackville*, II, 137; Clinton to William Eden, Aug. 22, 1779, Clinton Papers.

55. Clinton to Lord George Germain, Aug. 21, 1779, and Clinton to Frederick Haldimand, Sept. 9, 1779 (enclosed in Clinton to Germain, Oct. 9, 1779), C.O. 5/98; Clinton to Newcastle, August 14, 1779, Newcastle Papers; Clinton, *American Rebellion*, pp. 140, 151, 153. Although Clinton said in retrospect that he had hoped to subdue "the two Carolinas" (*American Rebellion*, p. 151), in August 1779 he talked of taking only South Carolina.

fected thousands of veterans serving at New York, Clinton's army was not at once stronger for the reinforcement.[56] Still he was able to send two thousand troops to Canada on September 9 and would have sailed for the Chesapeake and Charleston shortly thereafter had not a desperate plea for help arrived from the governor of Jamaica. Governor John Dalling, anticipating an attack by a French fleet under Admiral D'Estaing, asked for an immediate reinforcement. Clinton responded by postponing his expeditions to the South and by ordering General Cornwallis with four thousand troops to Jamaica. Cornwallis sailed on September 24 and returned on the thirtieth, having learned shortly after leaving port that D'Estaing had bypassed Jamaica and was on his way to Georgia or some other part of the mainland.[57] For the ensuing seven weeks no one at New York was sure where the French had gone or what the British should do. Clinton abandoned Stoney Point, Verplanks, and Rhode Island in an effort to consolidate his forces; considered various measures for counteracting D'Estaing; and talked of attacking Charleston as soon as the French were gone —provided, of course, Georgia did not surrender in the interim.[58] Not until November 18 did he learn that D'Estaing had tried and failed to capture Savannah in early October. Even then he was unwilling to proceed with his expeditions to the Chesapeake and Charleston until he was sure that the French had left North America. By the time he was sure, autumn had slipped away and he had decided to postpone operations in the Chesapeake until spring and to proceed directly to South Carolina.[59] He sailed from New York on December 23, reached South Carolina on February 11, and laid siege to Charleston on April 1. Six weeks later Charleston surrendered.[60]

Clinton had gone to Charleston in the hope of preserving Georgia

56. Lord George Germain to Clinton, Mar. 3, 1779, C.O. 5/97; Clinton to Germain, Sept. 4, 1779, C.O. 5/98.

57. Clinton to Frederick Haldimand, Sept. 9, 1779 (enclosed in Clinton to Lord George Germain, Oct. 9, 1779), Clinton to Germain, Sept. 26, 30, 1779, Clinton to Dalling, Sept. 16, 1779 (enclosed in Clinton to Germain, Sept. 26, 1779), C.O. 5/98; Marriot Arbuthnot to John Montagu, Earl of Sandwich, Sept. 19, 1779, Sandwich, *Private Papers*, III, 134–35.

58. Clinton, *American Rebellion*, pp. 428–30; Arbuthnot to Sandwich, Oct. 30, 1779, Sandwich, *Private Papers*, III, 136–38; Clinton to Germain, Sept. 30, Oct. 9, 26, 28, Nov. 10, 17, 1779, C.O. 5/98; Clinton to Arbuthnot, Oct. 24, 1779, *Facsimilies*, X, No. 1026.

59. Clinton to Germain, Nov. 19, 1779, C.O. 5/98; Clinton to Germain, Dec. 15, 1779, C.O. 5/99; extract of Arbuthnot to Clinton, Dec. 23, 25, 1779, and extract of Clinton to Arbuthnot, Dec. 26, 1779, Clinton, *American Rebellion*, pp. 437–38, 153.

60. Clinton to Germain, May 13, 1780, C.O. 5/99.

and recovering South Carolina. But reports from England as well as success in South Carolina soon led him to a more ambitious southern strategy. Even before Charleston surrendered he knew that the ministry was greatly pleased with his decision to go south—that it relied on his efforts in South Carolina and the Chesapeake to end the war and that it was willing to forego a summer offensive in the middle colonies. He also knew that the French were preparing to send another fleet to North America, presumably to Canada, and that he would have to embark reinforcements for Quebec as soon as possible.[61] These reports arrived just when he was achieving the most dramatic successes enjoyed by any British general during the war. At Charleston he captured nearly all of the rebel forces in South Carolina: six thousand soldiers and sailors, four frigates, and over three hundred cannon. Soon thereafter his troops advanced into the interior, dispersed the rebels, and established a line of armed camps from Cheraw to Camden to Ninety-Six. Protected by these posts, the colonists came forward in gratifying numbers to swear allegiance and enlist in various provincial units.[62] This striking success together with the ministry's encouragement soon persuaded Clinton to authorize more extensive operations in the South. The prospect of French intervention forced him to postpone once again his plans for going to the Chesapeake; he was not yet prepared to declare South Carolina at peace or to restore civil government.[63] But by the time he was ready to return to New York, by early June 1780, he believed South Carolina secure and was planning offensive operations into North Carolina and Virginia. His successor, Earl Cornwallis, was to

61. Lord George Germain to Clinton, June 25, 1779, C.O. 5/97 (received Sept. 1 and acknowledged in Clinton to Germain, September 4, 1779, C.O. 5/98); Germain to Clinton, Aug. 5, 1779 (received Oct. 23 and acknowledged in Clinton to Germain, Oct. 23, 1779), C.O. 5/98; Germain to Clinton, Dec. 4, 1779, C.O. 5/98 (acknowledged in Clinton to Germain, May 9, 1780, C.O. 5/99); Germain to Clinton, Jan. 19, 1780 (acknowledged in Clinton to Germain, May 9, 1780), C.O. 5/99; Germain to Clinton, Mar. 15, 1780 (received May 10 and acknowledged in Clinton to Germain, May 14, 1780), C.O. 5/99.

62. Clinton to Germain, May 13, June 4, 1780, C.O. 5/99; Clinton, *American Rebellion*, pp. 174, 181; Charles Earl Cornwallis to Clinton, June 30, 1780, Charles Marquis Cornwallis, *Correspondence of Charles, First Marquis Cornwallis*, ed. Charles Ross (2nd ed. rev., 4 vols.; London, 1859), I, 499–501. *The Toll of Independence Engagements & Battle Casualties of the American Revolution*, ed. Howard H. Peckham (Chicago, 1974), p. 70, estimates 3,371 Americans were captured. Clinton's 6,000 probably includes civilians deliberately excluded by Peckham.

63. Clinton to Germain, May 14, 1780, C.O. 5/99; Marriot Arbuthnot to Germain, May 2, 1780, *Manuscripts of Stopford-Sackville*, II, 161–62; [Andrew] Bruce's minutes of his conversation, June 7, 1780, *Facsimiles*, X, No. 1041.

consider the defense of South Carolina and Georgia his primary responsibility. He was also to consider, in the proper season, "a *solid* move into North Carolina," a move to be made overland in the interior and to be sustained both by loyalists and by small detachments of regulars posted from Cape Fear north along the coasts of North Carolina and Virginia.[64]

On assuming command Cornwallis was eager to pursue Clinton's ambitious plans. He was confident that with the help of the loyalists he would be able not merely to defend South Carolina but also to recover North Carolina, support Clinton's projected expedition to the Chesapeake, and, perhaps, reestablish royal government throughout the South. He intended to draw as much support as possible from the people and the land. He would begin in South Carolina by raising loyalist militia to assist his regular troops in maintaining order and defending the province and to release regulars for service elsewhere. Then, when the harvest was in—when there would be an abundance of provisions and cooler weather—and when he had established a supply depot at Cross Creek on the Cape Fear River, he would invade North Carolina. His primary objective would be the Piedmont where the loyalists were said to be most numerous. He would end organized resistance, establish secure outposts, and call upon the inhabitants to rise. So confident was he of being well supported by the people of the Carolinas and so sure that possession of North Carolina would provide security for South Carolina and Georgia that he saw no need for reinforcements. With only those troops that were in South Carolina after Clinton returned to New York, Cornwallis would do all that he planned and have troops to spare for operations in the Chesapeake.[65]

He was soon forced to revise his expectations of loyalist support as well as his plans for recovering North Carolina. By early summer he knew that Virginia and North Carolina were raising troops to defend themselves and attack South Carolina. Some of these troops had

---

64. Clinton to Germain, May 14, June 4, 1780, C.O. 5/99; Clinton to Cornwallis, June 1, 1780, and Clinton's "Instructions to . . . Cornwallis," June 1, 1780, Clinton-Cornwallis Letterbook No. 1, Clinton Papers; quoting Clinton, *American Rebellion*, p. 186, but see as well pp. 183–87, 213, 221–24; Wickwire and Wickwire, *Cornwallis*, pp. 133–35. Willcox, *Portrait of a General*, p. 321, believes that by the beginning of June Clinton was blinded by his success.

65. Cornwallis to Clinton, June 30, 1780, and Cornwallis to Germain, Aug. 20, 1780, Cornwallis, *Correspondence*, I, 499–505.

already succeeded in intimidating loyalists, inspiriting rebels, and annoying British outposts on the frontiers of South Carolina. To prevent any further erosion of confidence among the loyalists, Cornwallis knew that he would have to abandon, temporarily, his plans for recovering North Carolina and strike at the rebel forces gathering on the frontier. He would no longer have time for the careful preparations required to recover the province—for organizing militia, awaiting the harvest, and establishing a supply depot on the Cape Fear River. He could not even be sure of assembling a force capable of defeating the rebels. Yet to save South Carolina he would have to invade North Carolina at once, engage the enemy, and hope that Clinton would be able to support him with a diversion in the Chesapeake.[66] On August 9, while preparing to march, he learned that an army of six thousand rebels under General Horatio Gates was advancing on Camden. Unable to defend Camden against such a force, he had either to attack the enemy or to abandon the interior of South Carolina. He attacked and won a dramatic victory, killing, wounding, or capturing more than a third of the rebel army and scattering the remainder across the Carolinas. He then sent cavalry to disperse a second rebel force and gave orders for punishing those colonists who had defected to Gates on his approach to Camden.[67]

Although Cornwallis had gone to Camden to save South Carolina, his victory encouraged him to think once again of recovering North Carolina, if not the whole South. His renewed hopes rested in part upon the assumption that there would be little organized resistance in North Carolina and in part upon vague expectations that he would be supported by loyalists and by Sir Henry Clinton. The day after his victory at Camden he called upon the people of North Carolina to rise, urging them to fall on the remnants of Gates's army and promising to assist them as soon as he could gather supplies from Charleston. His plan was to send three separate forces into North Carolina: a detachment of militia to sweep through the moun-

66. Cornwallis to Clinton, July 14, Aug. 6, 1780, and Cornwallis to Germain, Aug. 20, 1780, Cornwallis, *Correspondence*, I, 50–54, 502–5; Cornwallis to Clinton, July 15, Aug. 6, 1780, C.O. 5/100.
67. Cornwallis to Clinton, Aug. 10, 1780, C.O. 5/100; Cornwallis to [John Harris] Cruger, Aug. 18, 1780, and Cornwallis to Germain, Aug. 21, 1780, Cornwallis, *Correspondence*, I, 56–57, 506–9. Cornwallis seems to have overestimated the size of Gates's army. Peckham, ed., *Toll of Independence*, p. 74, says that Gates lost 1,050 of his 3,050 troops.

tains, a small contingent of regulars to establish a base on the Cape Fear River, and a much more substantial body of regulars— under his command—to advance through Charlotte and Salisbury to Hillsborough. At Hillsborough he would attempt to arm and organize the loyalists and to form a magazine for the winter. To exploit the advantage he had won at Camden, he knew that he had to act quickly, that he could not wait to receive Clinton's reaction to these plans. Cornwallis did, however, ask the commander in chief for help and advice—not merely for a diversion in the Chesapeake (or reinforcements) but also for instructions on how to proceed after reaching Hillsborough.[68] He then set out for North Carolina.

Once there circumstances and events persuaded him to change his strategy—to set aside his plans for recovering the remainder of the South and to concentrate on defending South Carolina. He had hoped that his victory at Camden would break the rebellion in North Carolina. Quite the contrary. The rebels remained a formidable enemy, "mostly mounted militia, not to be overtaken by our infantry nor . . . safely pursued in this strong country by our cavalry"; and the loyalists were an almost worthless ally, too few and too frightened to be of any real assistance to the British. He also found after reaching Charlotte that his militia had been overwhelmed at Kings Mountain and that the triumphant rebels were again threatening the frontiers of South Carolina.[69] Although Cornwallis had a strong preference for offensive measures, and although in this instance he clearly found recovering North Carolina more appealing than trying to maintain a static defense of his outposts in South Carolina, he decided to retire toward Ninety-Six. Prospects of dispersing the rebels or raising a significant number of loyalists around Charlotte were simply too poor to justify leaving South Carolina open to attack. He would with-

68. Cornwallis to Clinton, Aug. 23, 29, 1780, and Cornwallis to Germain, Aug. 21, 1780, Cornwallis, *Correspondence*, I, 57–59, 506–9. In assessing Cornwallis's intentions after his victory at Camden, Wickwire and Wickwire, *Cornwallis*, pp. 192–93, blur chronology. They quote from his dispatch of Aug. 6 to suggest that he entered North Carolina to destroy the rebel army. I believe that having defeated Gates at Camden, Cornwallis went north to gather the fruits of his victory.

69. Francis Rawdon-Hastings, Lord Rawdon, to Alexander Leslie, Oct. 24, 1780 (quoted), Cornwallis to Clinton, Aug. 29, 1780, Rawdon to Clinton, Oct. 29, 1780, Cornwallis, *Correspondence*, I, 510, 58–59, 62–64; Cornwallis to Germain, Sept. 19, 1780, *Manuscripts of Stopford-Sackville*, II, 183; Wickwire and Wickwire, *Cornwallis*, pp. 212–16.

draw, cover the frontier, strengthen the defenses of Ninety-Six and Camden, and ask once again for a reinforcement.[70]

Thus far Cornwallis had received no help from Clinton. It is possible that Clinton did not wish to help—that he was too jealous of Cornwallis. It is more likely that since going to New York in June, his preference for a decisive victory over Washington together with the arrival of a French fleet and the necessity of working with Arbuthnot had kept him from sending troops to the Chesapeake, from creating a diversion for Cornwallis. Although Clinton knew that the ministry expected him to concentrate on recovering the South—that it was willing to maintain a defensive posture in the middle colonies during the summer of 1780—his first efforts on reaching New York were directed toward destroying the Continental army.[71] Those failing, he asked Arbuthnot to join in establishing a post at Norfolk, to favor Cornwallis and to prepare the way for much more extensive operations in the Chesapeake. But Arbuthnot refused, saying he was unwilling to spare ships until reinforced and until he knew what part the French would play in the campaign of 1780.[72] As waiting for the French and deciding not to attack them after they had reached Rhode Island consumed nearly six weeks, it was not until mid-August that Clinton again proposed helping Cornwallis: first, by destroying magazines at Philadelphia and then, after learning that Gates was invading South Carolina, by sending an expedition to the Chesapeake.[73] But preparations went forth so slowly that troops ordered to the Chesapeake were still at New York when Sir George Rodney arrived unexpectedly on September 16 with ten sail of the line. In an effort to cooperate with Rodney in capturing West Point—to take advantage of Benedict Arnold's offer to betray that fortress—Clinton further delayed the expedition to the Chesapeake.[74] Finally, on Oc-

70. Lord Rawdon to Alexander Leslie, Oct. 24, 31, 1780, and Rawdon to Clinton, Oct. 29, 1780, Cornwallis, *Correspondence*, I, 509–11, 64–65, 62–64.

71. Sir Henry Clinton to Lord George Germain, July 4, 1780, C.O. 5/100; Clinton, *American Rebellion*, pp. 189–92.

72. Clinton to Germain, Aug. 30, 1780, C.O. 5/100; Clinton, *American Rebellion*, pp. 195–96.

73. Clinton to Germain, July 4, Aug. 14, 30, Sept. 3, 1780, and Cornwallis to Clinton, Aug. 10, 1780 (received by Clinton, Aug. 24), C.O. 5/100; Clinton to Henry Fiennes Clinton, Duke of Newcastle, July 4, 1780, Newcastle Papers.

74. Clinton to Newcastle, Sept. 14–16, 1780, Newcastle Papers; Clinton to Germain, Oct. 11, 1780, C.O. 5/100; Clinton, *American Rebellion*, pp. 214–18.

tober 16, Major General Alexander Leslie left New York with twenty-five hundred men to destroy magazines at Petersburg and Richmond, capture Norfolk, and open a correspondence with Cornwallis. If all went well, Leslie would force the rebels to withdraw north of the James, leaving the Carolinas safely in British hands.[75]

Before Leslie sailed, 72 percent of all British troops in the rebellious colonies were at New York with only 28 percent in South Carolina and Georgia. Seven months later, the distribution would be remarkably altered: 41 percent at New York; 59 in Georgia, the Carolinas, and Virginia.[76] This remarkable redistribution, which would affect British strategy throughout America, was not the result of a deliberate or comprehensive alteration in plans. Rather it was the cumulative effect of Sir Henry Clinton's efforts to support Cornwallis, satisfy the ministry, and match the redeployment of French and American forces. In sending Leslie to the Chesapeake, Clinton did consider that he might one day wish to conquer Virginia. But his immediate purpose was to assist Cornwallis, and once that was achieved—once he knew that Leslie had gone on to Cape Fear to join his lordship—Clinton was willing to defer any further operations in the Chesapeake until prodded by the ministry.[77] In early December, after learning that the ministry was particularly eager to establish a base in the Chesapeake, he ordered nineteen hundred men under the command of Benedict Arnold to capture and fortify Portsmouth. Arnold was also to destroy rebel magazines along the James and to assist Cornwallis, but "the primary object of this Expedition" was

75. Clinton to [William Eden], Oct. 15 [Nov. 1], 1780, Additions to the Manuscripts, 34,417, British Museum, London; Clinton to Germain, Sept. 20, 1780, and Germain to Clinton, Nov. 28, 1780, C.O. 5/100; Clinton, *American Rebellion*, p. 221. Although Clinton said he would send about 3,000 men with Leslie, the "Distribution of the troops under . . . Clinton," Nov. 1, 1780 (enclosed in Clinton to Germain, Nov. 10, 1780, C.O. 5/100), shows that Leslie took about 2,500 officers and men.

76. Recapitulation of the army under Sir Henry Clinton, July 1, 1780 (enclosed in Clinton to Germain, July 4, 1780), and "Distribution of the troops under . . . Clinton," Nov. 1, 1780 (enclosed in Clinton to Germain, Nov. 10, 1780), C.O. 5/100; "Distribution of the Army under . . . Clinton," May 1, 1781 (enclosed in Clinton to Germain, May 13, 1781), C.O. 5/102. Whenever possible, I have used figures for rank-and-file "fit for duty"—rather than rank-and-file "effectives." The total listed as "fit for duty" usually comes much closer to expressing the actual strength of the forces in any given post.

77. Clinton to Charles Earl Cornwallis, Nov. 6, [1780] (enclosed in Clinton to Germain, July 13, 1781), C.O. 5/102; Clinton to Leslie, Nov. 2, 1780 (enclosed in Clinton to Germain, Nov. 10, 1780), and Clinton to Germain, Nov. 12, 1780, C.O. 5/100.

to take Portsmouth.[78] Arnold did his job so well that he soon provoked a formidable response. By March 1 Clinton knew that Washington had sent Lafayette to Virginia and that the French squadron
at Newport was preparing to sail, presumably for the Chesapeake.
To protect Arnold as well as to favor Cornwallis, plunder the bay,
and prepare a station for ships of the line, Clinton now sent Major
General William Phillips with a third expeditionary force of twenty-
four hundred men to the Chesapeake.[79] Although Phillips and Arnold
together had no fears for Portsmouth, they promptly began to argue
that with a modest reinforcement they would be able to do much
more than defend themselves—that they could attack Lafayette and,
if necessary, fight their way to Cornwallis. So it was that Clinton was
persuaded to send another nineteen hundred men to the Chesapeake
in early May.[80] But even then he expected Phillips and many of his
troops to return to New York for the summer, and he explicitly rejected a proposal to make Virginia the seat of the war.[81]

While Clinton shifted his forces to the Chesapeake, Cornwallis
was once again invading North Carolina. In October 1780, after his
militia were defeated at Kings Mountain, he had retired to Winnsboro to cover the interior of South Carolina. Although much discouraged by the failure of his expedition to Charlotte, he still dreamed
of raising loyalist troops in North Carolina; and he knew that he
would have to get control of that province to provide for the security
of South Carolina, that his forces were quite inadequate to prevent
infiltration and insurrection along an extensive and exposed frontier.
He first considered asking Major General Leslie, who was in the

78. Germain to Clinton, Sept. 6, 1780 (received Nov. 30 and acknowledged in
Clinton to Germain, Dec. 16, 1780, C.O. 5/101), C.O. 5/100. Clinton to Germain,
Dec. 16, 1780 (enclosing Clinton-Marriot Arbuthnot correspondence, Dec. 9–13,
1780), and quoting Clinton to Arnold, Dec. 14, 1780 (enclosed in Clinton to Germain, Feb. 27, 1781), C.O. 5/101. The total number of men in each detachment
has been computed by adding officers, noncommissioned officers, and rank and file
("fit for duty") from Clinton's returns of Nov. 1, 1780, Jan. 15, and May 1, 1781
(C.O. 5/100–102). It was necessary to estimate the number of officers and noncommissioned officers sent with Arnold and Phillips.

79. Clinton to Germain, March 1 [-16], 1781, and, enclosed therein, Clinton to
Phillips, Mar. 10, 1781, C.O. 5/101; Clinton to Germain, Apr. 5, 1781, and, enclosed therein, "Substance of Opinions given to . . . Phillips . . . previous to his Embarkation . . . ," n.d., C.O. 5/102.

80. Phillips to Clinton, Apr. 15, 1781, and Phillips and Arnold to Clinton, Apr.
18, 1781 (enclosed in Clinton to Germain, Apr. 23, 1781), C.O. 5/102; Clinton,
American Rebellion, p. 281.

81. Clinton to Phillips, Mar. 10, 1781 (enclosed in Clinton to Germain, Mar.
1 [-16], 1781), C.O. 5/101; Clinton to Germain, Apr. 23, 1781, C.O. 5/102.

Chesapeake with twenty-five hundred men, to go by sea to Cross Creek on the Cape Fear River. He would then march to join Leslie in restoring the loyalists to power in North Carolina.[82] But, finding the backcountry of South Carolina in turmoil, he decided to stay at Winnsboro and have Leslie join him by way of Charleston. Together they would be able to sweep the rebels before them into the Piedmont of North Carolina, destroying resistance and raising provincial units to help hold the countryside.[83] Their offensive began inauspiciously in January 1781 with the loss of more than eight hundred men at the Battle of Cowpens. Even so, Cornwallis was determined to carry through with his plans. Destroying his baggage to gain mobility, he plunged north in pursuit of the principal rebel forces under Daniel Morgan and Nathanael Greene. He reached Salisbury on February 4, Guilford Court House on the tenth, and the Dan River on the fifteenth—always too late to bring the rebels to action. Once Morgan and Greene had escaped over the Dan, Cornwallis turned back to Hillsborough to rest his men and to begin organizing loyalist units. His efforts were soon interrupted by Greene, who returned to harass the British and, finally, to offer battle. Cornwallis accepted, "being convinced that it would be impossible to succeed in that great object of our campaign, the calling forth the numerous loyalists of North Carolina, whilst a doubt remained on their minds of the superiority of our arms."[84] On March 15 he won a costly victory near Guilford Court House. Three days later he made one final, futile plea for popular support and began a slow withdrawal to Cross Creek and Wilmington.[85]

82. Francis Rawdon-Hastings, Lord Rawdon, to Alexander Leslie, Oct. 24, 31, 1780, and Charles, Earl Cornwallis, to Leslie, Nov. 12, 1780, Cornwallis, *Correspondence*, I, 509–11, 64–65, 69.

83. Cornwallis to Clinton, Dec. 3, 1780, and Jan. 6, 1781 (enclosed in Clinton to Germain, Feb. 27, 1781), C.O. 5/101; Cornwallis to Lord Rawdon, Dec. 30, 1780, Cornwallis to Germain, Mar. 17, Apr. 18, 1781, Cornwallis, *Correspondence*, I, 77, 516–20, 90–91. Smith, *Loyalists and Redcoats*, p. 150, argues that Cornwallis decided to go north primarily to carry out the ministry's plans for recovering the South. I believe that he did so as much to defend South Carolina as to raise loyalists and recapture North Carolina.

84. Cornwallis to Germain, Mar. 17, 1781, Cornwallis to Lord Rawdon, Feb. 4, 21, 1781, Cornwallis, *Correspondence*, I, 516–20, 84–85; Cornwallis to Clinton, Jan. 18, 1781 (enclosed in Clinton to Germain Feb. 27, 1781), and Nisbet Balfour to Clinton, Mar. 4, 1781 (enclosed in Clinton to Germain, Mar. 1 [–16], 1781), C.O. 5/101.

85. Cornwallis to Germain, Mar. 17, Apr. 18, 1781, Cornwallis, *Correspondence*, I, 520–23, 92; Cornwallis's Proclamation, Mar. 18, 1781, C.O. 5/102.

By the time Cornwallis reached Wilmington on April 7, he was willing to concede that he could not conquer North Carolina directly —that he did not have the forces required to impose royal government on such an inaccessible and hostile province. He was also willing to concede that while North Carolina remained in rebellion, it would be difficult to maintain order in the backcountry of South Carolina. Indeed, he had begun to think his only hope of holding the Carolinas lay in a conquest of Virginia.[86] But as Greene was then in the Piedmont of North Carolina, Cornwallis could not go safely to Virginia without reinforcements or without being sure that he would be supported there. On April 23 he learned not merely that there was a British army in the Chesapeake to cooperate with him and that he would not soon be reinforced at Wilmington but also that Greene had marched south to attack Camden. Although anxious about making a fundamental change in British strategy without consulting Clinton, Cornwallis decided at once to take his army overland to Virginia. To delay long enough to correspond with Clinton would give Greene time to return from Camden and block the route to Petersburg; and to go by sea to the Chesapeake would merely encourage further attacks on the frontiers of South Carolina. By leaving at once and marching toward Hillsborough, Cornwallis would have an excellent chance of getting through safely and might even force Greene to return to North Carolina, to give up temporarily his plans for attacking Camden. On April 25 Cornwallis left Wilmington to see whether conquering—rather than raiding—Virginia would help restore royal government in the Carolinas. He reached Petersburg on May 20.[87]

He soon discovered that he and Clinton had very different ideas about using the forces then in the Chesapeake. Cornwallis, who was thoroughly disillusioned with promises of loyalist support, gave up his plans for securing the Carolinas by conquering Virginia. But he continued to favor making Virginia the seat of the war and to oppose Clinton's proposal for a summer offensive at the head of Chesapeake

86. Cornwallis to Clinton, Apr. 10, 1781 (enclosed in Clinton to Germain Apr. 23, 1781), C.O. 5/102; Cornwallis to Germain, Apr. 18, 1781, Cornwallis, *Correspondence*, I, 90–91.

87. Cornwallis to William Phillips, Apr. 10, 1781, Cornwallis to Clinton, Apr. 23, 1781, and Cornwallis to Lord Rawdon, May 20, 1781, Cornwallis, *Correspondence*, I, 88–89, 94, 97, 99; Cornwallis to Germain, Apr. 23, 1781 (enclosed in Clinton to Germain, May 22, 1781), and Cornwallis to Phillips, Apr. 24, 1781 (enclosed in Clinton to Germain, May 18, 1781), C.O. 5/102.

Bay, an offensive designed to raise loyalists in Maryland and Pennsylvania and to create a sanctuary of the Eastern Shore.[88] Clinton, who was not at all pleased to find that Cornwallis had gone to the Chesapeake but who knew that the ministry was eager to recover Virginia, tried at first to persuade Cornwallis to accept his proposal for a campaign at the head of the Chesapeake—to make one more effort to enlist popular support. Failing to persuade, he ordered him to release some of the troops in Virginia for service in the middle colonies, for the defense of New York and, subsequently, for a raid on Philadelphia.[89] When Cornwallis replied that he would have to evacuate all of Virginia except Portsmouth in order to comply, Clinton countermanded his order.[90] Although thoroughly exasperated, Clinton was not willing to abandon Virginia—not, at least, while the ministry was demanding that he prosecute the war from south to north and while the navy was asking for a base in the Chesapeake that would accommodate ships of the line (as Portsmouth would not).[91] For the moment he seemed to be far more interested in justifying his own behavior and criticizing Cornwallis than in preparing to defend British forces against a French fleet expected from the West Indies.[92] He told Cornwallis to return to Williamsburg Neck, estab-

88. Cornwallis to Rawdon, May 20, 1781, Cornwallis, *Correspondence*, I, 99; Cornwallis to Clinton, May 20, 26, 1781 (enclosed in Clinton to Germain, June 9, 1781), and Cornwallis to Clinton, May 26, 1781 (enclosed in Clinton to Germain, July 13, 1781),C.O. 5/102. Clinton's plans had been set forth at length in "Substance of Opinions given to . . . Phillips," n.d. (enclosed in Clinton to Germain, Apr. 5, 1781), C.O. 5/102.

89. Clinton to Cornwallis, May 29, 1781 (enclosed in Clinton to Germain, July 13, 1781), C.O. 5/102; Germain to Clinton, Feb. 7, 1781 (received May 22 and acknowledged in Clinton to Germain, May 23, 1781, C.O. 5/102), C.O. 5/101; Clinton to Cornwallis, June 8, 1781 (enclosed in Clinton to Germain, July 13, 1781), Clinton to Germain, June 9, 1781, Clinton to Cornwallis, June 11, 1781 (enclosed in Clinton to Germain, June [9 –12], 1781), and Clinton to Cornwallis, June 15, 19, 26, July 1, 1781 (all enclosed in Clinton to Germain, July 13, 1781), C.O. 5/102.

90. Cornwallis to Clinton, June 30, 1781, and Clinton to Cornwallis, July 8, 1781 (both enclosed in Clinton to Germain, July 13, 1781), C.O. 5/102; Clinton to Alexander Leslie, July 23, 1781, C.O. 5/103.

91. Germain to Clinton, May 2, 1781, secret (received June 27 and acknowledged in Clinton to Germain, July 3, 1781, C.O. 5/102), C.O. 5/101; Clinton to Cornwallis, July 8, 11, 1781 (enclosed in Clinton to Germain, July 13, 1781), C.O. 5/102; Thomas Graves to John Montagu, Earl of Sandwich, July 20, 1781, Sandwich, *Private Papers*, IV, 175–77. Willcox, *Portrait of a General*, pp. 405–6, underestimates, I believe, the importance of Germain's instructions of May 2, 1781.

92. Clinton to Germain, July 13, 1781, C.O. 5/102; Clinton to Germain, July 18, 28, Aug. 9, 1781, and Clinton to Cornwallis, Aug. 2, 1781 (enclosed in Clinton to Germain, Aug. 9, 1781), C.O. 5/103. Cornwallis was also justifying himself:

lish a naval base at Yorktown or Old Point Comfort, and send to New York any troops that could be spared. Offensive operations in the Chesapeake would be deferred until autumn.[93] Cornwallis received these instructions on July 20 and began at once to give up Portsmouth and to fortify Yorktown. But before his works were completed a French fleet arrived to seal the Chesapeake and jeopardize his army. For the ensuing seven weeks all British forces were devoted to futile efforts to save Cornwallis.[94] Thus during the summer and autumn of 1781 the British had been unable to adopt any effective strategy in North America. Differences of opinion—aggravated by distance, personal pique, and pressure from London—kept Clinton and Cornwallis from acting together until the French intervened finally and decisively at Yorktown.

Well before Cornwallis surrendered Britain's southern strategy had proved a failure. The British had simply been unable to enlist enough loyalists to restore and preserve royal government throughout the South. Perhaps they could not have done so: perhaps no eighteenth-century army could have restored the loyalists to power over such an unruly population scattered across a remote and inhospitable country. But the British had never really given their strategy a full trial. They had agreed to that strategy; they had not agreed, except during the spring of 1780, that it should take precedence over other efforts to end the rebellion. At the beginning of the war ministers and commanders alike favored operations in the North. They believed that subduing New England and destroying the Continental army would reestablish royal government throughout America. To complement these measures, the ministry also sent seven regiments to exploit loyalist strength in North Carolina and encouraged Sir Wil-

Cornwallis to Clinton, July 24, 27, 1781, Cornwallis, *Correspondence*, I, 107–10. Although Clinton constantly warned the ministry not to allow the French to gain naval superiority in North America, and although he was sensitive to the advantages of sea power in laying his own plans, he could also ignore the threat of a French fleet—as he did during the summer of 1781.

93. Clinton to Cornwallis, July 8, 11, 11, 1781 (all enclosed in Clinton to Germain, July 13, 1781), C.O. 5/102; Clinton to Cornwallis, July 15, 1781 (enclosed in Clinton to German, July 25, 1781), C.O. 5/103.

94. Cornwallis to Alexander Leslie, July 20, 1781, Cornwallis to Charles O'Hara, Aug. 2, 1781, Cornwallis to Clinton, July 27, Aug. 22, 1781, Clinton to Cornwallis, Sept. 6, 1781, Cornwallis, *Correspondence*, I, 107, 112–13, 108-10, 117, 119–20. Cornwallis to Clinton, Sept. 2, 1781 (enclosed in Clinton to Germain, Sept. 7, 1781), Clinton to Thomas Graves, Sept. 17, 1781 (enclosed in Clinton to Germain, Sept. 26, 1781), Clinton to Germain, Oct. 29, 1781, C.O. 5/103.

liam Howe to campaign in the South during the winter of 1777–78. But not until Burgoyne surrendered and France entered the war, until it was clear that Britain lacked the troops for extensive campaigning in the middle colonies, did the ministry order Clinton to invade Georgia and make a systematic effort to employ loyalists in recovering the South. Thenceforth the ministry relied increasingly on its southern strategy. In 1779 it made one further proposal for prosecuting the war in the North, for bringing Washington to action and raising loyalists in New York and New Jersey. By 1780 it was willing to defer operations in the middle colonies, and the following year it told Clinton unequivocally to proceed from south to north. Clinton, who was reluctant to jeopardize New York and who continued to dream of ending the war with a decisive victory in the middle colonies, followed the ministry's instructions only fitfully. He sent no more than a token force to Georgia in 1778, spent the summer of 1779 seeking battle along the Hudson, and then, after capturing Charleston in 1780, returned promptly to New York to squander another summer considering ways to attack Washington and his French allies. Before Clinton agreed to commit more than a third of his army to the South, Cornwallis had been forced to modify British plans for restoring loyalists to control in the Carolinas. In the spring of 1781, he decided to abandon those plans altogether and conquer Virginia. So it was that a strategy inspired by necessity and pursued intermittently—a strategy that received only once the full support of the commander in chief—foundered at last on determined opposition in a difficult country.

Functions of the Partisan-Militia in the South During the American Revolution: An Interpretation

Clyde R. Ferguson   *Kansas State University*

On July 11, 1782, Colonel James Jackson of Georgia, at the head of his "Partisan Legion," led Major General Anthony Wayne's Continentals into Savannah in the wake of the evacuating British army. Five months later, when the redcoats finally abandoned Charleston, accompanied by four thousand loyalists and five thousand black slaves, the South Carolina state militiamen were barred from the triumphant reoccupation as "dangerous spectators." Guarded by Lieutenant Colonel Henry Lee's Legion and attended by Major General Nathanael Greene, Governor John Mathews proclaimed from the state house the "restoration of civil government throughout South Carolina." With the exception of a few senseless raids by "Bloody Bill" Cunningham and other diehard Tories, the fratricidal war that was the American Revolution in the South ended December 14, 1782.[1]

The partisans honored in the one state and the militia dishonored in the other did in fact play a major role in the victory of 1782, and

1. Thomas U. P. Charlton, *The Life of Major General James Jackson* (Augusta, Ga.: George F. Randolph, 1809), pp. 33, 43–44; John R. Alden, *The South in the Revolution, 1763–1789* (Baton Rouge: La. State Univ. Press, 1957), pp. 266–67; Allan Nevins, *The American States during and after the Revolution, 1775–1789* (New York: Macmillan, 1924), pp. 393–94, 396; William G. Simms, *The Life of Francis Marion* (New York: H. G. Langley, 1844), p. 329. William Cunningham had terrorized the backcountry since the fall of 1781. In February 1783 he murdered General Andrew Pickens's commissary of supplies. The South Carolina assembly authorized recruiting two companies of rangers to pursue Cunningham and offered a reward for his capture. The final dispersion of the Cunningham band by William Butler probably occurred in March 1783, not in the summer of 1782 as has often been claimed. Edward McCrady, *The History of South Carolina in the Revolution, 1780–1783* (New York: Macmillan, 1902), pp. 471–75, 627–31; *Gazette of the State of Georgia*, Mar. 6, 1783, p. 4; "South Carolina House of Representatives Journal," Mar. 4, 1783, S.C. Department of Archives and History, Columbia, S.C., pp. 248–49.

they have not been without their defenders. Russell Weigley has recently published a study of the partisan resistance against the British occupation of 1780–82. His partisans, however, seem to spring to arms as if by magic and in response to this British proclamation or that loyalist atrocity. Weigley seldom mentions militia in his *Partisan War*.[2] Robert Pugh has made a plea for recognition of the accomplishments of the southern militiamen in the year 1780. His study culminates in their excellent performance at Cowpens under Daniel Morgan, a Continental officer who understood their strengths and weaknesses. Pugh hardly ever refers to partisans; when he discusses the exploits of Francis Marion following the battle of Camden, he treats Marion as just another leader of a body of southern militia.[3] Of the two authors, Pugh, I believe, has the sounder perspective. A Continental officer who escaped capture at the fall of Charleston in 1780, Marion became a famous partisan by leading out those militiamen who were prepared to and who already knew how to fight. Once he demonstrated successful leadership he was commissioned a brigadier general of militia by the itinerant governor, John Rutledge. As John Barnwell has noted, "the partisan leaders depended not merely on volunteers, but sought to enforce the militia laws"—that "they held commissions was of importance."[4] The rise to prominence of Thomas Sumter was similar to that of Marion, though the Gamecock was first elected brigadier general by his militia followers, and Rutledge simply confirmed the choice. Andrew Pickens was commissioned brigadier general by the governor after his successful leadership of Carolina and Georgia militia at Cowpens.[5]

The matter of authority leads to a major contention of this essay: that much of the success in the guerrilla war or partisan resistance to British occupation was due to the preexisting colonial militia structure, which had been tempered by changes resulting from five years of war before the fall of Charleston. Furthermore, it is argued that the bulk of activities and experiences of the militia in the period 1775–

---

2. Russell F. Weigley, *The Partisan War: The South Carolina Campaign of 1780–1782* (Columbia: Univ. of S.C. Press, 1970), pp. 8, 12–15.

3. Robert C. Pugh, "The Revolutionary Militia in the Southern Campaign, 1780–1781," *William and Mary Quarterly*, 3d ser., XIV (1957), 154–75.

4. Robert W. Barnwell, Jr., "Rutledge, 'The Dictator,'" *Journal of Southern History*, VII (1941), 220.

5. Weigley, *The Partisan War*, p. 15; Rutledge to Daniel Morgan, Jan. 25, 1781, James Graham, *The Life of General Daniel Morgan* . . . (New York: Derby & Jackson, 1856), pp. 335–36.

80 can correctly be designated as irregular warfare or training for partisan war. And finally it is contended that the basic functions of the militia were clarified early in the war, long before any major combat with British regular forces occurred, and that the militia's success in performing those functions meant disaster for the royal government's troops when they turned to a "southern strategy" in 1779. The interpretation of those functions which follows is drawn mostly from examples in the colony-state of South Carolina and largely from the activities of the partisan-militiaman, Andrew Pickens.

Opposed to the basic contention of this essay are the views of two scholars who consider the South Carolina militia system as degenerate in the eighteenth century. John Shy and David Cole view the militia as little more than a social institution whose chief function was the control of slaves. Shy has suggested that blacks were no longer enrolled in the militia after the 1739 slave insurrection, but Lieutenant Governor William Bull specifically contradicted this view in 1770 when he made a very valuable, and by no means totally derogatory, assessment of the militia:

The Defense of the province as far as our own power can avail, is provided for by our militia against foreign and Patrols against domestic enemies. ... our militia is now encreased to about Ten Thousand men, divided into Ten Regiments unequal in numbers, but equal in want of discipline. ...

In the country almost every militia man marches on Horseback. ... In great danger the militia is to be reenforced with a number of Trusty Negroes (and we have many such) not exceeding one-third of the corps they are to join. To observe good order among the slaves, one fourth of the militia must be left at home which furnishes a constant Patrol to keep all quiet there. In these times the Governor does not proclaim martial Law, but publishes an alarm by the advice of council which puts the whole Province under arms, and then the only Martial Law is the Militia Act. It is thought unlawful to march the Militia out of the Province.

Bull has also given us a picture of the operation of the militia system in 1770 and thus a base from which to view various changes in the next decade.

Supporting Shy's derogatory evaluation of the southern militia was the thinness of the population in the early eighteenth century.[6] But

6. John Shy, "A New Look at Colonial Militia," *William and Mary Quarterly*, 3rd Ser., XX (1963), 180–81; David Cole, "A Brief Outline of the South Carolina

as Don Higginbotham has pointed out, contemporary New England-ers also held a dim view of southern military potential but were un-aware that in the years 1730–75 approximately 250,000 immigrants had been added to the southern backcountry. He saw a remarkably sound militia system responding in South Carolina during the Chero-kee War (1759–61) and in Virginia to Lord Dunmore's War (1774). "Whatever their traditions and inadequacies," wrote Higginbotham, "the Americans in 1775, unlike most other popular revolutionary movements in modern history, began their War of Independence in control of a large military organization, the militia."[7] In his study of the South Carolina interior during the 1760s Richard Brown found the militia organization vital when the threat was the hostility of the red men (a smoldering ember that would burst into flames again in 1776) but inadequate to control the social disruption that followed in the wake of the Cherokee War. In 1764 Bull created another back-country militia regiment between the Broad and Saluda rivers to give the settlers "some sort of Order and Government which they seem generally at present not sufficiently acquainted with, being chiefly from the back parts of the Northern colonies."[8] By 1775 twelve militia regiments had been created in South Carolina; the colony's military potential was then estimated at between twelve and fourteen thousand men. In spite of the fact that militiamen usually moved by horseback, the dozen regiments, based on twelve military districts, were designated infantry. There was also a cavalry regi-ment in the low country which was not tied to any single district.[9] One could surmise that the cavalry unit indicated that slave control remained a chief function for the low-country militia, whereas the growing population, the addition of new regiments, and the existence of an Indian threat suggested that the institution had real military functions in the upper part of the colony.

Colonial Militia System," *Proceedings of the South Carolina Historical Association 1954* (Columbia: South Carolina Historical Association, 1955), pp. 14, 19 ("The Report on Militia by Lt. Gov. William Bull in 1770," pp. 20–21).

7. Don Higginbotham, *The War of American Independence: Military Attitudes, Policies, and Practice, 1763–1789* (New York: Macmillan, 1971), pp. 7–10.

8. Richard M. Brown, *The South Carolina Regulators* (Cambridge, Mass.: Harvard Univ. Press, 1963), pp. 5–6, 14, 23. Hereafter cited as Brown, *Regulators*.

9. John Drayton, *Memoirs of the American Revolution* . . . (2 vols.; Charleston: A. E. Miller, 1821), I, 352–53; Edward McCrady, *The History of South Carolina in the Revolution, 1775–1780* (New York: Macmillan, 1901), pp. 10–12, hereafter cited as McCrady, *South Carolina 1775–1780.*

When the Revolution came to South Carolina, the militia had to add a third string to its bow, the suppression of loyalist sentiment and organization. Since in theory all male citizens between sixteen and sixty were members of the militia, the task proved formidable in areas where the majority of the leading men—and the South Carolina interior definitely had a deferential social structure—chose to back the king or at least to defy the revolutionary Provincial Congress. As the militia system had proved ineffectual as an instrument of social control during the Regulator movement, so it did now in areas where the people were strongly divided in their sentiments. This was necessarily so for the militia were the male citizenry; in an equally divided area half the people could not be expected to control the other half.[10] A great division of sentiment existed in an area bounded by the Saluda and Broad rivers, the Cherokee and North Carolina borders. Royal Governor William Campbell claimed the militia's allegiance as did the Provincial Congress. Before the latter adjourned in June 1775, it created an executive committee called the Council of Safety and to it delegated "full power and authority to carry the acts of Assembly for regulating the Militia of this colony, in all respects, into execution, as in time of alarm. . . ." The council was also given power to approve replacements for vacant positions in the militia and to remove officers upon "just complaint."[11]

Why so many leading figures in the forks of the Saluda chose the loyalist cause will probably never be completely ascertained. Andrew Pickens thought Robert Cunningham did so because of failure to receive command of the newly created regular regiment of Rangers: ". . . if Cunningham had been appointed Colonel at that time, we would not have had so violent an opposition to our cause in this country, and I never had a doubt but he would have made the best officer."[12] Some historians stress backcountry distrust of a political movement dominated by the coast, the inferior representation of the

10. My comments on the social structure and the Regulators are based on Brown, *Regulators*, pp. 23–27, 38–40, 43–45, 55–59, 83–95, 137. The analogy of 1775 with the period of the Regulation is my own.

11. Tennent to Laurens, Aug. 20, 1775, Drayton's proclamation, Sept. 13, 1775, Drayton, *Memoirs*, I, 323, 391–92, 411–12; *Extracts from the Journals of the Provincial Congresses of South Carolina, 1775–1776*, ed. William E. Hemphill and Wylma A. Wates (Columbia: S.C. Department of Archives and History, 1960), pp. 50–51, 54.

12. Pickens to Henry Lee, Aug. 28, 1811, Lyman C. Draper Collection, Thomas Sumter Papers, Series VV, I, 107[1], State Historical Society, Madison, Wisc. Hereafter cited as Dr., VV.

interior, the number of Germans on lands newly granted by the king; Wallace Brown has established a degree of correlation between recent European immigrants and the loyalist cause. Many common people were doubtless committed to Tory allegiance by rumors that the Provincial Congress was sending ammunition to the Cherokee for use against the king's adherents.[13] When Thomas Fletchall, commander of one of the militia regiments in the Saluda forks, denied Congress's powers, the decision was crucial. On September 5 the Council of Safety made "a Declaration of Alarm to the militia according to the militia acts. . . ."[14] Two rapidly mobilized forces, composed mostly of militia and supporting different causes, stalemated each other, and a truce was signed on September 16. For various reasons the pact broke down, and the two bodies of troops came to blows at Savage Old Fields on November 19. Patriot militiamen were outnumbered but fought well. The loyalists were well organized and aggressive, but had to break off hostilities upon receiving intelligence of a superior force marching to relieve the patriots.[15]

Rather than viewing this situation as an example of the inability of the militia to control the interior, I suggest that the events of June–November 1775 are evidence of the vitality of the militia structure. In the ability to mobilize and move against an opposing force the loyalist militia thus far had the best of it.

Representatives of the Council of Safety used several expedients to counteract the Tory militia in the forks. One was the authorization of numerous volunteer patriot companies of horsemen in adjoining militia districts. Andrew Pickens and James McCall gained their first prominence while leading such units at Savage Old Fields. According to the Reverend Mr. William Tennent, the strategy of the revolutionaries was the "hemming in the Dissidents on all sides as much as possible. . . ." In the regiment of Colonel Thomas Neel east

13. David D. Wallace, *South Carolina: A Short History, 1520–1948* (Chapel Hill: Univ. of N.C. Press, 1951), pp. 263–64; Wallace Brown, *The King's Friends* (Providence, R.I.: Brown Univ. Press, 1965), pp. 219, 222, 258–60, 269–70, 278; David Ramsay, *Ramsay's History of South Carolina* . . . (2 vols.; Newberry, S.C.: W. J. Duffie, 1858), I, 143–44, hereafter cited as Ramsay, *History of South Carolina*; McCrady, *South Carolina 1775–1780*, p. 89.

14. Drayton, *Memoirs*, II, 25.

15. Ibid., I, 399–403; *Documentary History of the American Revolution* . . . *1764–1776*, ed. Robert W. Gibbes (New York: D. Appleton & Co., 1855), pp. 209–10, 214–19, hereafter cited as *Documentary History, 1764–1776*; extract of a letter from an officer at Ninety-Six, Nov. 29, 1775, *South Carolina and American General Gazette*, Nov. 24–Dec. 8, 1775.

of Broad River Tennent helped organized a "troop of volunteer Horse Rangers," apparently the company of Ezekiel Polk. Gary Olson believes this unit was created to detach from Fletchall's command the uncommitted and those leaning toward the revolutionary cause.[16] An attempt to appease the grievances of the disaffected was doubtless behind the Provincial Congress's decision to grant more representation to the forks of the Saluda. Also, Congress or the Council of Safety sanctioned the promotion of Captain John Thomas to colonel and commander of a second regiment carved out of Fletchall's military district.[17]

The second Provincial Congress meeting in November undertook important reforms in the militia structure. At the same time the revolutionary legislature attempted to reduce the colony's dependence on militia units by promoting the newly authorized regular regiments. Nevertheless, when word reached Charleston of the seriousness of Fletchall's insurrection, the major response was a draft of contingents from eight of the militia regiments.[18] Reforms included mandatory fortnightly assemblies with substantial fines for nonattendance, an attempt to cut down on the use of horses in the regiments (a change that so went against the customs of the men that it never worked and caused trouble throughout the war), the subdivision of large regiments into battalions, and a major crackdown on those using membership in the volunteer companies to avoid militia patrols. For dereliction of duty, however, militiamen remained subject only to the militia laws, not the Articles of War governing the regulars. A major change, destined to be in effect for the duration of the War for

16. Drayton, *Memoirs*, I, 384, 412–13; *Extracts from Journals*, pp. 113–14; Gary D. Olson, "Loyalists and the American Revolution: Thomas Brown and the South Carolina Backcountry, 1775–1776," *South Carolina Historical Magazine*, LXVIII (1967), 210–11. Olson has written a very valuable article regarding the divisions in the Carolina backcountry as seen from the side of the loyalists. He thinks, and I agree, that most of Fletchall's men would have liked merely to be left alone. The Provincial Congress, taking the viewpoint that all who aren't with us are against us, made such neutrality impossible.

17. McCrady, *South Carolina 1775–1780*, p. 608; *Extracts from Journals*, pp. 57, 76, 101–2, 198; Drayton to Council of Safety, Aug. 21, 1775, Thomas to Drayton, Sept. 11, 1775, *Documentary History 1764–1776*, pp. 152–53, 170. Although McCrady believed Thomas took over Fletchall's regiment, the correspondence and the Provincial Congress journals provide a correction. Thomas was designated colonel when elected to Congress on November 1, 1775. On November 7 he was called regimental commander when contingents were chosen to march against Fletchall. The journal entry of Feb. 19, 1776, referred to drafts of militia both from the "Late Col. Fletchall's" regiment and from Thomas's regiment.

18. *Extracts from Journals*, pp. 39–40, 61, 101–4, 143, 151–52.

Independence, was the requirement that commanders "draught one third of their respective regiments, including volunteer companies, and hold them in constant readiness to march at a minute's warning" on call of the Congress or the Council of Safety.[19] The second session of the second Congress, by agreeing to send military assistance to North Carolina if necessary, ended the tradition that militia could not be ordered across colonial boundaries. This reform was an almost mandatory response to the aid the North State had given South Carolina against Fletchall.[20]

The militia army launched against the Tory commander by Colonel Richard Richardson of the Camden district was overwhelming and should have dispelled for all time the view that militia could not respond or that South Carolina was equally divided in terms of loyalists and patriots. The force ultimately reached four to five thousand men, which included some two hundred South Carolina regulars, about two hundred North Carolina regulars, perhaps a thousand North State militia, with the remainder coming from South Carolina militia regiments including Captain Polk's volunteers. Richardson displayed the velvet hand in the mailed gauntlet; the smallfry Tories "I dismiss with soft words and cheerful countenances, and admonish them to use their interest with their friends and neighbors. . . ." By December 22 the "spirit of discord being much abated, the most of the Captains" had surrendered "and a good part of the companies under them." The loyalist militia army virtually disintegrated before Richardson attacked it at the "Brake of Canes on the Cherokee Land." He forced those surrendering to sign a statement "by which they forfeit their estates, real and personal, if they ever take up arms against, or disquiet the peace and tranquility of the good people of this colony again, and to assist them if they are ever called upon."[21]

The Provincial Congress wisely followed Richardson's lead by

---

19. *Ibid.*, pp. 104, 135, 143–44, 146–47, 149. By 1775 slaves were no longer being mustered in time of alarm. A resolve of November 20 gave the militia colonels power "to enrol such a number of able male slaves, to be employed as pioneers and labourers, as public exigencies may require. And that a daily pay of seven shillings and six-pence be allowed for the services of each such slave, while actually employed." *Ibid.*, p. 141.

20. *Ibid.*, pp. 140, 246; Ramsay, *History of South Carolina*, I, 146; William Moultrie, *Memoirs of the American Revolution* . . . (2 vols.; New York: David Longworth, 1802), I, 120–21.

21. *Extracts from Journals*, pp. 101–2, 152. The quotes are from four letters from Richardson to Henry Laurens dated Dec. 12, 16, 22, 1775, and Jan. 2, 1776. *Documentary History 1764–1776*, pp. 239–48.

granting the insurgents pardon and amnesty "with certain exceptions." Opposing the revolutionaries in the future would bring disarmament and possible incarceration, no minor threat for an adherent
of the king living near the Indian boundary. All officers who had
been involved in the insurrection "or shall be convicted of having
been active in opposing the authority of Congress" were to lose their
commissions.[22] The forks of the Saluda were now formally reorganized to include John Thomas's "Upper or Spartan" regiment. The
purport of this move was doubtless to gerrymander disaffected militiamen into different districts, but the area was also given additional
representation in what was soon to be the new state government.[23]
The great mass of the dissidents had now been reconciled or coerced,
or had fled to the Cherokee nation or to the Floridas. After the dispersion of Fletchall's uprising control of loyalist sympathizers became a feasible function for the upcountry militia.

The protection of the frontier against the Indians, a task that became inextricably interwoven during the Revolution with suppression
of the Tories, became the foremost duty for the militia in the summer of 1776. In the fall of 1775 the patriots had accepted as an article
of faith that John Stuart, British Indian superintendent in the South,
and his deputy, Alexander Cameron, were trying to instigate Indian
intervention in behalf of British arms. That Stuart was deliberately
thwarting General Thomas Gage's orders that the red men "take
arms against his Majesty's Enemies, and to distress them all in their
power" was unknown. At the same time individual loyalists like
Thomas Brown, in exile after Fletchall's defeat, actively encouraged
Indian attacks on the patriot frontier. However, when the Cherokee
did strike in July 1776, they did so for their own reasons (essentially
white encroachment on their lands) and in their own way (concerted
surprise attacks from the Watauga boundary to Georgia).[24] Since

22. *Extracts from Journals*, pp. 230–32. The Provincial Congress's action was
much less severe than that of the new state government created by the Constitution of 1776. Taking up arms in opposition to government, urging others to do so,
or giving intelligence to enemies of government was made a felony punishable by
death. Estates of offenders were made forfeit. *Statutes at Large of South Carolina*,
ed. Thomas Cooper and David J. McCord (10 vols.; Columbia: A. S. Johnson,
1836–41), IV, 344–46.
    23. *Extracts from Journals*, pp. 182–83, 251.
    24. *Documentary History, 1764–1776*, pp. 147–48, 161–62; Philip M. Hamer,
"John Stuart's Indian Policy during the Early Months of the American Revolution,"
Mississippi Valley Historical Review, XVII (1930), 351–66; Philip M. Hamer,
"The Wataugans and the Cherokee Indians in 1776," *East Tennessee Historical*

the South Carolinians had long expected just such an action, the death toll of approximately sixty citizens indicates a decided failure for the upcountry militia in a defensive role. Patriot militiamen in the forks of the Saluda were the most effective; in one battle they took thirteen prisoners, all white, four of them "painted as Indians." Many loyalists joined the Cherokee and thus played a major role in the attack on South Carolina.[25]

The three-pronged retaliatory campaign composed essentially of militia contingents of the two Carolinas, Georgia, and Virginia (including the Wataugans) was devastating to the Cherokee nation. The strategy was the culmination of the entire colonial experience of warfare against the red man: burn out his villages, destroy his existing food surpluses, force him to sue for peace and yield coveted territory. Patriot leaders assumed their objective was to force the Cherokee out of hostile activities concerted with the British armed forces. Interstate cooperation in 1776 was superior to such intercolonial efforts as those in King Philip's War; the patriot militiamen were far more effective alone than they had been when actively assisted by British regulars in 1760–61. Among the results of the campaign were the weakening of the various southern Indian nations' ties to England, the immense strengthening of the patriot cause in the divided backcountry (particularly in South Carolina), and the effectual splitting of Cherokee unity via the defection of Dragging Canoe in 1777 and creation of the splinter band of Chickamauga.[26] Less evident results were the training of patriot militiamen for partisan warfare. South Carolina irregulars learned the value of rapid mobility, the

---

Society's Publications, III (1931), 108, 126; Jack M. Sosin, "The Use of Indians in the War of the American Revolution: A Re-Assessment of Responsibility," *Canadian Historical Review*, XLVI (1965), 113–15; Drayton, *Memoirs*, I, 412; James H. O'Donnell, III, *Southern Indians in the American Revolution* (Knoxville.: Univ. of Tenn. Press, 1973), pp. viii–ix, 14, 18, 29–31, 35–42.

25. *Documentary History of the American Revolution . . . 1776–1782*, ed. Robert W. Gibbes (New York: D. Appleton & Co., 1857), pp. 24, 27; "A South Carolina Protest Against Slavery Being a Letter from Henry Laurens . . . to . . . John Laurens Charleston . . . August 14th, 1776" (New York: G. P. Putnam, 1861), p. 27.

26. Helen L. Shaw, *British Administration of the Southern Indians, 1756–1783* (Lancaster, Pa.: Lancaster Press, 1931), pp. 15–17, 100–104; Samuel C. Williams, *Tennessee during the Revolutionary War* (Nashville: Tenn. Historical Commission, 1944), pp. 61–62, hereafter cited as Williams, *Tennessee in Revolution*; Ramsay, *History of South Carolina*, I, 100–107; O'Donnell, *Southern Indians*, pp. 14–15, 43–44, 49–50, 52–53. My comparison with King Philip's War is based on Douglas E. Leach, *Flintlock and Tomahawk* (New York: Norton, 1966).

ambush, good intelligence, the psychological impact of terror, and the concert of light troops' movements with those of the major force during the campaign of 1776.

The core of South Carolina's retaliatory force was the Ninety-Six district's militia regiment, which apparently was totally mobilized; seven hundred men were in the field by July 22. They were incensed at the regiments in the Saluda forks "for granting quarter to their prisoners, and declare they will grant none either to Indians or white men who join them."[27] Contingents from two new South Carolina regular rifle regiments (ninety-three men) and units from Thomas's and Neel's militia regiments (and possibly some men from Fletchall's old regiment in the forks) brought Andrew Williamson's command to about twelve hundred. Only a major in mid-July, Williamson had advanced to the leadership of the Ninety-Six regiment upon the incapacitation or death of Colonel John Savage. Though quickly promoted to colonel, Williamson had difficulty asserting authority over senior regimental commanders. "He is undoubtedly a brave man, and not a bad general," wrote Henry Laurens to his son, John. "You know his deficiency in education, what heights might he have reached if he could have improved his genius by reading."[28] Williamson was ambushed by Cherokee and loyalists at Seneca on August 1, while attempting a surprise night march to capture Alexander Cameron. In the following two weeks his army destroyed the Lower Cherokee towns on the headwaters of the Savannah River.[29]

Following the ambush at Seneca Captain Andrew Pickens took over reconnaissance duty for the main force. Mounted, his men armed with sabers, he skirmished daily with Cherokee patrols. When the red men attempted to concentrate on Williamson, Pickens struck and burned their villages. If the Indians dispersed their warriors to defend against the mobile troops, they had no chance against the main

27. *Documentary History 1776–1782*, pp. 24–27.

28. Ibid.; McCrady, *South Carolina 1775–1780*, p. 197; "South Carolina Protest Against Slavery," p. 28; Brown, *Regulators*, p. 209. Savage died in 1776, probably before the Cherokee attack. He may have been only incapacitated in July 1776, for Williamson was only a major when he began raising troops for the campaign. Francis Salvador begged William H. Drayton to have Williamson promoted to straighten out the command problem, and it apparently was done immediately. That would indicate that Savage was deceased by late July or early August.

29. *Documentary History 1764–1776*, pp. 125–26; *Documentary History, 1776–1782*, p. 32.

force. The basic role of partisan collaboration with a large offensive army had been discovered.[30] During the reconquest of South Carolina in 1781 Pickens would be the partisan leader who best understood the necessity of coordinating his moves with Nathanael Greene and the Continental army.

The use of militia in an offensive campaign that crossed old boundaries was not without its problems. In mid-August Williamson had to allow many of his militiamen to return home for provisions. Perhaps there was a major rotation of the active contingents deployed by the various regiments, but many of the same men rejoined him at the beginning of September. On the eleventh he was reenforced by Thomas Sumter and 330 of his regular riflemen; nine days later, during the campaign against the Valley Cherokee, these men became Continentals by act of the South Carolina assembly.[31] Williamson used the hiatus in the action to build a fort on Keowee River, an act which would enable the Carolinians to claim a land cession by right of conquest and possession.[32]

The Cherokee put up their strongest resistance against this South Carolina wing of the patriot offensive, and some of the actions were fierce and bloody. Pickens was ambushed August 12, both suffering and inflicting heavy casualties in a fight that ended hand to hand, corn knife versus tomahawk. Williamson ran into another ambush on September 19 that had been intended for Griffith Rutherford and the North Carolinians who had just wreaked havoc on the Middle settlements. Arthur Fairies, a member of Neel's regiment, casually noted in his journal the brutality that marked the last phase of the

30. John Swelling's Account of Indian Expedition, Dr., VV, XVI, 379–80; Cousin Andrew Pickens's notes, ibid., III, 140; Samuel Hammond's narrative of 1776 campaign, ibid., III, 128–29; Williamson to Griffith Rutherford, Aug. 14, 1776, *The Colonial Records of North Carolina*, ed. William L. Saunders (10 vols.; Raleigh: Printer to the State, 1886–90), X, 746–47.

31. Joseph McJunkin's narrative, Dr., VV, XXIII, 7–8; "Arthur Fairies' Journal of an Expedition in 1776 against the Cherokees," ibid., III, 162–67; Fragment of Diary of A. Williamson, ibid., III, 153, 156, 159; McCrady, *South Carolina 1775–1780*, pp. 197–98; Moultrie, *Memoirs*, I, 187. Williamson ordered Sumter to bring a major's commission for Andrew Pickens.

32. McCrady, *South Carolina 1775–1780*, pp. 198–99; Dr., VV, III, 160–61; Treaty of Dewitt's Corner, May 20, 1777, in *Public Lands*, Vol. I of *American State Papers* (38 vols.; Washington, D.C.: Gales & Seaton, 1832–61), 29–30. At the Long Island Treaty negotiations the Tassel successfully argued against ceding territory to the Wataugans on the grounds that they had failed to build a fort and take possession of the area through which their army campaigned. Williams, *Tennessee in Revolution*, pp. 265–68.

campaign. On September 21 his company wounded a squaw and forced her to give information regarding Cherokee plans: "Hearing this account, we started, and the informer being unable to travel, some of our men favored her so far, that they killed her there, to put her out of pain."[33] By September 26 the two Carolina wings, mostly militia, had burned out and destroyed all crops and supplies in thirty-six towns. The South Carolina militiamen were released by mid-October, having gained three months of partisan experience against the phantom Cherokee whose woes were still not over; the Virginians and Wataugans were only beginning their invasion of the Overhill settlements.[34]

The suppression of the loyalists in 1775 and the devastation of the Cherokee in 1776 provided the South Carolina revolutionaries a breathing time which they utilized to clamp a tight control on the new state. Under the leadership of John Rutledge, the legislature of 1778 completely rewrote the basic militia laws. Regimental size was approximately equalized at six hundred, all the regiments being re-assigned to three newly created brigades. For special duty up to three-fourths of a unit could be mobilized and used outside the regimental district; the remainder were to stay at home on constant patrol. Officers above the rank of captain were authorized to impress necessary supplies from the citizenry but had to issue receipts on the state for anything confiscated. A strict loyalty oath was made mandatory for all males over sixteen. Refusal of a militiamen to take the oath brought automatic disarmament, exile from the state, and the death penalty upon return. A law to dragoon "idle and disorderly persons" into the Continentals was also passed.[35] Aimed at the immediate threat of incursions from the Floridas and the raising of a body of loyalists under Joseph Coffell, the legislative measures helped spur resistance to British invasion in 1779 and improved the organization for resistance to occupation during 1780–81.

Also significant was the experience gained by the upcountry militia

33. *Colonial Records of North Carolina*, X, 747–48; J. G. Hamilton (ed.), "Revolutionary Diary of William Lenoir," *Journal of Southern History*, VI (1940), 251–52; Joseph McJunkin's narrative, Dr., VV, XXIII, 8–10; "Arthur Fairies' Journal," ibid., III, 170–71.

34. Robert L. Ganyard, "Threat from the West: North Carolina and the Cherokee, 1776–1778," *North Carolina Historical Review*, XLV (1968), 59–61; "Arthur Fairies' Journal," Dr., VV, III, 172–75.

35. Rutledge to assembly, Jan. 9, 1778, *North Carolina Gazette*, [date torn]; Cooper and McCord, *Statutes*, I, 147–50; IV, 410; IX, 666, 674–78.

in 1778. Called out on April 19 to assist General Robert Howe on his ill-fated invasion of Florida, elements of the new Ninety-Six brigade under Brigadier General Williamson actively campaigned against Tory raiders and small parties of hostile Indians until November. Though ineffective as auxiliaries to the Continental army, the brigade was seasoned in the field for nearly seven months in 1778, certainly marathon duty for irregular forces.[36] The important point is that before being called on to face British regulars, a major loyalist uprising, and Indians operating under British orders, the patriot militiamen had become veterans through months of field duty and had achieved organization superior to that of 1775. They had essentially broken the back of Cherokee power in 1776, and they had effectually suppressed most of the Tories since 1775. British hopes that both allies were as potent as they once had been were pipedreams. Though much misery lay ahead for the patriot militia, it had essentially already destroyed the two allies that would have given British plans for a southern strategy any realistic chance for success.[37]

The preliminary conditions in the South were thus decisive when the British shifted their advance forces to that theater in December 1778. Paul Smith has shown that the strategy pursued from the French entry into the war in 1778 until Yorktown was based on belief in the latent strength of southern loyalism. Hopeful of being able to retake Georgia with the aid of the Tories, and also expecting assistance from John Stuart's Indians, British strategists planned to secure conquered areas with a loyalist militia, thus freeing the regular army to campaign against South Carolina. Once that state fell, the procedure would be repeated, and American resistance would be smashed from the bottom upward, like rolling up a window shade. Rather than being discouraged by early setbacks to the loyalists and Indians, George Germain, colonial secretary, thought the fact they

36. *Documentary History, 1776–1782*, pp. 93–96, 99. Documents pertaining to the campaign of Robert Howe are found in Moultrie, *Memoirs*, I, 203–40. The relationship between the civil authorities of Georgia and Howe's army are dealt with in items 72 and 73, Papers of the Continental Congress, National Archives, Washington, D.C.

37. Walter Millis stated the point I make somewhat differently: "The patriots' success in infiltrating and capturing the old militia organizations, by expelling and replacing officers of Tory sympathies, was perhaps as important to the outcome as any of their purely political achievements. While the regular armies marched and fought more or less ineffectually, it was the militia which presented the greatest single impediment to Britain's only practicable weapon, that of counter-revolution." Walter Millis, *Arms and Men* (New York: Putnam, 1956), p. 30.

had risen without British assistance meant they would be invaluable allies if given military aid. Exiled royal governors continually fed this point of view to the ministry. Thomas Brown, leading a loyalist unit in East Florida, estimated that the Carolina backcountry would put sixty-three hundred men into the field in support of a British army landing in Georgia.[38] Considering that the loyalists had been badly bloodied in 1775 and that the revolutionary governments and militias had done everything within their power for three years to suppress dissidence, such estimates were sheer folly.

To test the new strategy, the British landed Lieutenant Colonel Archibald Campbell and thirty-five hundred men in Georgia; they captured Savannah on December 29, 1778. Five days later Campbell and Hyde Parker, commander of the naval force at Savannah, issued a proclamation announcing reinstatement of British government, calling loyalists to "rescue their Friends from Oppression, themselves from Slavery," promising "no parliamentary imposed tax," and threatening those who opposed "the Re-establishment of legal Government" with the "Rigours of War."[39] Georgia militia leaders issued a counterproclamation giving the disaffected three days to join the resistance or be "deemed as Enemies & dealt with accordingly." By January 15 the Georgia patriots knew Campbell's objective was Augusta, the purpose "to protect the disaffected of South Carolina," and this information they passed to leaders in the neighboring state.[40] Nevertheless the rapid movements by Campbell threw the South Carolina patriots off balance. On January 31 he captured Augusta and began organizing a loyalist militia.[41] Campbell was in a precarious position, however, if the large-scale uprising of backcountry Tories failed or if the Indians did not come to his assistance.

Andrew Pickens, by 1779 colonel and regimental commander in

38. Paul H. Smith, *Loyalists and Redcoats: A Study in British Revolutionary Policy* (Chapel Hill: Univ. of N.C. Press, 1964), pp. 25–26, 29–31, 72, 79, 83–84, 86–87, 92–93, 172–73; Gary D. Olson, "Thomas Brown, Loyalist Partisan, and the Revolutionary War in Georgia, 1776–1782," *Georgia Historical Quarterly*, LIV (1970), 8–9. The belief in the value of the southern loyalists had been imbedded in the minds of the British ministry since the abortive campaign of 1776 that had ended in the disaster of Moore's Creek Bridge.

39. *Facsimiles of Manuscripts in European Archives Relating to America . . . ,* ed. Benjamin F. Stevens (25 vols.; London: Malby & Sons, 1889–95), XII, No. 1238.

40. *Proceedings of a Council of War Held at Burke Jail . . . ,* ed. Paul L. Ford (Brooklyn, N.Y.: Historical Printing Club, 1890), pp. 13–15, 17, 19–20.

41. Olson, "Thomas Brown, Loyalist Partisan," p. 13; McCrady, *South Carolina 1775–1780,* pp. 336–37.

the Ninety-Six brigade, had been guarding the frontier against Indian incursions. He now took over leadership of both states' militias in the upper Savannah River area and began stabbing at Tory outposts and detachments. Only one major body of backcountry loyalists was organizing to join Campbell, and the patriot grapevine carried news of Colonel Boyd and his eight hundred men to Pickens. On February 14 he caught up with the Tories at Kettle Creek and virtually annihilated them.[42] Campbell had already begun his retreat, his newly organized militia companies collapsing even before his departure. By mid-February the loyalists of the backcountry who had rallied to the king's cause were left to the tender mercies of the revolutionary regimes.[43] When the promised Indian contingents from the Creek nation attempted in March to break through to the British at Savannah, Pickens and various Georgia partisan leaders intercepted, dispersed, and turned most of them back.[44]

The functions of the patriot militiamen were essentially the same in early 1779 as in previous years—controlling the Tories, protecting against the Indians. However, by 1779, as a result of the commitment to the southern strategy, a blow against either was a far more direct strike at the British than such actions had been in earlier years. Georgia was not reconquered by the minimal British effort of 1779, and the Tories would not rise again until protected by an army of occupation.

The patriot militia of Georgia and South Carolina now opened a

42. Clyde R. Ferguson, "General Andrew Pickens" (Ph.D. dissertation, Duke University, 1960), pp. 48–62.

43. Olson, "Thomas Brown, Loyalist Partisan," pp. 11–13; Extract of a letter from a camp near Adams' ferry, Feb. 20, 1779, *South Carolina and American General Gazette*, Mar. 4, 1779; Smith, *Loyalists and Redcoats*, pp. 101–6.

44. Pickens to Lee, Aug. 28, 1811, Dr., VV, I, 1075; Letter from Williamson's camp, Apr. 3, 1779, *Gazette of the State of South Carolina*, Apr. 7, 1779; Charles C. Jones (ed.), "Autobiography of Col. William Few of Georgia," *The Magazine of American History with Notes and Queries*, VII (1881), 349. Ordering the Creek warriors against the patriot frontier was one of John Stuart's last acts as superintendent since he died in March 1779. That Campbell tried to blame his own failure on Stuart was made clear by a letter from Germain to Stuart of June 2, 1779: ". . . Lieutenant Colonel Campbell has informed me that from his arrival in Savannah on the 3rd of December 1778, to his departure from that province on the 9th of March, 1779, he had not heard or seen an Indian; and that had he been joined as he expected, by any considerable body of them, when he was at Augusta, he should have been able to have opened communication with the loyal inhabitants of the back country of the two Carolinas and doubts not he could have effected other very important services which he was obliged to leave unattempted for want of their assistance." Shaw, *Southern Indians*, pp. 128, 130–32.

campaign of terror against those Georgians who were not openly supporting the revolutionary cause. Political in intent, of course, it was also military, designed to destroy transportation and supplies that otherwise might be used by the British army in lower Georgia. An elaborate intelligence system was created to keep the militiamen of both states informed as to enemy movements in the low country. South Carolina's John Rutledge heartily approved of warfare on cattle, horses, and other provisions belonging to Georgians who were either Tory or neutral. That the Continental commander, Benjamin Lincoln, argued vociferously against such tactics indicates that he failed to grasp the essential role of the militia as suppressor of the political dissident.[45]

Lincoln's concept of the militia's value was simply that it was a manpower source useful to augment the Continental army. Because of a British move against Charleston, the Ninety-Six brigade was ordered to the coast and was actually thrown into the useless assault at Stono Ferry on June 20. The withdrawal of these men from frontier defense, a primary function, led to massive desertions in July when rumors began to spread that the Cherokee were about to assault the backcountry.[46] The real contribution of the Indian to British success was pinpointed by Lieutenant Walter Scott of the Loyalist Refugees: "The Talk of their [Cherokee] going to war has certainly answered a very good intention by keeping a great many Rebels upon the Frontier which greatly help the Troops (Br.) by keeping so many men from them."[47] Returned to its proper sphere of operations, Williamson's brigade cut a bloody swath through the Valley Cherokee towns in August 1779. This put an end to active intervention of the red men in the war until the occupation of 1780. Almost unbelievably the backcountry militia returned to the low country for one final sanguinary action in 1779. While Pickens's regiment remained on frontier defense, five hundred men of the brigade marched for Savannah and took part in the Franco-American assault of October 9.[48] Until the

45. Williamson to Lincoln, Apr. 9, 1779, Revolutionary Collection, Duke Univ. Library, Durham, N.C.; Moultrie to Rutledge, Apr. 16, 1779, Moultrie, *Memoirs*, I, 368; McCrady, *South Carolina 1775–1780*, pp. 347–48.

46. Moultrie, *Memoirs*, II, 7, 11, 15–17.

47. Shaw, *Southern Indians*, pp. 136–37.

48. Letter from Whitehall, Sept. 17, 1779, *South Carolina and American General Gazette*, Sept. 24, 1779; Moultrie, *Memoirs*, II, 39–41; Alexander A. Lawrence, *Storm over Savannah* (Athens: Univ. of Ga. Press, 1951), pp. 111–12; Robert Long's pension statement, Dr., VV, XVI, 146.

middle of October these men were on virtually continuous duty, performing well in their accustomed role, not failing in the unaccustomed role of auxiliary to the regulars. The militia was not a degenerate institution nor was it likely to submit for long to the implementation of the British southern strategy after occupation.

Epilogue

One might expect from the foregoing that the Ninety-Six brigade would be the first to open partisan resistance against British occupation. Such was not the case. Though a few minor-level figures like James McCall and Samuel Hammond refused to surrender, the backcountry militia as a body only slowly became committed to full-scale resistance. One reason was undoubtedly fatigue; a large number of these men were in the field from January 1780 until the fall of Charleston in May. Then most capitulated. The conduct of officers probably influenced the troops. Their brigade commander, Williamson, and their most prestigious regimental commander, Pickens, accepted British protection. Williamson offered to continue the fight if his men desired, but they declined.[49] Ironically, Williamson's suspected defection to the enemy after capitulation elevated Pickens to leadership of the backcountry patriot militia. His decision to open partisan resistance would be decisive, but that did not come until October or November.

Another deterrent was the division of sentiment in the backcountry. With so many potential Tories resistance in the face of a British army of occupation seemed hopeless at first. Attempting to implement the southern strategy, Major Patrick Ferguson, British Inspector of Militia, gave priority to organization of the backcountry loyalists. He soon enrolled four thousand men in the militia; fifteen hundred he trained to campaign with the British army. When he took the best of these men into North Carolina and then lost them at King's Mountain in October, the situation in the backcountry quickly changed.[50]

49. Ferguson, "Andrew Pickens," pp. 92–100; Samuel Hammond's narrative, Joseph Johnson, *Traditions and Reminiscences Chiefly of the American Revolution in the South* . . . (Charleston: Walker & Jones, 1851), pp. 149–51; McCrady, *South Carolina 1775–1780*, pp. 529–32.

50. Smith, *Loyalists and Redcoats*, pp. 136–40; Excerpt, Cornwallis to Ger-

Apparently John Rutledge was in close touch with Pickens, for he was able to discount rumors that the Colonel was prepared to open resistance in September.[51] In October Pickens was at Gilbert's Town, North Carolina, where the overmountain men assembled before the attack on Ferguson. To William Campbell, leader of these partisans, Pickens recommended that no small patriot force be sent into the South Carolina backcountry, as it would serve "no other purpose than to draw upon our Friends in this Quarter the Resentment of our Enemies."[52] After King's Mountain, John Cruger, Tory commandant at Fort Ninety-Six, wrote Cornwallis that "the loyal subjects were so wearied by the long continuance of the campaign . . . that the whole district had determined to submit as soon as the Rebels should enter it."[53]

The arrival of Daniel Morgan's Continentals on the Pacolet River in December was crucial. Pickens immediately joined them with seventy men from his regiment. At Cowpens on January 17, 1781, he commanded six hundred militiamen, most of whom knew him only by reputation. Pickens was appointed brigadier general as a result of that battle; he then moved with Morgan into North Carolina and organized the militia resistance behind Cornwallis. Militia from South Carolina and Georgia followed him through that campaign in which Pickens screened General Greene's buildup and suppressed loyalist militia that attempted to assist Cornwallis. Returning to South Carolina in March, Andrew Pickens activated the old Ninety-Six brigade. It resumed its role of squelching the loyalist militia units. Another function the revolutionary militia undertook was the isolation of Tory garrisons from the small force of British regulars that might have assisted them. When Greene returned to South Carolina in April, the enemy was caught on the horns of a dilemma. If he concen-

main, Aug. 20, 1780, McCrady, *South Carolina 1775–1780*, pp. 607–8; Robert D. Bass, "The Last Campaign of Major Patrick Ferguson," *Proceedings of the South Carolina Historical Association 1968* (Columbia: S.C. Historical Association, 1968), pp. 16–28.

51. Rutledge to South Carolina delegates in Congress, Sept. 20, 1780, Joseph W. Barnwell (ed.), "Letters of John Rutledge," *South Carolina Historical and Genealogical Magazine*, XVII (1916), 136.

52. William Campbell to William Preston, Dec. 12, 1780, "The Preston Papers, Relating to Western Virginia," *Virginia Magazine of History and Biography*, XXVII (1919), 314–15.

53. Rawdon to Clinton, Oct. 29, 1780, *Correspondence of Charles, First Marquis of Cornwallis*, ed. Charles Ross (3 vols.; London: J. Murray, 1859), I, 63.

trated to face Greene and the Continentals, he would lose his posts to Marion, Sumter, and Pickens. If he dispersed to hold the posts against the partisan-militia, he could not prevent Greene's army from marching at will over the state and taking the garrisons one by one.[54]

The backcountry militia continued to have a complicated function until the end of hostilities. Not only did they coordinate actions with Greene's regulars and continue to wage war on the Tories, but they did so while continually looking over their shoulders at the Indian frontier. Significantly, the Ninety-Six brigade waged three final sorties against the Cherokee and closed the war of the Revolution in police actions against such diehard Tory-bandits as "Bloody Bill" Cunningham.

This brief résumé of the better known aspects of the war in the South should not divert our attention from the significant functions of the militia. These were control of the dissidents and suppression of the Indians, functions successfully carried out long before the British opened their southern strategy. Preconditions decided the outcome of the southern campaign; the reduction of Britain's potential allies by the partisan-militia made the strategy futile from its inception. When His Majesty's government allowed the loyalists to rise and fall and the patriot militia to organize and ride high in the saddle for three years, the chance for a victory in the South disappeared. The British lost their southern campaign before it began, and they lost it as early as the autumn of 1776.

54. Ferguson, "Andrew Pickens," pp. 112–225.

The British Withdrawal from the South, 1781–85

Eldon Jones   *Ford Foundation*

In the early afternoon of October 19, 1781, the British army under the command of Lord Charles Cornwallis marched out from its fortified positions surrounding the village of Yorktown, Virginia. With their colors furled and covered, eight thousand troops filed between long lines of American and French soldiers to lay down their arms. At the appropriate moment General Charles O'Hara presented his sword on behalf of Cornwallis, and Major General Benjamin Lincoln, acting for General George Washington, commander in chief of the Franco-American army, accepted O'Hara's offering. The defeated troops then returned to their lines to await marching orders to prison camps in Virginia, Maryland, and Pennsylvania. The last major campaign of the American War of Independence had ended.

The surrender of the army at Yorktown was the conclusion of a faltering British military effort in America. For six years England's soldiers had fought to crush the rebellion. Led by mediocre generals, hampered by poor communications across the Atlantic and within America, and confronted by an unfavorable terrain for European-style operations and an enemy that refused to be defeated, they had failed to restore the king's authority in the thirteen colonies. A few months after the news of Yorktown arrived in London, Parliament forced King George III and the cabinet to abandon offensive operations in America. Then, on March 27, 1782, a new government, led by the Marquis of Rockingham, came to power. Rockingham wanted peace, and, hoping that negotiations with the Americans could be opened quickly, he ordered the colonies evacuated. Sir Guy Carleton, who had been appointed to replace Sir Henry Clinton as commander in chief in America only a month before Rockingham took office, received the assignment. Carleton was known to favor the continuation of the war, but Rockingham chose to disregard this fact and ordered the general to depart for New York immediately and to carry out the withdrawal as rapidly as possible.

Carleton received his final orders shortly before he embarked at Portsmouth on April 8. The first object of his attention, according to the instructions, was to be the withdrawal to Halifax of all troops, artillery, provisions, stores, and other public property from New York, Charleston, and Savannah. The manner and time of the evacuations were left to his discretion, and when he arrived at New York he was to decide whether St. Augustine should be abandoned. If he were attacked in force or unable to remove these garrisions without severe loss, he was to capitulate rather than fight. All loyalists who wished to leave the colonies were to receive assistance, and any land grants which Carleton made for the people who desired to settle in other parts of British North America would be confirmed by the king. Finally, the general was directed to keep a close watch over British possessions in the West Indies and to dispatch to them whatever troops were necessary for their protection.[1]

Carleton reached New York on May 5, 1782. General Clinton, Admiral Robert Digby, commander of British ships in American waters, and Major General James Robertson, the royal governor of New York, were present to greet him on his arrival and to escort him to his headquarters. During the next ten days Carleton met repeatedly with these men and other officials, trying to gain an understanding of the British position at New York and in the South. The reports he received were not encouraging. The garrison at New York consisted of only eighteen thousand British, German, and provincial soldiers—an insufficient number to properly man the long and broken lines around the city; Digby had only three ships of the line and a few smaller vessels to protect the harbor; most of the British warships were in the West Indies and could offer no assistance should New York be attacked by sea; and many of the fortifications of the city were weak or incomplete. Carleton knew that if Britain's enemies launched a

1. Lord Shelburne to Carleton, Apr. 4, 1782, Colonial Office 5/106 (transcripts), Library of Congress, Washington, D.C.

strong combined sea and land attack on New York, he could do nothing but surrender, and he firmly believed that any indication of his plan to evacuate the city would precipitate such an assault.[2]

The situation in the southern colonies was equally depressing. The British position there had deteriorated badly during the past year. Clinton was not certain that troops could be maintained in them much longer, and he carefully described to Carleton what had happened in the South after the surrender of Cornwallis.

In October 1781 Clinton had sailed from New York with seven thousand troops and a large naval force under the command of Admiral Sir Thomas Graves to attempt a relief of the beleaguered British army at Yorktown. Upon his arrival at the mouth of the Chesapeake Bay, he received word that Cornwallis had already surrendered, and he ordered the expedition to return to New York. Before going back, however, he directed Lieutenant General Alexander Leslie to proceed to Charleston and to assume command of the troops in North Carolina, South Carolina, Georgia, and East Florida. Clinton intended to make certain that the capitulation of Cornwallis would not lead to a total loss of British control over the South. Accordingly, he instructed Leslie to retain as many interior posts as possible and, above all, to hold Charleston.[3]

Clinton had received no reports from Charleston since June 1781; when he issued these orders to Leslie he was not aware that the territory under British control in the far South had been severely reduced after Cornwallis had advanced from North Carolina into Virginia. All interior posts in South Carolina and Georgia had been abandoned or lost to the Americans. British forces in the South held only Wilmington, Charleston, Savannah, and St. Augustine, and the gar-

2. *New York Royal Gazette*, May 8, 1782; Carleton to Shelburne, May 14, 1782, Colonial Office 5/106 (transcripts), Library of Congress, Washington, D.C.

3. Clinton to Leslie, Oct. 28, 1781, General Sir Guy Carleton Papers (photostats), Colonial Williamsburg Research Center, Williamsburg, Va., XXXIII, 3850. These papers, which are composed of official records of the successive British commanders in chief in the American War of Independence, have had several titles. They have been named the British Army Headquarters Papers, 1775–83. The Royal Historical Manuscripts Commission published a calendar of them entitled *Report on American Manuscripts in the Royal Institution of Great Britain* (4 vols.; London: 1904–9). In addition, they have been called the Carleton or Dorchester Papers because most of the documents in the collection were written during the period 1782–83 when Carleton (later Lord Dorchester) was commander in chief and because they remained in Sir Guy's possession until 1798. Hereafter cited as Carleton Papers.

risons for these towns were too small to defend them effectively.

On November 8 General Leslie arrived in Charleston. The new commander soon realized that the British hold on the southern colonies was weak and moved quickly to try to strengthen it. He ordered Wilmington abandoned and brought the troops from there to Charleston. A detachment of two hundred men was sent to Savannah to assist in the defense of that town. In addition, Leslie wrote to Clinton, describing the situation he faced and warning that if reinforcements did not arrive soon, neither Charleston nor Savannah could be held.

Clinton considered Leslie's assertion that British power in the South was on the brink of collapse to be incredible.[4] The latest returns at New York had shown that there were 4,576 troops fit for duty in Charleston, 691 in Savannah, and 476 in St. Augustine—sufficient forces, in Clinton's opinion, to defend all three posts. Nevertheless, Clinton submitted the information he had received to a board of general officers for an opinion. The officers believed that no troops could be spared from the garrison at New York for the defense of Charleston or Savannah unless information came that a serious attack was being made against either place. They agreed, however, that Leslie should have the authority to evacuate Savannah if that town should be in danger of falling to the Americans. Clinton therefore denied Leslie's request for reinforcements, but he did send from New York to Charleston all officers and soldiers—537 men—who belonged to units in the southern colonies. Furthermore, he directed Leslie to decide whether Savannah needed to be evacuated, but not to order a withdrawal without the consent of the royal governor and council of Georgia.

The information that Clinton received from Savannah was as discouraging as that from Charleston. Sir James Wright, the royal governor of Georgia, and Brigadier General Alured Clarke, the British commander in the colony, believed that the Americans meant to attack Savannah and that the town could not be defended unless troops were sent immediately from New York. Clinton, however, thought that the Americans would not assault Savannah without the aid of a French fleet. He refused Wright's and Clarke's requests for reinforcements; and despite the information received from Leslie, he told

4. Leslie to Clinton, Nov. 30, 1781; Clinton to Leslie, Dec. 20, 1781, Carleton Papers, XXXIII, 3912; XXXIV, 3970.

the two men that any troops needed for the defense of Savannah could be sent from Charleston.[5]

During the next five months, before Sir Guy Carleton arrived at New York, Clinton steadfastly refused to change his mind and send additional forces to the South. In fact, when the British commander in chief learned in February 1782 of an impending attack on Jamaica by French and Spanish forces in the West Indies, he ordered two thousand men sent from Charleston to assist in the defense of that valuable island. In response to Clinton's decision, Leslie ordered his chief engineer, James Moncrief, to make a survey of the city's defenses. Moncrief reported that a minimum of forty-five hundred men were needed to hold Charleston. The garrison in the town at that time consisted of only five thousand men. If Moncrief were correct, few soldiers could be spared for an expedition to Jamaica. Leslie refused at first to comply with the order and determined that if two thousand men were removed, Savannah would have to be evacuated and that specific instructions from Clinton would be required for such an action. The British commander in Charleston intended to make certain that any blame for the loss of a southern post would fall upon Clinton. Eventually, Leslie decided to compromise and ordered two regiments—a force of about thirteen hundred men—to embark for Jamaica. Nevertheless he still considered the evacuation of Savannah to be necessary and informed Clinton that should Charleston or Savannah be abandoned, transports would have to be dispatched from New York because there were no ships available at either southern port.[6]

Despite the warnings of Leslie, the departure of the thirteen hundred troops from Charleston early in May 1782 did not radically affect military operations in the South. Charleston and Savannah remained under British control. The American armies, led by General Nathanael Greene at Charleston and by his subordinate, General Anthony Wayne, at Savannah, still did not have sufficient forces to assault the two towns. They continued to stop the British soldiers from foraging in the countryside and attempted to prevent supplies

5. Clinton to Wright, Jan. 6, 1782, Clinton to Clarke, Jan. 6, 1782, Carleton Papers, XXXV, 4041, 4042.

6. Minutes of the Council of War, Apr. 10, 1782; Leslie to Clinton, Apr. 17, 1782; State of the Detachment under O'Hara, June 15, 1782, Carleton Papers, XXXVIII, 4377, 4415; XC, 9985.

and loyalist refugees from reaching the enemy's lines. Leslie reduced his perimeter of defense to compensate for the loss of the troops going to Jamaica. The British general remained hopeful that reinforcements would arrive and enable him to hold Charleston and Savannah. Once more, however, he hoped in vain, for within a month after the detachment for Jamaica had left, Leslie learned that Carleton had assumed command in New York and that the southern colonies were to be abandoned.

It will be recalled that the orders Carleton received before departing from Portsmouth gave him authority to determine when to evacuate each of the British posts in America. These orders had been drafted by Lord Shelburne, secretary of state for home affairs in the government of the Marquis of Rockingham. Shelburne was the only member of the cabinet who did not wish to grant the colonies their freedom, and he insisted that it was his responsibility to negotiate with the Americans so long as their independence was not recognized. In the first few days of the Rockingham ministry, Shelburne discussed with Carleton the problems of securing an agreement with the colonies. Then, acting without the approval of the cabinet, he promised Carleton powers to treat for peace with the Americans. Carleton, therefore, left England believing that he was to have a direct role in the negotiations. But Shelburne failed to keep his promise. Carleton never received peacemaking powers, and he later became so angry that he asked to be relieved of command. Nevertheless Shelburne's promise had an important effect on Carleton's activities at New York and on the British withdrawal from the South.[7]

On May 7, 1782, only two days after arriving at New York, Carleton ordered a count of all transports and victuallers in America. He intended to carry out Shelburne's instructions for the evacuation of British forces as rapidly as possible. The results of the count were disappointing. There were thirty-one transports and victuallers and one hospital ship at New York; seven transports were in Charleston to take troops to Jamaica; and five additional vessels were employed on various duties in the South.

7. *Report on Manuscripts in Various Collections, Royal Historical Manuscripts Commission* (8 vols.; London, 1904–14), VI, 284; Diary of William Smith, Sept. 5, 1782, New York City Public Library, New York, N.Y.; Carleton to Shelburne, May 12, 1782, Colonial Office 5/106 (transcripts), Library of Congress, Washington, D.C.; Paul H. Smith, "Sir Guy Carleton, Peace Negotiations, and the Evacuation of New York," *Canadian Historical Review*, L (1969): 245–64.

Carleton realized that there were not enough ships available to re-move all of the British garrisons in 1782. He then had to determine which forces to evacuate first: those in New York or those in the South. Because he believed that he soon would be discussing peace terms with the Americans, he was reluctant to order a withdrawal from New York. He therefore resolved to abandon the southern posts before New York in order to improve his bargaining position, should peace negotiations begin there.[8]

The British withdrawal from the southern colonies was a complex operation that was protracted because of insufficient shipping and poor planning. In the first seven years of the American war, the Eng-lish merchant fleet suffered severe losses; nearly two thousand of its transports and victuallers were destroyed or captured. By 1782 there were not enough vessels to carry the recruits and provisions needed by the forces in America. The lack of ships, however, was not the only problem that affected these operations. The British government under the leadership of Lord North failed repeatedly during the war to develop policies for securing vessels for service in the colonies. The cabinet issued instructions for the movement of troops and sup-plies, but it did little to ensure that ships were made available. Be-tween 1775 and 1781 the activities of the British armies in America were consistently hampered by delays in arrivals of reinforcements and provisions and of transports for use in amphibious operations. The inability of the North ministry to perceive that the war could not be effectively waged without adequate shipping was the real cause of these delays. In March 1782 the Rockingham government likewise paid no attention to this matter. Although Rockingham desired the colonies abandoned as quickly as possible, neither he nor any member of his cabinet made any plans for the evacuation.[9] In fact, the only official to give the problem serious consideration was Sir Charles Mid-dleton, comptroller of the navy. Middleton, in a plan which he drew up before Carleton left London for New York, claimed that eighty-five thousand tons of shipping were needed to evacuate New York and Charleston—almost three times the amount that was readily avail-able in England and America. To overcome the shortages of trans-

8. Carleton to Shelburne, May 14, 1782, Colonial Office 5/106 (transcripts), Library of Congress, Washington, D.C.
9. David Syrett, *Shipping and the American War, 1775–1783: A Study of the British Transport Organization* (London: The Athlone Press, 1970), pp. 231–44.

ports and victuallers, he suggested that New York be evacuated first with about fifty thousand tons of shipping to be gathered in the American colonies, Quebec, Nova Scotia, St. Lucia, and Jamaica. The withdrawal from New York, Middleton estimated, could be completed by September. The ships retained in America, combined with those which were to leave England in April or May for Canada and the West Indies, could evacuate Charleston a short time later.[10] Rockingham and his cabinet ignored Middleton's plan. Furthermore, the government failed in the spring and summer of 1782 to order to America from any point ships that could be used in the removal of British forces. Carleton, Leslie, and Admiral Digby were required to use whatever vessels were already in America and the West Indies. These three men worked skillfully and patiently to make certain that every available ship was employed in the withdrawal, and they succeeded within seven months in evacuating Charleston and Savannah.

Middleton's plan to remove British troops from America probably could have been carried out successfully had the government approved it and provided Carleton with proper instructions before he left England. After he reached New York, however, the cabinet could not have put the plan into effect because Sir Guy quickly ordered the evacuation of the southern posts—just the opposite of what Middleton suggested. On May 23, 1782, Carleton wrote to Leslie, instructing him to abandon Savannah and St. Augustine. The troops and public stores were to be sent to New York; all loyalists who wished to depart were to be given transportation; plundering and the destruction of buildings and fortifications were forbidden; and after the withdrawals from those two towns were completed, Charleston was to be evacuated. Carleton apparently did not believe that many citizens would choose to leave the southern colonies, for he gave no instructions to Leslie indicating where the Loyalists were to be sent. He did order, however, that none of them were to be permitted to sail to New York.[11]

When Leslie received Carleton's orders, he immediately sent instructions for the evacuation of Savannah and St. Augustine to Sir James Wright and Patrick Tonyn, the royal governor of East Florida.

10. Charles Middleton, Lord Barham, *Letters and Papers of Charles Lord Barham, Admiral of the Red Squadron, 1758–1813*, ed. Sir John Knox Laughton, Publications of the Navy Records Society (Vols. XXXII, XXXIII, XXXIX; London, 1906–11), XXXIII, 47–50.
11. Carleton to Leslie, May 23, 1782, Carleton Papers, XLI, 4636.

Although British influence in Georgia had not extended beyond the fortifications at Savannah during the previous six months, Governor Wright was shocked by Carleton's instructions. He believed that Carleton did not understand the situation in the colony and told him that five hundred reinforcements could again secure Georgia for Great Britain.[12] Governor Tonyn was even more bitter than Wright about the directions of Carleton, and in conjunction with the Houses of Assembly of East Florida, he vehemently protested to Leslie and Carleton the abandonment of the colony.

Tonyn's fears were soon quieted. On May 27, only four days after the first orders to Leslie had been sent, Carleton conferred with Captain Keith Elphinstone, a naval officer who believed that there was not enough shipping available at that time to evacuate both St. Augustine and Savannah. Carleton agreed with Elphinstone and decided that Savannah should be abandoned before St. Augustine. Moreover, thinking that peace negotiations might soon begin at New York and that the large garrison from Charleston would strengthen his position more than would the few troops at St. Augustine, he ordered Leslie not to evacuate East Florida before South Carolina.[13] Carleton's new instructions, along with thirty-four transports and victuallers to be used in the withdrawal from Savannah, arrived at Charleston on June 20. Leslie notified Tonyn that Carleton had decided against evacuating East Florida, but directed him to encourage the inhabitants to dispose of their property in case that colony was later to be abandoned. Contrariwise, he instructed Wright to take advantage of East Florida as a refuge for the loyalists because no one would be allowed to land at Charleston; and he ordered the fleet commander, Captain William Swiney, to assist in the removal of all persons who desired to go to St. Augustine.[14]

The ships from Charleston reached Tybee Island at the mouth of the Savannah River early in July. Governor Wright and General Clarke had prepared the citizens and troops in Savannah for departure and had had fortifications constructed on Tybee for the protec-

12. Wright to Carleton, July 6, 1782, Carleton Papers, XLIV, 5025; Patrick J. Furlong, "Civilian-Military Conflict and the Restoration of the Royal Province of Georgia, 1778–1782," *Journal of Southern History*, XXXVIII (1972): 440–42.
13. Carleton to Leslie, May 27, 1782, Carleton Papers, XLI, 4667.
14. Leslie to Wright, June 20, 1782, and to Swiney, June 20, 1782, General Alexander Leslie Letter Books, 1781–82, Emmet Collection, New York City Public Library, New York, N.Y. Hereafter cited as Leslie Letter Books, 1781–82.

tion of the loyalists and soldiers who were to await embarkation there. The troops withdrew from the town on July 11 and joined approximately thirty-one hundred loyalists and thirty-five hundred Negroes who were camped on the island.[15] The evacuation lasted three weeks and was unfortunately complicated by a lack of transports to carry the loyalists to St. Augustine. Lieutenant Governor John Graham attempted to overcome the deficit in ships by hiring five private vessels at Savannah. These ships, however, made little difference, for most of the loyalists had to proceed to East Florida overland or in small boats and canoes along the inland waterways of the Georgia coast. The situation was further aggravated by an appeal to Leslie from Wright and several prominent loyalists in Savannah for shipping to convey their Negroes to Jamaica. Leslie approved the request and directed that transports to fifty loyalists and two thousand Negroes were to be made available for these people.[16] Captain Swiney obeyed the order, and on July 20 six transports with ten white families and 1,568 Negroes on board sailed for Jamaica. Two days later seven ships left for St. Augustine with 580 loyalists and 748 Negroes. Finally, on July 24, one ship filled with refugees—primarily royal officials bound for England—and twenty-three transports and victuallers with 1,996 British, German, and provincial troops and large quantities of public stores departed for New York.[17] More than five thousand whites and Negroes remained behind, and these unfortunate people had to make their own way to St. Augustine as best they could.

General Wayne occupied Savannah immediately after the British troops withdrew. He chose, however, not to interfere with the embarkation at Tybee. Clarke had scrupulously followed Carleton's orders, leaving intact the fortifications and buildings of Savannah, and Wayne was pleased by the orderly withdrawal of the British forces. Before the town was evacuated, Wayne had promised protection to all loyalists who wished to stay in Savannah and had granted a request from British merchants and traders to remain behind for a period of six months to dispose of their goods. Furthermore, he had agreed to permit anyone who had supported the enemy to serve in

15. Kenneth Coleman, *The American Revolution in Georgia* (Athens: Univ. of Ga. Press, 1958), p. 145.

16. Leslie to Swiney, July 6, 1782, Leslie Letter Books, 1781–82.

17. List of Ships from Savannah, Aug. 10, 1782, Colonial Office 5/106 (transcripts), Library of Congress, Washington, D.C.

the Georgia Continentals for two years or for the duration of the war and thereby regain full American citizenship.[18] The decisions of the American commander were merciful and wise. He retained in Georgia not only a large quantity of supplies but also many useful citizens.

The American occupation of Savannah did not last long. After a brief period of rest Wayne led his army back to Charleston where General Nathanael Greene anxiously awaited him. Greene feared that the British troops from Georgia would land at Charleston and that Leslie would take the offensive. To his great relief, most of the ships from Tybee sailed on to New York before Wayne arrived.

The fleet from Georgia reached Charleston on July 25. Leslie, disobeying Carleton's instructions, ordered 846 provincial troops and a large quantity of food brought ashore and retained the transports and victuallers which had brought the soldiers and provisions. Disease and the expedition to Jamaica had severely reduced the strength of the army at Charleston. Leslie considered reducing further his already restricted perimeter of defense in order to give the city better protection, but after he had taken part of the troops from Savannah, he hoped that this action would be unnecessary.

The fifteen remaining ships from Tybee reached New York in early August. This fleet, combined with twenty-eight victuallers which had arrived a few weeks before from England, gave Carleton the largest number of vessels at New York since he had assumed command.[19] Nevertheless there were still not enough ships available for a rapid evacuation of Charleston. Half of the vessels which had been sent to Savannah were in Jamaica or St. Augustine. In addition, the transports used to carry the troops from Charleston to Jamaica in May had still not returned to New York.

Carleton was now seriously concerned about the evacuation plans for America. He believed that the withdrawal from Georgia had taken too long and that the removal of the loyalists and their property was a burdensome task; he was uncertain whether the ships in East Florida and the West Indies could be collected in time to evacuate Charleston in 1782; and he doubted that he would be able to abandon

18. Wayne to Greene, July 12, 1782, Nathanael Greene Correspondence, Library of Congress, Washington, D.C.

19. Carl Leopold Baurmeister, *Revolution in America*, trans. Bernhard A. Uhlendorf (New Brunswick, N.J.: Rutgers Univ. Press, 1957), p. 516.

New York in the following year. Furthermore, he knew that he had employed all of the ships that he could obtain in the evacuation of Savannah and estimated that three times the amount of their tonnage would be necessary for the withdrawal from Charleston.[20]

Fortunately for Carleton, ships sufficient to carry out the evacuation of Charleston in 1782 were available before the end of September. Twenty transports and victuallers en route to the West Indies were ordered by Lord Shelburne to proceed to South Carolina after they had discharged their cargoes.[21] Carleton likewise directed several transports which had brought recruits to Halifax from England to sail immediately to Charleston. The ships used to carry troops to Jamaica returned to New York. Governor Tonyn and General Archibald Campbell, the British commander in Jamaica, sent to Leslie all vessels that had gone to St. Augustine and Jamaica from Savannah. Additionally, Admiral Digby finally received the warships that he needed to convoy the transports and victuallers at New York to South Carolina.

Meanwhile Leslie made preparations for the withdrawal from Charleston. The few ships that were anchored in the harbor he loaded with public stores. On August 7 he announced that Charleston was to be evacuated and directed that all persons who wished to leave the city were to register with the army, specifying their desired destinations and delivering an account of the property they wished to take. Within a week 4,230 loyalists and 7,163 Negroes were on the departure lists.[22] Leslie estimated that twenty-five thousand tons of shipping were necessary to remove these people and their belongings, but feared that this amount would never be available to him. He therefore ordered into the public service all private vessels which could be used in the evacuation. In addition, to reduce the demand for transports, he authorized that the merchants of the city who wished to remain behind to dispose of their goods and collect American debts could negotiate terms for staying with General Greene or John Mathews, the governor of South Carolina.[23]

By early August food supplies in Charleston had dwindled to such

20. Carleton to Shelburne, Aug. 15, 1782, Colonial Office 5/106 (transcripts), Library of Congress, Washington, D.C.

21. Shelburne to Carleton, June 5, 1782, Carleton Papers, XLII, 4741.

22. A Return of Inhabitants at Charleston, Intending to Leave, Aug. 13, 1782, Carleton Papers, XCVII, 10316.

23. Leslie to Carleton, Aug. 10, 1782, Carleton Papers, XLVI, 5263.

a low level that Leslie was forced to dispatch a large party of soldiers along the Santee River to raid American farms and plantations for provisions to feed his garrison and the city's inhabitants. He regretted the necessity of sending an expedition into the countryside to seize food, and after the troops had returned he asked Greene and Mathews for a cessation of hostilities and permission to buy provisions from the people of South Carolina. Leslie hoped that the American leaders, knowing that he intended to evacuate Charleston, would respond favorably to his requests. Greene, however, refused to end the fighting without authorization from Congress. Mathews was likewise unreceptive to Leslie's proposal and denied the British the privilege of purchasing provisions from American citizens.[24] Consequently, hostilities did not cease until the final day of the evacuation, and Leslie, against his wish, continued to send troops to forage in the interior of South Carolina.

The British commander also attempted in August to obtain Greene's approval for an exchange of prisoners. He told Greene that unless an exchange was agreed upon immediately, he intended to transfer all American soldiers in his custody to New York. Greene had hitherto been unwilling to trade prisoners because he wanted the British to pay his commissary accounts and because he feared the enemy would gain a decided advantage if he allowed an exchange of American militia for British regulars. For these two reasons he still opposed entering into a cartel with Leslie. Nevertheless, realizing that an exchange had to take place before Charleston was evacuated, Greene ordered all British prisoners sent from North Carolina to his camp.[25] Leslie insisted that his bills were as large as Greene's and refused to consent to negotiations concerning commissary accounts. He proposed only to exchange Continentals first and then militia for British troops. Greene, however, would discuss the matter no further until the prisoners arrived from North Carolina; and Leslie, who did not have enough ships to carry out his threat of sending American captives to New York, was forced to wait until October before an exchange was finally concluded.

While Leslie tried in vain to reach some kind of accord with

24. Mathews to Greene, Aug. 14, 1782; Greene to Leslie, Aug. 15, 1782, Carleton Papers, XLVI, 5296, 5312.

25. Greene to Leslie, Aug. 9, 1782, Nathanael Greene Papers, William L. Clements Library, Univ. of Michigan.

Greene and Mathews, Carleton and Digby prepared the ships for the voyage to Charleston. Seventeen victuallers and twenty-six transports were provisioned and refitted. The situation at New York became tense, however, after Carleton received intelligence indicating that a French fleet of thirteen ships of the line had left the West Indies and was sailing up the American coast. Admiral Digby had at that time only nine warships to defend the harbor, and Carleton was worried about the safety of the city and of the British ships which were then sailing toward it. Furthermore, he was concerned that the enemy's presence might cause more delay in the evacuation of Charleston. To his great relief, the French threat soon ended. The enemy bypassed New York and sailed to Boston, where some of their vessels underwent extensive repairs. With the French out of the way, more British warships, two small fleets of victuallers, and some transports from Antigua made their way safely to New York.[26] The two British commanders now hastened to complete the preparations for the ships going to Charleston. On September 20 the first contingent of vessels—twenty-seven transports and victuallers—finally sailed from New York.

The ships reached Charleston ten days later. Leslie arranged immediately to evacuate part of the troops and loyalists to East Florida and Nova Scotia. He withdrew his men from the most advanced posts and told Governor Tonyn to expect a fleet from Charleston within a few days. Two weeks passed, however, before any ships were ready to sail. Finally, on October 14, a large number of transports departed for East Florida with 1,383 loyalists, 1,681 Negroes, and 1,147 provincial troops. Several victuallers, loaded with six months' provisions for a thousand refugees and a thousand Negroes from Georgia and a large supply of ammunition, small arms, and light artillery for the garrison at St. Augustine, accompanied the transports. A few days later, Leslie dispatched the last nine ships to Halifax with 166 soldiers, 534 loyalists, and all of the heavy ordnance at Charleston.[27]

On October 8 Carleton sent Leslie the thirty-one transports and victuallers remaining at New York. Admiral Digby provided eight

26. Digby to Shelburne, Sept. 13, 1782, Colonial Office 5/186 (transcripts), Library of Congress, Washington, D.C.

27. Embarkation Returns, Oct. 9, 10, 20, 1782, Nov. 13, 1782, Carleton Papers, LI, 5823, 5836; LII, 5938; LIV, 6159.

warships to escort them to Charleston and to convoy the smaller fleets that were to leave from there. These ships reached Charleston on October 21. They were the last vessels to arrive, and they made possible the evacuation of the city before the end of the year.

The most vexing problem confronting Leslie before the final withdrawal was the disposal of Negroes upon whom neither the British troops nor the loyalists in Charleston had valid claims. Many of the Negroes had sought protection within the lines of the city and had been assigned to various departments of the army to work on fortifications, to carry supplies, and to perform other menial tasks. The great majority of these were considered as slaves without masters, under the control of the army. A sizable number of Negroes had also been brought into the town by British officers who had taken abandoned slaves to use as personal servants. The remaining Negroes, whose status was in question, were in the hands of the loyalists. During the occupation of South Carolina, the British had carried out an extensive program of sequestering American lands and slaves to compensate loyalists who had suffered because of their devotion to the king. Consequently, by 1782 many Tories in Charleston had acquired Negroes formerly owned by fellow South Carolinians. The difficult issue, then, that Leslie had to resolve before the evacuation was which of these Negroes, if any, should be returned to their owners and which should be allowed to depart with the army and the loyalists.

On February 26, 1782, the South Carolina Assembly retaliated against the British by passing laws for the confiscation and taxation of loyalist estates. The property of over two hundred Tories was declared subject to confiscation; the estates of forty-seven more were amerced at a rate of 12 percent of their value; and most of the men affected by the acts were banished from the state under penalty of death if they returned. The acts, however, did declare that American debts to British merchants and loyalist claims to estates by marriage settlements were valid.[28]

These measures caused great distress to the loyalists in Charleston. Leslie, upon learning of the inhabitants' alarm at the prospect of losing their property, sent a small party of troops across the Cooper River to collect "the slaves who belong to those in arms against the

28. Ella Pettit Levett, "Loyalism in Charleston, 1761–1784," *Proceedings of the South Carolina Historical Association*, VI (1936): 12–16.

British government" and told Mathews that he would take similar actions in the future unless the new laws were rescinded.[29] Mathews disregarded Leslie's warning and declared that there was no difference between British and American measures of confiscation, except that the American acts were more lenient.[30] Leslie, realizing that he could not prevent the confiscation of the loyalists' property and knowing that there were already too many American slaves in Charleston, decided not to execute his threat to seize more of the enemy's Negroes.

On May 23, in the same letter that contained the instructions for the evacuation of the South, Carleton had directed Leslie to allow no plundering during the withdrawals from Savannah and Charleston. Leslie sent a copy of Carleton's dispatch to Governor Wright in Savannah, but gave no explicit order prohibiting the removal of American slaves. Consequently Wright permitted the evacuation of many American Negroes. Leslie, however, was still not sure how Carleton wanted him to dispose of the slaves at Charleston. He therefore asked Carleton whether the Negroes in the service of the army and those who had been promised their freedom were to be carried away or returned to their owners. Carleton's answers were confusing. Initially, he told Leslie to decide for himself about evacuating slaves employed by the army but ordered that pledges of freedom made to deserving Negroes were to be respected. Later, though, he repeated his former injunction against plundering and directed Leslie not to remove any American property.[31]

In August, after the announcement that Charleston was to be evacuated, Governor Mathews notified Leslie that if American slaves were carried away, he intended to cancel American debts to British merchants and to invalidate loyalist claims to estates by marriage settlements. Leslie was disturbed by Mathews's threat, but he did not know how to prevent the governor from acting. He delayed a reply for over a month and then finally proposed negotiations to settle the problem. Mathews approved the suggestion, and on October 10 commissioners from both sides met to draw up an agreement for the restitution of slaves to the Americans. Leslie pledged that all Negroes, except those who had been given their freedom and those "particu-

---

29. Instructions to Major Frasier, Mar. 27, 1782, Leslie Letter Books, 1781–82.
30. Mathews to Leslie, Apr. 12, 1782, Carleton Papers, XC, 9964.
31. Carleton to Leslie, July 15, 1782, Aug. 15, 1782, Carleton Papers, XL, 5072; XLVI, 5306.

larly obnoxious" to the Americans because they had assisted the British, would be returned, that American inspectors would be permitted to reside in Charleston to assist in recovering the slaves, and that the British government would pay the Americans within six months for every Negro removed from the city. In return Mathews promised not to annul American debts to British merchants or claims to property secured by marriage settlements and to permit loyalists to sue for the recovery of their property in the courts of South Carolina.[32]

The agreement between Leslie and Mathews had no chance of success. There were too many interested parties within Charleston who did not wish to comply with its provisions. The loyalists who had been banished and whose property had been confiscated resented the additional loss of the slaves they had obtained. The army officers regarded their servants as their own property and wanted them included among the Negroes who were to be evacuated. General Leslie believed that the slaves were afraid of being punished by their masters and unwilling to return to the hard labor on American plantations.[33] None of these considerations, however, was responsible for ending the agreement. Instead, a trivial incident led to its collapse. The American inspectors appointed by Mathews had gone aboard several ships bound for St. Augustine and had discovered 136 Negroes belonging to citizens of South Carolina. When they asked that these slaves be released in their custody, Leslie refused to deliver them until three of his soldiers recently taken by an American patrol were returned to British lines. Leslie considered the action by Greene's army an affront to the pacific policies which he was following at that time. Mathews, however, was so enraged by Leslie's refusal that he ordered the inspectors out of the city and declared the agreement to be void.

Before Mathews nullified the pact, Leslie sent a letter to Carleton, describing the difficulties in returning the slaves and asking him to specify the number of Negroes to be removed and the amount to be paid for them. Carleton did not consider himself authorized to order payment for any Negroes and recommended to Leslie that the time period in the agreement be extended from six to twelve months so that the government in London would have adequate time to decide upon

32. Agreement for the Restoration of American Slaves, Oct. 10, 1782, Carleton Papers, LI, 5844.
33. Leslie to Carleton, Oct. 18, 1782, Carleton Papers, LI, 5924.

the matter. He also instructed that no slaves were to be carried away "under pretence of belonging to the Departments" and that the loyalists were to pay for any Negroes that were not their own. Carleton did approve, however, the removal of those slaves who had been promised their freedom or who were offensive to the Americans.[34]

Carleton's final orders arrived in Charleston too late to affect the evacuation. Many Negroes had already departed for East Florida; preparations for the withdrawal were nearly complete; and the pact with the Americans had been canceled. Moreover, a few days after Mathews ended the agreement for returning the slaves, Leslie appointed a board of officers to decide which Negroes could be evacuated in accordance with Carleton's first directions. The board, however, paid little heed to Leslie's instructions and recommended the removal of many Negroes who should have been left in Charleston. Governor Mathews later asserted that the board had found every Negro worth carrying away to be "obnoxious" to the Americans.[35] The exact number of slaves that the board saved for the people of South Carolina is unknown, but, as Mathews indicated, it must have been very small. Most of the Negroes at Charleston departed on ships bound for Jamaica or East Florida.

In February 1783, after Charleston had been evacuated, Mathews sought Carleton's assistance in recovering the slaves. Carleton refused to help him and referred the problem to the cabinet for consideration.[36] Governor Tonyn likewise declined repeated requests from Benjamin Guerard, Mathews's successor, and from several planters in South Carolina to send back the Negroes who had gone to East Florida. Notwithstanding Tonyn's opposition, a few of these slaves were returned during the next two years while East Florida was being evacuated, but most of the citizens of South Carolina who had lost Negroes never recovered them.

The government of South Carolina did not retaliate against the British for the removal of American Negroes. Some merchants in Charleston had obtained permission from Mathews to remain in the city for six months after the British troops had departed so that they could sell their goods and collect American debts. Mathews and Guerard abided by this agreement, and the South Carolina Assembly

34. Carleton to Leslie, Nov. 12, 1782, Carleton Papers, LIV, 6145.
35. Mathews to John Rutledge, Feb. 1, 1783, Carleton Papers, LI, 6850.
36. Carleton to Rutledge, May 31, 1783, Carleton Papers, LXX, 7832.

later extended the period of time to eighteen months. Many of these merchants did not wish to stay in Charleston very long and applied to Carleton soon after the city had been evacuated for ships to remove themselves and their property. In March 1783 Carleton granted their request. The Assembly, however, did carry out its acts for the confiscation and taxation of the loyalists' property, but it soon modified even these measures and removed many of the names from the banishment lists.[37]

In October 1782, while Leslie and Mathews tried to settle the problem of restoring slaves to the citizens of South Carolina, General Greene finally consented to a prisoner exchange. Leslie had asked the American commander again in September for negotiations to conclude an agreement for returning captured soldiers. After the British prisoners arrived from North Carolina, Greene responded favorably to the request. On October 20 British and American commissioners signed a cartel for the exchange of captives. Each side agreed to release unconditionally all noncommissioned officers and privates. Officers were to be exchanged as far as possible according to rank, and any remaining officers were to be paroled.[38] Leslie and Greene complied with these provisions within ten days after the agreement was signed. The British received 1,152 soldiers, excluding officers, from Greene. The number of American prisoners who were returned is unknown. It is evident, however, that Leslie held more officers than Greene, for a large number of American officers were on parole in South Carolina after the British departed from Charleston.

At the end of November the transports and victuallers that had gone to East Florida in October returned to Charleston. Bad weather along the Florida coast had delayed the fleet, and a few vessels had been lost in a storm. Leslie now had enough ships to remove the troops, loyalists, and stores remaining in the city. He ordered that the final preparations for the withdrawal were to proceed as quickly as possible.[39]

Meanwhile General Greene and Governor Mathews realized that the British occupation of Charleston was rapidly coming to an end.

---

37. Levett, "Loyalism in Charleston," pp. 16–17.
38. Agreement to Settle an Exchange of Prisoners of War, Oct. 20, 1782, United States Revolution Collection, Library of Congress, Washington, D.C.
39. Leslie to Carleton, Nov. 18, 1782, Carleton Papers, LIV, 6199.

Greene feared that Leslie would send out a foraging expedition before quitting the town, and he prepared his troops to check such an action. Mathews was more concerned about the safety of Charleston. He believed that if large numbers of people outside the lines returned soon after the evacuation, extensive damage might be done to the city. Accordingly, he instructed Greene that no one was to enter the city without permission, that no goods were to be sold, that no boats in the harbor were to depart, and that all ownerless Negroes and other unclaimed property were to be detained until further orders.[40] Greene transmitted these directions to General Wayne, whom he had chosen to lead the first troops into Charleston, and ordered him to maintain peace in the city until the civil authorities were able to establish a government. In the final days before the evacuation, however, Greene came to believe that these precautions would not be sufficient for ensuring the safety of the city. He was afraid that if Wayne's force entered Charleston while the enemy was leaving, fighting would break out, causing the British soldiers and loyalists to loot and burn the town. He therefore directed Wayne to avoid contact with the British until the city was abandoned and gave him permission to make arrangements with Leslie to allow the enemy's troops to leave unmolested if the British commander promised to prevent the destruction of Charleston.

General Leslie was likewise anxious to make certain that his troops would be able to depart in peace. On December 13 he sent Wayne a plan for the evacuation. When the British troops left their positions at nine o'clock on the following morning, Wayne and his men were to follow the rear guard at a distance of two hundred yards. A complete cessation of hostilities would exist until the British soldiers were on board their transports.[41] Leslie declared that if Wayne refused to approve these arrangements and allowed his men to attack the British forces while they were leaving, the city would be destroyed. Wayne quickly agreed to follow Leslie's plan, and on December 14 the last British troops departed from Charleston without incident.

The transports and victuallers in the harbor did not leave immedi-

40. Mathews to Greene, Nov. 17, 1782, Greene Papers, Clements Library.
41. James Wemyss to Maurice Simmons, Dec. 13, 1782, General Anthony Wayne Papers, The Historical Society of Pennsylvania, Philadelphia, Pa., XVIII, 116.

ately. The naval officers spent four days organizing the ships and waiting on the tides. Finally, on December 18, five fleets left Charleston. Three of these sailed southward. Eight ships with 134 loyalists, 142 Negroes, and a large quantity of provisions departed for St. Augustine; five transports and victuallers, loaded with supplies, a few provincial soldiers, and fifty cavalry horses, went to St. Lucia; and twenty-nine ships with 1,265 British troops, 597 colonists, and 1,550 Negroes left for Jamaica. The fleets bound for England and New York sailed northward together for two days before parting. Twenty ships with 506 army officers and invalids, a large number of inhabitants, and the royal officials from Charleston turned toward the east; and 48 transports and victuallers carrying 4,071 British, German, and provincial troops and large quantities of provisions and stores continued to the north. All told, 126 transports and victuallers—35,289 tons of shipping—were used in the evacuation of Charleston.[42] The British never made an exact count of how many persons, excluding the soldiers, left Charleston. An American estimate of 3,794 whites and 5,237 Negroes, however, is probably close to accurate.[43]

During 1782 East Florida had been the principal refuge for the loyalists and Negroes of South Carolina and Georgia. British immigration returns indicate that at least 5,090 whites and 8,285 Negroes from these two states went to East Florida, swelling its estimated previous population of 4,000 to 17,375.[44] The evacuation of most of these people occurred after the British had abandoned the rest of the American colonies and Carleton had returned to England.

The refugees who fled to East Florida soon realized that the opportunities for starting a new life were limited. The colony was blessed with neither a fertile soil nor a healthy climate; there were no roads to travel or rivers to navigate; except for St. Augustine, no large communities existed in East Florida; the Indians, although friendly at that time, were a threat to the stability of the colony; and until crops could be raised and Carleton could send more provisions

42. List of Ships at Charleston, Jan. 3, 1782, Carleton Papers, XCVI, 10277.

43. Joseph W. Barnwell, "The Evacuation of Charleston by the British in 1782," *South Carolina Historical and Genealogical Magazine*, XI (1910), 26, citing Miscellaneous Papers, 1769–93, Mass. Historical Society, V, 139.

44. Returns of Refugees and Negroes in East Florida, Nov. 13, 1782, Dec. 31, 1782, Apr. 20, 1783, Carleton Papers, LIV, 6159; LVI, 6204; LXVII, 7468. See also Wilbur H. Siebert, *Loyalists in East Florida, 1774 to 1785* (2 vols.; Deland: Fla. State Historical Society, 1929), I, 130–31.

to replenish the insufficient amount of food furnished by Leslie, the new inhabitants were confronted by the grim prospect of starvation. But despite these hardships some loyalists and their slaves did penetrate deep into the interior and begin new homes in the backlands. Many settled along the coast above St. Augustine and near the St. John's and St. Mary's rivers. Had these people remained in East Florida, they probably would have created a self-sustaining, if not prosperous, colony.[45]

As previously stated, in May 1782 Carleton decided not to evacuate East Florida until the troops and loyalists in Savannah and Charleston had been removed. Yet early in 1783 after these objectives had been achieved he still refused to order a withdrawal from the colony. He was preparing for the evacuation of New York, and he was worried because he did not have enough ships even for that service. The orders that Carleton received before he departed from England had given him permission to use his discretion in ordering the abandonment of East Florida. In the end, though, he had no voice in the matter, for the decision to evacuate the colony was made in Paris. On January 20, 1783, the preliminary peace treaty between Spain and Great Britain was signed. England retained control of Gibraltar, but ceded West Florida, East Florida, and Minorca to Spain. Thus British rule in East Florida came to an end. The Spanish delegation in Paris, however, agreed to permit the inhabitants of the colony to remain for eighteen months after the final treaty had been signed so that they could sell their property and remove their families and possessions.

Carleton and Digby received copies of the preliminary treaty between Spain and England early in April. Carleton immediately wrote Brigadier General Archibald McArthur, the military commander at St. Augustine, informing him of the terms of peace and asking him to ascertain where the provincial troops and loyalists in East Florida desired to go.[46] At the same time Admiral Digby promised Governor

---

45. For detailed accounts of the refugees in East Florida, see Charles Loch Mowat, *East Florida as a British Province* (Gainesville: Univ. of Fla. Press, 1964), pp. 135–49; Siebert, *Loyalists in East Florida*, I, 101–59; J. Leitch Wright, Jr., *Florida in the American Revolution* (Gainesville: Univ. Presses of Florida, 1975), pp. 125–43; idem, "Blacks in British East Florida," *Florida Historical Quarterly*, LIV (1976), 439–42; Linda K. Williams, "East Florida as a Loyalist Haven," *Florida Historical Quarterly*, LIV (1976), 473–78.

46. Carleton to McArthur, Apr. 7, 1783, Carleton Papers, LXVI, 7347.

Tonyn all possible assistance in the removal of those persons who wished to leave the colony.

Before the letters of Carleton and Digby reached St. Augustine Tonyn received from London a copy of the preliminary treaty between England and Spain. On April 21 he announced the cession of East Florida to Spain and ordered the people to settle their affairs and to prepare for evacuation. However, Tonyn soon decided not to relinquish control of the colony so quickly. Eight victuallers, loaded with provisions for the soldiers and refugees, had recently arrived at St. Augustine from New York, and Tonyn estimated that there were enough provisions to last the people until October. Because the final treaty was not yet signed, he correctly predicted that the colony was not to be abandoned that summer. Another proclamation was then issued informing the citizens of the arrival of provisions and asking all persons who wished to depart, except those who had established their farms, to register their names and preferred destinations with British authorities. Those people already engaged in farming were to continue raising crops for the colony.[47]

The announcement of England's cession of East Florida to Spain caused confusion and discontent among the loyalists. A small number of citizens reluctantly decided to go back to South Carolina and Georgia and to take their chances on being punished by those states. The remaining loyalists were in an equally difficult position. They preferred to move to another British possession, namely Nova Scotia, Jamaica, or the Bahamas, rather than live under Spanish rule. Choosing a final destination, however, was not easy, for the future in any of these locations was uncertain. Moreover, these people were faced with the unhappy prospect of having to sell their property quickly with no guaranteed means of survival until transports arrived from New York. Some loyalists became so disgruntled because of their situation that they turned to violence. Small bands of malcontents robbed and plundered along the frontier of the colony, and Tonyn, knowing that the troops were soon to be removed, was worried about controlling these lawless citizens after the soldiers had gone.[48]

The provincial troops under McArthur were also uncertain about

47. *East Florida Gazette*, May 17, 1783.

48. Tonyn to Evan Nepean, Oct. 1, 1783, Colonial Office 5/560 (transcripts), Library of Congress, Washington, D.C.

where they wanted to go when the colony was evacuated. Like the civilians, a few decided to return to their families in the United States and face a hostile American reception, but most desired to be removed to another British colony. They did not, however, want to leave St. Augustine until they were certain that land grants had been allocated for them at their destinations. Some refused to choose a destination until they learned what was promised for them at each place.[49]

The Indians in East Florida were an additional problem to British authorities. The Seminoles, Creeks, and Cherokees were allies of the British and frequent visitors at St. Augustine, where the superintendent of Indian affairs, Lieutenant Colonel Thomas Browne, liberally supplied them with rum and presents. When Browne announced that the Spanish were soon to take control of the colony, the Indians refused to believe that the king intended to abandon them. The chiefs of the Creeks and Cherokees declared that if the British left East Florida, the Indians would accompany them. Browne was disturbed by the unfortunate predicament of the Indians, but he realized that none of them should be removed from the colony. Nevertheless, he asked Carleton to furnish transports for them if they insisted on departing.[50]

Carleton could do little to relieve the distressing conditions in East Florida. In the summer of 1783 he was concerned exclusively with the evacuation of New York, and he did not have sufficient transports and provisions to remove and to feed the refugees who wished to leave East Florida. He did, however, take some limited measures to solve the problems of the loyalists and British authorities in East Florida. He ordered Lieutenant John Wilson, the chief engineer at St. Augustine, to survey the Bahamas for the purpose of determining the suitability of the islands for farming. He instructed General McArthur to notify the troops that they could be removed to either the Bahamas or Nova Scotia. Those soldiers who decided to go to Nova Scotia were to receive grants of land, but since Wilson's report was not yet complete, no promises for farms in the Bahamas could be given. He sent a few more provisions to St. Augustine and promised to dispatch excess foodstuffs which would otherwise be left behind when New York was evacuated. To assist Governor Tonyn in curbing the lawless behavior of citizens after the provincial troops were

49. McArthur to Carleton, May 20, 1783, Carleton Papers, LXIX, 7731.
50. Browne to Carleton, June 1, 1783, Carleton Papers, XCII, 10016.

removed, he detached 150 British regulars to St. Augustine. Finally, he directed Colonel Browne to use every conceivable argument to induce the Indians to remain in the colony but agreed to provide the necessary transports if the native Americans were determined to leave.[51]

On September 12, 1783, both transports for removing the troops and victuallers with additional provisions reached St. Augustine. Half of the provincial soldiers chose to be discharged at St. Augustine and to await later transports. A few of the remainder wanted to be sent to the Bahamas, but most of the soldiers decided to go to Nova Scotia.[52] McArthur completed the evacuation of his men within a month after the transports arrived. He had been appointed commander of British forces in the Bahamas by Carleton, and he accompanied the troops who went to New Providence. A few months later, however, he returned to St. Augustine, in accordance with Carleton's instructions, to await the final evacuation. In November the troops which Carleton had promised Tonyn landed at St. Augustine. During the interim between the departure of McArthur's men and the arrival of the British regulars Tonyn had organized two troops of loyalist cavalry to check the banditti on the frontier. After the soldiers from New York had come to his support, he considered the colony to be secure again.

Only a very small number of refugees departed from East Florida in 1783. There were few ships at St. Augustine, and Carleton was unable to provide any vessels for the removal of the people. In June one transport bound for Jamaica and one for New Providence left St. Augustine with loyalists aboard, and on July 9 two ships filled with refugees sailed for England. McArthur used four of the victuallers that had brought provisions from New York to carry loyalists and Negroes to New Providence. However, before sending them on to Nova Scotia, he directed them to return to St. Augustine for one more load. Those persons who had resided in East Florida before the great immigrations of 1782 were allowed to leave first. The refugees from South Carolina and Georgia had to await later transports before they were removed from the colony.

In December 1783 Carleton completed the evacuation of New

51. Carleton to McArthur, June 19, 1783, Aug. 22, 1783, Carleton to Browne, Oct. 4, 1783, Carleton Papers, LXXII, 8084; LXXVIII, 8780; LXXXIII, 9289.
52. McArthur to Carleton, Sept. 15, 1783, Carleton Papers, LXXXI, 9136.

York. He had been unable to provide additional food to East Florida before he departed, and Admiral Digby had dispatched only a few ships to assist Tonyn in the removal of the inhabitants. Tonyn, however, was still determined not to order the abandonment of the colony until he received definite instructions from London. Those instructions finally reached St. Augustine in the spring of 1784, more than six months after the final treaty between Spain and England had been signed. Governor Tonyn then reluctantly directed the withdrawal to proceed as quickly as possible.

The evacuation took far longer to complete than either the Spanish or the British expected. Many of the transports that were used had been employed by Carleton at New York and had to be refitted and sent from Nova Scotia or England.[53] By June 1784, when the Spanish governor arrived at St. Augustine to assume control of the colony, many British citizens had not yet departed. The Spanish graciously allowed Great Britain an additional six months to complete the withdrawal. Yet even this increase in time was not sufficient. The evacuation of East Florida continued until November 1785. About half of the colony's inhabitants chose not to live under Spanish rule. Approximately 1,000 loyalists and 2,200 Negroes went to the Bahamas; 725 settlers with 159 slaves sailed to Nova Scotia; 421 whites and 1,185 Negroes departed for Jamaica or Dominica; and 462 loyalists and 2,561 slaves returned to the United States.[54]

The departure of the loyalists from East Florida in 1785 was the final operation in the British withdrawal from the South. The failure of each British government in the American war to develop policies for the procurement of ships to serve in the colonies was the basic reason for this withdrawal being so delayed. Other factors, such as the large number of loyalists who had to be taken away and the lack of shipping caused by losses incurred by the British merchant fleet, did, of course, also extend the length of time required to complete the evacuation. Nevertheless the removal of troops and loyalists would have proceeded more quickly if it had been properly planned. The Rockingham cabinet, however, followed the pattern set by the North ministry and did little to secure ships for use in America. The government led by Lord Shelburne, which came to power in July 1782,

53. Charles Middleton et al. to Philip Stephens, Nov. 10, 1783, Home Office 28/3, Public Record Office, London, England.

54. Siebert, *Loyalists in East Florida*, I, 208.

did likewise. As a result, the evacuation of the South was not completed until four years after Cornwallis surrendered at Yorktown.

The inability of Britain's political leaders to see the need for shipping in America caused severe hardships to Carleton, Digby, and Leslie. Yet the three commanders overcame these difficulties by executing the withdrawal in a skillful and patient manner. Ships were carefully gathered at New York and sent to Charleston. The loyalists and soldiers were prepared to depart when the ships arrived. Carleton, for the most part, provided explicit instructions on how the evacuation was to take place, and Leslie obeyed his instructions. The British forces departed peacefully from Savannah and Charleston. Little damage was done to either of these two cities, and, except for the removal of their slaves, the Americans suffered only slightly from the British withdrawals. Finally, the removal of British troops and loyalists from Charleston and Savannah went quickly, despite the shortage of shipping. These two cities were abandoned within seven months after Carleton assumed command at New York, and credit must be given to him and his subordinates for these rapid evacuations. The withdrawal from East Florida took more time because after the loyalists and soldiers at Charleston and Savannah had been removed Carleton had to attend to the evacuation of New York. Only after this task was finished could the withdrawal from the South finally be completed.

Index

DATE DUE

PRINTED IN U.S.A.